PURGATORIO

Also by Mary Jo Bang

POETRY

A Doll for Throwing
The Last Two Seconds
The Bride of E
Elegy
The Eye Like a Strange Balloon
Louise in Love
The Downstream Extremity of the Isle of Swans
Apology for Want

TRANSLATION

Inferno, by Dante Alighieri

PURGATORIO

Dante Alighieri

Translated,
with an Introduction and Notes, by

MARY JO BANG

Graywolf Press

This publication is made possible, in part, by the voters of Minnesota through a Minnesota State Arts Board Operating Support grant, thanks to a legislative appropriation from the arts and cultural heritage fund. Significant support has also been provided by Target Foundation, the McKnight Foundation, the Lannan Foundation, the Amazon Literary Partnership, and other generous contributions from foundations, corporations, and individuals. To these organizations and individuals we offer our heartfelt thanks.

MINNESOTA STATE ARTS BOARD

CLEAN WATER LAND & LEGACY AMENDMENT

Published by Graywolf Press
250 Third Avenue North, Suite 600
Minneapolis, Minnesota 55401

www.graywolfpress.org

Published in the United States of America

ISBN 978-1-64445-057-4

2 4 6 8 9 7 5 3 1
First Graywolf Printing, 2021

Library of Congress Control Number: 2020944210

Cover design and art: Henrik Drescher

Contents

Acknowledgments

Thanks to the editors of the following magazines, anthologies, and websites where individual cantos have appeared:

LIT Magazine: Canto XXXIII, Spring 2020, Issue 33
The *New Yorker* (online): Cantos I, IV, VI, and IX, December 23, 2019
Dante, Purgatorio: Translations by Contemporary Poets: Cantos I, IV, and V (Todmorden, UK: Arc Publications, forthcoming)

Thanks to Kevin Young, poetry editor at the *New Yorker*, for the podcast interview that accompanied the publication of Cantos I, IV, VI, and IX on the NewYorker.com website.

Thanks to Nick Havely and Bernard O'Donoghue, editors, for including Cantos I, IV, and V in their multitranslator *Poets in Purgatory: After Dante*.

Thanks to Regina Galasso, director of the Translation Center, Department of Languages, Literatures, and Cultures, University of Massachusetts Amherst, for publishing the essay "Today in the Temple of Language: Translating Dante," which included portions of "A Note on the Translation," in *This Is a Classic* (Bloomsbury Publishing, forthcoming).

VIRGIL
DANTE

introduction

Finally, you're here, where the sea meets the feet of Mount Purgatory. You did it, you survived Hell and its horrors. You traveled through Hell's ugly inner lobby and all nine hideous circles, each smaller than the one above. You met and spoke to countless souls serving timeless sentences. On the ninth circle, you walked across three icy zones of betrayal, all the way to Satan—who stood, as he will stand for eternity, surrounded by giants and locked in a lake forever frozen over. From there, you found your way out through the underground where Satan's legs dangle in the void. You went against gravity through middle-earth to get to the mountainous landmass formed by the rock displaced by Satan when, tossed out of Heaven, he landed on earth.

That's all behind you now and yet, it's never out of mind. You never forget the lessons you learn by looking into the souls of others, nor should you. But here, unlike in Hell, things will get better. It's safe to lift the metaphoric sails. All you have to do is walk up seven flights of steps, circle seven terraces, and you'll be at the Terrestrial Heaven—where Beatrice, beloved since childhood, is waiting. That's only seven stories, a cinch. But hold on, only in fairy tales do wishes work, *Snap! Just like that!* This is real life. On each of these terraces, you have to evolve, feel the weight of your earthly errors, pay down the debt of every mistake you've made, learn compassion. That's what this long haul is for.

Fortunately, you're not alone, there's Virgil, the Roman poet who guided you through Hell. He's here to pave the way, which is good, because here comes someone to question your right to arrive on foot, instead of by a boat steered by an angel. (Those Heaven-sent messengers, you'll soon discover, work here as greeters.) The questioner is Cato, a general from Roman history who now has an endless gig guarding the coastline. Virgil explains how Beatrice came down to Limbo and begged him to rescue you when you were in dire straits. Virgil says he took you to Hell to show you what could happen if you didn't pull yourself together. And now, he says, he's brought you here to see how people better themselves. And Cato, who knows firsthand what it is to seek freedom, says, fine, but first Virgil needs to wash the grime of Hell from your face and tie a reed around your waist to show humility. So, that's what he does. And that's what's called a beginning.

Of course, you're not the only one beginning. Here comes a boatload of new beginners. The angel steering is so bright you have to look away. The souls it leaves at the shore ask you for directions, as if you would know. Virgil explains we're all strangers here. As he's talking, one of the new recruits walks toward you. What a surprise, it's someone who used to set your poems to music. Could he sing one now? you wonder. Is it allowed? Your body and mind would find that extremely consoling. He sings and not only you but all the others too are mesmerized. It feels (small-scale) divine until, here comes Cato. This is not betterment, he says, this is time-waste. Get over to the mountain *now.*

Virgil's embarrassed, feels he should have been a better father figure than to let you fall into a trap like that. Even so, here comes a group of slowpokes. Maybe they can say where the mountain incline is gradual enough for a human to climb. They're shocked to see your body throws a shadow. Whatever semblance the dead have, it's not solid matter. Virgil informs them, yes, you are alive but clearly this trip must have been cleared upstairs. How else could you be here? Fine, they say, we'll show the way. As you go along, one asks whether you knew him on earth. It's Manfred, king of Sicily, excommunicated by three popes but still, because he accepted God when he was stabbed on the battlefield, here he is. So expansive is God's forgiveness. He asks if you'll let his daughter know that he's here so she can offer up prayers of intercession.

The souls show you where you can enter the first flight of stairs. They'll stay here in Ante-Purgatory, since they took their sweet time working out their relationship with God. The entrance reminds you of the proverbial gap between a rock and a hard place; it looks like a needle's eye. You climb until you get to a ledge where you take a well-earned break. While Virgil explains why shadows fall the odd way they do here, you suddenly hear a voice steeped in sarcasm. In the shade behind a boulder, who is it but the lute-maker Belacqua from Florence, a past master of indolence? This is ridiculous. Don't you want to go up, Belacqua? He tells you he has to stay here thirty times however long he resisted God's grace, unless friends pray for him and how likely is that?

You move along and run into a group who met a violent end, so had no time to make amends. You speak with them, then off you go. Virgil's always saying, "This day will never come again," or "Those who know the most, most hate wasting time." He's right, this day will never come again and it's getting late. But where to go next? Luckily, you see a soul sitting all alone who Virgil thinks may know. The soul acts aloof until he discovers, surprise, he and Virgil are both from Mantua. Then it's a lovefest. It's Sordello, the bad-boy troubadour poet who died thirty years ago and who is still quite heated (as you are) about the way the country's been allowed to die a painful death while those in charge have stuffed their piggy pockets and purses and stroked their own fragile egos.

He says you can't climb at night, so he takes you over to a group of kings and VIPs. As you stand there, two angels fly in and chase off a garden snake.

You then see a judge you knew and you both come out of the dimly lit closet to say hello. He's bitter because his widow remarried a much younger man, a pol from another party. He rants on and on. Perhaps that's what's keeping him here: anger and envy and pride. That last, sadly, is the essence of being human. Maybe that was Eve's problem, too proud to stay in a cloud of unknowing. Although Adam comes off no better. Aren't they one and the same: A and E, a diphthong? Being human, you still have Adam in you, so you go to sleep and dream of being carried off like Ganymede, that beautiful, much-beloved boy. But when you wake, Virgil says it was Saint Lucy, not Zeus, who carried you up, after which, she and soft-handed sleep went off together. She left you at the gate: three steps up and then—a Saint Peter key-holder, who acts like a halogen lamp that's always on, unlocks the gate and finally, you're an insider. That angel inscribes seven Ps across your forehead, one for each *pecatto*, those seven deadly sins. You're warned not to look back or else, right back out you'll go.

What you do look at, on the first terrace, is a scroll of photorealist etchings on the white marble bank. The figures are so active they remind you of stop-motion animation. Each scene is an object lesson on the danger of hubris and the worth of humility. But what's this? Something that doesn't seem human is coming toward you. Finally, you realize, it's the crushed bodies of those carrying rocks on their shoulders, each boulder the size and weight of the person's hubris. Their squat bodies look like corbels, those well-carved men and women one sees holding up the eaves of buildings. You can see yourself in them, smashed beyond recognition. You won't forget this. Leaving this level, an angel erases one of the Ps from your forehead. You notice how much lighter you feel as you enter the second cornice. Unlike on the first, there are no illustrations here, only the stone itself: top to bottom, the livid color of envy. Voices fly by. What's that? you ask. Virgil says they're the words of those who showed a noble concern for others. The exact opposite of those who, out of envy, took pleasure in watching harm come to others. Schadenfreude, it's called. You'd think every language would have such a word, but no, only Greek and German.

Those you speak with here don't seem very aware; they lack sincerity and it shows in what they say and how they compose their faces to try to make you think they are nicer than they are: a shy look, an unassuming shrug. But you aren't fooled, you see them for what they are. Until *they* see the light, they'll stay right here, their eyes sewn shut with fine wire, crying over the spilt milk of their envy of others. The lesson that has to be learned is: delight in damage done to others is actually damage done to the self. One of them says something that puzzles you and you make a note to ask Virgil. But not right now because here comes another of those high-octane angels. As you look away from the brightness, it erases another P from your forehead. And now, you ask the question that's been gnawing at you: it's about attachment. Virgil tries to answer, using the example of how light gets refracted, making you even more bewildered. He says you may have to wait until you reach Beatrice: he deals with reason; she deals with faith.

On the way to the third terrace, you have two brief visions. This makes you realize, even thoughts that seem outside the self—since they're made by the mind and the mind is real—are also real. Such is the imagination. As you try to explain this bright idea to Virgil, smoke comes rolling in and now, like those with their eyes sewn shut, you can't see. Out of the darkness, there's a voice. Perhaps this one can give you a clue as to how to get to where you're going. You talk as he walks alongside you. He says something similar to what that other soul said that confused you, something about picking the right partner. So, you ask him, if humans have a problem being true to one another, is it because fate interferes, or, are we our own problem? Oh boy, he says, you *are* wearing a blindfold. If it were fate, there would be no free will. When humans begin, he says, everything is fine and dandy, but then, they see others eating candy and say, why not, I'll have some of that, and then they don't want their dinner. That's the way, he says, in the Church and in the State: the so-called leaders do whatever they want and now the whole world is following their sad example.

Now we're almost at the angel, so the soul has to go back. Until he understands his anger, he has to stay there, where everyone is breathless, unable to see past their wrath. Throughout this level: anger over this, anger over that, a slight here, a slight there. Anger is natural, Virgil says, but vindictive anger, that's another story. That injures others and so it's a sin. There is, he says, the ego-tripper who's angry when others have the things they want; the smug ones who fear they'll lose out if someone else gains; and then, those king-babies who get so good at perceiving slights, they fabricate errors in others just so they can sadistically release their payload of anger.

But what about love? That's what you want to know. Virgil says love is the alpha and omega of all good and all evil. Good *and* evil? Say more, you say. So, he does: since everything is programmed on high, every kind of love is fine, if it's in the image of the Divine. Bees do what bees do, fires rise to get what they require, all is as it should be. But, too little attachment, or too much, or to the wrong object, that's where the problem lies. What one needs is the right kind of love and to the right degree. This is the opposite of apathy, which is the level you've now arrived at. The punishment here, a payback yes, but also what brings about the insight needed to move up, is to run nonstop around the circular terrace. One minute, the souls are in front of you; the next, they're coming from behind; and now, they're passing you by. On earth, it was all: maybe later, I'm too tired, what about tomorrow . . . Here, it's now or never.

On the way to the next terrace, you have a daydream: a woman who's more than a bit messed up becomes just what you want when you deceive yourself into seeing her as a charming, sexy Siren. That can't last because in the dream, Beatrice shows up, calls Virgil over, and together they unmask the woman for the botch-job she is. You come to your senses just as you come to the terrace for greed, where there, everyone is lying facedown, having an up-close and personal conversation with the ground. The path is acting as stand-in for the earthly goods the souls never looked away from in order to see what good they could do. You meet a pope who says the punishment for greed is the most bitter pill the mountain has to offer. He and others call out the names of those who learned that lesson the hard way, like Midas, whose touch turned his plate, and everything on it, to gold. And now, something like a minor earthquake makes the mountain shake.

Someone comes up behind you and says, Hello! What do you know, it's another Roman poet, Statius, whose poems have a debt to your docent, Virgil! When Statius learns he's talking to his idol, he wants to bend and touch his feet, but Virgil says, No, remember, we're nothing now but shadows. Statius is on his way up to Heaven, having served his sentence here, not for greed, but for its converse: being a spendthrift. Too much, it turns out, is just like too little. The key is moderation. He explains that the mountain shook from the host of hosannas the other souls shouted, as a celebratory send-off because, yay, after five hundred years here, he's now going up.

Now another P gets erased and the three of you proceed to the next level, where you see a tree. The problem here is gluttony, says a former friend who you can see has been whittled down to his skeleton plus his skin, which is now caved in. The tree, he says, makes them crave the ambrosia it's watered with. The longing never ends as they circle the cornice. To go forward, they have to give up wishing for what they can never get enough of. And now, here comes someone else who recognizes you. He tells you what will happen in the future—you'll move to a new city, meet a delightful lady. He's a poet and wants to know whether you wrote a verse he still remembers. You say, yes, in fact, you did. To which he says, your verse really was no better than those written by him and his friends. Hmm.

Leaving that terrace, you can't help asking Virgil: If a dead soul has no body, how can they starve? Virgil has Statius answer that, which becomes a long TED Talk on the birds and the bees and how babies are made and how the seed gets infused with the soul—which is, he says, at the point when thinking begins—and this gives the soul a semblance and senses, both of which outlive the body. While you're taking this in, flames suddenly shoot from the cliff face. Two groups come and go, each calls out the name of a biblical city or a mythical figure, examples that stand for the rules they broke. The problem, it seems, is an excess of sexual energy. Let's just call it lust. You meet another poet here, one to whom you and your friends owe so much. He talks about how fleeting fame is and points out a soul up ahead, who, he says, was a far better wordsmith than he was. It's Arnaut Daniel, who speaks as he once wrote, in code, but you know what he means: you too have to refine yourself. You do this by walking through fire while following the voice of an angel.

On the other side, it's night. You sleep and dream of a woman picking flowers. A Leah-type, active and able. And then, it's morning. Light as air now, you run up the last flight of stairs, and you're back to the garden. Virgil makes you ruler of yourself and tells you to no longer look to him for help, you're on your own. So, off you go, into the Elysian forest, where, on the opposite side of two streams, you see a woman picking flowers, just like in the dream. You think, maybe the two of you can play Adam and Eve. To which she says, Hello, but no, this is not the kind of love we practice here. She teaches you about this place, and how Adam and Eve had to be banished because they couldn't follow the rules. She says one stream is Lethe, which erases the memory of sin, and the second is Eunoe, which brings back every bit of goodness you ever knew. You have to actually drink the water, she says, Lethe first, then Eunoe, in that order.

And now, a flashing light and a chorus of hosannas, and a procession led by seven candelabras, each on its own stand: Elders, Evangelists, Virtues, a griffin, a chariot, angels, flowers, and over it all, rainbow streamers of the finest light. It is all very biblical, very Book of Revelation. You look back to share this with Virgil—but oh, no, Virgil is no more. You begin to cry, and a woman exits the chariot. She is not at all happy with you. The angels tell her to give you a break, but no, she explains, she can't. Unless you understand the error of your ways, there's no going forward and no going back. She then becomes judge and jury, with you in the box. She wears down your lame resistance, and, in a moment of self-recognition, you lose it and faint. When you come to, the woman you saw in the forest is getting you into Lethe and pulling you across. And then, there you are, on the same side as the procession, facing your accuser. The angels beg her to remove her veil and when she does, you see it's Beatrice. Of course, it is. Who else would know you so well?

The griffin delivers the chariot to the Tree of Knowledge, then leads the procession back to Heaven. And now, an eagle, a fox, and a dragon rip the chariot apart; then a loose woman climbs up on it and tries to flirt with you, until her pimp catches on and drags her and the chariot, which meanwhile has become a many-headed monster, into the forest. And now, the few who are left—you, Statius, the Seven Virtues, Matelda (the one who pulled you across), and Beatrice—walk together over to the river of Eunoe. On the way, Beatrice gives you a quick lesson in theology and tells you to write everything you saw. Next thing you know, you're in the water again: Eunoe, the river that takes you straight to Paradise. A sip of that and now you're pure and ready to reach for the stars.

A Note on The Translation

There are many stand-alone translations of Dante's *Inferno* into English; there are far fewer of the second canticle, *Purgatorio.* We humans seem both amused and horrified by the concept of Hell. If we include ourselves in the equation error equals punishment, the idea of Hell as a place where the mistakes we make on earth will forever torment us in the afterlife is terrifying. On the other hand, the idea of eternal punishment is delightfully satisfying when we remove ourselves from the equation and consider Hell simply as no less than what our earthly tormentors deserve. Because the notion of Hell is so elastic—in terms of what eternal punishment might look like and who might be a worthy recipient—when stretched even a little, it becomes the basis of humor, of high art, and especially of popular culture—that transient, now you see it, now you don't, type of art.

Although cursory internet searches cannot, of course, be put forth as solid evidence, it's interesting that "Hell in the arts and popular culture" has its own Wikipedia page with references to depictions of Hell in art, cartoons, comics, film, games, literature, music, radio, and television. No such easy-access equivalent exists for Purgatory. Perhaps Purgatory earns less attention because of the general lack of clarity attached to it. Compared to its afterlife counterparts, its location is murky and unfixed in our imaginations: we have assigned Heaven the space above us, Hell the territory below us, but where is Purgatory situated? As a theological idea, Purgatory is grounded in the Old Testament book of 2 Maccabees (12:43–46), where it is said that it is a "holy and wholesome thought to pray for the dead, that they may be loosed from sins." The Catholic Church embraced the idea of a necessary penitential step between death and acceptance into Heaven only sometime in the late twelfth century, which is also when the word, from the Latin *pūrgātōrium* (purgation or cleansing), came into use. Since then, it's been unclear whether Purgatory should be considered an actual place, or a suspended state. What is clear is that it is where the soul waits and hopes that prayers of intercession offered by the living will shorten the waiting. This association with an agonizing wait that feels interminable gives Purgatory what it needs to hold its own metaphorically with Heaven and Hell—how many purgatorial situations have we all suffered our way through? But in the end, it's a transient space, lacking the permanence of Heaven and Hell, the vast territory of the eternal.

After I published a colloquial translation of *Inferno* in 2012, I was frequently asked whether I intended to translate *Purgatorio*, and if I did translate *Purgatorio*, would I also translate *Paradiso*? At that time, I said I didn't know. I said, in all honesty, that I'd spent six years hand in hand with Dante, and his docent, the Roman poet Virgil, slowly descending, circle to circle, that funnel-shaped Hell, meeting figures from history and myth, understanding their errors and marveling at the inventive punishments, each aptly suited to the offense, that the author Dante had devised for them, and it was possible that that was enough time spent in that company. I was also concerned that translating *Purgatorio* would then require me to translate *Paradiso*, the final book of the trilogy, because one could translate *Inferno* and leave it at that, many had, but how could one translate the two books and not do the third? That alone made me ambivalent since I wasn't at all sure I would enjoy translating *Paradiso*. It's an idea-heavy book I had found difficult to read when I tried years ago.

What I didn't say, because I didn't want to get locked into a commitment I wasn't yet certain of, was that I had already begun translating *Purgatorio*. I began in March 2012, before the publication of *Inferno* in August of that year. By early June, I had finished the first three cantos and most of the notes for Canto I. But then I ran into a problem. I had promised myself—after having put off writing the notes to *Inferno* until the end, and then having to work on nothing but the notes for a wearying eighteen months—that if I were to translate *Purgatorio*, I would do the notes to each canto as I went along. And yet, here I was, still at the beginning and already two cantos behind. I couldn't find the energy and focus to do the notes, not having just finished those of the *Inferno*, and I couldn't allow myself to translate Canto IV until the notes for Cantos II and III were finished.

Things might have stayed that way forever but for the fact that in February 2014, I received a kind email from Nick Havely, a noted British Dantist and emeritus professor of English and Related Literature at the University of York, asking whether I would be willing to contribute to a multi-translator *Purgatorio* that he and the Irish poet, translator, and medievalist Bernard O'Donoghue intended to curate. Honored to be asked, I agreed to translate whichever cantos they wished to assign me. They asked for Cantos I, III, IV, and V, which seemed an ideal way to escape my painted-in corner. I went back and completed the notes for Cantos II and III and then went forward through Cantos IV and V. At that point, for fear I might get stuck again if I tried to keep pace with the notes, I gave up that admirable idea and just carried on with the translation, accepting that there would be a future purgatorial stretch when I would have to pay down the debt of having done only what gave me pleasure.

That's *how* I came to translate *Purgatorio* but not *why* I translated it. At the end of *Inferno*, the character named Dante emerges from an underground cavern, still shaken by the horrors he witnessed while traveling with Virgil through the nine circles of Hell. Hearing the stories told by those confined there for eternity, he had sometimes found his eyes filling with tears, or, in the case of the two ill-fated lovers, Francesca and Paolo, he was so moved by their story, he fainted. He was chased by demons, had to cross a river of boiling blood on the back of a centaur, was scolded by Virgil for gawking at the petty bickering of a couple of counterfeiters. Now, having made his way through a dimly lit, winding underground channel, accessed by climbing down the dangling hairy legs of a huge, three-faced Satan frozen in a block of ice called Lake Cocytus, he steps outside. Here is how *Inferno* ends:

> Down there, in a remote corner—
> The distance of Beelzebub's tomb times two—
> Is an area one can't find by sight in that low light
>
> But only by the sound of a stream that,
> As it trickles down a slight incline,
> Has carved a winding canyon through the rock.
>
> My teacher and I entered that secluded passage
> That would lead us back to the lit world.
> Not wanting to waste time resting, we climbed—
>
> Him first, then me—until we came to a round opening
> Through which I saw some of the beautiful things
> That come with Heaven. And we walked out
>
> To once again catch sight of the stars.

Since the *Commedia* is a trilogy, the final scene of the *Inferno* is only the moment when someone hits the pause button; *Purgatorio* is the next chapter in the ongoing story. As I stood with the character named Dante on the hopeful shore of the ocean surrounding Mount Purgatory—and looked up and saw what he saw, the convulsive beauty of the stars in a place where no light pollution washes out the night sky—I wanted to know what happened next. I felt attached to this character in the midst of an existential crisis; I wanted to stay with him to see who and what he would encounter now. I could have simply read an existing translation. There are some excellent ones, but, in general,

I find the elevated register of those a continually distracting reminder of the fact that the poem was written in a long-ago era. In *Camera Lucida*, Roland Barthes argues that when looking at photographs taken in the past, there are two possible reactions: one, *studium*, an intellectual curiosity about the historical, or two, a state of *punctum*, a piercing recognition of likeness so profound it is sometimes perceived as physical. For me, the elevated register of most Dante translations makes the experience of reading the poem pure *studium*, not only by reminding me that the poem is a literary artifact but also by blunting the subtle differences between the voices of the characters, which is a key element of how the poem works.

The *Commedia* timelessly mimes what it is to be a human being. Although written in the 1300s, it feels both before its time and one with our time. The work was so radical in its own era, it inspired many in other parts of Italy to learn the Tuscan dialect so they could read it. Dante's conception of Purgatory is a seven-terrace mountain, each level devoted to atoning for one of the seven deadly sins; at the top is the Terrestrial Heaven, the long-ago abandoned Eden. As in *Inferno*, the reader finds, among those on the mountain, enduring examples of the human behaviors that fracture the social fabric into feuding groups, each hell-bent on the destruction of the other, and the myriad types of bad actors who willingly sacrifice everyone—except the yes-men and yes-women who prop them up, and those too are sacrificed if ever a yes isn't forthcoming. Because the characters are meant to represent humanity from the beginning of time until now, Dante draws equally on real people and on invented figures from myth. The drunken, half-man/half-horse centaurs, who carry off the bride and bridesmaids at a wedding, can serve as an illustration of the dangers of impulsive behavior as easily as an Italian archbishop named Ruggieri degli Ubaldini can demonstrate human cruelty by locking a former associate in a castle with two of his sons and two grandsons and allowing all of them to starve to death. Dante makes it clear: it's the offense that is the problem, not the perpetrator. Individuals may be punished, yes, but unless society gains insight, spiteful and vicious behavior will simply continue with new players. And so it has. We have only to look at the news.

While religion, specifically medieval Catholicism, is the stage setting for the poem, and source of the character Dante's hope for redemption, for himself and for others, the author, Dante Alighieri, draws on early-Christian and non-Christian thinkers to construct his arguments for a better world. He exposes the hypocrisy of the leadership, Church and State, demonstrating over and over again the crookedness of the shepherd's rook, and the greed and meanness of those who wield power. He allows the pagan Roman poet

Virgil to be the voice of reason until they reach the edge of Lethe, the River of Oblivion, where a woman named Beatrice assumes the role. At the end of the poem, she tells Dante he should have recognized that the features of the Tree of Knowledge—its enormous height, a canopy so wide it overwhelms the trunk, the fact that the branches point up—speak not just to the prohibition not to eat from the tree but also to the need for obedience to a moral code that protects society. She instructs Dante to write this poem, based on what he's seen and learned.

Dante was aware that his poem, which he called a "comedy," needed to have warmth if it were to adequately reflect the psychological complexity of human behavior. In Book I of *Convivio* (*The Banquet*), he explains why the vernacular is more appropriate for poetry than the literary Latin of the past: Latin was so beautiful, virtuous, and noble, its sovereignty would overwhelm the poem; plus, these elements make it feel remote. The vernacular has intimacy, familiarity, and a sense of generosity; it's not reliant on special learning but is simply given to one as a child. Latin is frozen in time and therefore can't change; the Latin of yesterday will be the same Latin of tomorrow. The vernacular is unstable, corruptible, and will change over time. Latin was limited to a small group of readers, the "learned"; the poem needed to be written in a language that could be read by many.

I've taken Dante's stated aims as my own. As in the earlier *Inferno* translation, in order to bring *Purgatorio* forward into the present, I've used spoken English. For sound patterning, because Dante's interlocking *terza rima*—a rhyme scheme devised by him for this poem—is impossible to sustain in rhyme-poor English with a degree of elegance in a poem of this length, I've relied on the less regimented phonic echoes common to contemporary English poetry: internal, slant, and sight rhyme, alliteration and assonance. I've included occasional glimpses of contemporary life—to extend threads that run through the original work. I've tried to make those contemporizing moments brief enough so the flash of recognition doesn't distract from the narrative, or from the essential pillars on which the story rests: Italian history; medieval Catholic theology; Greek and Roman myth. Those are still there but there are also (to name a few) the fable of The Little Red Hen; The Princess and the Pea fairy tale; Goldilocks and the Three Bears; the musical *West Side Story*; a photo-op close-up of the MGM logo, Leo the Lion; the painting *Census at Bethlehem*, by Pieter Bruegel the Elder; Tootsie Fruit Chews; and Chutes and Ladders—called Snakes and Ladders in Britain, where it began as a Victorian-era revision of the ancient Indian game Moksha Patam. There are lines from poems that extend the lineage of Dante and his Roman poets: Shakespeare,

Emily Dickinson, Gertrude Stein, Allen Ginsberg, Alice Dunbar-Nelson, and Oscar Wilde, among others. There are snippets of songs from contemporary musicians, meant to echo the singers and songs Dante weaves into the poem: Bob Dylan, Cyndi Lauper, Led Zeppelin, Amy Winehouse, John Coltrane, Marvin Gaye, Talking Heads, Richie Havens, and others.

Shared culture creates both a sense of lineage and the illusion of verisimilitude, the way a mirroring store window confirms that the world behind you is today's world. My hope is that these allusions will create a recognizable backdrop against which the reader will see that Dante's remarkable intelligence, considerable humor, vast erudition, and subtly drawn characters are one with our world. As in *Inferno*, I have followed Walter Benjamin's argument that the life of any translated work is indebted to its afterlife. A poem is a delicate apparatus (W. H. Auden once referred to it as a "verbal contraption," which seems brilliantly apt) that performs multiple functions. How a poem comes to mean can't be totally deconstructed and yet, in spite of that, the translator's task is to find language and pattern it in a way that will echo the effects of the original.

Here, too, I followed the advice of Charles Singleton and relied on previous translators as readers: I was guided most often by Singleton himself, both his 1973 *Purgatorio* translation and his *Commentary*; by Robert Hollander and Jean Hollander, their 2003 translation and notes; by William Warren Vernon and his 1889 (third edition, 1907) translation of *Purgatorio*, which traces the commentary back to Benvenuto da Imola (d. 1388) and other early commentators; by John D. Sinclair (1939); and by Allen Mandelbaum (1981). I also consulted *Purgatorio* translations by Robin Kirkpatrick (2007), Mark Musa (1981), and many others. I've relied on countless online sources for research for the notes and for assistance in the translation. With *Purgatorio*, I've also had the extraordinary good fortune to have a Virgil in the person of Nick Havely, who, with great patience and remarkable generosity, fielded multiple questions and gave guidance where it was most needed. That said, all of the shortcomings of this work are my own. My hope for this translation of *Purgatorio* is the same as my hope for the *Inferno* translation: that it will bring new readers to Dante. And that having read my translation, readers will want to read other translations of the poem. The differences and similarities speak to the way translation works and more generally to how language works.

I happily thank Timothy Donnelly, with whom I first read *Inferno* and *Purgatorio*—and whose continued friendship and conversations about poetry give support to all of my work. It was his insistence twenty-five years ago that we read two different Dante translations that first led me to appreciate the malleable relationship between a translation and the original. I again thank William Weaver, now deceased, with whom I took a translation workshop at Columbia University in 1995. I'm especially grateful for his demonstration (using three translations of the first pages of Cervantes's *Don Quixote*) of how language shifts in register over time, and how, by keeping current with those changes, a translator keeps pulling a text into the ever-evolving present (a clear echo of Benjamin's theory). His teaching has more than once given me the necessary courage to engage with Dante's poem in the time-bending manner I've chosen. I thank Mark Bibbins for his significant contribution to the *Inferno* translation and his friendship then and now; Mónica de la Torre, for her translation insights and her friendship; Kevin Young, for graciously featuring four of the *Purgatorio* cantos, and an interview about the translation process, on the *New Yorker* website; to Bill Clegg, whose friendship and support sustain me; and to Jeff Shotts, Katie Dublinski, Fiona McCrae, Chantz Erolin, and all of those at Graywolf Press—this book would not exist in this form without their collaboration. Thanks also to Mary Byers for her expert copyediting of both this manuscript and the previous *Inferno*.

Thanks to Henrik Drescher, whose amazing illustrations and cover for *Inferno* gave that book a physical form and presence that perfectly echoed the biting wit and high drama of Dante's Hell. And more thanks for this cover, which is, once again, an ingenious echo of Dante's poem; thanks to him as well for the typography that ties the two volumes together. Continued thanks to Ken Botnick for introducing me to Drescher's work and for his support of my work. Thanks to friends and colleagues at Washington University, especially David Schuman, Edward McPherson, Heather McPherson, and Danielle Dutton. Thanks to Kathleen Finneran, for her discerning prose-writer's eye—which she applied to this note and to the introduction—and for her steadfast friendship. In the English Department, special thanks to Miriam Baillin, Guinn Batten, Joe Loewenstein, William Maxwell, Steven Meyer, Anca Parvulescu, Vivian Pollak, Vincent Sherry, Julia Walker, Rafia Zafar—and to Steve Zwicker, for long ago pointing me to Dryden's writing on translation. Thanks to Ignacio Infante, associate professor of Comparative Literature and Spanish, for his thoughts about translation. Thanks to Timothy Moore, John and Penelope Biggs Distinguished Professor of Classics, for help with a translation of Virgil. Thanks to former students with whom I've discussed this translation at one time or another over these eight years: Aaron Coleman, Robert Whitehead, Neil Rosenthalis, James Scales, Paige Webb, Cassie Donnish, Paul Tran, Larry Ypil, and Philip Matthews. Thanks to fellow translators who have supported this and other translations: Aditi Machado, Yuki Tanaka, Matthias

Göritz, Susan Bernofsky, and Aníbal Cristobo: I learn from all of you. Thanks to friends, especially Lynn Melnick, Claudia Rankine, Joni Wallace, Richard Greenfield, Jessica Baran, Matthea Harvey, Rob Casper, Brett Fletcher Lauer, Mark Wunderlich, Marjorie Perloff, Sylvia Sukop, Karla Kelsey, Carmen Giménez Smith, Gabe Fried, Susan Wheeler, Stephanie Burt, Tara Ison, and Eleanor Sarasohn. Thanks to Jennifer Kronovet, who fits into several of the above categories: former student, fellow translator, and friend. Thanks to Nick Havely, for the invitation that prompted me to return to the translation, and for being a *dolce* Virgil. Thanks to Caroline Bergvall for her poem "Via (48 Dante Variations)," which led me to translate the *Inferno*, without which there would be no *Purgatorio*. To the late Marni Ludwig and Lucie Brock-Broido, you were both here when I began this project: I wish you were here now, at this moment of completion.

June 15, 2020 (St. Louis)

PURGATORIO

Canto I

Heading over waters getting better all the time
My mind's little skiff now lifts its sails,
Letting go of the oh-so-bitter sea behind it.

The next realm, the second I'll sing,
Is here where the human spirit gets purified
And made fit for the stairway to Heaven.

Here's where the kiss of life restores the reign
Of poetry—O true-blue Muses, I'm yours—
And where Calliope jumps up just long enough

To sing backup with the same bold notes
That knocked the poor magpie girls into knowing
Their audacity would never be pardoned.

The fluid blue of the eastern sapphire
Pooling in the cloudless mid-sky,
Clear down to the first curved horizon-line,

Was an even more delightful sight,
Having left behind the sad-making dead air
That had so messed with my chest and eyes.

The gorgeous planet that says yes to love
Was turning the east into a total glitter fest,
Veiling the fish that formed her entourage.

I looked right. Focusing on the South Pole,
I saw four stars that had gone unseen
Since the first human beings.

It was like the sky was having a wild night
With these tiny blinking lights; O sad-eyed lady North,
Widowed of a sight you would so love to see!

After this mini stargazing party, I turned
A bit toward the other pole, where there,
The shuddering Bear had already lumbered off

Nearby, I saw a man on his own;
He looked like an elder statesman, one worthy
Of no less respect than a child owes a parent.

His beard was long and salted white,
Ditto his hair, which fell forward
Onto his chest in two thick bands.

The rays of the four sacred stars
Gave his face the glint of a minted coin;
I pictured a searchlight sun in front of him.

"Who are you, who've turned the dead-end river
On its head by getting out of jail without a card?"
He said, his venerable feathers ruffled.

"Who guided you, or acted like a flashlight,
When you fled the fathomless night-gloom
That keeps the Infernal Valley forever in the dark?

Have the laws of the Abyss been broken? Or,
Has Heaven weakened the law, so you damned ones
Can come right up to my rockface anytime you like?"

My teacher gave me a look—then,
Using head nods and hand gestures,
Made me kneel and bend my head in deference.

"I didn't come here on my own," he said.
"A woman came down from Heaven
And begged me to help this one by coming with him.

But since you want to hear the whole story,
The unabridged version of how and why
We came to be here, I can't say no to that.

This man hasn't seen his final evening hour;
Playing a fool's game, however, he was so close
There was very little time for a turnaround.

As I told you, I was sent to help him stay alive.
There was no other way to do that
Except the one I set for myself.

I've shown him the guilty ones,
And now I need to show him those spirits
Who purify themselves under your sovereign say-so.

It's a long story, how I brought him this far; power
Descended from on high and helped me bring him
To this place, where he can see and hear you.

I hope you'll agree to his coming here.
He's seeking freedom, the price of which is known
By those who give their lives for it.

You know this. Death for the sake of it wasn't bitter
In Utica, where you shuffled off your mortal coil,
Which will be so bright on that one fine day.

We haven't violated any eternal edicts: he's alive
And I'm not tied to Minos; I'm of that circle
Where the innocent eyes of your Marcia

Show how much she longs to still belong
To your pure and most-most loving breast.
For her love then, I hope you'll give us the go-ahead.

Let us travel through your seven kingdoms;
I'll take word of your kindness back to her, that is,
If you don't mind your name being dropped below."

"I so loved setting eyes on Marcia
When I was far from here," he said,
"That I never said no to whatever she asked for.

But now that she's on the far side of the river
Of pain, she no longer moves me—that law
Was decreed when I was airlifted out of there

But if, as you say, a Heavenly woman moves you
To act and acts as your handler, there's no need
To flatter; it's enough to ask in her name.

So, go, tie a simple reed around his waist,
And wash his filthy face—
Make sure you scrub off all the grime.

There's no way he can go in front
Of the first of the ministers from Paradise
Looking as if he got caught in a smoke cloud.

All around this small island, at its lowest-most
Point where the sea-waves' sway tugs
At the rough stones, rushes grow in the soft silt.

Plants with leaves or woody stalks don't last
There; they get badly broken
By the surf's steady rasp and after-rasp.

Don't travel back this way;
The sun, now rising, will show you how
To take an easier route up the mountain."

With that, he vanished into the air.
I got up without speaking and turned
To my teacher, looking straight into his eyes.

He said, "Son, you can follow me.
Let's go back. The plain slopes that way
Down to its lowest point."

Dawn was outracing the after-midnight hours
Running in front of it. I could see, even
From this distance, the fluttering edge of the shore.

We made our way over the desolate plain
Like someone looking for a lost path,
Who, until it's found, feels like it's all in vain.

When we came to an area where,
Because of a cool breeze, the dew held its own
Against the sun's evaporative reach,

My teacher opened both hands
And placed his palms lightly on the wet grass;
Now seeing what he had in mind,

I offered him my tear-stained cheeks,
And, right there, he revealed all my true colors,
Which Hell had kept hidden.

We then went down to the deserted coastline,
Which had never seen anyone navigate
Its waters and come back after the fact.

There, he tied the reed around my waist
As the other had directed: Oh, one for the books!
When he pulled up the lowly plant by its roots,

Another at once sprang up in its place.

1–3. *waters getting better all the time . . . the oh-so-bitter sea behind it*: The poem begins by suggesting the metaphoric sea voyage through Purgatory will be far easier than the one just taken through the storms of Hell. The sails can now be safely raised. Conditions steadily improve in Purgatory as the souls climb the mountain and sequentially do penance for the seven deadly, or cardinal, sins—pride, envy, wrath, sloth, avarice (and its opposite, prodigality), gluttony, and lust. The soul becomes gradually purified, and finally, worthy of Paradise. "Getting better all the time" is a refrain from the song "Getting Better," written by John Lennon and Paul McCartney of the Beatles (*Sgt. Pepper's Lonely Hearts Club Band*, 1967).

4–6. *The next realm, the second I'll sing, / Is here where the human spirit gets purified / And made fit for the stairway to Heaven*: Purgatory, the "second realm," is divided into three parts: Ante-Purgatory, Purgatory, and Post-Purgatory, which is more often referred to as the Terrestrial Paradise. Recalcitrant spirits—those who delayed their repentance, or those who refused to accept the Holy Church—are forced to remain at the foot of the mountain, outside the gate to Purgatory proper, for thirty times the length of their delay. Prayers of intercession offered by those on earth can shorten the time spent there. Purgatory proper comprises seven cornices, or ledges, connected by stairways; each ledge is the width of three times the height of a man, and each is devoted to penance for one of the seven deadly sins. The song "Stairway to Heaven" was written by Jimmy Page and Robert Plant of the British rock band Led Zeppelin; it appeared on their 1971 album, *Led Zeppelin IV*.

9. *where Calliope jumps up just long enough*: In Greek mythology, Calliope is the Muse of epic poetry. Dante follows Virgil (*Aeneid* 9, 525) in calling on her for inspiration.

10–12. *the same bold notes / That knocked the poor magpie girls into knowing / Their audacity would never be pardoned*: Ovid (*Metamorphoses* 5.290–678) tells the story of how the Pierides, the nine daughters of Pierus, the king of Thessaly, challenged the Muses to a singing contest. The Muses chose Calliope to represent them. Not only did she win, but she afterward changed the Pierides into magpies as punishment for their hubris.

13. *The fluid blue of the eastern sapphire*: Dante refers to the color of the sky as *orïental zaffiro* (Oriental, or eastern, sapphire—a cobalt blue). The East, for Dante, would have been India. In *Dante and the Orient*, Brenda Deen Schildgen (123) points out that the description of the sky "signals not just the start of a new day but the beginning of new hope and delight. . . . Its transparent blue color was linked to the bright early morning light, which comes from the East." One of the tenets of "Orientalism," as established by Edward Said in his 1978 groundbreaking book *Orientalism*, is the tendency to regard the East as exotic, a viewpoint first adopted during the medieval era with the establishment of academic departments devoted to the translation of texts from Arabic to Latin.

17–18. *the sad-making dead air / That had so messed with my chest and eyes*: In the underworld, the air was so dark that Dante was sometimes unable to see clearly, causing him to initially misread the giants that guard the ninth circle of Hell as towers.

19–21. *The gorgeous planet that says yes to love . . . Veiling the fish that formed her entourage*: In the medieval era, Venus was thought to have two manifestations, chaste love and lustful desire. Dante's language encodes sexual desire. Venus's "entourage" is composed of the stars in the constellation Pisces, the fishes; since she outshines them, they seem less bright relative to her. They may also be "veiled," however, in order to give Venus the privacy she requires for the lovemaking she prompts.

22. *I looked right. Focusing on the South Pole*: Facing east, the Antarctic Pole would be on the speaker's right. Dante refers to this as the "other pole"; as Charles S. Singleton (2:9) points out, "The South Pole is the 'other' pole for those of us who inhabit the northern hemisphere of land."

23–24. *I saw four stars that had gone unseen / Since the first human beings*: Some scholars have argued that these four stars represent the Southern Cross, while others maintain that Dante could not possibly have been aware of the existence of that constellation since it wasn't yet recorded. On the figurative level, it's possible that the four stars are meant to allegorically represent the four cardinal virtues: prudence, justice, fortitude, and temperance. The first humans are Adam and Eve. After the Fall, the couple would have relocated to the Northern Hemisphere, where they and their descendants would have been deprived, or "widowed," of the stars. The arrangement of the stars indicates it is April 10, 1300, Easter Sunday. On that date, Pope Boniface VIII welcomed the pilgrims arriving in Rome for the first jubilee and promised "the fullest forgiveness of all their sins" for those who were contrite and confessed if they would visit the Basilica of Saint Peter or that of Saint Paul.

25. *It was like the sky was having a wild night*: Emily Dickinson (269): "Wild nights – Wild nights!": "Wild nights – Wild nights! / Were I with thee / Wild nights should be / Our luxury!"

26–27. *O sad-eyed lady North, / Widowed of a sight you would so love to see*: "Sad-Eyed Lady of the Lowlands," written by Bob Dylan, appeared on his 1966 album, *Blonde on Blonde*: "And your flesh like silk, and your face like glass / Who among them do they think could carry you? / Sad-eyed lady of the lowlands."

28–30. *I turned / a bit toward the other pole, where there, / The shuddering Bear had already lumbered off*: This is the North Pole. The seven brightest stars of the constellation Ursa Major (the Great Bear) are known today as the Big Dipper; in the medieval era they were called Charles's Wain (or Wagon). Many Native American tribes have myths that explain the origin of these seven stars, among them: seven boys are turned into seven geese; seven hunters chase a bear into the sky; seven girls climb a tree to escape a bear; a girl adopts seven brothers and they climb a tree to escape a buffalo; the seven stars represent the boat that carries the dead to their final resting place (Lynch and Roberts 12–14). T. S. Eliot, "Gerontion": "De Bailhache, Fresca, Mrs. Cammel, whirled / Beyond the circuit of the shuddering Bear / In fractured atoms."

31. *Nearby, I saw a man on his own*: Marcus Porcius Cato Uticensis (95–46 BCE), commonly known as Cato the Younger to distinguish him from his great-grandfather Cato the Elder, was a late Roman Republic statesman and follower of Stoicism. He was highly regarded by ancient writers and included in Plutarch's *Lives of the Noble Grecians and Romans*. In an era of political turmoil dominated by strong factions, not unlike Dante's own moment, Cato was outspoken, principled, and scrupulously honest. The idea of Cato as the warden of Purgatory may have come from Virgil's *Aeneid* 8, 670: "Cato privately granting just rewards to the pious" ("Secretosque pios, his dantem iura Catonem").

35–36. *his hair, which fell forward / Onto his chest in two thick bands*: Some Roman coins featured Cato's head, with long hair and wreathed in ivy; the verso side had a seated winged victory (www.coinarchives.com). It's possible that Dante saw one of these coins and used that image for the description of Cato.

37–38. *The rays of the four sacred stars . . . the glint of a minted coin*: These stars, allegorically forming the foundation of a virtuous life (prudence, justice, fortitude, and temperance), are so bright that their combined effect is like the sun. These four moral principles were first delineated in Plato's *Republic* (4.426–435). The verb Dante uses (*fregiare*) to describe the effect of the light on Cato's face can mean "to adorn or be adorned with something: to boast a medal" (*Enciclopedia italiana di scienze, lettere ed arti*) (Italian encyclopedia of science, letters, and arts).

39. *a searchlight sun in front of him*: Dante is clearly anxious lest Cato not find him worthy of being there.

53–54. *A woman came down from Heaven / And begged me to help this one by coming with him*: The woman is Beatrice. In *Inf.* II, 52–114, Beatrice explains to Virgil how Saint Lucy, prompted by the Virgin Mary, alerted her to Dante's plight and how she then immediately left her seat beside Rachel (who represents the contemplative life) in Heaven and came down to Limbo to entreat Virgil to help Dante.

58. *his final evening hour*: Albert Camus, *The Plague*: "That evening hour which for believers is the time to look into their consciences is hardest of all hours on the prisoner or exile who has nothing to look into but the void" (182–183).

66. *Who purify themselves under your sovereign say-so*: Cato guards the shore of Purgatory the way Charon guarded the shore of Hell. Commentators point out that as a champion of liberty, Cato is an appropriate choice to oversee the souls who are struggling to free themselves from the chains of sin in order to achieve Heaven.

73–75. *You know this. Death for the sake of it wasn't bitter / In Utica, where you shuffled off your mortal coil, / Which will be so bright on that one fine day*: The day in question is Judgment Day. At the onset of the civil war, Cato opposed Caesar and sided with Pompey. In 46 BCE, after Caesar prevailed at the Battle of Thapsus, Cato took his own life in Utica, rather than serve Caesar. Shakespeare, *Hamlet* (III.i.74–77): HAMLET. "For in that sleep of death what dreams may come, / When we have shuffled off this mortal coil, / Must give us pause."

77–80. *I'm of that circle / Where the innocent eyes of your Marcia // Show how much she longs to still belong / To your pure and most-most loving breast*: Marcia, Cato's wife and mother of three of his children, resides in Limbo with Virgil and other pre-Christian figures (*Inf.* IV, 128). Lucan's *Pharsalia* tells the story of how Cato's friend, L. Hortensius, asked for Cato's daughter's hand in marriage; deeming that match inappropriate, Cato instead, after first asking for her father's consent, gave him Marcia. After Hortensius's death, Marcia returned to Cato (2.327–349) and asked him to again recognize their marriage: "Give me / the bond of my first marriage bed, give me the mere empty / name of spouse: allow me to carve on my gravestone 'CATO'S MARCIA'" (trans. Jane Wilson Joyce). Shakespeare, Sonnet 110: "Then give me welcome, next my heaven the best, / Even to thy pure and most most loving breast."

82. *Let us travel through your seven kingdoms*: These kingdoms are the seven cornices of Purgatory.

94. *So, go, tie a simple reed around his waist*: The simple reed is to signify humility. Dante was also girded in the *Inferno*, there with a knotted cord like those worn by Franciscan monks. In the Franciscan order, the knots symbolize the monks' vows of poverty, chastity, and obedience.

95–96. *And wash his filthy face— / Make sure you scrub off all the grime*: The grime on Dante's face is the residue of the noxious atmosphere of Hell.

98–99. *the first of the ministers from Paradise . . . as if he got caught in a smoke cloud*: The *primo ministro* is the angel of God that guards the entrance to Purgatory. Dante will encounter it in *Purg.* IX, 78.

101–102. *where the sea-waves' sway tugs / At the rough stones*: Lord Byron, *The Prophecy of Dante* (2, 109): "Her sandy ocean, and the Sea-waves' sway"; Hilda Doolittle (H.D.), "The Wind Sleepers": "tear us an altar, / tug at the cliff-boulders, / pile them with the rough stones—."

104–105. *broken / By the surf's steady rasp and after-rasp*: Hilda Doolittle (H.D.), "Sea Gods":

> They say you are twisted by the sea,
> you are cut apart
> by wave-break upon wave-break,

that you are misshapen by the sharp rocks,
broken by the rasp and after-rasp.

107–108. *The sun, now rising, will show you how / To take an easier route up the mountain*: The sun, metaphorically divine grace, will guide them. The hour is just before dawn, the beginning of a new day.

109. *With that, he vanished into the air*: Lewis Carroll, *Through the Looking Glass and What Alice Found There*: "Whether she vanished into the air, or whether she ran quickly into the wood ('and she *can* run very fast!' thought Alice), there was no way of guessing, but she was gone" (45).

112. *you can follow me*: The song "Follow" was written by Jerry Merrick and sung by Richard P. "Richie" Havens on his 1967 album, *Mixed Bag*: "Then don't mind me 'cos I ain't nothin' but a dream. / And you can follow; And you can follow."

125–127. *And placed his palms lightly on the wet grass . . . I offered him my tear-stained cheeks*: Commentators point out both the echoes of the sacred rite of Christian baptism and of that moment in the *Aeneid* (6, 637–659) when Aeneas sprinkles himself with water at the threshold of the Elysium, an Edenic "garden-like region wrapped in unearthly sunshine. There are games, and music, and chariot-driving, each one following the pursuit which was his delight in life" (Conington).

128. *And right there, he revealed all my true colors*: "True Colors," written by Billy Steinberg and Tom Kelly, is the title song of Cyndi Lauper's second album (1986): "And I'll see your true colors / Shining through / I see your true colors / And that's why I love you."

134–136. *Oh, one for the books! / When he pulled up the lowly plant by its roots, // Another at once sprang up in its place*: Dante has borrowed from Virgil the trope of a plant that when plucked miraculously regenerates (*Aeneid* 6, 136–144). In Virgil's tale the plant, a golden bough, is both beautiful and valuable; in Purgatory, the plant is appropriately a humble rush, which gestures to the fact that it is only through humility that a purgatorial soul can ever reach Paradise.

Canto II

The sun had already reached the horizon
Of the meridian circle that,
At its height, covers Jerusalem like a lid.

On the circle's other side, Night was emerging
From the Ganges with the Scales that fall
From Libra's hand when dark outweighs the day.

So that from where I stood,
The white-and-red cheeks of pretty Aurora
Had, after so long, become washed-out.

We were still alongside the sea, like those
Who conjure the road in their minds,
Then set out, while their bodies remain behind.

Just then, like when caught red-handed
By morning, Mars blushes red behind a thick mist
Low in the west over the ocean,

That's the way I saw—I can still see it—
A bright light traveling so fast across the sea
That nothing with wings could equal its speed.

In the few seconds that it took me to turn
And ask, "What's that?"
It had grown much larger and brighter still.

Then, on either side, something indecipherable,
A seeming whiteness, and underneath it,
Little by little, another emerging whiteness.

My teacher didn't say a word
Until the first white areas resolved into wings.
When he saw it was the coxswain, he shouted,

"Get down, down on your knees. Look—
It's one of God's angels! Put your hands together;
From now on, you'll see overseers like these

See how it rejects human methods:
It doesn't want an oar, no sail
Other than wings, even on a long haul like this.

See how its wings point toward Heaven,
Handling the air with those eternal feathers
That never lessen, unlike human hair."

As the divine bird came closer and closer,
It kept growing brighter. Finally,
I looked down to avoid the blinding light.

It came to shore in a sort of airboat, so light
And swift the boat only skimmed the surface;
The hull hung in the wind above the water.

The celestial navigator stood at the stern,
Looking as if blessedness had been etched upon it.
More than a hundred spirits sat before it,

Singing in unison, maintaining a single melody,
"When Israel went out of Egypt"—
On and on until the end of the psalm.

It made the sign of the Holy Cross over them,
After which the spirits all rushed onto the shore.
Then it left the way it had come, quick as a wink.

The crowd that stayed, looking all around,
Seemed like strangers in a strange land
Pondering a brave new world.

The sun, having already booted
Capricorn out of the mid-sky, was now
Shooting dart-like rays of daylight everywhere,

When the new people turned and faced us,
Saying, "If you know, please show us
The on-ramp for the road up the mountain."

"You probably think we know everything
About this place," Virgil answered,
"But we're also travelers, just like you.

We arrived just before you by another road
So steep and rough, it'll make this one
Seem like a game of Chutes and Ladders."

The spirits, once they could see
I was breathing, and thus, clearly still alive,
Turned a whiter shade of pale in astonishment.

The same way no one shies away
From the messenger holding an olive branch
But instead presses in to get the breaking news,

So, every last one of these fortunate souls
Fixed their eyes on my face, as if forgetting
To go and better themselves.

I saw one approach with obvious affection,
As though wanting to hug me; I was so touched
I found myself moved to do the same.

O spirits, empty except as simulacra!
Three times I clasped my hands behind his back,
And each time they came back to my own chest.

Amazement must have been written on my face,
Because the ghost smiled and stepped back;
I pressed forward, following him.

He gently told me I should let it go,
At which point I realized who he was. I asked
Whether he could stay a little bit longer and talk.

"The way I loved you when I wore my mortal state,"
He said, "I love you the same released from it.
So, I'll stay. But why are you coming through?"

"Here, my dear Casella, is where I hope
To return to, so I'm taking the road now.
But why were you passed over for so long?"

"I don't feel slighted," he said, "if the one
Who decides who it will pick up, and when,
Has more than once said no to my going;

It only ever wants what's fair and just.
For three months now it's actually been willing
To take on anyone who wanted to go.

I was just standing there, facing the shore
Where the water from the Tiber enters the sea,
When it kindly said I could join it.

Right now, it's flying back to the river delta:
That's the eternal meetup spot for those
Who aren't dropping down to Acheron."

"If there's not a rule that wipes your memory,
Of those love songs that used to soothe me
When desire was burning down the house,

Would you be willing to give a little aid
And comfort to my soul? It's utterly exhausted
After having lugged my body all the way here."

"Love reasoning out inside my mind—"
He began to sing, so smoothly
That the cool melody still plays deep inside me.

My teacher, I, and all the others with him,
Seemed totally content, as if our minds
Were emptied of everything but this.

We were mesmerized, intent on the music,
When hello! here was the venerable old man
Shouting, "What's this, you spiritual slugs?

What's this foot-dragging? Get to the mountain
Now and throw off that checkered snakeskin
That holds you back from knowing God."

Suddenly, like pigeons at a breakfast buffet—
Calmly pecking at a rolled oat or shredded wheat,
Showing no signs of their usual puffed-up hubris—

If something frightens them, they instantly
Abandon what had acted like a lure,
Hijacked now by a far more pressing concern,

That's how I saw this new group stop listening
To the singing and run toward the slope,
Like those who go with no idea where they'll end up.

Nor was our own departure any less quick.

1–3. *The sun had already reached the horizon / Of the meridian circle that . . . covers Jerusalem like a lid*: The meridian is a theoretical circle that defines the spherical nature of the cosmos. It is perpendicular to the horizon and extends from the celestial zenith through the celestial nadir. When it's day on one side of the meridian circle, it's night on the opposite side. Dante uses Jerusalem as a point of reference for tracking time: in Jerusalem, the sun is at the horizon and setting, while on Mount Purgatory—Jerusalem's antipodal opposite—the sun is rising.

4–6. *Night was emerging / From the Ganges with the Scales that fall / . . . when dark outweighs the day*: With the longer days that follow the autumn solstice, Libra is no longer a nighttime constellation; the scales, therefore, "fall from her hand"—which means she and her celestial scales are invisible. It is now spring in the Northern Hemisphere, however; thus, on the opposite side of the meridian circle where it is nightfall, Libra is coming into view. Night comes to Jerusalem from the east, the direction of the Ganges River.

8–9. *The white-and-red cheeks of pretty Aurora / Had, after so long, become washed-out*: As the sun rises higher in the sky, the blushing cheeks of Aurora, the Roman goddess of dawn, undergo a visible change. Similarly, in *Purg.* IX, 1–3, where Aurora is identified as the lover of ancient Tithonus, she is seen whitening on the eastside balcony.

40–42. *It came to shore in a sort of airboat . . . above the water*: The boat is light because the souls are weightless. Similarly, when Dante boarded the boat steered by Phlegyas across the river Styx in *Inf.* VIII, 26–27, only his weight caused the boat to sink in the water.

46–47. *Singing in unison . . . "When Israel went out of Egypt"*: Dante uses the Vulgate Latin: *In exitu Israel de Aegypto.* Dante could reasonably expect that this first verse of Psalm 114 would bring the entire psalm to a reader's mind. The psalm is a song of thanksgiving for the Exodus out of Egypt. Since it celebrates a form of rebirth, it was part of the traditional Catholic Easter liturgy; it was also sung at the burial of the dead. In a much-quoted letter to his patron, Cangrande I della Scala, Dante writes that the psalm refers to "the passing of the sanctified soul from the bondage of the corruption of this world to the liberty of everlasting glory" (Toynbee, trans.).

53. *like strangers in a strange land*: *Stranger in a Strange Land* is a 1961 science fiction novel by Robert A. Heinlein. The title is taken from Exodus 2:22: "And she bare him a son, and he called his name Gershom: for he said, I have been a stranger in a strange land."

54. *Pondering a brave new world*: Shakespeare, *The Tempest* (V.i.186–187): MIRANDA. "How beauteous mankind is! O brave new world, / That has such people in't." *Brave New World* is the title of a 1932 dystopian futuristic novel by Aldous Huxley. The novel,

set in London in CE 2540, depicts a society defined by consumerism and industrial exploitation, where unhappiness is treated with an antidepressant.

55–57. *The sun, having already booted / Capricorn out . . . Shooting dart-like rays of daylight*: It is approximately a half hour past sunrise and Aries is now alone in the sky. The shooting of the rays evokes the figure of Apollo, the Roman god of the sun who was depicted as an archer.

66. *a game of Chutes and Ladders*: The game Chutes and Ladders, based on the ancient Indian game Moksha Patam, was introduced in America in 1943 by Milton Bradley Company. The original game, which incorporated elements of Hindu philosophy and moral principles, was brought to England from India in 1892. At that time, it was renamed Snakes and Ladders and the "vices and virtues" were replaced by Anglican values of thrift, penance, and industry; the consequences for failure included illness, disgrace, and poverty.

69. *a whiter shade of pale*: "A Whiter Shade of Pale," a 1967 hit single by the British rock band Procol Harum, written by Gary Brooker, Keith Reid, and Matthew Fisher, appeared that same year on the group's first studio album, *Procol Harum*.

80–81. *I clasped my hands behind his back, / And each time they came back to my own chest*: The souls in Purgatory, like those in Hell, have a semblance that matches their appearance at the time of their death. In Hell, the substance appears to have materiality—one hits another in the stomach and we hear a hollow sound; Dante pulls the hair of another and he screams—in this case, however, the spirit appears to lack material substance; when Dante attempts to embrace the soul, his arms encounter nothing but only come back to his own chest.

86. *I realized who he was*: As with the living, the voice of the spirit appears to keep its distinctive qualities. In *Inferno*, Dante could recognize those souls who had Florentine accents. Here, it appears he recognizes the voice of someone he knew.

87. *Whether he could stay a little bit longer and talk*: "Stay (Just a Little Bit Longer)" is a song written in 1953 by Maurice Williams. It was first recorded as a demo record in 1960 by his doo-wop band, the Zodiacs. Later that year, Herald Records released it as a single; the following year it appeared as the title song on the group's first album.

88. *when I wore my mortal state*: Shakespeare: *King Henry VIII* (II.iv.226–230): Henry. "We are contented / To wear our mortal state to come with her, / Katherine our queen."

91. *Here, my dear Casella*: Casella, a musician, and someone Dante clearly knew and was fond of, has never been identified with confidence by commentators. Singleton (2:36) mentions a document archived in Siena, dated July 13, 1282, that records a fine levied against someone named Casella for "wandering the streets at night." *Here, My Dear* is a double studio album by Marvin Gaye, released in 1978 by Tamla Records.

98–99. *For three months now it's actually been willing / To take on anyone who wanted to go*: Dante appears to be assuming that the Christmas papal bull announced by Pope Boniface VIII, which granted indulgences to pilgrims attending the jubilee in Rome during the year 1300, would naturally be extended to the souls waiting in Ante-Purgatory. The three months of leniency to which Casella refers would have covered the period from December 25, 1299, until March 25, 1300, the Easter setting for the poem.

101–105. *Where the water from the Tiber enters the sea . . . those / Who aren't dropping down to Acheron*: The Tiber River passes through Rome before emptying into the sea near Ostia, an ancient Roman seaport. It's here, near the seat of Saint Peter and his papal descendants, that the dead souls depart for Mount Purgatory. The transporting angel is apparently allowed to use its discretion as to which souls are ready to be carried over. Those who are not Purgatory-bound sink down to the River Acheron, where, if their only sin was their failure to stand for right when they had an opportunity to do so, they will languish in the vestibule of Hell; if their sins were more significant, Charon will ferry them across to Hell proper and Minos will assign them a circle.

108. *When desire was burning down the house*: "Burning Down the House" is a song written and performed by the band Talking Heads (David Byrne, Chris Frantz, Jerry Harrison, Tina Weymouth). It was released first as a single and then on their 1983 studio album, *Speaking in Tongues* (Sire Records).

112. *Love reasoning out inside my mind*: The third section of *Convivio* (*The Banquet*), an unfinished work in praise of Lady Philosophy that interweaves prose and canzoni (lyric poems) written by Dante between 1305 and 1308, begins with a poem, the first line of which is "Amor che ne la mente mi ragiona" (Love that reasons out inside my mind). It is possible that Casella set the poem to music, although there is no evidence of it apart from Dante's claim in *Purgatorio*.

119–120. *here was the venerable old man / Shouting, "What's this, you spiritual slugs"*: Cato not only guards the shore of Mount Purgatory but he also appears to be in charge of keeping the new arrivals on track. The secular music they have stopped to listen to is not contributing anything to the souls' penitential betterment. This moment serves as yet another object lesson about the need not to waste time.

122. *throw off that checkered snakeskin*: Shakespeare, *Henry VI, Part II* (III.i.228–230): Queen. "Or as the snake rolled in a flowering bank, / With shining checkered slough, doth sting a child / That for the beauty thinks it excellent."

CANTO III

While the others were quickly scattering
Across the field, headed for the mountain
Where justice tracks us down,

I clung to my faithful friend.
Where would I be now, if it weren't for him?
Who would lead me up the mountain?

He seemed overcome by guilt—
You noble, unstained conscience,
How sharper than a serpent's tooth is a tiny fault!

When he stopped his frantic rushing,
Which undermines the gravity of any action,
My mind, until now laser-focused,

Became curious to see more. I looked up
At the mountain's height, a measure of how far
It had once been hurled from the sea bottom.

The sun, a red flame behind my back,
Threw a shape in front of me that exactly matched
The sunlight blocked by my body.

Since the ground was only dark in front of me,
I looked to one side,
Worried I'd been abandoned.

And my reassurance: "You still don't trust me?
You don't believe I'm with you
And acting as your minder?

It's time for vespers back there, where they buried
The body I lived in when I cast a shadow.
Naples has it now; it was moved from Brindisi.

No shadow in front of me shouldn't surprise you
Any more than the fact that one bottomless lake of sky
Doesn't block the light coming from another.

The Purest of the Pure designs our bodies
To suffer discomfort—extremes of heat and cold—
And doesn't care to tell us how He does it.

We're foolish if we think we can use reason
To unlock the mystical process
By which Three Persons become One Substance.

Limit yourselves, human beings, to the simple *that*
That is. If you'd been able to grasp everything,
Mary could have turned down the job of baby-maker.

You've seen the fruitless questing by some men,
Who, if they'd been successful,
Wouldn't be grieving for all eternity—

I'm speaking of Aristotle and of Plato
And of countless others." He looked down,
Said nothing more, but still seemed upset.

Meanwhile, we'd arrived at the foot
Of the mountain, where we found a cliff so sheer
Not even trained legs could have made it up.

Compared to this, the roughest and most desolate
Rock-bound path between Lerici and Turbìa
Would seem like an easy open-air escalator.

"Who knows on which side the slope
Is more graded," my teacher paused to think,
"Where someone without wings could climb?"

While he stood there with his head bent,
Trying to sort out which way was best,
And I was staring at the cliff face above,

From the left a group of souls suddenly appeared
To be walking toward us, but so slowly
They seemed not to be moving at all.

"Look up, sir," I said. "Over there.
They might offer us advice,
If you can't figure it out by yourself."

He looked up with obvious relief and said,
"Since they're moving so slowly, let's go to them,
And you, dear son, hang on to that hope."

Even though we'd taken quite a few steps,
I'd say they were still as far away
As the distance a good pitcher can throw,

When they all pressed against the hard rock
Of the high wall and huddled, stock still—
The way stunned people freeze-stop and stare.

"You who've come to a good end,
The true spiritual elite," Virgil began,
"By the peace I trust is waiting for each of you,

Could you tell us where the incline is least steep
So we can make the climb: the more one knows,
The more one hates to waste time."

Like sheep leave the pen, one, then two, then three,
While the others stand there, pure timidity,
Eyes and snouts to the ground,

Then, what the first does, the others do—silently,
Simplemindedly, ending up, if one stops, smack-dab
Against the one in front of it, without knowing why—

That's how I saw the first line of that fortunate flock
Move slowly forward, artlessly
And with humility.

As soon as those in front saw the break
In the light on the ground to my right,
And my shadow on the rock wall,

They stopped short and stepped back;
Then all the others coming up behind
Did the same, clueless as to why.

"Before you even ask, yes, what you see here is,
In fact, a human body taking a man-sized bite
Out of the light on the ground.

Don't overreact, but think," my teacher said.
"It can't be without Heaven-sent clearance,
That he's trying to scale this wall."

To which those decent people responded,
"In that case, turn around and walk in front of us,"
Fanning the air forward with the backs of their hands.

One of them then began: "Whoever you are,
As you're walking, look back at me and consider
Whether you ever saw me on the other side."

I turned and gave him the once-over:
Blond hair, handsome, a rather refined look,
But one eyebrow split where it had suffered a cut.

When I politely said no to ever having seen him,
He said, "Look at this!"
And showed me a wound above his collarbone.

Smiling, he then said, "I'm Manfred,
Grandson of the Empress Constance.
Given that fact, I beg you, when you return,

Go and see my lovely daughter, the progenitor
Of the paragon kings of Sicily and Aragon,
And tell her the truth, if she's been told otherwise.

After my body was slashed
With two mortal stab wounds,
I turned in tears to Him who willingly pardons.

My sins were horrific
But the expansive arms of Infinite Goodness
Embrace any who walk into them.

If the Archbishop of Cosenza,
Sent by Clement to locate me,
Had better understood this aspect of God,

The bones of my body would still be at the bridgehead
Near Benevento, marked and guarded
By a mound of heavy boulders.

Now they're rain-washed and wind-scattered
Outside the kingdom, near the banks of the Verde,
Where he had them carried with candles snuffed.

In spite of being cursed, no one is so lost
That Eternal Love can't restore them,
As long as hope still has a speck of green left in it.

The truth is, if at the hour of death, one's a heretic
Of the Holy Church, even if they repent,
They wait at the foot of this precipice

Thirty years for each one spent being presumptuous,
Unless that sentence gets reduced
By prayers said by the righteous.

Now you see how happy you could make me
By telling my good Constance you saw me,
And also about this exception:

There's much to be gained here from those back there."

9. *How sharper than a serpent's tooth is a tiny fault*: Shakespeare, *King Lear* (I.iv.285–86): LEAR. "How sharper than a serpent's tooth it is / To have a thankless child!"

13–15. I *looked up / At the mountain's height, a measure of how far / It had once been hurled from the sea bottom*: Mount Purgatory was formed as a result of the displacement of rock when Satan was thrown from Heaven. Dante positions it directly opposite Jerusalem.

25–27. *back there, where they buried / The body I lived in when I cast a shadow. / Naples has it now; it was moved from Brindisi*: Virgil was born near Mantua in 70 BCE and died in Brindisi in 19 BCE. Augustus arranged for his body to be taken to Pozzuoli, just outside Naples, and interred in a tomb that bears a Latin inscription Virgil himself is said to have composed: "Mantua me genuit, Calabri rapuere, tenet nunc Parthenope. / Cecini pascua, rura, duces." (Mantua gave birth to me, Calabria whisked me away, now Naples holds me. / I sang of pastures, the countryside, and those who lead.)

29. *that one bottomless lake of sky*: William Styron, *Lie Down in Darkness*: "Late in April he and Helen went on the train for a three-week vacation to a resort near Asheville, and there among the smoky hills, in the cool ferny air where the sky seemed to be spread like a bottomless lake above them, they both calmed down" (258).

35–36: *the mystical process / By which Three Persons become One Substance*: Virgil's point is that the mystery of the Trinity—God as three persons: Father, Son, and Holy Ghost—is beyond the limits of human reason. One needs faith.

38–39. *If you'd been able to grasp everything, / Mary could have turned down the job of babymaker*: Had humans been able to perceive the nature of God, it would not have been necessary for Christ to come to earth, die, and be resurrected.

40–44. *You've seen the fruitless questing by some men . . . Aristotle and of Plato / And of countless others*: Virgil reminds Dante of the brilliant pagan philosophers he encountered in Limbo, saying if anyone could have penetrated these mysteries, it would have been them. Having lived in the pre-Christian era, however, they sadly can't know the very truths that might have led to their deliverance but are instead consigned to Limbo, where they remain in a state of endless longing for something better. Virgil himself is in this group.

49. *most desolate / Rock-bound path between Lerici and Turbìa*: Dante is referring to what was then a nearly impassible mountainous area between the fortified town of Lerici on the Gulf of La Spezia on the eastern edge of Liguria, and the village of Turbìa, on the far western edge of Liguria. Today, Turbìa (now La Turbie) is located in France.

58–60. *From the left a group of souls suddenly appeared . . . so slowly / They seemed not to be moving at all*: Vernon (1:95) mentions Benvenuto da Imola's belief that the slow pace of these excommunicated souls is meant to echo their having delayed repentance until the very end of their lives.

67–69. *Even though we'd taken quite a few steps . . . the distance a good pitcher can throw*: Dante and Virgil have walked a Roman mile, approximately 5,000 feet, but are still almost 500 feet away from the group. According to the *Guinness Book of Baseball World Records*, Glen Gorbous, a Canadian, holds the world's record for the longest pitch; he threw a ball 445 feet and 10 inches on August 1, 1957. The record for the longest throw by a woman is held by Mildred "Babe" Didrikson who, on July 25, 1931, threw a baseball 296 feet.

104–105. *look back at me and consider / Whether you ever saw me on the other side*: As we'll discover in v. 112, this is Manfred (d. 1266, age thirty-four), the offspring of Holy Roman Emperor Frederick II and Bianca Lancia, a noblewoman. Manfred was king of Naples and Sicily from 1258 to 1266. Dante would have been less than a year old when he died, but Manfred can't help but hope that Dante will know him and will want to take word of him back to his family.

108–111. *one eyebrow split where it had suffered a cut . . . a wound above his collarbone*: These are the wounds Manfred suffered at the Battle of Benevento.

112–113. *I'm Manfred, / Grandson of the Empress Constance*: Manfred's grandparents were Henry VI, Holy Roman emperor from 1165 to 1197, and Empress Constance of Sicily. Commentators note that Manfred identifies his lineage through his paternal grandmother, whom Dante placed in Paradise, and not through his father, whom Dante placed with the heretics in *Inf.* X, 119. Although not married at the time to Manfred's mother, Frederick II recognized him as his legitimate son and stipulated in his will that Manfred should rule as regent during his half brother Conrad IV's absence.

115–116: *Go and see my lovely daughter, the progenitor / Of the paragon kings of Sicily and Aragon*: Constance, queen of Aragon, was the only daughter of Manfred and his wife, Beatrice of Savoy. She married Peter III, the eldest son of King James I of Aragon. When James I died in 1276, Peter III ascended to the throne with Constance as queen. Upon Manfred's death at the Battle of Benevento in 1266, she became queen of Sicily. She had two daughters and four sons, three of whom were kings: Alfonso III served as king of Aragon (1285–1291); James II reigned as king of Sicily (1285–1295) and king of Aragon (1291–1327); Fredrick III was king of Sicily (1296–1327).

117. *And tell her the truth, if she's been told otherwise*: His daughter would have had no way of knowing about his last-minute repentance; she would have assumed that because he had died in a state of contumacy, he would go to Hell.

118–119. *After my body was slashed / With two mortal stab wounds*: Manfred's half brother Conrad IV died of malaria in 1254; at that time, his son Conradin, the rightful heir to the kingdom, was only three years old. The authority would have passed to Conradin's tutor, Pope Innocent IV (from 1243 to 1254), except that a consortium of Sicilian barons asked Manfred to serve as regent. Since Manfred was an ardent antipapist and Ghibelline supporter, this was unacceptable to the pope; in retaliation, he excommunicated Manfred. Innocent's successor, Alexander IV (1254–1261), also excommunicated Manfred, as did Urban IV (1261–1264). Clement IV (1265–1268) offered the kingdom to Charles, Count of Anjou, who accepted. Charles was crowned in Rome in January 1266 and by February had moved his troops south to battle Manfred. The rival armies met on February 26, 1266, at the Battle of Benevento. Manfred refused to flee and died on the battlefield.

120. *I turned in tears to Him who willingly pardons*: According to Charles Hall Grandgent (*The Divina commedia*, 2:30): "In the *Imago Mundi* of Jacopo da Acqui, written only some ten or twenty years after Dante's time, it is recorded that Manfred saved himself by exclaiming just before death: 'Deus propitius esto mihi peccatori!' [God be gracious, I am a sinner.] The incident as it appears in the *Purgatorio* is, therefore, presumably based on a tradition already current." Manfred appears to be quoting Luke 18:13: "And the publican, standing afar off, would not lift up so much as his eyes unto heaven, but smote upon his breast, saying, God be merciful to me a sinner."

124–126. *If the Archbishop of Cosenza, / Sent by Clement to locate me, / Had better understood this aspect of God*: The archbishop would have been either Bartolomeo Pignatelli or his successor, Tommaso d'Agni. Manfred appears to be referring to John 6:37: "Him that cometh unto me I will in no wise cast out."

127–129. *The bones of my body would still be at the bridgehead / Near Benevento, marked and guarded / By a mound of heavy boulders*: Manfred's body was originally buried at the foot of a bridge near the battlefield. Since this was sacred Church land, Clement IV ordered the body moved.

130–132. *Now they're rain-washed and wind-scattered / Outside the kingdom . . . carried with candles snuffed*: Church law dictated that when the bodies of those who had been excommunicated were transported to the grave, candles had to be snuffed and carried upside down. Candles were expensive and frequently limited to special liturgical services; they would not have been wasted on the burial of a heretic.

138–141. *They wait at the foot of this precipice // Thirty years for each one spent being presumptuous, / Unless that sentence gets reduced / By prayers*: The belief that time spent in Purgatory can be shortened by prayers said by the living became part of Church doctrine in the twelfth century, but nowhere is it stated that the excommunicated must spend a period of thirty years in Purgatory for each year spent cut off from the Church; this is Dante's invention.

canto IV

When any of the mind's inherent
Capacities sense pleasure, or pain,
The soul focuses on that alone

And seems to ignore the other potentials—
This versus the mistaken claim that one soul
Above another gets lit up in us—

So, as a result, when a sight or a sound
Holds the soul in its grip,
We lose all sense that time is ticking.

The faculty watching the clock isn't the one
That ties up the mind; the first moves around
While the hands of the other are bound.

I had that actual experience: while I was
Listening to that spirit and marveling,
The sun had climbed a full fifty degrees.

I hadn't noticed until we came to a place
Where the souls all called out,
"Here's what you were asking about."

When the late grapes turn brown,
A groundskeeper will often take a garden fork
Of thorn shrub and plug a larger opening

Than the narrow gap that my teacher first,
Then I, climbed through—alone now
Since the group had gone on without us.

One can make it up to San Leo, or down
To Noli, or reach the diadem of snow that crowns
Bismantova on foot, but here one had to fly—

By which I mean with streamlined wings
And featherlight intense desire behind the guide
Who gave me hope and lit the way

We climbed where the rock was broken open,
A hermitage, squeezed between two walls;
The ground beneath required both hands and feet.

When we'd reached the highest rim of the precipice,
Where it opened out onto a hillside,
I asked my teacher, "Which way?"

"Don't backslide," he said, "not even one step.
Just stay behind me and keep gaining ground
Until someone arrives who can guide us."

The summit above soared out of sight;
The incline was difficult and much steeper even
Than the line that divides a right angle in half.

Having reached the point of exhaustion, I said,
"You've been a very kind father, but turn and look:
If you don't stop to rest, I'll be left here by myself."

"And you, my son, keep going," he said, "just
Up to there," pointing to a slightly higher ledge
Circling that side of the mountain.

What he said flipped a switch; as tired as I was,
I forced myself to scramble after him
Until the narrow beltway was firm beneath my feet.

There we sat to rest, facing east—
Which was for us the mooring of starting out.
It helps to see how far one has come.

I first looked down at the shores below,
Then raised my eyes to the sun,
Amazed that its light was striking us from the left.

The poet realized I was totally baffled
By the fact that the sun's aerial car
Was cutting a path between us and the North.

He said, "If it were Castor and Pollux
In the company of that big reflecting mirror
That conducts its light in both directions,

You'd see the zodiac's wheel revolve even closer
To the Bears, unless, that is,
It were to suddenly jump its well-worn track.

If you want to understand how this can be,
Picture Mount Zion and imagine
Both it and this mountain located on Earth

In such a way that they share one horizon
But occupy two different hemispheres; the path
That poor Phaeton sadly failed to navigate,

If you consider it closely, you'll see,
Must pass this mountain on one side,
When it's passing Zion on the other."

"Of course!" I told my teacher.
"Before this, I could never figure it out—
My mind kept missing the point, which I now get:

The mid-circle of celestial motion,
Or what's called the equator in some sciences,
Forever lies between the sun and winter weather,

At the identical angle that—for exactly the reason
You just gave—it once lay for the Hebrews
To the warm-weather South.

But if you don't mind my asking, I'd love to know
How much farther we have to go; the mountain rises
Higher than I can see with my naked eye."

"The design of the mountain is such," he said,
"That when you begin at the base, the climb's harder;
The higher you get the less painful the effort

So, when you seem to be enjoying the ascent,
And the path up feels as effortless as coasting
Downstream in a beautiful pea-green boat,

Then you will have reached the end
And can hope to rest and catch your breath.
Of that much I'm sure. I really can't say more."

As soon as he'd said those words,
We heard a voice nearby, "But maybe first . . .
You'll find you really need a bit of a sit-down."

Hearing that, we both turned
And saw on our left a huge boulder,
Which neither of us had noticed before.

We went over to the rock and found people
Lounging in the shade behind it, as if
They were a bunch of good-for-nothing slackers.

One, who seemed quite listless, was sitting
On the ground, arms loosely circling his bent knees.
His lowered head hung between them.

"Whoa, my good lord," I said. "Take a look
At this one. He's showing more indifference
Than if laziness were his little sister." At that,

He slowly turned his head. Resting it on his thigh,
While keeping his eyes fixed on us, he said,
"Fine, Mister Lightning Bolt, you go right on up."

I now realized who he was.
Not even the lingering effects of my recent effort
Stopped me from going straight over to him.

When I got there, barely raising his head, he said, "So,
Is your understanding of why the sun drives his chariot
Along your left upper arm now complete?"

His sluggish manner and curt remarks
Prompted a slight smile; I said, "Belacqua,
From now on, I'll no longer worry about you.

But why are you sitting here like this?
Are you waiting for an escort?
Or simply going back to your old bad habits?"

"O brother, what's the point of trekking up?
God's feathered messenger in charge of the gate
Isn't going to let me in to do my penance.

First, I have to wait outside for as long
As in my lifetime the heavens spun around me; this
Because I put off my pious sighs until the very end—

Unless, that is, someone whose heart's in a state
Of grace helps me out by sending up a few prayers.
What good is anyone, if Heaven can't hear them?"

The poet, without waiting for me, had already begun
The climb, calling back: "Come on now, look how
The sun is crossing the meridian, and at the edge,

The boot of the Western night is about to cover Morocco."

5–6. *the mistaken claim that one soul / Above another gets lit up in us*: Plato maintained there was a vegetative spirit, located in the liver; a sensory spirit, located in the heart; and an intellectual spirit, located in the brain. And further, that each of these remained completely separate, hierarchically resting one on top of the other. Dante follows Aristotle and Aquinas in refuting this idea. In *Convivio* (3, 2, 11–16), he argues that all three "powers"—life, sense, and reason—are integrated in the human soul and can't be teased apart. The senses not only can't exist independently, but they also form the bedrock on which rational thought rests.

In *Vita nuova*, Dante describes the moment when he is nine years old and first sees Beatrice as involving all three aspects of his being: "I can honestly say that at that moment, the animating spark of life that lives in the deepest recess of the heart exploded with such force that I felt it in every fiber of my being. I was shaken by what it implied: *A stronger god than I is about to take control.* That's exactly when the animal within—which occupies that attic room where all the sense perceptions travel, especially the visual—was filled with awe and said to the eyes: *Get ready to see blessedness.* Then the primitive part of nature, at the most basic level of the gut, began to cry and crying said: *Hello misery, my suffering is going to go on forever.*"

7–9. *when a sight or a sound / Holds the soul in its grip, / We lose all sense that time is ticking*: As evidence against the Platonic argument, Dante points out that the rational aspect of the integrated soul can lose track of time when it's totally preoccupied with sensory experiences. If there were three separate souls, the rational soul would continue to track time while the sensory soul was otherwise engaged.

13–15. *while I was / Listening to that spirit and marveling, / The sun had climbed a full fifty degrees*: This cryptic and complicated philosophical discourse is a long prelude to Dante's noting that he was so fascinated by Manfred's story that he had lost all awareness of the passage of time. Since the sun revolves fifteen degrees per hour, an elevation of fifty degrees means that three and a half hours have elapsed since sunrise, making the time approximately 9:30 a.m. Not all of that time has been spent listening to Manfred; Dante includes the time it took to find the path and reach this point.

18. *Here's what you were asking about*: In *Purg.* III, 76–77, Virgil had asked the group where the mountain was least steep.

22–24. *the narrow gap that my teacher first, / Then I, climbed through—alone now / Since the group had gone on without us*: Commentators note the echo of Matthew 7:13–14: "Enter ye in at the strait gate: for wide is the gate, and broad is the way, that leadeth to destruction, and many there be which go in thereat: Because strait is the gate, and narrow is the way, which leadeth unto life, and few there be that find it."

25. *up to San Leo, or down / To Noli*: San Leo was a remote fortress town in the district of Monteveltro, in the duchy of Urbino. Located at the top of a mountain, and surrounded by high peaks, it was difficult to reach. Noli is on the northernmost Ligurian coast (the Gulf of Genoa), at the base of a steep and rugged mountain; in Dante's time the only way to reach Noli by land was to descend the mountain.

26–27. *or reach the diadem of snow that crowns / Bismantova*: The Pietra di Bismantova is a geological rock formation with a flat summit and nearly perpendicular walls that juts above the neighboring peaks. During Dante's time, there was a single tortuous footpath to the top. Lord Byron, *Manfred* (I.i): "Mont Blanc is the monarch of mountains; / They crown'd him long ago / On a throne of rocks, in a robe of clouds, / With a diadem of snow."

32. *A hermitage, squeezed between two walls*: Lord Byron, "The Prisoner of Chillon": "These heavy walls to me had grown / A hermitage—and all my own!"

41–42. *much steeper even / Than the line that divides a right angle in half*: In other words, the incline was much steeper than a forty-five-degree angle.

53. *Which was for us the mooring of starting out*: John Ashbery, "Soonest Mended": "Making ready to forget, and always coming back / To the mooring of starting out, that day so long ago."

56–57. *Then raised my eyes to the sun, / Amazed that its light was striking us from the left*: In the Northern Hemisphere, the midmorning sun would be in the southwest quadrant of the sky; if someone were looking east, the sun would be on his or her right and a shadow would be cast to the left. Since Mount Purgatory, however, is in the Southern Hemisphere, the sun is in the northeast quadrant of the sky and would strike a person facing east from the left side and cast a shadow to the right.

59. *the sun's aerial car*: In Greek myth, the sun god, Helios, rose each dawn from his palace in the east and drove a chariot pulled by four fiery horses across the sky. Natalie Clifford Barney, "A Parisian Roof Garden in 1918": "Reclining love will make the heavens dance; / And if the enemy from aerial cars / Drops death, we'll share it vibrant with the stars!"

61–65. *If it were Castor and Pollux . . . You'd see the zodiac's wheel revolve even closer / To the Bears*: Today is Easter Sunday and the sun is in Aries. Virgil is explaining that if it were later in the year, the sun—that reflecting mirror that alternates sending light to the Northern and Southern Hemispheres—would be in Gemini (Castor and Pollux) and therefore farther north and closer to the Bears (Ursa Major and Ursa Minor).

68–71. *Picture Mount Zion and imagine . . . that they share one horizon / But occupy two different hemispheres*: The medieval Catholic conception of earth was that Mount Zion—the highest of the four hills that make up Jerusalem, and the biblical site of King David's palace—was the center of the Northern Hemisphere. It was assumed that the Southern

Hemisphere was entirely covered with water. Dante imagines Mount Purgatory, the sole landmass in that vast body of water, as antipodal to (i.e., directly opposite) Mount Zion. The shared horizon is the equator.

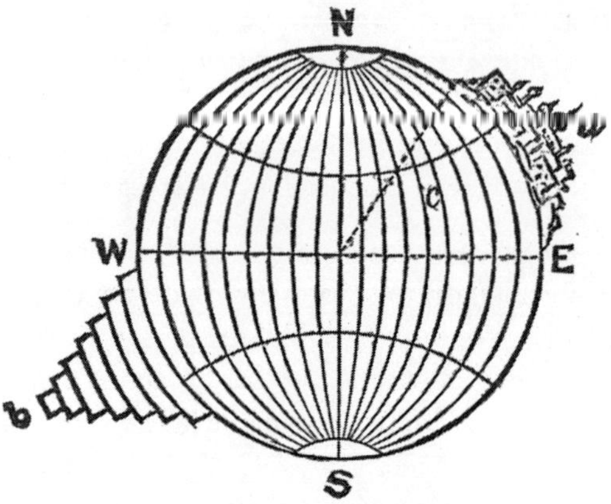

The Earth of Dante.

***a.* City of Jerusalem.**
***b.* Mountain of Purgatory.**
***c.* Inferno within the Earth.**

71–72. *the path / That poor Phaeton sadly failed to navigate*: Phaeton, the offspring of the sun god Helios and the sea nymph Clymene, insisted, against his father's sage advice, on driving the horse-drawn sun chariot across the sky. He lost control and dropped the reins. After the fiery chariot singed the plains of Africa, Jupiter saved earth by killing the boy with a lightning bolt.

74–75. *Must pass this mountain on one side, / When it's passing Zion on the other*: In the Northern Hemisphere, where east is on one's left, the path of the sun goes from left to right; in the antipodal Southern Hemisphere, where east is on one's right, it goes from right to left.

83–84. *it once lay for the Hebrews / To the warm-weather South*: The sun once passed to the south of Jerusalem to the very same degree that here, in the Southern Hemisphere, it is now passing to the north of Mount Purgatory.

93. *a beautiful pea-green boat*: Edward Lear, "The Owl and the Pussy-Cat": "The Owl and the Pussy-cat went to sea / In a beautiful pea-green boat."

114. *Fine, Mister Lightning Bolt, you go right on up*: Usain Bolt (b. 1986), a Jamaican runner who holds the record of 27.8 mph—as measured at the 2009 World Championships in Athletics in Berlin on August 16, 2009—is considered by many to be the fastest runner in recorded history. The media has dubbed him "Lightning Bolt."

122. *Belacqua*: Commentators have identified Belacqua, who is delaying his repentance by lounging in the shade of a boulder, as a Florentine lute-maker and musician, most likely Duccio di Bonavia, who died sometime between 1299 and 1302, and whom Dante was said to have known and often teased about his indolence. Belacqua appears in several of Samuel Beckett's novels. *Molloy* begins with the speaker beneath a rock: "I crouched like Belacqua, or Sordello, I forget." In the novel *How It Is*, the speaker describes himself as "Belacqua fallen over on his side tired of waiting forgotten of the hearts where grace abides asleep." The story "Echo's Bones" begins with a resurrected Belacqua smoking a cigar atop a cemetery fence.

127–128. *what's the point of trekking up? / God's feathered messenger in charge of the gate / Isn't going to let me in to do my penance*: Belacqua not only sees no point in going up to the gate, but one suspects, given his apathy, he may even prefer the comfort of the shade to the torments he'll have to endure once he's been admitted to Purgatory proper.

129–131. *I have to wait outside for as long . . . Because I put off my pious sighs until the very end*: As Belacqua once delayed his "pious sighs," he's now delaying his active repentance. Since those in Ante-Purgatory have to wait thirty times the period they delayed accepting God (see the note to *Purg.* I, 4–6), Belacqua—if he lived to be seventy, the lifespan suggested in Psalm 90:10, "The days of our years are threescore years and ten," and only accepted God on his deathbed—will have to spend twenty-one thousand years there.

133–135. *someone whose heart's in a state / Of grace helps me out by sending up a few prayers. / What good is anyone, if Heaven can't hear them*: Belacqua undoubtedly knows that not having exerted energy to help anyone else, it's highly unlikely anyone would go out of their way to help him. His attitude—what good are friends if one can't use them?—implies he would not have made many friends.

136. *The poet, without waiting for me, had already begun / The climb, calling back*: Virgil has no patience for this kind of self-pitying indolence, especially given that Belacqua has been given an opportunity that is closed to him.

139. *The boot of the Western night is about to cover Morocco*: Allen Ginsberg, *Howl* (Part III): "in my dreams you walk dripping from a sea-journey on the highway across America in tears / to the door of my cottage in the Western night." In the medieval era, the horizon dividing the Northern and Southern Hemispheres, which Dante places equidistant between Jerusalem and Mount Purgatory, was believed to extend from the Ganges in the east to Gibraltar in the west; Gibraltar in the poem is indicated by Morocco, which is on the northwest coast of Africa, directly across from it. If the sun is crossing the meridian, it's noon on Mount Purgatory and 6:00 p.m.—or just before nightfall—in Morocco. Commentators point out the similarity of these verses to Ovid's *Metamorphoses* 2.142–43: "Dum loquor, Hesperio positas in litore metas / umida nox tetigit; non est mora libera nobis!" (Even while I speak, the goal of the distant western shore / has been reached by dewy night; we must not delay anymore!)

Canto V

I'd already left those ghostly shades,
And was following in the footsteps of my guide,
When behind me, one pointed an indicative finger

And shouted, "Look how there's no sunlight
To the left of the lower one, and how the way
He moves makes it seem like he's alive."

Hearing that remark, I turned and saw
How they were staring in awe at me, and only
At me since it was my body blocking the light.

"What's so captivating," my teacher asked,
"That it's causing you to dawdle?
What do you care what they whisper about here?

Come along behind me, and let people talk.
Stand like a tower of strength, one that won't fall
Even if the wind batters it, tower-top to ground.

People who allow their thoughts to flit around
Soon lose sight of the end goal;
Every new thought splashes cold water on the last."

What could I possibly say except "I'm coming"?
As I said it, my face blushed bright red, suggesting
I was someone who might still deserve forgiveness.

Meanwhile, just ahead of us, people were coming
Across the mountain slope, singing
In alternate parts the verses of "Have Mercy on Me."

When they realized there was no way
For the sun's rays to pass through my body, their song
Became one long-drawn-out, rasping *Ohhh*—!

Two of them, sent as messengers by the others,
Ran over to meet us, insisting,
"Fill us in on your condition."

My teacher said, "You can go back now
And tell the others who sent you that, yes,
This man's body really is still flesh and blood.

I assume seeing his shadow is what stopped
Them; if so, that's all the truth you need to know.
They show him respect, it might benefit them."

I never saw a shooting star slice through
A clear twilight sky,
Or lightning rip apart August clouds at sunset,

As fast as those two ran back up. Once there,
They and all the others turned and ran back down
Like a mob breaching a barricade.

"This crowd pressing in on us," said the poet,
"They're hoping you'll help them,
But keep walking; you can listen as you go."

They came shouting, "Soul, on your way
Seeking bliss with the same frame
You were born with, please stop here for a while

To see whether you know any of us,
So you can carry news back to the other side—
Hey! Why are you going? *Hey*! Why don't you stop?

In our past lives, we all died a violent death;
Sinners to the end, at our final hour
A perspective pushed through like light from Heaven,

And at that point, penitent and all-forgiving,
We abandoned our lives fully reconciled to God,
Our hearts aching with the desire to see Him."

I said: "I'm carefully examining your faces,
But I don't recognize anyone. But if there's something
You want me to do, you spiritual elite, just say it.

I promise to do it, by the peace for which
I'm searching as I go from world to world
Following in the steps of this model guide."

One spoke up: "Each of us trusts, even without
Your swearing it, that you'll do your best for us,
Unless the power to do as you wish suffers a setback.

Speaking first, and only for myself, if you ever
Lay eyes on the territory between Romagna
And Naples, where Charles reigns,

I beg you to kindly pray for me in Fano,
Where through your devout prayers
I might wash away my grievous sins.

I was from there. But the wounds, from which
My blood and life force leapt like a fish from a lake,
Were delivered in the lap of Antenori land,

Which was where I thought I'd be safest.
It was Azzo of Este who was out to get me;
His anger toward me was far more than I deserved.

If I'd kept high-tailing it toward La Mira,
Instead of stopping off at Oriaco, I'd still be back
Where one breathes and the heart brags, I am.

Instead, I rode into the marsh, and got so tangled
In the reeds and muck, I stumbled and fell. There
In the mud, I watched a lake of venous blood gush out."

Another spoke up: "To help you get that wish
That draws you up the steep mountain,
Show some kind pity and help me realize my own.

I was a Montefeltro, I'm Buonconte: no one cares
About me, not even Giovanna. So, I go around,
My head bowed down, with this bunch."

I asked, "What power or fate led you
To wander so far from Campaldino,
That no one knows where you were buried?"

"Oh, that," he said. "The base of the Casentino
Valley is crossed by a river called the Archiano
That begins in the Apennines above the Hermitage.

I arrived just where it enters the Arno
And loses its name; stabbed in the throat, fleeing
On foot, making the plain a bleeding piece of earth,

I lost my sight and my voice,
Which ended on the name of Mary.
And there I fell and only my onyx flesh was left.

I'll tell the truth, and you tell it to the living.
God's angel grabbed me, just as the Hellhound cried,
'Hey, you from Heaven, why're you robbing me?

He shed a little tear, so you're gonna swipe this guy
From me and carry off his eternal part?
Fine, I'll deal in my own way with what's left.'

As you're well aware, as soon as moist air rises
And merges with the cold,
The vapor condenses and turns to water.

The evil one linked his ever-vigilant wickedness
To his intelligence and, using the force
Nature gave him, exploited the wind and fog.

When the day had faded, the entire valley,
From Pratomagno all across the ridge,
Was covered in fog; and, just as he intended,

The superhumid air in the sky overhead quickly
Turned to water. The rain fell; whatever
The ground couldn't absorb filled the ditches

And, when those widening streams met,
Rushed toward the actual river with such
Devastating speed nothing could hold it back.

The swollen Archiano found my frozen body
At its mouth and swept it into the Arno,
Undoing the cross my arms had made on my chest

When I'd been overtaken by pain. It rolled me—
On the banks then along the bed, finally
Burying me in a shroud of silt the river had pillaged."

"When you've gone back to the world,
And have rested up from your long time away,"
A third began where the other left off,

"Please remember me, I'm the wishful Pia.
Seine made me, Maremma undid me. As is known
Well by the one who ringed me, then did me in,

After first having had me with his family jewel."

4–6. *there's no sunlight / To the left of the lower one, and how the way / He moves makes it seem like he's alive*: Dante is now headed west, so the sun is to his right. The spirit may be commenting on Dante's shortness of breath, noted in the previous canto, or he may have noticed, like the centaur Chiron did in *Inf.* XII, 80–82, that Dante's feet dislodge the stones as he climbs.

15. *tower-top to ground*: Gerard Manley Hopkins, "The Alchemist in the City": "I mark the tower swallows run // Between the tower-top and the ground / Below me in the bearing air."

23–24. *singing / In alternate parts the verses of "Have Mercy on Me"*: Psalm 51, a biblical song of repentance composed by Ruth for her great-grandson David—who murdered Uriah and committed adultery with Bathsheba—is known as the "Miserere," after the first verse of the Latin: "Miserere mei, Deus: secundum magnan misericordiam tuam." (Have mercy upon me, O God, after Thy great goodness.) In medieval England, knowledge of the Miserere was used in the courts as a test of clerical literacy; success allowed the petitioner to claim a "benefit of clergy," which transferred the case from the strict secular court to the more lenient ecclesiastical one. In time, the psalm became known as the "neck verse" since by reciting it, one could quite literally save one's neck from hanging. Dante writes that the souls were singing *a verso a verso*; commentators have variously interpreted this as "verse by verse," or "alternating verses." In *Dante's Journey to Polyphony*, Francesco Ciabattoni (117) argues that Dante was describing the then-common practice of psalm singing called *alternation*, a form of monophonic plainsong where two halves of a choir alternated singing verses in unison.

35. *that's all the truth you need to know*: John Keats, "Ode on a Grecian Urn": "'Beauty is truth, truth beauty,—that is all / Ye know on earth, and all ye need to know.'"

36. *They show him respect, it might benefit them*: Since Dante will return to earth, he can let the souls' loved ones know that they are in Purgatory and encourage them to offer the prayers of intercession that can shorten the souls' time there and allow them to more quickly achieve Paradise.

37–39. *I never saw a shooting star slice through / A clear twilight sky, / Or lightning rip apart August clouds at sunset*: Dante refers here to *vapori accesi*, lighted or kindled vapors, a category that in the Middle Ages included shooting stars, lightning, and meteors. Commentators often cite Virgil's *Georgics* 1, 365–367, as a possible source for this description:

> Often, the stars keep coming, falling
> Headlong from the heavenly heights

Through the dusky night, long flames hauling
Behind them brush strokes of white light.

52. *In our past lives, we all died a violent death*: The souls Dante and Virgil encountered in *Purg.* IV were negligent in seeking absolution; the souls in this group died violently, so without last rites.

54. *a perspective pushed through*: Amy Winehouse, "Tears Dry on Their Own": "Even if I stop wanting you, / And perspective pushes thru, / I'll be some next man's other woman soon."

67. *Speaking first, and only for myself*: It would have been clear to Dante's original readers that the speaker is Jacopo del Cassero, a Guelph from Fano who, when he was a podestà (chief magistrate) in Bologna, opposed the powerful Azzo VIII d'Este. On his way to serve as a podestà in Milan in 1298, he traveled from Fano to Venice, intending to proceed to Milan via Padua, but was instead murdered at Oriaco, presumably by assassins hired by Azzo. In *Inf.* XII, Azzo's stepfather, Obizza da Este, is encountered in the river of boiling blood where the violent suffer eternal punishment—a centaur-guide tells Dante and Virgil that he was murdered by his stepson.

68–69. *territory between Romagna / And Naples, where Charles reigns*: He died in the marshes between Romagna to the north and Naples, then ruled by Charles d'Anjou, to the south.

74. *My blood and life force leapt like a fish from a lake*: Janet Flanner ("Genet"), letter to Natalia Danesi Murray: "Man is so wicked and cruel, so strong of arm in torture, so violent of mind in his notions of improving the world that he scatters blood like a fish leaping from a lake, merely in pleasure and strength."

75. *the lap of Antenori land*: According to legend, the city of Padua was established by the Trojan prince Antenor. In the Middle Ages, the prevailing belief was that Antenor plotted with the Greeks to destroy Troy. In *Inf.* XXXII, 88, the second ring of the ninth circle is identified as Antenora; there, those who betrayed their political party or country remain frozen up to their chins in Lake Cocytus for all of eternity. That Jacopo del Cassero died in "Antenori land" gestures to the treachery of those who conspired with Azzo VIII d'Este to murder him.

79–80. *If I'd kept high-tailing it toward La Mira, / Instead of stopping off at Oriaco*: The main highway between Venice and La Mira passed by Oriaco (today, Oriago). When Jacopo was surprised there by Azzo's men, he tried to evade capture by riding into the marsh.

81. *one breathes and the heart brags, I am*: Sylvia Plath, *The Bell Jar*: "I took a deep breath and listened to the old brag of my heart. I am, I am, I am."

88. *I was a Montefeltro, I'm Buonconte*: Buonconte da Montefeltro, like his father, Guido (*Inf.* XXVII), was a Ghibelline leader. He was killed in a losing battle at Campaldino on

June 11, 1289—a battle in which the twenty-four-year old Dante Alighieri was known to have fought on the side of the Guelphs. Buonconte's body was never located.

88–90. *No one cares / About me, not even Giovanna. So, I go around . . . with this bunch.* Giovanna was his wife. He was also survived by a daughter and a brother. His progress up the mountain is delayed because none of the family members offer prayers for his salvation.

94. *Casentino*: The river Arno runs through the Casentino Valley. In 1209, Saint Francis of Assisi established the Order of Friars Minor (Franciscan Order) in the Apennine Mountains, above the river valley.

96. *Hermitage*: The hermitage is Camaldoli, a Benedictine monastery located above the Casentino. It was established in the eleventh century by Romuald, a monk who preached and practiced asceticism—hermetic withdrawal from the world and renunciation of worldly pleasures.

99. *making the plain a bleeding piece of earth*: Shakespeare, *The Life and Death of Julius Caesar* (3.i.279–280): ANTONY. "O, pardon me, thou bleeding piece of earth, / That I am meek and gentle with these butchers!"

102. *only my onyx flesh was left*: Ralph Ellison, *Invisible Man*: "Barbee stood with his arms outstretched now, beaming over the audience, his Buddha-like body still as an onyx boulder" (133).

104. *God's angel grabbed me*: Similarly, in *Inf.* XXVII, Saint Francis struggles with a fallen angel for the soul of Buonconte's father.

116. *Pratomagno*: A mountain range that lies between the Casentino Valley to the west and the Italian Alps to the east.

124. *Archiano*: The Archiano River feeds into the Arno River in the Casentino Valley.

133–136. *wishful Pia . . . Maremma undid me . . . by the one who ringed me . . . first having had me with his family jewel*: The word *pia* in Italian means "pious" and "charitable"; Pia's manner of speaking demonstrates her modesty: she not only kindly suggests that Dante should first rest up from his journey but she also uses the polite imperfect imperative to request that he remember her. She refers to herself as *la* Pia, suggesting the secondary meaning of *pia*, "innocent" or "naive." The term for wishful thinking in Italian is *pia illusione*. Commentators have speculated that she was a Sienese noblewoman who, once widowed, married someone else who was said to have murdered her in order to marry another. The marriage ceremony may have consisted only of a private declaration of fidelity and the gift of a family ring. There is, however, a clear double entendre in the original, suggesting that the consummation of the marriage was an act of deception and that the pious Pia was naive.

CANTO VI

When the dice game breaks up,
The sad-sack loser stays behind,
Replays each move, and dismally learns.

The crowd surrounds the winner:
One's in his face, one taps his back; at his side,
One reminds him: "I knew you when."

He doesn't stop but listens to this, to that;
The ones to whom he slips a little something
Fade away. Like that, he manages the pack.

That was me in that press of people,
Facing first one, then another;
With a promise for each, I finally escaped.

Here was the Aretine killed by the long arm
Of grisly Ghino di Tacco; another drowned
On the run from a band holding a grudge.

The one begging with his hands out
Was Federico Novello; plus the Pisan
Who'd forced Marzucco to show his moral courage.

I saw Count Orso, and another soul
Split from his body by spite and envy,
And through no fault of his own, or so he said: i.e.,

Pierre de la Brosse. And the Lady of Brabant,
Who's still in the world, had better watch her step
Lest she land in a flock far worse than this one.

As soon as I'd freed myself from that group
Of shadows, whose only prayer was for others
To pray and speed them into blessedness,

I began, "It seems to me, O light of mine,
That in a certain passage, you expressly deny
Prayer can ever bend a fate decreed in Heaven,

And yet, these people are praying for exactly that.
Does that mean they're hoping in vain,
Or am I missing the sense of what you said?"

He told me, "My writing is clear;
The hope they have isn't a fallacy,
Which you can see if you think it through.

The high standards of divine justice aren't lowered
If a moment of great fire in someone's soul below
Satisfies the debt of one who struggles here.

Back there, where I made that point,
Mistakes couldn't be corrected by prayer,
Because prayer wasn't yet connected to God.

Even so, don't let these profound doubts stop you
Before speaking to that one who'll shed light
On the line between the truth and the intellect.

I'm not sure you understand: I mean Beatrice.
You'll see her above, at the top of the mountain,
Lighthearted among the blissful."

"Sir," I said, "let's pick up the pace.
I'm not as tired as I was. Also, look,
The mountain's already casting a shadow."

"We'll keep going as long as there's daylight,"
He said, "as far as we can. But the fact is—
Things here aren't quite as you imagine.

Before you reach the summit, you'll see the return
Of what's now tucked so far behind the cliff
Your body no longer blocks its rays.

But that soul you see over there
Who's sitting all alone and looking toward us;
He'll let us know the fastest way."

We approached him: O esteemed Lombard soul,
You seemed so lofty and detached,
As your cool eyes slowly scanned the horizon!

He spoke not a word to us
But let us keep coming, watching us warily,
Like Leo the Lion posing for a close-up.

Nonetheless, Virgil kept moving toward him, asking
If he'd please be willing to show us the best way up.
Even then, he didn't answer the question

But instead asked where we were from and what life
Was like there. My modest guide began, "Mantua . . ."
At which the shade, who'd been so distant,

Jumped up and ran toward him, saying,
"O Mantuan! I'm Sordello, from the same place!"
At which they hugged each other.

Servile Italy, pain hostel, no pilot at the helm
In a hurricane. No longer a mistress
Of the provinces, but a brothel.

How quick that generous spirit was, at the mere
Mention of the precious name of his city,
To extend a warm welcome to his fellow citizen.

Now it's one war after another, and those who live
Barricaded behind a single wall and moat
Eat each other up.

Look around, you lame excuses,
From sea to shining sea, then look into the heartland,
And see if you find peace worth rejoicing over.

What good did it do you, Justinian refitting the bit
Like he did, if no one's in the saddle?
If he hadn't done that, there'd be less shame.

You, who ought to be observant and put Caesar
In the saddle, if you'd read the text
God wrote for you, render to him, et cetera—

Ever since you grabbed the bridle ring
But refused to use it to correct the animal,
It's become wild and vicious.

O Albert of Austria, you've abandoned it
Now that it's a brute and can't be subdued,
You should be *on* the horse, sitting in the saddle.

May a well-deserved plague fall from the stars
And hit your house. One so novel and obvious
Your successor will live in fear and trembling.

A bad case of greed led you and your father
To stay up there, allowing the garden
Of the empire to turn into a wasteland.

Come and see, Sir Fancy-Free, the Montecchi
And Cappelletti, the Monaldi and Filippeschi,
Some already hopeless, others keeping both eyes open.

Come and see, cruel one, how your nobles bully
One another. Come and cure what ails them.
Come and see how gloomy it is in Santafiora.

Come and see your suffering Rome,
Widowed, alone, calling night and day:
"Caesar, why aren't you here with me?"

Come and see the people, how they *love* one another.
If pity for us doesn't move you, come out of shame
For how your name will be remembered.

And if one is allowed to ask, O Jove on High,
Who was crucified on earth for us,
Are your righteous eyes turned elsewhere?

Or, are you preparing something fine
In the council chamber of your unfathomable mind
That we can't grasp because of our brokenness?

Every town and city in Italy is swarming
With tyrants and every partisan chucklehead
Comes to play the part of Marcellus.

And Florence, my own, you should be happy
With this digression, which, thanks to your people
And how they handle matters, doesn't concern you,

Many have justice in their hearts, but are slow;
The arrow keeps asking the bow for advice.
But your mouth is filled to the brim with it.

Many refuse the burden of public office, but you,
Even before being asked, hoist the weight and cry
Like the Little Red Hen, "*I* will, *I* will, *I* will."

Now you're happy, and with good reason;
You have wealth, peace, a sense of direction!
If I speak the truth, the facts can't mask it.

Athens and Sparta framed the ancient laws
And modeled what it was to be civilized,
Only hinting at what the good life might be—

Unlike you people, who so narrowly define
Your steps that the hairs you split in October
Fray and break by mid-November.

How often, in your memory, have you modified
Your laws, currency, precedents, and policies,
And thrown people out and brought others in?

If you think carefully about your past,
You'll see you're like the princess and the pea:
Twenty feather beds atop twenty mattresses, and yet

No rest; pain makes her toss and turn all night.

NOTES TO CANTO VI

1. *the dice game*: The game Dante mentions, *zara* (Arabic for "dice"), is much like the game of craps—played, however, with three dice. When the dice total equaled the most statistically probable numbers (3, 4, 17, and 18), the word "zara" was called out and a player received zero points for those throws. To win a toss, the player was required to correctly call out the number of pips before the throw. According to Hollander and Hollander (120), the winner would distribute some of his winnings, much like contemporary players might tip a croupier at a gaming table.

13–14. *Here was the Aretine killed by the long arm / Of grisly Ghino di Tacco*: The Aretine is Benincasa de Laterina, a judge and assessor in Siena who once sentenced a relative of Ghino di Tacco's—an exiled Sienese noble turned infamous highwayman—to death. Fearing retribution at the hands of di Tacco, Laterina arranged to be transferred to Rome; Ghino di Tacco was said to have entered the papal court there and stabbed and beheaded him, then escaped out a window. Pope Boniface VIII later pardoned di Tacco.

14–15. *another drowned / On the run from a band holding a grudge*: The unnamed Aretine is believed to be Guccio de' Tarlati, a Ghibelline leader from Arezzo who drowned when his runaway horse ran into the Arno. He was either trying to escape from a battle with the Bostoli—Guelphs who'd been exiled from Arezzo—or else he was pursuing a group of Bostoli who were in retreat. The text is unclear since the Italian *correndo in caccia* (running in the hunt) can equally indicate running away or toward an object of prey. "Band on the Run" is the title song from the Paul McCartney & Wings 1973 album of the same name; the song was written by Paul and Linda McCartney: "Band on the run; band on the run / And the country judge, who held a grudge."

17. *Federico Novello*: Federico Novello, son of Count Guido Novello, was killed while fighting to defend Guccio de' Tarlati (see the preceding note). The counterfeiter "Master Adam," in *Inf.* XXX, blames the count and his brothers for his having been sent to Hell, saying they hired him to add base alloys to gold florins.

17–18. *the Pisan / Who'd forced Marzucco to show his moral courage*: The Pisan is most likely the son of Marzucco degli Scornigiani, a judge and public official in Pisa. Most commenters concur that the son's politically motivated killing in 1287—by beheading—was directed by Ugolino, who was then coruler of Pisa with Archbishop Ruggieri. The courage the father showed is also unclear, but many believe that Marzucco had joined an order of Franciscan monks and forgave the killing instead of seeking revenge. His humility may also have convinced Ugolino to reverse an order that the son's body should not be buried. In 1288, Ruggieri imprisoned Ugolino, with his two sons and two grandsons, and starved them all to death. In *Inf.* XXXII, Ugolino and Ruggieri are eternally locked together in the ice of Antenora, the zone of the ninth circle reserved for political traitors; there Ugolino enacts a just form of retribution by eternally gnawing on Ruggieri's head.

19. *Count Orso*. According to Benvenuto da Imola, author of the earliest commentary on the *Commedia* (*Comentum super Dantis Aligherii comoediam*), Orso degli Alberti della Cerbala was brutally killed by his cousin in what he describes as a "bear mauling," verbally playing on the fact that the word *orso* in Italian refers to both "bears" and "misanthropes." The fathers of the two cousins had also killed each other. Dante places the fathers, Napoleone and Alesandro, in Caina, the outermost third zone of the ninth circle of Hell, reserved for those who betray family members.

19–22. *another soul / Split from his body by spite and envy, / . . . or so he said . . . Pierre de la Brosse*: Pierre de la Brosse was chamberlain to Louis IX, and subsequently to Louis's son Philip III. When Philip's son and heir to the throne died suddenly in 1276, the queen, Marie of Brabant, accused de la Brosse of poisoning him. In 1278, the king ordered his arrest and had him hanged.

22–23. *the Lady of Brabant, / Who's still in the world, had better watch her step*: Stories abounded after Pierre de la Brosse was hanged; while the exact nature of the complaint isn't known, all the stories implicate the queen and her courtiers and gesture to a false accusation that was the result of court envy due to de la Brosse's position as a favorite of the king.

29–30. *in a certain passage, you expressly deny / Prayer can ever bend a fate decreed in Heaven*: In Virgil's *Aeneid* (6, 376), the Cumaean Sibyl tells the unburied Trojan helmsman Palinuru—who now wishes to accompany Aeneus to the underworld after having been swept overboard at sea by Sleep, and then murdered when he reached shore and his body left to the elements—that no amount of prayer can cancel the divine decree that the unburied must not be allowed to cross the river Styx: "Stop hoping the gods will soften and bend fate based on your prayers." ("Desine fata deum flecti sperare precando.")

This Stoic premise was first stated by the Roman philosopher and statesman Seneca the Younger (ca. 4 BCE–65) in his *Ad lucilium epistulae morales* (*Moral letters to Lucillius*) (77.12): "Why are you crying? What do you want? You are wasting your energy. Stop hoping that through prayer you can bend the fates decreed by the gods. They are fixed, inviolable, great, and eternal, and derive from necessity. You will go where everything goes." ("Quid fles? quid optas? perdis operam. Desine fata deum flecti sperare precando. Rata et fixa sunt et magna et aeterna necessitate ducuntur: eo ibis quo omnia eunt.")

37–39. *The high standards of divine justice aren't lowered / If a moment of great fire in someone's soul below / Satisfies the debt of one who struggles here*: Letter from Vincent van Gogh to Theo van Gogh, "Cuesmes, Between about Tuesday, June 22 and Thursday, June 24th 1880"; original manuscript (155), Amsterdam, Van Gogh Museum, inv. nos. b153 a-b

V/1962: "Someone has a great fire in his soul and nobody ever comes to warm themselves at it, and passers-by see nothing but a little smoke at the top of the chimney and then go on their way."

40–42. *Back there, where I made that point, / Mistakes couldn't be corrected by prayer, / Because prayer wasn't yet connected to God*: In Christian theology, with the exception of those few lifted up at the time of Christ's brief descent into Hell prior to his ascension to Heaven (the Harrowing of Hell), only Christians can commune with God.

44–46. *one who'll shed light / On the line between the truth and the intellect . . . Beatrice*: In v. 28, Dante refers to Virgil as *luce mia* (my light); now Virgil reminds Dante that his light only goes so far. As a pagan, he cannot grasp Christian mystery. It will fall to Beatrice, who waits for him above, to guide him in those matters.

54–56. *Things here aren't quite as you imagine. // Before you reach the summit, you'll see the return / Of what's now tucked so far behind the cliff*: Virgil, who is able to know Dante's thoughts, is trying to correct his mistaken assumption that the mountain can be scaled in a single day. It is now early afternoon and Virgil and Dante are on the shaded eastern side of the slope. Thus, Dante's human body isn't casting a shadow.

61. *esteemed Lombard soul*: As we'll learn in v. 74, this soul is the poet Sordello da Goito (fl. 1220–1269). Like Virgil, he's from the town of Goito, in the province of Mantua, in the region of Lombardy. He wrote not in Italian but in Provençal. He was exiled from Italy after a court political scandal, in which he is said to have abducted Cunizza da Romana, the wife of Count Ricciardo di San Bonifazio, and was later employed by Charles of Anjou. His forty-three known poems are mostly love poems and satires; however, the one that most impressed Dante, "Ensenhamen d'onor" (Instruction in honor), was a 1,325-line didactic poem on courtly honor that takes to task the kings and princes of Western Europe for their lack of courage and virtue.

Sordello's life was fictionalized in *Sordello*, a narrative poem written by Robert Browning between 1836 and 1840. Oscar Wilde includes both Sordello, whose passion he praised, and Dante, "the seven-fold vision of the Florentine," in his sonnet "Amor intellectualis." Of his time in prison, Wilde is quoted as having said, "I read Dante every day, in Italian, and all through, but neither the *Purgatorio* nor the *Paradiso* seemed written for me. It was his *Inferno* above all that I read—could I help liking it? Cannot you guess? Hell, we were in it—Hell, that was prison!" Ezra Pound alluded to Sordello in an early version of his first three cantos, published in *Poetry* magazine in 1917:

> Hang it all, there can be but one *Sordello*!
> But say I want to, say I take your whole bag of tricks,
> Let in your quirks and tweeks, and say the thing's an art-form,
> Your *Sordello*, and that the modern world
> Needs such a rag-bag to stuff all its thought in.

Sordello also appears in Samuel Beckett's novels *Molloy* and *Malone Dies*, and in Roberto Bolaño's novella, *By Night in Chile*.

66. *Leo the Lion*. Leo the Lion, the MGM mascot and logo, was depicted in black and white from 1916 to 1924. In the twenties, Leo appeared in color and began to roar.

76. *Servile Italy, pain hostel*: This verse begins a diatribe that continues until the end of the canto. It is a long and bitter lament about the political conditions in Italy. Dante indicts the meddling clergy, Christ ("Jove on High"), and Albert of Austria, for their collective failure to resolve the internecine feuds and battles. He accuses the Florentines of being smug in their dysfunction because of their relative wealth and comfort.

88–90. *What good did it do you, Justinian refitting the bit . . . If he hadn't done that, there'd be less shame*: Justinian I, known as Justinian the Great, was the emperor of Constantinople from 527 to 565. He convened a panel of jurists to rework existing law and later added to that. The entire four-volume work, issued as the *Corpus iuris civilis*, became the foundation of Roman law in Europe.

91–93. *You, who ought to be observant and put Caesar / In the saddle . . . render to him, et cetera*: Dante, as he made clear in the *Inferno*, held Pope Clement V (who abdicated after six months) and Boniface VIII (who succeeded him) responsible for the political manipulations that continued the factional struggles that eventually resulted in his own banishment from Florence. The text to which Dante refers is Matthew 22:21: "Render therefore unto Caesar the things which are Caesar's; and unto God the things that are God's."

97. *Albert of Austria*: Albert I (whom Dante calls the "German Albert"), the son of King Rudolf I of Hapsburg, was Duke of Austria until 1298, when he was chosen as the German king by a group of electoral princes after defeating his predecessor, Adolf of Nassau, in a battle. He was never officially crowned because Pope Boniface VIII—who maintained it was the right of the pope to select the king, consecrate him, and crown him—refused to recognize his election. In 1303, after an alliance with King Philip IV of France, who was committed to usurping the rights of the Church, failed, Albert wrote to the pope confirming the pope's right to choose the king and promising never to take sides against him. In return, Boniface confirmed Albert's election as king of the Romans. He was then assassinated in 1308 by his nephew John.

102. *Your successor will live in fear and trembling*: Henry VII of Luxembourg succeeded Albert in 1308 (and ruled until 1313), but it's not known whether Dante is specifically referring to him, or to a hypothetical successor. Since the fictional allegory is set in 1300, the successor would not yet be known.

103–105. *A bad case of greed led you and your father . . . allowing the garden / Of the empire to turn into a wasteland*: Neither King Rudolf I (1273–1291), nor his son Albert I, ever visited

Italy, the "garden of the empire." Each remained intent on consolidating his power and extending his wealth in Germany.

106–108. *Come and see, Sir Fancy-Free, the Montecchi / And Cappelletti, the Monaldi and Filippeschi, / Some already hopeless*: These powerful families represent factions in the political life of northern Italian cities. Their fortunes rose and fell depending on their feuds and shaky alliances that were always based in self-interest. Shakespeare's *Romeo and Juliet*, an adaptation from a story by Matteo Bandello (1554) reset in Verona, was based on the conflict between the Cappelletti, the Guelph political party in Cremona, and the imperial Ghibelline Montecchi party. Previous literary sources for the story include Salernitano (1476) and Luigi da Porto (1524).

109–111. *how your nobles bully . . . how gloomy it is in Santafiora*: Santafiora was a Sienese fiefdom that belonged to the Ghibelline Aldobrandeschi family continuously from the ninth century until it fell to the control of the Guelph party of Siena in 1300 (Count Omberto Aldobrandeschi appears in *Purg.* XI, 55–72).

112–113. *your suffering Rome / Widowed, alone, calling night and day*: The personified Rome is envisioned as lonely and mourning its lack of leadership, a metaphorical widowing.

115. *Come and see the people, how they* love *one another*: This is said with bitter sarcasm, given the continual feuding that characterized the social and political landscape in Italy.

118–119. *Jove on High / Who was crucified on earth for us*: Jove, the principal god or "sky-father," was an older Roman name for Jupiter, which was a Roman reimagining of the Greek god Zeus. Jove's name occurs nine times in the *Commedia*. By conflating Jove with the crucified Christ, Dante appears to be reviving the merger of Greek and Roman mythology with Christianity, a feature of early Christianity. He does this intermittently throughout the *Commedia*.

126. *play the part of Marcellus*: During the reign of Julius Caesar, there were at least three Roman consuls named Marcellus, all of whom opposed him. Dantists continue to debate which of the three Dante had in mind. Hollander and Hollander (127–28) argues that Marcus Claudius Marcellus, consul in 222 BCE, referred to as "the Sword of Rome" for his success against Hannibal, and mentioned by Virgil in the *Aeneid*, should also be given consideration.

135. *Like the Little Red Hen, "*I *will,* I *will,* I *will."*: "The Little Red Hen and a Grain of Wheat" is a folktale in which three barnyard animals—a cat, a rat, and a pig—refuse to help an industrious red hen plant a grain of wheat, or take the ripened wheat to the mill to be ground to flour, or make bread from the flour. Each time she asks the three animals who will help her, each says "*I* won't." Once the bread is baked, she asks who

will eat it; now each one answers, "*I* will." In the event, the red hen refuses to share and eats the loaf herself. Like the animals who say "*I* will" only when there's something to be gained, Dante is portraying the Florentines as overeager to serve but only in order to use their positions for self-aggrandizement.

139–141. *Athens and Sparta framed the ancient laws / And modeled what it was to be civilized, / Only hinting at what the good life might be*: Dante uses the name Lacedaemon for Sparta. A set of Greek laws was drafted ca. 621 BCE by the Athenian statesman Draco; the punishments, regardless of the severity of the crime, were harsh—leading to the adjective "draconian." The laws established debtor slavery and led to extreme income inequality. A later statesman, Solon, was responsible for reforming the laws and abolishing debt slavery. His reforms were considered the basis of Athenian constitutional democracy. Sparta's constitution, the Great Rhetra, was said to have been given to Lycurgus in verse by the Oracle of Apollo at Delphi. His reforms included a citizens' council and a strong military.

143–144. *the hairs you split in October / Fray and break by mid-November*: It is possible that the November in question is that of 1302. In March 1302, Dante traveled with six others to Rome on a diplomatic mission to try to convince Pope Boniface VIII to intervene in the internecine struggle between the Black and White Guelphs in Florence. The rest of the party was subsequently discharged, but Dante was held in Rome by the pope. With the pope's backing, Charles of Valois arrived in Florence on November 1, 1301. His support of the Black Guelphs allowed them to assume power and to banish the White Guelphs. On January 27, 1302, a vote was approved to banish Dante for a period of two years for unsubstantiated wrongdoing during the two months he served as a podestà in 1300. After his failure to pay the fine, new charges were brought based solely on hearsay evidence. Those charges are archived in the Book of Nails (so-called for the actual nails in its binding) in the Florence State Archive (*Il libro del chiodo*, Archivio di Stato di Firenze):

> Alighieri, Dante is convicted for public corruption, fraud, falsehood, fraud, malice, unfair extortion practices, illegal proceeds, pederasty, and is sentenced to a fine of 5000 florins, perpetual disqualification from public office, permanent exile (in absentia), and if detained, condemned to die at the stake, so he dies.

On June 12, 2008, a motion was approved by the Florence City Council to revoke the condemnation and, however belatedly, exonerate Dante.

149–151. *the princess and the pea: / Twenty feather beds atop twenty mattresses, and yet // No rest; pain makes her toss and turn all night*: The story "The Princess and the Pea" (originally "The Princess on the Pea"), by the Danish author Hans Christian Andersen, describes a sensitive young woman who is troubled all night by a pea buried under twenty feather beds atop twenty mattresses. Her sensitivity proves that she's of noble birth and worthy to marry the prince. There are even older stories of disturbed sleep due to objects buried beneath mattresses. An eleventh-century Sanskrit collection called *Kathasaritsagara* (A continuous ocean of stories) by Somadeva, includes a story in which a highly sensitive young man has a restless night on seven mattresses and wakes to find the imprint of a hair on his back; a hair exactly matching the imprint is then discovered when the mattresses are lifted.

In the medieval and Renaissance eras, the mattresses of nobility were usually stuffed with straw (sometimes mixed with wool or feathers) with a feather comforter on top. Peasants slept on mattresses stuffed with pea shucks and other dried vegetable matter. The story of the princess rests on the presumption that had she been of lower birth, she would have been used to the occasional pea in her mattress; the fact that she was unable to sleep suggested she was used to a better mattress. Dante compares the comfortable Florentines who live in a state of extreme dysfunction to a sick woman on a feather bed who, in spite of her comfortable bed, can't sleep but spends all night turning from one side to another. In Dante's metaphor, the feather mattress doesn't help because her sickness represents an underlying problem, a figurative pea.

Canto VII

After three or four sincere and joyful embraces
Sordello drew back and asked,
"So, who are you?"

"Long before there were souls deemed worthy
Of reaching God at the top of this mountain,
My bones were buried by Octavian.

I'm Virgil—I lost out on Heaven
For no other reason than not having faith."
That was how my leader answered *that* question.

Like when you suddenly see something
Amazing right in front of you, you do and don't
Believe, saying to yourself, "It is . . . it isn't . . ."

That's how it seemed with the other.
He came forward again, his head bent in respect,
And gave him a clingy hug, like a little kid.

"O Glory of the Romans," he said,
"Who showed us what one could do with language.
Timeless treasure of the place I came from.

What credit due or god's gift is letting me see you?
If I deserve to hear you, tell me,
Do you come from Hell, and from which lockup?"

"I've been through every circle of the Kingdom
Of Woe," he said. "Moral virtue, Heaven's
Polestar, first stirred me and comes with me.

Not for what I did, but through what I didn't do,
I lost the chance to see the highest sun
You long for and that I learned about too late.

There's a place below that's not sad with misery
Only with gloom, and where sorrow sounds
Like a sigh, not a sobbing woe-is-me

I live there with innocent kiddos
Who were shredded by the red teeth of Death
Before being released from human guilt.

I live there with those who were never vested
With the three holy virtues; we, of course,
Knew and flawlessly followed all the others.

But if you know, and are allowed to say,
Can you tell us the fastest way to reach the point
Where Purgatory proper begins?"

"We're not confined to a given area.
I'm free to wander up and turn around;
I'll go with you as far as I can.

But see how day's already fading?
Climbing at night isn't possible; instead,
It's best to think about a nice place to stay.

Over there, farther on the right, are some souls.
If you let me, I'll take you to them,
Seeing who they are won't fail to delight you."

"How is it?" he asked. "If someone tried
To climb at night, would others stop them?
Or would someone just not be able to climb?"

Kind Sordello drew his finger through the dirt,
Saying: "See this? You couldn't even cross
This line after the sun sets;

No one would try to hold you back,
Only the dark night. The absence of light
Traps the will and makes it helpless.

It would be easy at night to descend again
And aimlessly wander around the slope,
While day remained locked behind the skyline."

At that, my master said, almost admiringly,
"Lead on then, to the place where you say
We'll enjoy taking a break."

We'd only gone a short distance when I noticed
The mountainside was dropping down,
The same way a valley drops down here.

"Let's go over there," said the shade, "to where
It slopes and the grass makes a mother's lap.
That's where we'll wait for the new day."

A slanting path between steep and level
Brought us to the sloping bank of a hollow
With an incline drop well over fifty percent.

Gold and refined silver, scarlet and lead-white,
Indigo blue, bright lucent black,
Rough emerald after the first facets,

Each of these colors, if placed in that valley,
Would be outdone by the flowers and grass,
The way lesser is always outdone by better.

Not only had Nature made a landscape painting
There, but a thousand delicate fragrances
Wafted into one impossible to name.

I saw "Hail, Holy Queen" being sung by souls
Who, sitting on the grass and flowers,
Hadn't been visible outside the valley.

"Until the last bit of sun is settled in its nest,"
Began the Mantuan who'd led us here,
"Don't ask me to take you down to them;

From this ledge, you'll have a better view
Of their faces and can see how they act,
Than if you were mixed in with them below.

The one seated highest up,
Who looks guilty of dereliction of duty,
And whose mouth isn't moving with the others,

That was Emperor Rudolph, who could have
Cured the plague that killed Mother Italy;
Now it's too late for others to bring her back.

The other, who's consoling him, ruled Bohemia,
Which gives rise to the waters the Moldau
Carries to the Elbe, and the Elbe out to sea.

Ottocar was his name, and even as a baby,
He was smarter than his bearded son,
Wenceslaus, who feeds on lust and leisure.

See the pug-nosed one, who seems
To be confabbing with the bland-looking one;
He died in flight, deflowering the fleur-de-lis;

Look how he beats his chest. See how
The other sighs and puts his cheek to sleep
In the well-padded palm of his hand:

They're father and father-in-law of France's
Cancer; they know the son's filthy blighted life,
And from that comes the grief that turns the knife.

The stocky one who's harmonizing
With the one with the strong nose,
He had a notch on his belt for every virtue,

And if his young son sitting behind him
Had stayed on the throne longer, all that virtue
Would have passed from one vessel to the next,

Which can't be said of the other heirs.
Frederick and James possess the kingdoms
But neither inherited the better attributes.

Integrity rarely rises through a family tree;
God, who grants it, wants us to know
That we have to look to Him for it.

My words also apply to the strong-nosed one
And equally to Pedro, singing with him, which
Is why Naples and Provence are now grieving.

The degree to which the plant's inferior to the seed,
Means Constance can brag on her husband
More than Beatrice and Margaret can on theirs.

See the king said to live a simple life,
Sitting there by himself, Henry of England,
He added better offspring to his family branches.

The lowest of all, sitting on the ground
And gazing up, is William the Marquis;
He's why Alessandria and its war

Are making Montferrat and Canavese cry."

4–6. *before there were souls deemed worthy / Of reaching God . . . My bones were buried by Octavian*: Virgil was buried in 19 BCE, during the rule of Augustus, emperor from 27 BCE to 14 CE (a tenure that included the birth of Jesus). Augustus was born Gaius Octavius; he took the name Octavian after Caesar's death.

23–24. *Moral virtue, Heaven's / Polestar, first stirred me and comes with me*: The *Analects* (edited conversations) are assumed to be a collection of aphorisms and ideas attributed to Confucius and compiled by his followers after his death in 479 BCE. "The rule of virtue can be compared to the Pole Star which commands the homage of the multitude of stars without leaving its place" (2:1; trans. D. C. Lau).

28–30. *a place below . . . where sorrow sounds / Like a sigh*: This is Limbo of the Forefathers, *limbus partum* ("border" plus "brought forth from"), a holding area outside Hell proper, which houses Virgil and other pre-Christian poets and thinkers who are barred from Paradise only because they died before Jesus Christ was said to absolve humans of original sin.

31–33. *innocent kiddos . . . Before being released from human guilt*: This is the Limbo of Infants, *limbus infantium*, the afterlife residence of children who died before being given the rite of baptism. The concept is not biblical but was introduced in the fifth and sixth centuries by early Christian authors. In the Catholic Church, the sacrament of baptism is thought to absolve one from the collective guilt of original sin, sinfulness believed to be inherited from the first humans, whose sin was to disobey God by consuming forbidden knowledge in the form of a piece of fruit, possibly an apple.

34–36. *I live there with those who were never vested / With the three holy virtues; we . . . flawlessly followed all the others*: The three holy (or theological) virtues are faith, hope, and charity (or love). According to Catholic theology, these come only with salvation; the other virtues are called the cardinal virtues: prudence, temperance, justice, and fortitude. Virgil is saying the pagans followed the latter but didn't have access to the former because those came only after Christ's redemption.

46–48. *some souls set apart . . . Seeing who they are won't fail to delight you*: Sordello imagines that Dante and Virgil will both be delighted to see that those responsible for Italy's current misery are having to pay a price for their political negligence.

68. *the grass makes a mother's lap*: Walt Whitman, "The Song of Myself" (1900): "Tenderly will I use you curling grass . . . And here you are the mothers' laps."

73–75. *Gold and . . . emerald after the first facets*: These colors correspond to pigments used by painters in the medieval era. Resin, often derived from sticky insects, boiled and reduced to powder, was sometimes added to enhance their translucency.

82. *I saw "Hail, Holy Queen" being sung*: "Salve, Regina" is a Catholic hymn that was first recorded in the twelfth century and, at least since that time, has been traditionally sung at the final church service of the day, the compline or "contemplative hour." Hollander and Hollander (144–145) note an echo of the hymn in the scene of the penitents sitting in the valley ("To thee do we send up our sighs, mourning and weeping in this valley of tears"); he also mentions that Poletto (1894) thought Dante might be echoing the scene in *Aeneid* 6, where Musaeus sits with the dead in the Elysian Fields, singing "glad hymns in chorus / within a fragrant laurel grove" ("laetumque choro paeana canentis / inter odoratum lauri nemus").

94–95. *Emperor Rudolph, who could have / Cured the plague that killed Mother Italy*: Rudolph I was the son of Albert IV. Following the death of Frederick II in 1250, during the subsequent Great Interregnum period, when power wasn't consolidated but was spread among competing princes, Rudolph I was unanimously elected emperor in 1273 over Ottokar II of Bohemia. He ruled until his death in 1291. While he increased his wealth and land base in Austria and Swabia through strategic marriages between his children and allies, he failed to take control of Italy, so didn't establish peace between the warring princes.

97–100. *The other, who's consoling him, ruled Bohemia . . . Ottocar was his name*: Rudolf's rival in life, Ottokar II, King of Bohemia from 1253 until he died in battle in 1278, is now his comforter in Purgatory. Singleton (2:149) notes that the same is true in the *Aeneid* (4, 827). Those who were rivals in arms above, "now oppressed by perpetual night, they work in harmony" ("concordes animae nunc et dum nocte premuntur"). The Moldau River begins in what was then Bohemia and enters the Elbe just north of Prague; the Elbe then courses through Germany and ends in the North Sea.

101–102. *his bearded son, / Wenceslaus, who feeds on lust and leisure*: When Ottokar died, his six-year-old son, Wenceslaus II (b. 1271), succeeded him. Due to his young age, others initially ruled in his stead. In 1285, at the age of thirteen, he married Judith of Habsburg, the daughter of Rudolf I. He began to actively rule in 1290. During his reign, silver was discovered in Bohemia. Wenceslaus assumed control of the mine and began to mint his own silver coins, including the "penny of Prague," which remained in use for centuries. He died in 1305 at the age of thirty-three, possibly of TB. Along with having eleven children with his two wives, he fathered many children outside his marriages.

103–105. *the pug-nosed one . . . confabbing with the bland-looking one; / He died in flight, deflowering the fleur-de-lis*: Philip III of France, nicknamed "the Bold," and also "the Pug-Nosed," reigned from 1270 to 1285. His boldness was said to be evident, not in political matters, where he was seen as being indecisive, but from his comportment in battle. He died of dysentery while in retreat from an ill-advised and unsuccessful battle to conquer Aragon, a battle that nearly bankrupted the French government. He is depicted here having an intimate conversation with Henry I of Navarre. Philip III's son King Philip IV ("the plague of France") was married to Henry's daughter. Through that marriage, Philip IV would become both king of France and of Navarre. The fleur-de-lis is an ancient symbol—three gold stylized flowers, thought to be lilies, bound together on a blue background—associated with French royalty and with heraldry.

112–114. *The stocky one . . . the one with the strong nose . . . every virtue*: The stocky one, Pedro III of Aragon, was described by Villani (VII, 103) as "a worthy lord, skilled in arms, very brave and wise"; quoted in Singleton, *Purgatorio* (2:153). The one with the large nose is Charles I of Anjou—son of King Louis VIII and brother of Louis IX—king of Naples and Sicily. Pedro III wrested control of Sicily from Charles I during the Sicilian Vespers (1282), an uprising by nobles against the reign of Charles. Pedro III was a supporter of the arts, and especially of troubadour poetry. The wish that Pedro III would usurp Provence from Charles I is mentioned by a shepherdess in a troubadour poem attributed to Paulet of Marseilles (Chaytor, 95–96).

115. *his young son sitting behind him*: Pedro's eldest son, Alphonso III of Aragon, called "the Liberal," or "the Free," reigned only for six years (1285–1291) and died at the age of twenty-five.

119–120. *Frederick and James possess the kingdoms / But neither inherited the better attributes*: James was the second son of Pedro III and Frederick was the third. They vied for power over Sicily, and each was king at various times. In Dante's estimation, neither was as good as Pedro III.

127–129. *The degree to which the plant's inferior to the seed, / Means Constance can brag on . . . / More than Beatrice and Margaret*: Charles II (the plant) is worse than Charles I (the seed), to the same degree that Charles I is inferior to his successor, Pedro III of Aragon. Pedro III was married to Constance of Sicily. Therefore, Charles I's current wife, Margaret, and his first wife, Beatrice, have less to boast about than Constance.

130–133. *the king said to lead a simple life . . . Henry of England . . . added better offspring*: Henry III was king of England from 1216 to 1272. He was said to be sincere, devout, and a supporter of the indigent, orphans, monasteries, and universities. However, he enacted policies that were oppressive to Jews. His son, King Edward I, who reigned from 1272 to 1307, was responsible for many legal reforms and for increasing the power of Parliament, although he too was extremely cruel to Jews and exerted pressure to make them convert to Christianity.

134–136. *William the Marquis . . . He's why Alessandria and its war / Are making Montferrat and Canavese cry*: The marquisate of William VII, in the Piedmont area in northwestern Italy, included both Canavese and Montferrat. As a powerful Ghibelline leader, he tried to extend his reach but only ended up acquiring and then losing many areas, including Milan. When he entered Alessandria in 1290 to quell an uprising, he was captured and placed in a cage and kept on display until his death in 1292. His only son, John I, inherited the territory and title and fought against Alessandria to avenge his father's death and reclaim the territory. It is this war that is making the inhabitants in those areas weep.

Canto VIII

It was now the hour that melts the heart
And wakes the wish of those in a boat for the friends
To whom they said goodbye earlier that day,

Or pierces with love those just driving away
If they hear the toll of a far-off bell
Crying over the dying day,

When I began to tune out what I was hearing
And focus on one soul who had stood up—
Gesturing with his hand for the others to listen.

He then clasped both hands together
And turned his eyes east, as if to tell God,
"Nothing else matters to me."

He began to sing "To Thee Before the Close
Of Day," with such devotion and with such
A lovely melody, it took me out of myself.

The others then joined in, softly
And reverently, singing the entire hymn,
Keeping their eyes raised to the celestial tribunal.

Here, Reader, keep your eyes on the prize;
The curtain over the real is so thin
The light makes certain you can see within.

I watched as that sublime army went quiet;
They kept looking up, as if in anticipation:
Ashen, unassuming.

I saw two angels emerge and descend
From above with two flaming swords,
The tops cut off so the tips were missing.

Green as just-opened leaves, their robes
Billowed out behind them,
Fanned by the beating of their green wings.

One came and posted itself a little above us,
The other set down on the opposite side,
Keeping everyone between.

I could make out their platinum hair
But lost it trying to look at their faces;
Too much of a good thing can mess up the senses.

"Both come from Mary's lap," Sordello said,
"Security for the valley because of the serpent,
Who'll come along its usual way."

Not knowing by *which* way, I spun around and froze
Like a wheel in a winter scene by Bruegel,
Pressed up against the one I trusted.

Sordello went on, "Now let's make our way down
And talk to the shades of the once-great;
They'll be very happy to see you."

I think I only went down three steps and there
I was, at the bottom, where someone was staring
At me, as if wanting to know how he knew me.

It was late enough that the sky had begun to darken,
But not so dark that between his eyes and mine
We couldn't come out from behind the closed door.

He moved toward me; I moved toward him—
Noble Judge Nino, I was delighted
To find you weren't with the Damned!

We greeted each other every which way;
He then asked, "How long have you been at the foot
Of the mountain since making the crossing?"

"Oh," I told him, "I came here this morning
Via the Kingdom of Woe; I'm still in my first life,
But hoping to earn another by coming here."

As soon as they heard my answer,
He and Sordello drew back,
The way one does when suddenly at a loss.

One turned to Virgil, the other to someone
Sitting there, "Up, Currado, get over here
And see what God in His grace has sent us."

He then turned to me: "By that unique status
You owe Him, who so hides His whys
And wherefores they're impossible to fathom,

When you're back across the vast sea, please
Ask my Giovanna to send her calls here, where
Those of the innocent actually get answered.

I don't think her mother loves me anymore,
Not since she traded her white widow's veil
For what suits her, little tart! She craves it still.

Watching her, it's easy to see how weak
The bonfire of love is in a woman like that,
Unless a look or hand keeps fanning it.

The viper on the Milanese camp banner
Won't make her tomb look nearly as nice
As the cock on my coat of arms would have."

So he said, his face stamped with the ink
Of straight-up jealousy that matched
The fire flashing in his heart.

My greedy eyes kept wandering to the heavens,
To the area where the stars are slowest,
Like where spokes insert on a wheel axle.

My teacher: "What are you staring at
Up there, son?" I: "At those three lights
Burning up the pole on our side."

He: "The four bright stars you saw this morning
Are so low you can't see them now,
These have climbed to where those were."

While he was speaking, Sordello gestured to him
To come closer: "See, there's our adversary!"
He pointed to where he should look.

On the little valley's unsheltered edge,
There was the serpent, possibly the very same
That served Eve that bitter-tasting dish.

Through grass and flowers, the evil streak slid,
Time and again turning its head to lick its ridge
Like a fawning beast that sleeks itself.

I didn't see, so can't say just how those
Celestial hawks began to move, but I did clearly
Catch sight of one, then the other, in motion.

At the sound of their green wings slicing the air,
The snake fled. The angels wheeled and,
Like pair skaters, flew back as one to their posts.

The soul that had come when the judge
Had called him had, during the entire attack,
Never taken his eyes off me.

"So the lamp leading you finds enough power
In your will to do the job of getting you up
To the peak of the slippery slope," he said.

"If you have any real news
From the Magra Valley, or anywhere nearby,
Tell me—I was once a VIP there.

I was called Currado Malaspina,
Not the old guy, but one of his offspring.
The love I showed my own is evolving here."

"Oh," I told him, "I've never visited those areas,
But is there anyone alive in Europe
Who doesn't know all about them?

The fame that honors your house speaks loudly
Of your family, and of the area, so they're known
Even to those who have never been there.

I promise you, if I get upstairs,
Your honorable people will lose nothing
Of their market value nor their might.

Born to privilege, they use it well; as a wicked
Head twists the world into a pretzel, they alone
Keep theirs straight and hate the wrongheaded."

He said, "Go on now—the sun won't lie down
Seven times in a bed blanketed by
The Ram's fleece, its four feet acting like anchors,

Before this very gracious opinion of yours
Will get hammered deep into your head by studs
Far more enduring than other people's rantings—

That is, if the legal system doesn't shut them up."

1–6. *the hour that melts the heart / And wakes the wish . . . Crying over the dying day*: Byron, *Don Juan* (3.955—960):

> Soft hour! which wakes the wish and melts the heart
> Of those who sail the seas, on the first day
> When they from their sweet friends are torn apart;
> Or fills with love the pilgrim on his way
> As the far bell of vesper makes him start,
> Seeming to weep the dying day's decay.

13. *He began to sing "To Thee Before the Close of Day"*: "Te lucis ante terminum" is an ancient Latin hymn sung at compline, the final church service of the day. It is a prayer for protection from Satan and from *polluantur corpora* (polluting of the flesh). It begins: "To Thee before the close of day, / Creator of the world, we pray / That, with Thy wonted favour, Thou / Wouldst be our guard and keeper now" (trans. J. M. Neale [1818–1866]).

18–21. *Keeping their eyes raised to the celestial tribunal . . . The curtain over the real is so thin / The light makes certain you can see within*: Dante was tried by a people's tribunal, which considered only hearsay evidence. The truth behind the thin curtain he's drawn is that only Heaven's judgment is reliable. The canto will end with an indictment of the legal system that resulted in his exile from Florence.

19. *keep your eyes on the prize*: "Keep Your Eyes on the Prize" is a 1956 civil rights song written by Alice Wine. The song adapts a traditional hymn, "Gospel Plow," inspired by Philippians 3:14: "I press toward the mark for the prize of the high calling of God in Christ Jesus." The song title was used for *Eyes on the Prize*, a 1987 PBS series that documented the history of the American civil rights movement from 1954 to 1964; a second series documenting the years 1965–1985 was broadcast in 1990.

25–27. *I saw two angels emerge . . . with two flaming swords, / The tops cut off so the tips were missing*: Commentators link the two angels to the two cherubim in Genesis 3:24, left to guard the Tree of Life after the Fall: "So He drove out the man; and He placed at the east of the garden of Eden Cherubims, and a flaming sword which turned every way, to keep the way of the tree of life." The lack of tips on the phallic swords androgenizes the angels, who are said to have come from Mary's lap (or breast). "Green" (*verdi*), which appears twice in the next tercet, also means "unripe." The combination of green plus the blunted swords could signify prepubescent males. Ganymede, the beautiful boy taken up to Heaven by Zeus, is mentioned in the next canto in the context of a dream Dante has in which he is picked up in the claws of an eagle, and together, he and the bird "burn" until, scorched, Dante shakes himself awake. This "burning" echoes that moment in the *Inf.* (XV, 82–86) when Dante meets Brunetto Latini on the seventh circle. Latini is running with those who are tormented by a rain of fire. Dante tells the reader he would join that group except for wishing not to be burned.

28–30. *Green . . . robes . . . green wings*: Green is the color of hope but also the color of nature. It is as if the angels and the snake are of the same family, but antipodal opposites: bad nature (green snake in green grass) and good nature (angels with green wings, wrapped in green robes). The angels' green is said to be like new leaves being fanned open, effectively turning the angels into just-blooming flower buds.

33. *Keeping everyone between*: All who are in a state of penance are guarded by the angels.

34–35. *their platinum hair / But lost it trying to look at their faces*: Like the coxswain in *Purg.* II, the light radiated by the angels is too dazzling for Dante's human eyes to tolerate. In both cases, he is forced to look away. The same will be true in *Purg.* IX, when Dante encounters the angel who guards the gate to the first cornice.

36. *Too much of a good thing can mess up the senses*: Too much light can overcome the ability to see; similarly, too much of any sensory pleasure can be problematic. The idea of the value of moderation recurs often throughout the *Commedia*.

37. *Both come from Mary's lap*: The Italian word *grembo* variously means "lap," "womb," or "figurative bosom."

38–39. *the serpent, / Who'll come along its usual way*: Sordello may mean that the serpent will come, as it always does, to those on the shore who are still at risk of giving in to temptation, and that will subsequently delay their upward trajectory. Or, Sordello may mean the serpent will come as it always does *in the evening* since Satan is known as the "Prince of Darkness"—from the Latin *princeps tenebraum*, which first appeared in the medieval apocryphal Gospel of Nicodemus, based (in part) on the fifth-century Acts of Pilate (Acta Pilati). The most venomous snakes in Italy are nocturnal pit vipers; they have sense organs that allow them to hunt in the dark by detecting infrared radiation emitted by small warm-blooded animals.

40–42. *Not knowing by* which *way, I . . . froze / Like a wheel in a winter scene by Bruegel . . . the one I trusted*: Dante takes Sordello's words literally and assumes there is a particular path the snake always follows. Not knowing whether he's standing in the middle of that path, he moves behind Virgil, his protector, and—*tutto gelato*, completely freezes. *The Census at Bethlehem*, painted ca. 1566 by Pieter Bruegel the Elder, and later copied a dozen times by his sons, pictures Mary and Joseph on their way to pay their taxes in a Flemish snow scene littered with wagon wheels. There is a disembodied wheel at the center of the painting, which some art critics read as the wheel of fortune.

50–51. *But not so dark that between his eyes and mine / We couldn't come out from behind the closed door*: One could read into the language of coming out and declaring oneself from behind what had been shut tight ("dichiararsi ciò che prima serrava") not just uncertainty about recognizing one another but an initial reluctance on one or both sides to announce their prior association. *Dichiararsi* means "to makes facts public." Today the word is used to "come out," to declare one's homosexuality. *Serrava* means not just "closed" but "closed very tightly," possibly "locked."

53–54. *Noble Judge Nino, I was delighted / To find you weren't with the Damned*: In 1288, Nino Visconti of Pisa was a Guelph captain, sharing power with his grandfather, Count Ugolino della Gherardesca (whom Dante places in the ninth circle in *Inf.* XXXII). That same year, betrayed by the grandfather and expelled from Pisa, Nico fled to Florence, where commentators note that he and Dante may have met. For the next five years, he intermittently fought against Pisa, which had become Ghibelline. When peace was declared in 1293, he moved to Genoa and from there he went to serve as a judge in Sardinia, an island belonging to Pisa, where he died in 1296. Commentators make the point that Dante's pleasure doesn't indicate that he has any special knowledge about Nino that leads him to be surprised to find him in Purgatory instead of in Hell, but only that no one knows who will be saved. Other readings, however, are possible.

65. *Up, Currado, get over here*: Currado Malaspina was a Ghibelline marquis. He and his daughter, Spina Malaspina, appear in Boccaccio's *Decameron* (2, 6) in a drama that includes a woman hermit who breastfeeds kid goats and who later gets rescued by Currado and his wife; a sexual dalliance between Spina and one of Currado's young manservants; and a denouement in which the manservant is revealed to be the woman's son and of noble birth, and so is encouraged to marry Spina—after which, all live happily ever after!

71–72. *my Giovanna to send her calls here, where / Those of the innocent actually get answered*: In 1309, Nino's daughter, Giovanna Visconti, broke off her engagement to Corradino Malaspina, the Ghibelline nephew of Currado Malaspina, and married Rizzardo da Camino, Lord of Treviso and a loyal Guelph. Nino wants Dante to convey the information that he is in Purgatory and would benefit from her prayers of intercession, lest she think he's in Hell, where her prayers would be in vain.

73–75. *I don't think her mother loves me . . . she traded her white widow's veil / For what suits her, little tart! She craves it still*: Giovanni's mother, Nino's widow, was Beatrice d'Este. Nino died in 1296; in 1300, at the age of thirty-two, she married the twenty-three-year-old Galeazzo Visconti of Milan, a Ghibelline. In Nino's mind, had she not remarried, she might be saying prayers that would shorten his time in Purgatory. Instead, she has given up her white, virginal, widow's veil and is arranging a trip to the altar—to gain "what suits her," implying that the celibacy of widowhood didn't agree with her. The Italian *convien*, "to suit or agree with," also means "to come together," suggesting conjugal sex, possibly the real source of Nino's furious jealousy, since "She craves it still." The word *misera* can mean "sleazy" as well as "unhappy"; just as "tart" in English can mean "unpleasant" and "sluttish." The unhappiness that is upcoming, and about which Nino in Purgatory has advance knowledge, is that her new husband will be exiled from Milan in 1302. So, she will later pay for any pleasure she has today.

The word *misera* may also refer to Nino's misery—since it's isolated in the original by a comma followed by a rare exclamation point ("le quai convien che, misera! Ancor brami") and followed by his statement about her continuing to lust.

79–81. *The viper on the Milanese camp banner . . . as nice / As the cock on my coat of arms*: Nino foresees his widow's future death where, instead of his family crest with a cock on it (the wordplay here is obvious), her tomb will bear the heraldic crest of her new husband, Galeazzo Visconti of Milan: a blue viper swallowing a red man. There are multiple echoes between the serpent just witnessed on the green, the heraldic viper swallowing a red-faced man that will decorate the wife's tomb, and Nino's red-faced fury at having lost his wife to her new, much younger, Ghibelline husband, making the wound both personal and political.

82. *his face stamped with the ink*: The red ink matches the fire of jealous indignation in his heart. Dante may be suggesting that this envy and rage might be what are keeping Nino from advancing up Mount Purgatory, not the lack of prayers from relatives. In any event, Dante loses interest in Nino's diatribe and looks up at the stars.

86–87. *where the stars are slowest, / Like where the wheel spokes insert on a wheel axle*: In the medieval era, nobility and royals replaced their two-wheeled oxen carts with horse-drawn carts. In order to lighten the carts to match the lighter animals, solid wood or stone wheels were replaced by those with spokes.

89–90. *those three lights / Burning up the pole on our side*: Commentators are unable to say with certainty which three stars these might be; they instead emphasize the possibility that they can be read as the theological virtues of faith, hope, and charity (love).

91–93. *The four bright stars you saw this morning / Are so low you can't see them now, / These have climbed to where those were*: Virgil is referring to the four stars seen in *Purg.* I, 23, which were said to be previously visible only to Adam and Eve. Those four, plus these three that are now visible, will make up "the seven-starred North / Of the first Heaven," described at the beginning of *Purg.* XXX, 1–2.

97. *On the little valley's unsheltered edge*: The unsheltered edge, where one could still fall off, is away from the cliff face. Dante will be warned by Virgil in *Purg.* XXV, 118–120, to watch his feet as he walks so as not to slip off.

101–102. *to lick its ridge / Like a fawning beast that sleeks itself*: The figurative meaning of *liscio* (sleek) in Italian, as it was in earlier English, is "fawning." John Milton, *Paradise Lost* (9, 524–526): "Oft he bowd / His turret Crest, and sleek enamel'd Neck, / Fawning, and lick'd the ground whereon she trod."

115–117. *news / From the Magra Valley . . . I was once a VIP there*: Currado's castle was located at the mouth of the Marga River, in the province of Lunigiani. The entire river valley was ruled by the Malaspina family.

118–119. *Currado Malaspina, / Not the old guy, but one of his offspring*: The "old guy" is Currado II's grandfather, Currado I, who died in 1255. Vernon (1:194–195) states that Currado II's cousin, Moroello, a son of Manfred, was "a personal friend and protector of the poet, who is said in the letter which bears the name of Fra Ilario (possibly apocryphal) to have dedicated the *Purgatorio* to him, and he and his son Franceschino welcomed Dante as a guest in 1306, in the earlier period of his exile. An earlier Malaspina was conspicuous among the patrons of the Provençal Troubadours, and the taste for culture may have been inherited by his descendants. The whole passage that follows is obviously the utterance of the poet's gratitude."

120. *The love I showed my own is evolving here*: The sin of pride, including in one's family, is punished on the first cornice. The point is made here that pride in family leads one to arrogantly forget that everyone is equally a child of Mother Earth. In Purgatory, Currado's love for his relatives is evolving into a love of all human beings.

127–129. *if I get upstairs, / Your honorable people will lose nothing / Of their market value nor their might*: Even though Currado hasn't asked Dante to pray for him when he returns to earth, Dante reassures him that he will put in a good word for him and his family, should he reach the summit.

130. *Born to privilege, they use it well*: The high esteem in which Dante holds the Malaspina family, commentators note, is quite likely due to his gratitude. See note to vv. 118–119. During the period Dante remained with the family, he served as their notary at the signing of the prenegotiated Castelnuovo Peace Treaty on October 6, 1306 (Santagata, *Dante*).

130–131. *a wicked / Head twists the world into a pretzel*: The bearer of the head is unnamed but it's possible to read it as any or all of the following: the snake/Satan; Pope Boniface VIII; all the failed rulers Dante called out in *Purg.* VII, who allowed "Mother Italy" to die, especially those responsible for exiling him from Florence. Pretzels existed in the medieval era, although the country of origin is unknown. "The history of the word *pretzel* accords with the widespread tradition that a monk living in France or northern Italy invented the knotted shape of a pretzel in order to symbolize arms folded in prayer" (*American Heritage Dictionary of the English Language*).

133–135. *the sun won't lie down / Seven times in a bed blanketed by / The Ram's fleece*: As noted in *Purg.* IV, 61–65, the sun is currently in Aries, the zodiac sign of the ram, as it was on Easter Sunday in 1300. Currado says that fewer than seven years will pass before the Malaspina family will give Dante refuge (1306). Vernon (1:200) notes, "The ram has always been represented in the ancient astronomical maps as lying down, and with his body reclining on the ecliptic, the bed of the Sun, and with his folded legs covering and bestriding this section of the ecliptic."

136. *this very gracious opinion of yours / Will get hammered deep into your head by studs / Far more enduring than other people's rantings*: The rantings of others may be the hearsay

evidence on which Dante was tried and sentenced to death. Currado claims that his prophecy has more weight, because it is actual fact, than whatever has been said by those who have wrongly indicted Dante.

138. *That is, if the legal system doesn't shut them up*: This final verse circles back to the celestial tribunal mentioned in v. 18, and notes the failure of the legal system in Dante's case. This is the "thin curtain" through which Dante has shone a light, allowing fiction to reveal fact. In the event, the legal system didn't "shut them up."

Canto IX

The glowing mistress of ancient Tithonus,
Having just left her lover's warm arms, was
Becoming snow-white on the eastside balcony;

The gems in the diadem fit to her glittering
Forehead were set in the shape of a scorpion,
That cold-blooded creature with a stinging tail.

Night, where we were, had just taken two steps
Up time's staircase, while a third step was
Bending its feathered edge down to meet her,

When I, who had with me the essence of Adam,
Won over by sleep, lay down on the grass
Where all five of us had been sitting.

At the morning hour,
When the swallow begins her sad song,
Perhaps in memory of her earlier ordeal,

And one's mind, wandering further from flesh
And less rooted in thought,
Tends to have visions that are almost divine,

I thought I saw a golden eagle suspended
In a dream, underneath him steady air,
Wings outstretched, set any second to swoop.

I seemed to be exactly where Ganymede
Gave up those he was with to be carried off
To the high-level meeting on the mountaintop.

I thought: Perhaps it's only here
Where he strikes, and everywhere else
He refuses to grasp anything in his claws.

He seemed to wheel for a while, then struck
Like a terrible cloud-to-ground lightning bolt,
And took me up, as far as the realm of fire.

He and I both seemed to be in flames;
The heat of the dream-fire was so hot,
It made sense that sleep would crash and burn.

Not unlike Achilles's sudden coming to,
Eyes wide open, looking all around,
Not knowing where he was

After his mother smuggled him, asleep
In her arms, from Chiron to the isle of Skyros—
From which he later went off with the Greeks—

I was shaken, sleep having flown from my face,
I became lifeless and,
Like someone scared stiff, I froze.

There by my side, alone, was my comforter;
The sun had been up for over two hours.
My face was now oddly turned toward the sea.

"Don't be afraid," the kind sir said. "You're safe.
Things are well underway for us;
Don't clench up but give it everything you've got.

You've arrived now at Purgatory proper.
See the cliff that wraps around it?
See the entrance over there where it's split?

Earlier, right before daybreak,
While you and your innermost soul were sleeping
On that bed of roses on the grassy knoll below,

A woman came and said, 'I'm Lucy.
Let me take this one while he's sleeping,
So I can help him on his way.'

Sordello stayed put, as did the other noble figures;
She took you and as soon as it was light,
Made her way up, and I followed her.

She laid you down here, first indicating
With her bright eyes the entryway opening,
Then she and soft-handed sleep left together."

The way those in doubt reassure themselves
And that turns their fear into a form
Of comfort once they've discovered the truth—

I made that same exchange. When my teacher
Saw how at ease I was, he got up and moved on,
And I behind him, toward the summit;

Reader, you can clearly see how I'm elevating
My subject matter, so don't be surprised
If I prop it up with greater artifice.

We made our way, and were now where I saw
What I'd first imagined was a crevice—
Like a crack that splits a wall in two—

Was actually a gate, and below it, three steps
Leading up to it, each a different color,
And a gatekeeper who hadn't as yet said a word.

As the gatekeeper gradually took shape,
I could see it was sitting above the highest step,
But I couldn't bear to stare directly at its face.

The naked sword in its hand flashed back
Such blinding radiance
I kept trying and failing to get a look at it.

It spoke, "Tell me from there, what do you want?
Where's your escort? Be careful
That coming up here doesn't get you in trouble."

"There's a lady from Heaven, who's sure
About these things," my teacher said,
"Who just told us, 'Go that way, that's the gate.'"

"May she speed you on your way,"
The gracious gatekeeper continued,
"Come along, these are our stairs."

We moved ahead. The white-marble first tier
Was so flawless and polished I saw myself
Mirrored as if I were one of a pair.

The second was darker than absence-black
With hints of purple, the stone rough and crumbling,
An aggregate of cracks, length- and widthwise.

The third, its hefty mass resting on top,
Looked like porphyry, as close to flame red
As blood that rushes from a vein.

Planted on top of this were the two feet
Of the angel of God, seated on a stone threshold
That made me think of a lap of adamant.

My teacher climbed the three steps
While I let myself be led. He said,
"Kneel, and ask it to undo the lock."

I dropped down in front of the holy feet, begging
For it to please show me mercy and open the gate,
This after striking my chest three times.

Using the point of its sword, it lightly inscribed
Seven Ps across my forehead, then, "Make sure
You wash away these wounds when you're inside."

Ashes or dry dirt dug from the earth,
That was the color of its robe.
From beneath it, it took two keys,

One gold, the other silver; using first the white,
Then the yellow, I was quite happy
With the way things worked at the door.

It told us, "Whenever one of these keys fails
To turn the right way in the lock,
This narrow door won't budge.

The one's worth more, but the other requires a lot
Of skill and ingenuity. Before releasing,
It has to first line up the notches in the lock-body.

They came from Peter and I keep them; I err
As he told me to in opening it, rather than in
Keeping it shut, as long as the soul humbles itself."

It pushed open the door of the holy entrance,
Saying, "Come in, but I have to warn you,
Anyone who looks back goes right back outside."

As the pins in the heavy metal hinges
Of the holy gate turned, the echoing was louder
And even harsher than the roar

Of the door of the Tarpeian treasury being opened—
Along with good-guy Metellus being dragged off—
After which there was very little left.

I turned my attention to a new thunderous sound,
A mixed-voice choir with a held-note undertone;
I thought I could hear "Thee, O God, We Praise"—

The impression, in a nutshell, was something like
Trying to account for what's being said when listening
To organum, plainchant plus reinforced harmony:

No, you can't—yes, you can—understand the words.

1. *The glowing mistress of ancient Tithonus*: Eos, the Greek goddess of dawn (Roman: Aurora), took as her lover Tithonus, a mortal prince of the house of Troy. Tithonus is ancient, and continues to age, because Eos, when she asked Zeus to make her lover immortal, neglected to also ask for eternal youth.

4–5. *The gems in the diadem fit to her glittering / Forehead*: Emily Dickinson (597), "'Tis little I – could care for pearls": "A Diadem to fit a Dome – / Continual upon me –."

10. *who had with me the essence of Adam*: Since Dante alone is still in a human body, like mortal Adam, only he experiences fatigue.

14–15. *the swallow . . . in memory of her earlier ordeal*: In Ovid's *Metamorphoses* (6.438–674), Philomela is raped by her sister Procne's husband, King Tereus of Thrace. To keep her from telling her sister, Tereus cuts out Philomela's tongue and imprisons her in a forest. She, however, weaves a tapestry showing the assault and sends it to Procne, who then finds her sister and takes revenge for her silencing by killing her and Tereus's son, Itys. She serves the meat of the dead child to the king for dinner. The king realizes the subterfuge after he calls for his son and Procne says that his son is inside him. Philomela then enters, bearing the son's head. Tereus reaches for his sword but the two women have been changed by the gods into birds—Procne into a red-breasted swallow and Philomela into a nightingale, both songbirds. Tereus is also changed, into a crested hoopoe. Dante appears to believe that Philomela is the swallow. See note to *Purg.* XVII, 19–20.

20. *Underneath him steady air*: Gerard Manley Hopkins, "The Windhover: *To Christ our Lord*": "in his riding / Of the rolling level underneath him steady air."

22–24. *Ganymede . . . carried off / To the high-level meeting on the mountaintop*: Zeus, in the form of an eagle, abducts Ganymede, a beautiful mortal prince from Troy, who, accompanied by his guardians, is out hunting with dogs on the slopes of Mount Ida. Zeus carries him up to Mount Olympus, makes him immortal and forever young, and gives him the job of cupbearer to the gods. After his consort, Hera, jealous of the boy, refused the cup he offered, Zeus turned him into the constellation Aquarius. Both Virgil and Statius include the story of Ganymede. Statius, in *Silvae* 3.4.15, writes, "[Ganymede] to whom Juno gives a dirty look and withdraws her hand and says no to the nectar." Virgil, *Aeneid* 5, 252 ff. (trans. C. Day-Lewis): "Ganymede, hunting on leafy Ida, with his javelin, hunting down swift stags—you could almost see him panting, the nimble boy; he was pictured, too, being snatched up aloft from Ida in the claws of Jupiter's fast-flying eagle—his aged guardians are raising their impotent hands to heaven, his dogs are furiously barking up at the sky above them."

30. *as far as the realm of fire*: The medieval conception of space was that a sphere of air surrounded earth, then a ring of fire, then the lunar ring.

34–38. *Achilles's sudden coming to . . . smuggled . . . from Chiron to the isle of Skyros*: Achilles was the son of Peleus, the king of the Myrmidons at Phthia in Thessaly, and Thetis, a Nereid (sea nymph). Before Achilles's birth, Themis, the goddess of divine law, prophesied that he would die in battle. To make him immortal, his mother held him by his heel and dipped him in the river Styx; unfortunately, the spot where she held him remained mortal and vulnerable, his "Achilles' heel." Initially, Achilles was educated and trained in weaponry by Chiron the Centaur. When he was nine, Calchas, a seer, prophesied that a battle would take place at Troy that the Greeks could only win if Achilles fought on their side. Because of the earlier prophecy, his mother disguised him as a girl, renamed him Pyrrha (red-haired girl), and took him to live in the court of King Lycomedes on the island of Skyros. There he fell in love with the king's daughter, Deidamia, and fathered a child by her.

39. *From which he later went off with the Greeks*: When Achilles was fifteen, Odysseus, having heard the Calchas prophecy, and having learned that Achilles was on the island of Skyros, sailed there and convinced Achilles to set sail with him for Troy. Achilles left, accompanied by an army of soldiers from Phthia, fifty ships, and his friend Patroclus.

54. *On that bed of roses on the grassy knoll below*: "Bed of roses" is an idiom that gestures to luxury and ease. A "grassy knoll" is a grass-covered rise or hillock. In America, the phrase came to represent a grass-covered slope inside Dealey Plaza in Dallas, Texas, from which shots were reportedly heard during the assassination of President John F. Kennedy on November 22, 1963. The plaza is next to the Texas School Book Depository, the building from which Lee Harvey Oswald fired the shots that killed the president and wounded the Texas governor, John Connally.

55–57. *I'm Lucy . . . so I can help him on his way*: Saint Lucia, Lucia of Syracuse, was a martyr executed during the Roman Empire's "Great Persecution" of Christians. Her name means light and she is often portrayed with two eyes on a plate. Born of noble birth, she became a Christian and gave her riches to the poor, angering the man to whom she had been betrothed. He exposed her as a Christian and she was killed. In Heaven, she has clearly regained her eyes and her sight.

63. *she and soft-handed sleep left together*: John Keats, "Ode to Psyche":

As if disjoined by soft-handed slumber,
And ready still past kisses to outnumber
    At tender eye-dawn of aurorean love:
        The winged boy I knew;
But who wast thou, O happy, happy dove?
        His Psyche true!

70–72. *Reader . . . don't be surprised / If I prop it up with greater artifice*: This is the second address to the reader in the poem, the first being *Purg.* VIII, 19–21. It seems unlikely that the poet would stop to brag about what is to come next, or to alert the reader that the poem will now require an increase in the suspension of disbelief, especially following Saint Lucy's carrying the human body up the steep incline. It's possible that the alert here is to cue the reader to look for a political reading woven into the allegory. The poem ends with the confirmation that one might have difficulty deciphering the words of the hymn, just as one might have difficulty deciphering coded meanings in a poem, unless one knows to look for them. A contemporary term for such language is Aesopian, language that sounds innocent to outsiders but carries special political meaning for insiders.

88. *There's a lady from Heaven, who's sure*: Led Zeppelin, "Stairway to Heaven" (see note to *Purg.* I, 4–6).

93. *these are our stairs*: Commentators differ on the meaning of the three stairs. Many claim Dante meant them to represent the three steps to absolution: contrition, confession, and satisfaction. All three colors align with Christ: white for faith and purity, perse or purple for nobility, and red for charity or love.

94–96. *The white-marble first tier / Was so flawless and polished I saw myself / Mirrored*: The fact that the stone embodies perfection and perfectly mirrors the onlooker may also indicate the newborn soul.

97–99. *The second was darker than absence-black / With hints of purple . . . rough and crumbling . . . cracks*: *Perse* in Italian also means "lost," "absent," or "missing." Since black corresponds to the absence of color, even if hints of royal purple shine through, the overall effect is what's missing. With virtue, on the other hand, nobility reigns over grief, so virtue is associated with good. In *Convivio* 4, 20, Dante writes: "*Perse* is a mixed color of purple and black, but black wins, and dominates it. . . . Similarly, virtue is a mixture of nobility and suffering but because nobility wins in that matchup, it's named virtue, and labeled good."

100–102. *The third . . . like porphyry, as close to flame red / As blood that rushes from a vein*: If the purity of the first step represents the untried soul, and the stained and cracked second step, the struggle to be virtuous, the blood-red third step might be both death and also regeneration. In *Convivio* 4, 21, Dante quite explicitly discusses creation from a corporeal point of view: "Therefore, I say that when human seed falls into its receptacle, that is into the uterus, it is accompanied by the power of the generative soul and the power of heaven and the power of the combined elements. . . . The seed prepares and disposes the menstrual matter for the formative power . . . which produces the soul from the potentiality of the seed."

105. *a lap of adamant*: Emily Dickinson (363), "I know a place where Summer strives": "And she pours soft Refrains // Into the lap of Adamant –."

112–113. *inscribed / Seven Ps across my forehead*: The Italian word for sin is *peccato*, so each of these Ps stands for one of the seven cardinal sins: pride, envy, wrath, laziness, avarice, gluttony, and lust. Each time Dante leaves a cornice, the P that corresponds to that sin will be erased.

136. *the Tarpeian treasury*: The Tarpeian Rock is a cliff on the summit of Capitoline Hill in Rome; in the Roman Era, the state treasury was located there in a temple of Saturn and criminals were sometimes thrown from it.

137–138. *good-guy Metellus . . . After which there was very little left*: Caecilius L. Metellus, a tribune loyal to Pompey, attempted in 49 BCE to guard the treasury so Caesar couldn't plunder it. Lucan, *Pharsalia* 3, 153–157: "Straightaway Metellus was taken aside and the temple laid bare. Then the Tarpeian Rock sounded, and with loud screeching bore witness to the opening of the doors; then the wealth of the Roman people, stored in the depths of the temple and untouched for many a year, was dragged out" (trans. H. T. Riley). After the looting, there was less noise, and also little left in the way of money in the bank.

140. *A mixed-voice choir with a held-note undertone*: A mixed choir includes male and female voices and also includes soprano, alto, tenor, and bass. A prolonged bass note under a melodic line is called a drone bass.

141. *Thee, O God, We Praise*: "Te deum laudamus" is a fourth-century Latin hymn of unknown authorship. A song of praise, it incorporates elements of the Apostles' Creed.

144. *organum, plainchant plus reinforced harmony*: Organum is an early form of musical polyphony that has its beginning in plainchant (also called plainsong), liturgical Gregorian chants that incorporated a second voice.

145. *No, you can't—yes, you can—understand the words*: Once inside, the harsh sounds of the gate are replaced by sounds so complex that Dante isn't sure how to interpret them. They sound like the familiar hymn but he can't be certain. Similarly, the reader cannot be certain how to interpret the allegorical action in this canto.

Canto X

Once we'd crossed the threshold of the gate,
Unused by souls whose hurtful love
Makes them think their crooked ways are straight,

Its echoing told me it was closed;
If I'd turned my eyes to look,
What excuse could have justified *that* mistake?

We were climbing through a crevice in the rock
That switched this way and that
In a zigzag flame-stitch pattern,

When my teacher said, "Here's where it helps
To be creative; move side to side,
Until you find which way veers off."

This made for such slow going
That the yo-yo moon had gotten back into bed
And was dead to the world

Before we were outside the needle's eye.
Now free and in the open,
With the mountain rolled back behind us,

I exhausted and both of us unsure of the road,
We rested on a level stretch even more
Abandoned than Wall Street on a weekend.

From the outer border, the edge of the abyss,
To the base of the upstanding embankment,
Measured three men laid head to toe.

My eyes darted left, then right:
As far as I could see,
The cornice seemed the same throughout.

Our feet hadn't yet reached the wraparound
Cliff face that stood so straight,
There was no way of getting up it,

When I could already tell it was white marble
Inlaid with engravings, the likes of which
Would outclass Polycletus and Nature.

The Angel Gabriel—who landed on earth
With the long-awaited and wept-for peace decree
That undid the ban on Heaven—

Was animated in front of us, an etching that acted
Like a delicate form of stop-motion animation,
Lifelike and unlike any silent film still;

One could have sworn he was saying, "Hello!"—
Since the one pictured with him was the one
Who turned the key to unlock a love supreme.

The phrase "Here I am, the Lord's handmaiden"
Was imprinted on her character with the clarity
Of a die-cut seal pressed to warm wax.

My ever-helpful teacher said,
"Don't get fixated on one spot."
He had me on his heart side.

At that point, I turned my head
And saw how past Mary, on the same side
As the one who kept moving me along,

There was another story set in stone.
I crossed in front of Virgil and got closer,
So that I could get a better look.

There, also in marble, was the Holy Ark
In an ox-drawn cart, the lesson of which is:
People who try to play God should be very afraid.

A crowd made up of seven choirs
Led the procession; one of my senses said, "No,"
While the other argued, "Yes. Singing."

Likewise, the depiction of the incense smoke
Caused my eyes and nose to argue
With Yes and No.

Before the blessed chest, the modest Psalmist,
Dancing with his robe hiked up, was
In that case, more *and* less the essence of a king.

In contrast, in a plateglass window
Of a grand palace, Michal is sizing him up
And bitterly finding him sadly lacking.

I moved a few steps from where I was
To check out more closely another storyboard
I saw in the whiteness beyond Michal.

Here were the plot points of the story
Of the glorious Roman prince whose gallantry
Made Pope Gregory achieve a victory;

I'm talking about Emperor Trajan.
A young widow, her hand on his bridle,
Strikes a pose: tears and grief.

All around him, trampled ground and a throng
Of knights: gold eagles in needlepoint
Flutter in the wind above him.

One could imagine her in the thick of it saying,
"Sir, my son's death needs to be punished.
My heart is ripped apart."

And his answer, "Not now, wait until I'm back."
She says, "My sir,"
Like someone pushed forward by sorrow—

"What if you don't come back?" He:
"Whoever has my job will do it." She: "What good
Will it do you if you're living in oblivion."

Then, he: "Okay, calm yourself. I'll stay
And pay my debt before I go.
Justice says please, and pity keeps me here."

He, in whose sight nothing is ever new,
Invented this form of talking pictures,
Brand-new to us since it's unique to here.

While I liked looking at these images
Of so many serving as examples, and to see
What the locksmith holds in esteem,

"Here they come, over there," murmured
The poet. "So many, although their steps are few
And far between; they'll point us to the next level."

My eyes, happy to stare at these images
But also always looking for something new,
Quickly turned toward him.

I don't want, Reader, to lessen
Your good intentions when you find out
How God wants you to pay off your debt.

Don't focus on the form of suffering; think
Instead of what happens after, and how the worst
Can't outlast the great Judgment.

"Master," I said, "what I see coming our way,
They don't seem like humans; I don't know
What they are: it's like I can't see straight."

He said, "They're so bent down by the weight
Of their grief, they're nearly on the ground:
At first, I couldn't believe my eyes either.

Look carefully, see if you can't tease apart
The face from what's under the rocks.
You can already see how each is beaten down."

O arrogant Christians, pitiful and derelict:
From the vantage of your feeble minds,
You keep trusting your backsliding feet.

Don't you see how we're worms,
Born to be angel-butterflies, defenselessly
Winging our way toward judgment.

How is it you're a pompous cock of the walk?
You're nothing but misshapen bug bodies,
The larva that hasn't yet found its form.

Sometimes, to hold up a ceiling or an eave,
Instead of a support beam, there's a figure,
Crouched, knees pressed against chest—

However unreal, it creates real terror
In someone who sees it; once I made them out,
That's how I felt about these.

They were more or less bent over
Based on more or less weight on their backs;
Even the most patient ones, crying,

Seemed to say, "I can't go on (I'll go on)."

16. *outside the needle's eye*: There are clear biblical echoes here. Matthew 7:13–14: "Enter ye in at the strait gate: for wide is the gate, and broad is the way, that leadeth to destruction, and many there be which go in thereat: Because strait is the gate, and narrow is the way, which leadeth unto life, and few there be that find it"; and Matthew 19:24, Christ to his disciples: "And again I say unto you, It is easier for a camel to go through the eye of a needle, than for a rich man to enter into the kingdom of God."

20–21. *more / Abandoned than Wall Street on a weekend*: Dante's *strade per diserti* can be roads through deserts or abandoned streets. Once an actual wall at the northern limit of the New Amsterdam settlement, the eight-block-long Wall Street in New York City is the financial capital of America. Since banks, corporate offices, and stock exchanges are closed on weekends, it is all but deserted then.

33. *Would outclass Polycletus and Nature*: Polycletus was a classical Greek sculptor who excelled in carving statues of the male body that expressed ideal proportions. While nature imitates the perfection of God, God is said to have directly created the images on the cornice; therefore, they are more perfect than any imitation or artistic rendering, even those sculpted by the most talented.

34–36. *Angel Gabriel—who landed on earth . . . undid the ban on Heaven*: This scene depicts Archangel Gabriel's appearance to the Virgin Mary (the Annunciation), when she is told she will give birth to a child she is to name Jesus, and that he will be the Son of God. The proscription against humans entering Heaven is at that point lifted since the life and death of Christ will redeem Adam and Eve's error and allow those who accept Christ to enter the Kingdom of Heaven.

38. *a delicate form of stop-motion animation*: The first known use of stop-motion animation was in 1897 (*The Humpty Dumpty Circus*); the first film by an American woman animator using stop-motion figures sculpted from clay was Helena Smith Dayton's 1917 *Shakespeare's Romeo and Juliet*.

39. *silent film still*: A film still is an on-set photograph used for promotion of a film before and after the film's release.

40. *One could have sworn he was saying, "Hello!"*: Luke 1:28–29: "And the angel came in unto her, and said, Hail, thou that art highly favoured, the Lord is with thee: blessed art thou among women. And when she saw him, she was troubled at his saying, and cast in her mind what manner of salutation this should be."

41–42. *the one / Who turned the key to unlock a love supreme*: Since Mary conceived Christ, the Redeemer, she is said to have made God's divine love available to humankind. *A Love Supreme* is a jazz album by the saxophonist John Coltrane, recorded in 1964 and released in 1965 by Impulse! Records. It's a four-part suite ending with a section titled "Psalm." A poem by Coltrane in the liner notes ends, "ELATION-ELEGANCE-EXALTATION / All from God. / Thank you God. Amen."

43. *The phrase "Here I am, the Lord's handmaiden"*: Luke 1:38 tells of Mary's response to the Annunciation: "And Mary said, Behold the handmaid of the Lord; be it unto me according to thy word. And the angel departed from her." The Latin *Ecce* can mean "Behold," "Look," "Here," or "Here I am."

48. *He had me on his heart side*: Dante is standing to the left of Virgil. Less than 1 percent of the population has their heart on the right side. When that occurs, the congenital anomaly is called dextrocardia.

55–57. *the Holy Ark / In an ox-drawn cart . . . People who try to play God should be very afraid*: After defeating the Israelites in battle, the Philistines carried off the Ark of the Covenant. They subsequently found that disaster came to any who housed it. The men of Kiriath Jearim later reclaimed the Ark and moved it to the house of Abinadab, where it was guarded by Abinadab's son Eleazar. After forty years, King David brought the Ark to Jerusalem, moving it in a newly made cart and accompanied by Uzzah, another of Abinadab's sons. II Samuel 6:6–7 tells the story of how when Uzzah, although not a priest but wishing to steady the cart, reached out and touched the Ark, he was killed by God for his presumption in acting as if he were a priest and in thinking that God wouldn't be able to manage on his own.

58. *seven choirs*: The seven choirs occur in the Vulgate Bible but not in the King James Version.

60. *Yes. Singing*: The figures are so lifelike, it's difficult for Dante not to conjure the sound of singing and then to actually believe in what he's conjured.

64. *Before the blessed chest, the modest Psalmist*: Seventy-three psalms in the book of Psalms are linked by name to King David, two psalms in the New Testament.

65–66. *Dancing with his robe hiked up . . . more* and *less the essence of a king*: The *tresconeto* is a lively triple-meter Tuscan folk dance that incorporates leaping. It features a single dancer or a couple and gets progressively faster. By participating in the dance, his royal robes hiked up to allow freer movement, David was less kingly in the eyes of his wife Michal, who is watching with disdain from a window, and yet more kingly in the eyes of God because he can humble himself and join with his people in dance. His lack of pretension also endears him to his people.

67–69. *a plateglass window / Of a grand palace, Michal is sizing him up / And bitterly finding him sadly lacking*: Michal, the youngest daughter of King Saul, was the wife of King David of Judah (and later of Israel). Some versions of this story have her punished with barrenness for her scorn; other versions contradict that.

73–74. *Here were the plot points of the story / Of the glorious Roman prince*: This is the Roman emperor Trajan (Marcus Ulpius Traianus), as we will learn in v. 76. He ruled from 98 to 177 CE.

74–75. *whose gallantry / Made Pope Gregory achieve a victory*: A widely believed medieval legend was that Pope Gregory the Great (590–604), after learning of Trajan's magnanimous gesture to the woman, and offering prayers of intercession for him, actually succeeded in having Trajan recalled from Hell so that he could repent. This is counter to the doctrine that those in Hell can't be freed by prayer.

76. *I'm talking about Emperor Trajan*: According to Vernon (1:360): "No emperor ever extended the Roman Empire so far as Trajan. He was renowned for valour, justice and clemency, and for a statesman-like grasp of the events passing in his time, he was unsurpassed if not unrivalled by any other emperor. In the progresses he made through his different provinces, he won for himself through all history a name as a model of a prince. The episode recorded here is supposed to take place when he was just setting off on a military expedition of considerable importance, surrounded by his great officers of state, and his mind occupied with great matters."

90. *if you're living in oblivion*: *Living in Oblivion* is a 1995 independent film about making an independent film that takes place over the course of one day, written and directed by Tom DiCillo and starring Steve Buscemi and Catherine Keener.

95–96. *Invented this form of talking pictures, / Brand-new to us since it's unique to here*: Since God invented everything, nothing can be new to God. Dante's imagined *visibile parlare* (visible speech) anticipates talkie films by some six hundred years.

99. *What the locksmith holds in esteem*: Dante again uses the word *fabbro*, a metalworking or locksmith term. Only figuratively does the word mean "maker," in the general sense. "Locksmith" emphasizes that the ways of the maker are unfathomable.

106–108. *I don't want, Reader, to lessen / Your good intentions when you find out / How God wants you to pay off your debt*: This is another self-referential moment where Dante cautions the reader that what they are about to be told might scare them off.

110–111. *the worst / can't outlast the great Judgment*: The Final Judgment, based on Old and New Testament sources, is a concept common to many religious faiths. On that day, all will be judged by Christ; the repentant will go to Heaven, the others to Hell.

113–114. *They don't seem like humans; I don't know / What they are*: The prideful souls are crushed into crouching positions by the weight of the boulders they have to carry on their backs. Their human forms are so distorted Dante can't identify what he's seeing.

130–132. *to hold up a ceiling or an eave . . . there's a figure, / Crouched, knees pressed against chest*: These architectural supports, corbels, are structural elements that support an overhanging weight. In the medieval era, they were often carved into animal or human figures, often naked or partially clothed, sometimes engaged in obscene sex acts. Fudgé (92): "On the twelfth century abbey Church of St-Genès in Châteaumeillant under the words 'Hac rusticani mixti' (This is what the peasants do), we find two men kissing, one holding his erection in his left hand. All of these sexual positions and variations challenge the assumption of an uptight Middle Ages. Of course, many corbels are less arresting."

133–134. *However unreal, it creates real terror / In someone who sees it*: This is the ability of art to so accurately mirror a situation that we experience a subjective reaction, a reaction Roland Barthes refers to as *punctum* (piercing) in *Camera Lucida*.

136–137. *They were more or less bent over / Based on more or less weight on their backs*: Each carries a weight equal to the pride they manifested while living.

139. *Seemed to say, "I can't go on (I'll go on)"*: Samuel Beckett's 1953 novel *The Unnamable*, first published in English in 1958 by Grove Press, is the third work of a trilogy that also includes *Malloy* and *Malone Dies*. The work is a push-of-speech monologue that ends with:

> Perhaps they have carried me to the threshold of my story, before the door that opens on my story, that would surprise me, if it opens, it will be I, it will be the silence, where I am, I don't know, I'll never know, in the silence you don't know, you must go on, I can't go on. I'll go on.

Dante ends the canto with "Più non posso" (I can't go on); the shade, however, has no way of stopping, so it will go on, which is exactly the sentiment expressed by Beckett's ending. Beckett borrows characters and language from Dante in several of his works.

Canto XI

"Our father, who art in Heaven, not hemmed in
There on high but because you love best
The cosmic effects that you created first.

Let every creature praise your name and worth;
It's right to give thanks for your clouds,
Those delicate white-suited workers.

May the peace of your kingdom come,
Since with all of our intelligence,
We can't reach it if it doesn't come to us.

Just as your angels sacrifice their wills
To yours with an anthem of hosannas,
So let humans do the same with theirs.

Give us this day our daily bread,
Without which, those who strive to advance
Go backward through the waste land.

And as we forgive everyone for the harm
We've suffered, mercifully forgive us
And judge us not on our merits.

Don't test our morality, so easily overcome,
Against the timeless adversary, but deliver us
From that one who would egg us on.

We make this last request, Dear Lord,
No longer for ourselves, there's no need,
But for those who remain behind."

Praying for their and our progress, those souls
Went on under their ponderous weights,
Like one does sometimes in a dream,

Each anguished in its own way,
All of them wearily rounding the first cornice,
All of them purging the world's pollution

If they're always up there wishing us well,
What can be said and done by those on earth,
Who have good reason to wish them well?

We should help them wash away the stains
They carried here, so they, purified
And light, can enter the cosmic sphere.

"That justice plus compassion might soon
Lighten your load, and give you wings
To rise to whatever height you wish,

Please point out the shortest path
To the ascent—and if there's more than one,
Indicate which is the least steep.

Since the one with me is still weighed down
With Adam's flesh, he's slow at climbing,
In spite of wishing it were otherwise."

Some words were then returned in response
To those spoken by the one I was following,
Although it wasn't clear from whom they came.

What was clear was: "Come with us
To the right along the bank, and you'll arrive
At an incline that someone living can climb.

If I weren't prevented by this millstone
That's breaking in my proud neck,
And forcing me to keep my face down,

I'd look up at this unnamed, still-living man
To see whether I know him, and make him pity me
For the dead weight with which I've been saddled.

I was Italian, the son of a great Tuscan;
Guglielmo Aldobrandeschi was my father,
I don't know if you ever came across his name.

My ancient family line and their storied deeds
Made me so arrogant that I,
Never aware we all share a common mother,

Had extreme contempt for everyone else.
It led to my death; those in Siena know how,
As does any Jessy or Jack from Campagnatico.

I'm Omberto. It's not only me that was messed up
By pride, my whole family got swept up in it;
Now they have to deal with the same sickness.

And I have to bear the burden of it here,
With the dead, until God is satisfied
Since I didn't do it when I was with the living."

I'd bent my head down to listen, and one,
Not the one speaking, twisted himself beneath
That weight that acts like a ball and chain,

And saw me and knew me and called out,
Struggling to keep his eyes fixed on me, as I,
Completely bent over, went along with them.

"Oh," I said, "aren't you Oderisi, the honor
Of Gubbio, and the darling of the art
Of what in Paris is called illumination?"

"Brother," he said, "the brushwork
Of Franco of Bologna is far more charming:
All the honor goes to him now; and me in part.

I certainly wouldn't have been so courteous
While I was alive; what I wanted most
Was to be the best; my heart was set on it.

Here we pay the price for that sort of pride.
I wouldn't even be here, except that
When I was still able to sin, I turned to God.

O human powers, pull down thy vanity!
The green at the end of the branch is brief
Unless followed by a period of latency.

Cimabue believed he was the ace painter,
But now that Giotto's staked his claim,
The other's fame has faded.

So the poetic glory of one Guido is displaced
By another, and someone else might be born
Who'll push one, then the other, from the nest.

Worldly fame is nothing but a puff of wind,
Here it comes, there it goes;
It changes its name when it changes direction.

Are you the better for your desperate deal,
If you and your body part ways when it's old, versus
Going before you outgrow saying *din-din* and *lolly*,

Once a thousand years have passed? That,
Compared to infinitude, is less than an eye-blink
Next to the slowest-moving orbit in Heaven.

The one gaining so little ground in front of me,
All of Tuscany once echoed his name,
Now there's barely a whisper of him in Siena.

He was a lord there when they razed the rabble
Of Florence, which was as haughty
In that era, as now it's just like a hustler.

Your name is grass-colored, it comes and goes,
What bleaches it brown is the same thing
That brings it green from the ground."

"Your truth-telling moves me to real humility
And to deal with my own great arrogance,
But who were you talking about just now?"

"That one," he said, "is Provenzan Salvani.
He's here because he was cocky enough
To think he could put all of Siena in his pocket.

He's gone on this way since he died, and will keep
Going on without rest; this dime pays down the debt
For too much wise-guy audacity below."

I asked him, "If a spirit who puts off repentance
Until he's at death's door has to stay below,
Before coming up to this level,

For as long as they were living—
Unless helped out by holy prayers—
By what largesse was he allowed to come here?"

"When he was alive and at the height of his glory,
He openly sat in the public square in Siena,
Willingly enduring the shame

While managing to shake each veined wrist
In order to shorten the sentence
Of a friend doing hard time in Charles's prison.

I won't say more, and this may sound obscure,
But in a short time, your neighbors will behave
In such a way that you'll be able to decipher this:

That generous act let him escape those limits."

1–3. *Our father, who art in Heaven . . . that you created first*: The Lord's Prayer (Pater Noster) is found twice in the New Testament, in Matthew 6:9–13 and Luke 11:2–4. Dante takes liberties with his paraphrase, especially in his emphasis that God isn't limited to Heaven but is there because he's so delighted by what he first created (the cosmos). Genesis 1:1: "In the beginning, God created the heaven and the earth." This, the only complete prayer in the *Commedia*, is especially appropriate for those on this first cornice, where the penitents pay for having too much pride on earth; the prayer recognizes the superiority and perfection of God and asks for his assistance.

5–6. *your clouds, / Those delicate white-suited workers*: Vladimir Mayakovsky, "A Cloud in Trousers," trans. P. Lemke:

> Suddenly,
> clouds
> and various cloud-like things in the sky
> will kick up a fuss,
> as if white-suited workers were dispersing
> after calling an embittered strike against the sky.

Dante uses the word *vapore*, which can mean "steam," "smoke," "warmth," "heat," "mist," "fog," or "the ardour of love." Hollander and Hollander (226) note that some commentators argue this word gestures to the Holy Spirit, which is often associated with breath. Throughout *Purgatorio*, the natural behavior of clouds and mist is noted and is often put to creative use by both Satan and God.

15. *the waste land*: Dante may have in mind the Israelites being sustained by manna while crossing the desert. T. S. Eliot's 1922 long poem, *The Waste Land*, is a defining work of the modernist era. Eliot originally considered titling the poem *He Do the Police in Different Voices*. Ezra Pound suggested *The Waste Land* as a title and made other radical revisions to the poem.

20. *the timeless adversary*: This is Satan, the tempter. In *Purg.* VIII, 95, Sordello points out the serpent's arrival to Virgil, saying, "See, there's our adversary!" In *Purg.* XIV, 146, Dante mentions how "Using a lure line, the ancient adversary reels you in."

22–24. *this last request . . . No longer for ourselves, there's no need / But for those who remain behind*: Since the penitents can no longer succumb to earthly temptation, the prayer is sent up for those still on earth.

28–30. *Each anguished in its own way . . . All of them purging the world's pollution*: Each penitent will spend varying amounts of time on each cornice; some are able to skip a cornice if they are not guilty of that particular sin. They all, however, begin here, where they pay for various kinds of hubris. No one is free of that sin.

32. *What can be said and done by those on earth*: These are the prayers of intercession that can shorten someone's time on one of the cornices, and shorten their time overall. There is a theme that runs through *Purgatorio* about helping one another, and conversely, how the sins of one person make things worse for those close to them. The hair shirts on the second cornice, where one pays for the sin of envy, demonstrate this. Each shade leans against the other, which increases their discomfort, and the cliff presses against them all. Throughout the *Commedia*, Dante is concerned with the social fabric and what humans do to damage it. Religion and family can hold a society together only as long as the leadership has not been corrupted.

58–59. *the son of a great Tuscan; / Guglielmo Aldobrandeschi was my father*: As we'll learn in v. 67, this is Omberto Aldobrandeschi. His father, Guglielmo, Count of Santafioa, in the Sienese Maremma, began as a Ghibelline but later became a follower of the Florentine Guelphs. The son, Omberto, lord of the fortified castle of Campagnatico, died there in 1259 while fighting the Sienese. In the early thirteenth century the family was at the height of their power. Their fortune suffered from the continual fighting with the Sienese.

63. *we all share a common mother*: This verse is usually read as Mother Earth, not biblical Eve. Mother Earth nourishes all equally. Virgil in the *Aeneid* 11, 68–71: "Like a flower pinched by a maiden's fingers, a delicate violet or fading hyacinth . . . Mother Earth no longer feeds and cares for it, keeps it alive."

65–66. *It led to my death; those in Siena know how, / As does any Jessy or Jack from Campagnatico*: The *ogli fante* at the Castle of Campagnatico is variously understood as any Jack, knave, infantryman, or any child (Jack or Jill). The Sienese know the circumstances of his death because they killed him, either in a nearby field or in his bed; sources vary. Gerard Manley Hopkins, "The Candle Indoors": "I plod wondering, a-wanting, just for lack / Of answer the eagerer a-wanting Jessy or Jack / There / God to aggrándise, God to glorify."

76. *And saw me and knew me and called out*: The two men recognize one another, but it's unclear whether they knew each other well, or knew of each other only in passing.

79–81. *Oderisi, the honor / Of Gubbio, and the darling of the art / Of what in Paris is called illumination*: Gubbio is a town in Umbria. Little is known about Oderisi except that he was called to Rome in 1295 to illustrate papal manuscripts. Singleton (2:233) quotes Benvenuto: "This Oderisi was a great miniature-painter in Bologna at the time of our author, and he was very vain and boastful about his artistic talents, quite sure that he had no peer. Dante, who was well aware of his hunger for praise and glory, deliberately praised him as being without equal, to see if he had lost the wind that formerly inflated him."

83–84. *Franco of Bologna . . . All the honor goes to him now; and me in part*: A student of Oderisi da Gubbio, Franco Bolognese was an Italian painter and manuscript illuminator. Like Oderisi, he was employed by Boniface VIII to illustrate manuscripts in the papal library in Rome. He is said to have exceeded Oderisi in skill. As Benvenuto says in the preceding note, Dante appears to use this knowledge to test Oderisi's new-found humility. Oderisi still hasn't given up all of his self-regard; even though he says "all" honor goes now to Franco, he claims "a part" for himself, presumably for having taught Franco.

86–87. *what I wanted most / Was to be the best*: The grand desire for excellence ("lo gran disio de l'eccellenza"), Singleton (2:234) points out, is "a standard definition of pride." He quotes Thomas Aquinas (235): "Pride is said to be *love of one's own excellence*, inasmuch as [this] love makes a man presume inordinately on his superiority over others, and this belongs properly to pride."

91. *O human powers, pull down thy vanity*: In his Canto LXXXI, Ezra Pound uses "Pull down thy vanity" as a refrain. Dante similarly decries the many types of vanity: family lineage, talent, fame, wealth, privilege, and military might.

93. *Unless followed by a period of latency*: Fame occurs only if the artist remains unbested for some period.

94. *Cimabue believed he was the ace painter*: Cimabue was a Florentine painter and mosaicist; he was the teacher of Giotto and influenced the shift away from the stylized Byzantine manner toward a more painterly style.

95. *now that Giotto's staked his claim*: Giotto di Bondone was a Florentine painter and personal friend of Dante's. In 1332–1337, he painted a portrait of a young Dante, dressed in red, at the center of a fresco of Paradise in the Chapel of the Palazzo del Podestà, now the Bargello Museum.

97–98. *the poetic glory of one Guido is displaced / By another*: Oderisi shifts now from artists to poets. Commentators most often parse this sentence as: the younger Guido Cavalcanti (1250–1300) has taken the attention from the older Guido Guinizzelli (ca. 1225–1276). In *Purg.* XXVI, 97–99, Dante will refer to Guinizzelli as "the father: / Mine, and all the best among the rest of us— / Never have love poems been so freshly elegant."

103–107. *Are you the better for your desperate deal . . . That, / Compared to infinitude, is less than an eye-blink*: Alice Dunbar-Nelson, "The Idler": "Are you the better for your desperate deal, / When you, like him, into infinitude are hurled?"

105. *you outgrow saying* din-din *and* lolly: Dante uses the Italian nursery words *pappo* (to eat or gobble up) and *dindi* (money). *Din-din* is American baby talk for dinner and *lolly* is both a shortening of "lollipop" and a (primarily British) slang word for money.

110–112. *All of Tuscany . . . Now there's barely a whisper of him in Siena // He was a lord there*: Provenzan Salvani will be named in v. 121. Singleton (2:239–240) quotes Villani VII, 31: "He was an important man in Siena in his time, after the victory of Montaperti. He controlled the whole city, and the entire Ghibelline faction of Tuscany looked to him as its leader. He was very imperious in manner."

118–120. *Your truth-telling moves me to real humility / And to deal with my own great arrogance, / But who were you talking about just now*: Dante is admitting to the sin of pride; he, however, immediately brushes that aside to satisfy his curiosity. In a sense, it's proof that he will, as he predicts in *Purg.* XIII, 133–138, have to spend quite a bit of time on this cornice when he returns here after death.

121–123. *Provenzan Salvani . . . he could put all of Siena in his pocket*: Singleton (2:239): "After the battle of Montaperti (September 4, 1260) he [Salvani] was virtual dictator of Siena, and it was he who at the council of Empoli after the battle advocated the destruction of Florence, which was averted by the firmness and patriotism of Farinata (*Inf.* X, 91–93). . . . He met his death in an engagement with the Florentines at Colle in Val d'Elsa, in June [11, 1269], when he was taken prisoner and beheaded." Commentators note that Dante oddly places Salvani, who would have razed Florence, in Purgatory and yet consigns Farinata, who saved Florence, to Hell.

132. *By what largesse was he allowed to come here*: Those who delay asking for salvation are forced to remain in Ante-Purgatory for thirty times the number of years they were alive. Salvani died at the age of forty-seven and yet, if he is in Purgatory at the time of Dante's journey in 1300, he only spent thirty-one years in Ante-Purgatory (instead of 1,410). Dante appears to assume it was more than simply prayers of intercession that shortened his wait time.

134. *in the public square in Siena*: The square is the Campo di Siena, a well-known plaza in front of the Palazzo Pubblico.

135–136. *Willingly enduring the shame // While managing to shake each veined wrist*: The suggestion is that he humiliated himself by allowing the veins of his wrists to show as he was shaking an alms cup.

140–141. *But in a short time, your neighbors will behave / In such a way that you'll be able to decipher this*: Oderisi is prophesying Dante's 1302 exile at the hands of his "neighbors," the Florentine Black Guelphs.

142. *That generous act let him escape those limits*: Oderisi is also suggesting it will be to Dante's advantage in the afterlife to practice humility while he's living.

canto XII

Like equals, like oxen locked in a polished yoke,
I stayed even with that downtrodden soul
For as long as my dear schoolmaster allowed.

But when he said, "Leave him, and pick up
The pace, it's good here to use one's limbs or oars,
Whichever's best, to nudge one's boat along,"

I straightened, yes, like a person primed
To walk upright, although I had a sinking feeling,
And thought-wise I was getting nowhere.

Moving forward, I was happy to match my feet
To my teacher's stride,
Both of us now enacting our lightness.

He said to me, "Keep your eyes down,
It'll do you some good, and keep you quiet,
To study the bed beneath your feet."

The same way, for the sake of memory, designs
Are drawn on the lids of subterranean crypts
To signify and suggest what someone used to be—

And it's often right there that the innocent feel
The pinprick of remembrance,
Tin-white, like arsenic, nipping at their heels—

Just so, I saw portraits there, far more artfully
Rendered: a graphic storyline all along the rim-
Road that edged the mountain.

I saw, on one side, the one created nobler
Than any other creature,
Falling, lightning-like, from the sky;

I saw, on the other side, Briarèus, lying there,
Pinned to Earth with a lightning bolt,
Death heavy and cold as ice.

I saw Apollo Timbreo, Pallas Athena, and Mars,
Still armed, near their father, staring with
A wild surmise at the giants sprawled spread-eagle.

I saw Nimrod at the foot of his grand Babel Project
As if lost for words, anxiously looking back
At the crowd who'd been proud with him.

O Niobe, I saw your anguished eyes, scarified
On the path between your twice-seven children,
All snuffed out like candles in the wind.

O Saul, having fallen on your own sword,
Shown dead on Mount Gilboa—
Which, after that, never felt rain or dew!

O daft Arachne, I saw you in the middle
Of becoming a spider, wretched on the threads
Of the tapestry that turned out so badly for you.

O Rehoboam, here your image isn't menacing;
Your face, filled with horror, is racing away
In an armored car, with no one chasing after it.

It showed also, there along the hard rock road,
How Alcmaeon made his mother pay
A pound of flesh for an ill-fated necklace.

It showed how Sennacherib's sons jumped him
In the temple and then untwisted the last strands
Of manhood from him and left him dead.

It showed the defeat and raw slaughter Tomyris
Incited, that time she said to Cyrus, "You had . . .
A little bloodlust? I'll glut you up with blood."

It showed the Assyrians routed and fleeing
Following the slaying of Holofernes,
Plus the mess that was left behind.

I saw Troy bombed out and burned to ash;
O Ilion, the likenesses displayed there
Portrayed you as vulgar and vile and nothing else.

What ink-brush or steel-pen master drew these
Lines and stippled the shadows, astonishing
Even to someone adept at subtle detail.

The dead, doornail dead; the living, as if living.
Those seeing the events in real time, saw them
No better than I, walking there, my head bent.

Now, boys and girls of Eve, so full of yourselves,
Go off with your arrogant selfies and don't
Look down to see where your evil ways lead.

More of the mountain's curved road was covered,
And much more of the sun's path elapsed
Than my mind, preoccupied, had imagined,

When he, ever aware of the coming attractions,
Said, "Lift up your head. You can't keep acting
As if we have all the time in the world.

See over there, an angel is getting ready
To come over to us. See how the sixth-hour servant
Is coming home, after having served the day.

Look humble and assume a reverent attitude,
So it'll be happy to send us on to the next level.
Think about it, this day will never come again."

I was quite used to his cautionary talk
About never wasting time, so the gist
Of what he was saying wasn't lost on me.

The fantastic creature came toward us dressed
Wholly in white; and in its face, something
Luminous, like Venus in the morning

The arms opened, then the wings opened;
"Come, the graded walkway is near," it said.
"From there on out, the ascent will be easy.

Only very rarely does one get this invitation.
O human beings, you're born to fly straight up,
Why does a little gust of wind bring you down?"

He took us over to a cleft in the rock face; there,
He tapped my forehead with his wing, then
Promised that from here, it would be steady-on.

The way one climbs the hill on the right,
Over Rubaconte Bridge, where the church that keeps
The well-managed under its thumb is perched,

And the daunting pitch of the slope is broken
By stairways built back in an era
When measures and ledgers were sacrosanct,

So here too, the steep incline coming off
The higher terrace levels out a bit, except
For where the high stone wall infringes on it.

As we were in the midst of making the turn:
"Blessed are the poor in spirit," in a singsong voice,
Nothing at all like how it sounds in a sermon.

Ha! How different the hallways here are
From those in Hell. Here songlike chanting
Ushers one in; down there, shrieks and moans.

Now, mounting the sacred stairway, it seemed
To me that I was already much lighter,
Lighter even than before on the flat plain.

Which led me to ask my teacher, "What type
Of gravity have I been released from, that climbing
The steps is now more or less effortless?"

His answer: "When the remaining Ps
Still on your forehead—although fading—
Will, like the other one, be completely removed,

Your wish to do good will so convince your feet,
They'll not only feel no fatigue, they'll be
Even happier when you hurry them along."

At that point, I did what people caught unaware do
When they suspect, based on how others are acting,
That they may have something on their face—

Which is to use the hand to help settle
The question by feeling around and finding out
What can't in the moment be solved by seeing—

With the fingers of my right hand, it was easy
To find that of the letters carved on my forehead
By the one with the key, there were now only six.

Glancing over at that, my guide smiled.

1. *Like equals, like oxen locked in a polished yoke*: William Vernon (1:412) notes a similar description in Homer's *Iliad* (13, 791–796), and quotes the 1864 blank-verse translation by Edward Stanley, 14th Earl of Derby: "But as on fallow-land, with one accord, / Two dark-red oxen drag the well-wrought plough, / Streaming with sweat that gathers round their horns; / They, by the polish'd yoke together held, / The stiff soil cleaving, down the furrow strain; / So closely side by side those two advanced."

3. *my dear schoolmaster*: Hollander and Hollander (246) note that Dante's use here of the word *pedagogue* is one of the first vernacular uses of the word in Italian. He also notes that in 1867, Longfellow connected the word to its biblical appearance in Galatians 3:24: "Wherefore the law was our schoolmaster to bring us unto Christ, that we might be justified by faith." In the original Greek, the term referred to slaves who guided children to their lessons; by the fourteenth century, it was used to refer to teachers or schoolmasters. While Dante frequently calls Virgil his teacher or master, Vernon (1:412) suggests that Dante pairs the more formal term *pedagogo* with *dolce*, a capacious term in Italian that implies kindness and pleasure, to suggest that Virgil isn't one of those stern headmasters that metes out punishment but one who embodies the mnemonic device "the principal is your pal."

21. *Tin-white, like arsenic*: Sylvia Plath's "Elm," dedicated to the poet Ruth Fainlight, first appeared in the 1965 posthumous edition of *Ariel*, edited by Ted Hughes: "This is rain now, this big hush. / And this is the fruit of it: tin-white, like arsenic."

25. *one created nobler*: Satan, the fallen angel, is pictured here literally falling like a bolt of lightning. Luke 10:18: "And he said unto them, I beheld Satan as lightning fall from heaven."

28. *Briarèus*: In Greek myth, Briarèus, also known as Aegaeon, was one of three giant brothers known as the Hecatoncheries, the "Hundred-Handed-Ones," who overthrew the Titans.

31–32. *Apollo Timbreo, Pallas Athena, Mars / Still armed*: Timbreo, or Thymbraeus, is an epitaph for Apollo, derived from the temple in Thymbra dedicated to him. Pallas Athena is the Greek goddess of wisdom, crafts, weaving, war, and diplomacy (Roman: Minerva), often pictured in armor. Mars is the Roman god of war (Greek: Ares) and the protector of Rome.

32. *their father*: Their father is Jove (Roman: Jupiter). Orpheus's song in Ovid's *Metamorphoses* 10.150–151 begins: "My parent Muse, begin my song with Jove . . . the Giants / and Jove's victorious bolts of lightning / hurled down upon the plains of Phlegraea."

32–33. *with / A wild surmise*: John Keats's "On First Looking into Chapman's Homer":

> Then felt I like some watcher of the skies
> When a new planet swims into his ken;
> Or like stout Cortez when with eagle eyes
> He star'd at the Pacific—and all his men
> Look'd at each other with a wild surmise—
> Silent, upon a peak in Darien.

33. *the giants, sprawled spread-eagle*: The giants were the offspring of Gais (earth) and Uranus (sky), and each had a hundred hands and fifty heads. They were associated with hurricanes, tsunamis, and earthquakes. Singleton (2:248): "They made an attack upon Olympus, the abode of the gods, armed with huge rocks and trunks of trees, but the gods with the aid of Hercules destroyed them all and buried them under Etna and other volcanoes."

34–36. *Nimrod at the foot of his grand Babel Project / As if lost for words, anxiously looking back / At the crowd*: Nimrod, a tyrannical Mesopotamian king who appears both in the Old Testament and in the Qur'an (where he goes unnamed), was said to have led those who built the Tower of Babel, which God destroyed for fear that humans who all spoke the same language might gain too much power. Genesis 11:6–7: "And the Lord said, Behold, the people is one, and they have all one language; and this they begin to do: and now nothing will be restrained from them, which they have imagined to do. Go to, let us go down, and there confound their language, that they may not understand one another's speech." "Lost for Words" is a song by the British rock band Pink Floyd, written by David Gilmore and Polly Samson; it appeared on their 1994 album, *The Division Bell.*

37–39. *Niobe . . . your twice-seven children, / All snuffed out like candles in the wind*: Ovid (*Metamorphoses* 6.146–312), tells the story of Niobe, wife of Amphion, king of Thebes, who bragged that she, having seven daughters and seven sons, was better than Latona, who only had Apollo and Diana. Latona told her children what had been said and they proceeded to kill all fourteen of Niobe's children. In sorrow, Niobe's husband fell on his sword and Niobe, rigid with grief, turned to stone: "A whirlwind carries her to a mountain peak and sets her there to melt away, her tears even today flow from the marble." The story is also told in Homer's *Iliad* (24, 602–618). "Candle in the wind" is an idiom suggesting fragility. It is the title of a pop song lament, written by Elton John and Bernie Taupin, for Marilyn Monroe, who died in 1962 at the age of thirty-six; it appeared on their 1973 album, *Goodbye Yellow Brick Road*. The song was rewritten and re-released as "Candle in the Wind 1997" as a tribute to Diana, Princess of Wales (d. 1997).

40–42. *Saul, having fallen on your own sword . . . on Mount Gilboa . . . never felt rain or dew*: Abandoned by God because of his refusal to obey him, Saul, the first king of Israel, was wounded in a battle with the Philistines. He chose to commit suicide rather than be taken captive. David, on learning of Saul's death (II Samuel 1:21), cursed the site: "Ye mountains of Gilboa, let there be no dew, neither let there be rain, upon you, nor fields of offerings: for there the shield of the mighty is vilely cast away, the shield of Saul, as though he had not been anointed with oil."

43–45. *daft Arachne, I saw you in the middle / Of becoming a spider . . . turned out so badly for you*: Ovid (*Metamorphoses* 6.1–145) tells the story of how Arachne, a mortal shepherd's daughter, and a weaver since childhood, bragged that not even Athena, goddess of crafts, could weave as well as she could. Athena, overhearing the boast, came down disguised as an old woman and first gave Arachne a chance to ask forgiveness for her hubris; when Arachne remained defiant, Athena then revealed herself and the two began to weave. When Athena saw that Arachne had used the tapestry to mock the gods, she shredded the weaving and struck Arachne on the head. Arachne hanged herself in despair. Athena poured poison on her, which caused her to change from a girl to a spider. From then on, Arachne hangs and spins a web and serves as an example of unrepentant hubris.

46–48. *O Rehoboam . . . is racing away . . . with no one chasing after*: 1 Kings 12:1–18 recounts how when Rehoboam succeeded his father Solomon as king of Israel, he was asked to "lighten the heavy yoke" that Solomon had put on the Israelites. He ignored the advice of the elders and refused. Ten of the tribes rebelled and chose Jeroboam as their king; only two tribes, Judah and Benjamin, stood with him. When Adoram, his overseer, was stoned to death, Rehoboam sped off in his chariot to Jerusalem, even though no one was pursuing him.

50–51. *How Alcmaeon made his mother pay . . . for an ill-fated necklace*: Both Statius (*Thebaid* 2, 265–305) and Virgil (*Aeneid* 6, 445–446) tell the story of Amphiaraus, the seer who, having foreseen his own death in a battle of the Seven against Thebes, hid himself to avoid being conscripted. His wife informed on him in exchange for the necklace of Harmonia, a necklace crafted by Hephaestus, metalsmith to the gods, and previously worn by queens and princesses of the Kingdom of Thebes. The necklace, however, was said to cause misfortune to whoever owned it. Amphiaraus avenges the betrayal by having the son Alcmaeon kill his mother. Her pride in wanting to wear the necklace is her fatal flaw.

51. *a pound of flesh*: In Shakespeare's *Merchant of Venice*, a cosigned loan of 3,000 ducats is extended on the condition that if it's not paid on time and in full, "a pound of flesh" will be owed in its place.

52. *Sennacherib's sons*: Sennacherib was king of Assyria (705–681 BCE). He twice attacked Hezekiah, the king of Judah, and tried to take Jerusalem. The second time, his troops were annihilated in one night. He managed to escape to Nineveh, but while he was worshipping at the temple of his god, Nisroch, his sons assassinated him and fled to Armenia. His son Esarhaddon succeeded him (Isaiah 37:37–38).

53. *then untwisted the last strands / Of manhood from him*: Gerard Manley Hopkins,

> Not, I'll not, carrion comfort, Despair, not feast on thee;
> Not untwist—slack they may be—these last strands of man
> In me ór, most weary, cry *I can no more*. I can;
> Can something, hope, wish day come, not choose not to be.

55–57. *Tomyris . . . to Cyrus, "You had . . . / A little bloodlust? I'll glut you up with blood*: In 529 BCE, the Scythian queen, Tomyris, battled Cyrus the Elder, founder and king of the Persian Empire. Her son fought and died in the battle, as did Cyrus. Herodotus, *The Histories* (1, 214): "Tomyris, when she found that Cyrus paid no heed to her advice, collected all the forces of her kingdom, and gave him battle. . . . The greater part of the army of the Persians was destroyed and Cyrus himself fell, after reigning nine and twenty years. Search was made among the slain by order of the queen for the body of Cyrus, and when it was found she took a skin, and, filling it full of human blood, she dipped the head of Cyrus in the gore, saying as she thus insulted the cor[p]se, 'I live, and have conquered thee in fight, and yet by thee am I ruined, for thou tookest my son with guile; but thus I make good my threat, and give thee thy fill of blood'" (trans. Rawlinson).

58–60. *the Assyrians routed and fleeing . . . the slaying of Holofernes . . . the mess that was left behind*: After the besieged Jews in the city of Bethulia were on the verge of surrender, Holofernes, the chief captain in the army of the Assyrian King Nebuchadnezzar of Nineveh, invited a beautiful and very intelligent Jewish widow into his tent. After he drank a great deal of wine, he fell asleep and she beheaded him. When she showed the head to her people, they took courage and routed the Assyrians from their camp. The story is a frequent subject of painting and sculpture. The book of Judith is included in the Old Testament of the Catholic Bible (and the Greek and Eastern Orthodox) but not the Hebrew Bible. Some contemporary scholars believe the book is a historical novel that uses elements of history to construct a morality tale.

61–63. *I saw Troy bombed out and burned to ash; / O Ilion . . . vulgar and vile and nothing else*: Singleton (2:257) quotes Virgil (*Aeneid* 3, 2–3) as a possible source for Dante's depiction of Ilium, the main fortress of Troy, after it's been razed: "Proud Ilium fell, and all Neptune's Troy smokes from the ground." Commentators point out how the Italian anaphoric openings of the tercets that form vv. 25–64—*Vedeva, O, Mostrava*—acrostically form VOM (UOM), the Latin word for "man." Hollander and Hollander cleverly use "My eyes beheld," "Ah," and "Now was shown" to achieve MAN in English. I follow Vernon, Singleton, and others, in using "I saw," "O," and "It showed" to achieve IOI, a pronominal form of the human.

70–71. *Now, boys and girls of Eve . . . your arrogant selfies*: The word "selfie" refers to a self-portrait taken with a smartphone, usually held at a distance with a straightened arm or by using an extension device called a "selfie stick." Obsessive selfie taking, selfie syndrome (or selfitis), has been shown to correlate with narcissism.

78. *we have all the time in the world*: Louis Armstrong (d. 1971), nicknamed Satchmo, a jazz musician—trumpeter, composer, and singer—sang the song "We Have All the Time in the World" (composed by John Barry, lyrics by Hal David) on the soundtrack for the James Bond film *On Her Majesty's Secret Service* (1969). The song was also released as a single.

79–80. *an angel is getting ready / To come over to us*: An angel stands guard over each of the seven cornices; each erases one of the seven Ps etched on Dante's forehead.

80–81. *See how the sixth-hour servant / Is coming home, after having served the day*: The hours are seen as handmaidens to the sun. Singleton (2:259) quotes Ovid (*Metamorphoses* 2.116–119): "Titan . . . bade the swift Hours to yoke his steeds. The goddesses quickly did his bidding." Six hours having passed, it is now past noon.

99. *Promised that from here, it would be steady-on*: John Berryman, "Dream Song 20: The Secret of the Wisdom": "When worst got things, how was you? Steady on?"

101–102: *Rubaconte Bridge, where the church . . . is perched*: The bridge was built in 1237, and its original name comes from its builder, a podestà of Florence, Messer Rubaconte da Mandello of Milan. Today the bridge is known as Ponte alle Grazie. A small chapel sits there.

104–105. *an era / When measures and ledgers were sacrosanct*: Singleton quotes multiple sources (2:264–265) that document the fraud of Florentine overseers who were in charge of the distribution of salt or grain; they skimmed some off the top of whatever was owed by removing a stave from the measuring basket to make it smaller. In time, to prevent deception, the basket was replaced by a metal container.

110. *"Blessed are the poor in spirit," in a singsong voice*: Dante uses the Latin, *Beati pauperes spiritu*. The eight "blessings," known collectively as "the beatitudes," are found in Matthew 5:1–12. The first (Matthew 5:3) proclaims, "Blessed are the poor in spirit: for theirs is the kingdom of heaven." Seven of the eight blessings are spoken by angels, one on each of the seven cornices. Here, however, Dante uses the plural "voices," which has led some commentators to hear multiple angelic voices. The original Greek word for what has been translated as "blessed" means "happy," "rich," or "supremely blissful." Arthur Conan Doyle, *A Study in Scarlet*: "Here is Gregson coming down the road with beatitude written upon every feature of his face."

118–119. *What type / Of gravity have I been released from*: The removal, in v. 98, of the first of the seven Ps inscribed on Dante's forehead by the angel has made Dante feel lighter.

121–125 *When the remaining Ps . . . Will, like the other one, be completely removed . . . feel no fatigue*: Virgil reiterates what he previously explained to Dante in *Purg.* IV, 89–90: it is in the design of the mountain that the climb up gets progressively easier. This is because penitence removes the weight of sin; in this conception, pride must be the gravest sin, since the gravity in terms of seriousness of the sin correlates with the gravitational force felt by a body on the surface of the earth.

canto XIII

We were at the top of the stairs where
For a second time the mountain the others go up
To better themselves gets cut down a notch.

Like the first, a belt-like ledge
Ties into the graded base, except here
The bend of the arc is sharper.

There seemed to be no shaded drawings,
Only the cliff face, and the flat path:
A livid-blue quarry marble.

"If we wait for people to come so we can ask,"
The poet reasoned, "and delay too long,
Our choice could be narrowed to nothing."

Making his right side the pivot point,
He twisted his left side forward
And fixed his eyes on the sun.

"O fair glass of light," he said, "I'm counting
On you at the entrance of the new, please lead us,
Since one needs to be led here in order to enter.

You warm the world, you're the bulb above it.
Unless another reason overrides this one,
You'll always come out on top."

What you'd consider a mile
Is how far we'd already gone, and in very little time
Since we were so ready.

Flying toward us, heard but not seen,
Were spirits going on about courtly invitations
To the banquet hall of love.

The first that flew past kept saying,
In an elevated voice, "They have no wine,"
And then kept repeating it once it was behind us.

Before it was totally out of earshot,
Another sped by, shouting out, "I am Orestes";
It didn't bother to stop either.

"Father," I said, "what are these voices?"
And as soon I asked, Hello! A third appears,
Saying, "Love those who've harmed you."

My clever mentor said, "It's this beltway
That whips the sin of envy;
Here, however, love cracks the whip.

A counter-sound is needed to make it stop;
You should hear that, I would think,
Sometime before you get to Absolution Pass.

But for now, look closely and keep looking,
And you'll see people seated ahead of us,
All of them huddled along a recess in the cliff face."

Looking straight ahead, eyes even more wide open
Than before, I could make out shades in coats
No different from the color of the stone.

Once we were just a little farther along,
I heard crying: "Mary, pray for us now":
More crying: "Michael," and "Peter," and "All Saints."

I doubt there's anyone running around earth today
So coldhearted they wouldn't feel a quick stab
Of compassion at what I saw next.

When I was almost to where they were,
And certain now of what I was seeing, grief
Like spilt milk was wrung from my eyes.

They looked to be covered in coarse haircloth;
The shoulder of one held up the next
And the cliff face leaned against them all.

Like the sightless who don't have enough—ready
To tap the just-pardoned, as they must to meet
Their needs—the head of one falls on the other,

Because in others, pity leans in not to hear
The sound of words, but for the sight,
Which is better at begging.

And just like the sun doesn't arrive for those
Deprived of sight, Heaven's light doesn't
Lavish itself on the souls here:

At the lash line, a wire thread pierces the lids,
Suturing the eyes shut—the way you do
With a wild-caught falcon that won't stay still.

Since it seemed insulting for me
To go around observing others and not be seen,
I turned to my wise advisor.

Knowing full well what I, the tongue-tied, wanted
To say, he didn't wait for my "may I," but instead
Said, "Go on, but keep it short and sweet."

Virgil positioned himself behind me on the curved side
Of the cornice where there's no guardrail
At the edge, so one could easily fall off;

On the other side were the faithful shades
From whose ghastly suture-lines
Was squeezed out whatever ran down their cheeks.

I looked straight at them, "O people,
Certain to someday see the divine light—which is,
I know, your one and only wish—

So grace might soon scrub off that pond scum,
And with a purified conscience,
Your stream of conscious thoughts run clear,

What I'd consider a real favor—worth a lot to me,
And possibly helpful for the soul—
Is for any Italians among you to identify yourselves."

"O fellow traveler, everyone here is a citizen
Of the City of Truth—what you *meant* to ask is, who
Led the high life, footloose and fancy-free in Italy?"

The comeback, from the sound of it,
Seemed farther along from where I was standing,
So I pricked up my ears and moved forward.

I saw a shade that appeared to be waiting—
If you want to know "How so?"—that one's chin
Was held higher, like someone straining to see.

"Soul," I said, "giving in, in order to go up,
If it was you who answered,
Tell me about yourself by name or by place."

"I was from Siena," she said. "I'm here now
With the others, making amends for the guilty life,
Crying out to someone for a helping hand.

Sapient I wasn't, though by chance I was named
Sapìa; seeing damage done to others made me
Happier than any luck I might have had.

So you don't think I'm putting you on,
And can see, like I said, how crazy I was near the end
Of a slippery slope I'd been on for years.

When the people of my town were near Colle
And engaged with the enemy,
I prayed to God to let His will be done.

When they'd been routed there,
And were beating a bitter retreat, I watched them
Chased off, filled with a joy unlike any other,

So much so, I raised my smart-aleck face
And shouted, 'I'll never again be afraid of you,'
Like the blackbird did when the wind let up.

On my deathbed, I wanted to make peace
With God but that little bit of birdbrained
Penitence wouldn't have gotten me anywhere,

If it weren't for Peter Pettinaio, the comb seller,
The prayers he'd memorized included my name,
Which is how his offerings benefited me.

But who are you, going around asking
Who we are, hotshot with your eyes unstitched,
Or so I suspect, since you're still breathing."

"I'll be deprived of my eyes," I said,
"When I get here, but only briefly—they did
Very little damage by looking around in envy.

I'm much more worried about the agony
I suspect is ready to torment my soul below—
I already feel the weight of it on my shoulders."

She (to me): "So, who brought you up to us
If you think you're going back down?"
And I: "Someone with me who's not talking.

I'm quite alive, soul who chose to tell all,
Just ask if when I'm back there
You want me to move these mortal feet for you."

"O, wonder, O brave new world!" she said.
"What a huge sign that God loves you.
I could use your prayers now and then.

And I beg you, by all you most desire,
If you're ever stomping around Tuscany, you'll
Restore my good name to my nearest and dearest

You'll meet them among those people hoping
In vain in Talamone—they're set to lose more
In the way of hope than finding the river Diana—

But the nautical men there have the most to lose."

2–3. *For a second time the mountain . . . gets cut down a notch*. This is the second cornice, where the sin of envy is remunerated. Since the mountain is cone-shaped, the circumference of each successive cornice is smaller than the previous one.

9. *A livid-blue quarry marble*: Livid literally denotes a grayish blue or purple bruise-like color, but figuratively it is the color of envy. Today, green is the color associated with envy.

16. *O fair glass of light*: Shakespeare, *Pericles* (I.i.119–120): "Fair glass of light, I loved you, and could still, / Were not this glorious casket stored with ill."

22. *What you'd consider a mile*: A Roman mile was considered to be a thousand paces.

25. *heard but not seen*: Since the shades on this level can't see, their eyes having been sewn shut at the lash line, sound alone is used for their instruction. The voices are all linked to narratives that demonstrate concern for others, the opposite of envy.

26–27. *courtly invitations / To the banquet hall of love*: Love denotes an unselfish concern for others, as opposed to an envious concern for the self alone.

29. *They have no wine*: John 2:1–11 describes the first of Christ's miracles. At the marriage feast at Cana of Galilee, when told by his mother that the wine has run out, Jesus turns water into wine. Or else, he serves water that is so appreciated that it is like the best wine, or he serves water that is believed to be wine. In an article titled "Absolut® Memory Distortions: Alcohol Placebos Influence the Misinformation Effect," Seema L. Assefi and Maryanne Garry found that there is a "placebo effect" when subjects are given a nonalcoholic beverage but told it is alcoholic. Assefi reported: "We found people who thought they were intoxicated were more suggestible and made worse eyewitnesses in comparison to those who thought they were sober. In fact the 'vodka and tonic' students acted drunk, some even showing physical signs of intoxication. When students were told the true nature of the experiment at the completion of the study, many were amazed that they had only received plain tonic, insisting that they had felt drunk at the time."

32. *I am Orestes*: Orestes's friend, Pylades, claims to be Orestes in order to spare Orestes punishment for having killed his adulterous mother, Clytemnestra, and her lover, Aegisthus, a deed undertaken to avenge those two having killed his father, Agamemnon. Orestes then shouts out that he is truly Orestes. John 15:13: "Greater love hath no man than this, that a man lay down his life for his friends."

36. *Love those who've harmed you*: Matthew 5:44: "But I say unto you, Love your enemies, bless them that curse you, do good to them that hate you, and pray for them which despitefully use you, and persecute you."

37–39. *It's this beltway / That whips the sin of envy . . . love cracks the whip*: Love extinguishes envy because if one loves one's neighbor, one doesn't resent their good fortune but rejoices in it. The whip (*ferza*) here is a flexible leather lash made of three cords, possibly signifying the Christian virtues of faith, hope, and charity (or love).

40–42. *A counter-sound is needed to make it stop; / You should hear that . . . before you get to Absolution Pass*: In the secular sense, *perdono* means "to pardon or forgive"; in the religious sense, it means "absolution." Virgil is referring to the entrance to the third cornice (*Purg.* XV, 34–39), where the angel who welcomes them in will erase the P for the *peccato* (sin) of envy from Dante's forehead.

47–48. *I could make out shades in coats / No different from the color of the stone*: Since they are dressed alike in cloaks that match the livid-blue stone of the mountain, the color associated with envy, if any shade should manage to glimpse another through the narrow seam at the lash line, they won't envy the other based on their being better dressed.

50–51. *"Mary, pray for us now": / More crying: "Michael," and "Peter," and "All Saints"*: The penitents are presumably reciting the Litany of the Saints, a prayer that begins with an address to God, Christ, and the Holy Spirit, and then invokes the Virgin Mary, the angels Michael, Gabriel, and Raphael, then all the angels. It then adds the Patriarchs and Prophets, then the Apostles and Disciples, then the Martyrs, then the Bishops and Doctors, then the Priests and Religious, then Laypeople. These are all followed by an invocation to Christ, then prayers for "various necessities," and finally a conclusion that again invokes Christ and either asks for God to show them mercy and teach them to love or (in an alternative version) to answer their prayers.

56–57. *grief / Like spilt milk was wrung from my eyes*: The "tears milked from the eyes" simile may be meant to suggest the regret the penitents feel and their wish that they could return to a state of innocence. Crying over the fact that one can't expunge one's sins by avoiding them in a prior life is the equivalent of "crying over spilt milk." What's done is done and now the price must be paid.

58–60. *haircloth; / The shoulder of one held up the next / And the cliff face leaned against them all*: Hair shirts made of coarse goat's skin are associated with asceticism, the principle of cultivating an austere hermetic life as a means of escaping earthly temptations and of growing closer to God. Wearing hair shirts was practiced by the early Christians.

62. *To tap the just-pardoned, as they must*: Singleton (2:275): "In Dante's time it was a familiar sight to see the blind begging at churches and shrines on the days when crowds gathered for special indulgences (pardons) granted to the faithful." The practice appears to have continued for some time since Vernon (1:460), writing in 1889, states, "I have very frequently seen blind beggars sitting at church doors in Italy in the attitude Dante describes."

70–71. *At the lash line, a wire thread . . . Suturing the eyes shut*: Because these penitents looked around in envy during their lifetimes, their eyes are now sewn shut both to prevent any longing for what others have and as punishment for the longing they previously engaged in.

72. *a wild-caught falcon that won't stay still*: The eyes of a falcon are sewn not with wire but with thread; called seeling, it allows the falconer to acclimate the bird to the presence of people while it is being trained. The eyes are gradually opened so the bird can go after prey.

76. *Knowing full well what I, the tongue-tied, wanted*: As always, Virgil is aware of Dante's thoughts before they are voiced.

79–81. *Virgil positioned himself behind me . . . no guardrail . . . so one could easily fall off*: The point is made, as it has been before, that Virgil is the one thing between Dante and disaster.

90. *Your stream-of-conscious thoughts*: William James introduced the term "stream of consciousness" in 1890 in his book *Principles of Psychology.* The author and suffragist May Sinclair, using the pseudonym Mary Amelia St. Clair, introduced the term in a literary context in the *Egoist* magazine, in a 1918 review of a novel sequence titled *Pilgrimage*, by Dorothy Richardson.

92. *And possibly helpful for the soul*: Helpful in that Dante can inform those on earth who might be willing to offer prayers of intercession, which would shorten the soul's time spent in Purgatory.

94–96. *everyone here is a citizen / Of the City of Truth . . . footloose and fancy-free in Italy*: The soul reminds Dante that the penitents, by the time they arrive on this cornice, are so removed from their lives on earth that they no longer think of themselves as belonging there. Hebrews 11:16: "But now they desire a better country, that is, an heavenly: wherefore God is not ashamed to be called their God: for he hath prepared for them a city."

106–108. *I was from Siena," she said. "I'm here now . . . Crying out to someone for a helping hand*: This Sienese woman, named in v. 109, was a noblewoman once married to the Ghibelline Ghinibaldo Saracini. She was also the aunt of Provenzan Salvani (*Purg.* XI, 121–142). Singleton (2:280) notes that she died sometime after 1274, the date affixed to a document stating she made a donation to a hospital she and her husband founded in 1265.

109–110. *Sapient I wasn't, though by chance I was named / Sapìa*: In Italian, there's a play on words. Sapìa says she wasn't *savia*, meaning sapient, wise, sensible, or savvy.

110–111. *seeing damage done to others made me / Happier than any luck I might have had*: "Schadenfreude" is a loanword from German formed by combining *Schaden* (damage) and *Freude* (delight). The first recorded usage of "schadenfreude" in English as "malicious joy in the misfortunes of others" was in 1922 (*Online Etymology Dictionary*).

115–116. *When the people of my town were near Colle / And engaged with the enemy*: The battle at Colle was fought on June 17, 1269. The Sienese Ghibillines were routed by the Florentine Guelphs, who were aided by seven hundred French soldiers sent by King Charles. See the note to *Purg.* XI, 121–123, for more about the capture and beheading of Sapìa's nephew Provenzan Salvani, the Ghibilline leader who led the attack.

123. *Like the blackbird did when the wind let up*: An Italian fable tells the story of a blackbird who mocks a twenty-eight-day month of January. January punishes the bird by asking February for three of its days and adding those to the original twenty-eight.

127–129. *Peter Pettinaio, the comb-seller / The prayers he'd memorized . . . how his offerings benefited me*: This is the religiously observant Pietro Pettinaio (d. 1289). According to his biographer, Pietro de Monterone (*Vita del beato Pietro Pettinaio*) (The life of blessed Pietro Pettinaio), his final words were "Woe to you Pistoia; woe to you, Florence; and woe also to you, Siena!" Quoted in Thompson, 384. Because Sapìa's name can sound like *savia* (wisdom), it's possible that his prayers for Sapìa were inadvertent.

138. *I already feel the weight of it on my shoulders*: Dante is making it clear that he expects he will be burdened far longer on the first cornice—where he will have to pay down the sin of pride by carrying the weight of a heavy stone on his shoulders—than he will on this second cornice for the envious.

145. *O, wonder, O brave new world*: Shakespeare, *The Tempest* (V.i.181–184): Miranda. "O, wonder! How many goodly creatures are there here! / How beauteous mankind is! O brave new world, / That has such people in't!"

150. *Restore my good name to my nearest and dearest*: She appears to assume her friends and relatives would have thought her delayed repentance and envious ways would result in her being consigned to Hell, instead of to Purgatory.

151–153. *hoping / In vain in Talamone—they're set to lose more / In the way of hope than finding the river Diana*: Talamone in Dante's day was a small seaside town. Legend had it that there was a subterranean river beneath the town that the townspeople hoped could be excavated to create a seaport. The hypothetical river was referred to as "the Diana" after a statue of the Roman goddess that stood in the central market square in Siena and after a twelfth-century well named Diana's Well in the Cloister of Carmen. The townspeople searched obsessively for it. In 1303, the harbor was purchased by the Sienese with the hope of excavating the river, but the dredging operations proved so expensive the project was abandoned. Today the cloister is used as a hotel. Her "nearest and dearest" will lose the hope of finding the river but also, she's imagining, the hope of going to Heaven.

154. *But the nautical men there have the most to lose*: Since the tone of this statement is obviously playful, the inference may be that the nautical men have the most to lose because their loss of wealth and prestige will be added to the losses they share with the others. There is some discussion in the commentary as to whether Dante's *ammiragli* is meant to refer to naval commanders or to navigators hunting for the river.

Canto XIV

"Who's running rings around our mountain
Before death has given him a send-off,
Batting his eyes at whatever he wants?"

"I don't know, but I know he's not alone.
You ask him, since you're closer,
And talk nice, so he'll answer."

These two on my right were leaning in,
Having a little confab about me; they then
Fawningly looked up at me to speak.

One then said, "O Soul, still tucked
Into your body, headed toward Heaven,
Kindly encourage us by telling us

Who you are and where from; we marvel
How you're the very button on Fortune's cap;
How much one wants what they've never been."

I said, "Cutting Tuscany in two, there's a river
That's born in Mount Falterona and goes on
Without faltering for well over a hundred miles.

All of the above gave birth to the person I am.
To mention my name would be useless
Since it still wouldn't ring a bell."

"If I catch the drift of what you're saying,"
The one who'd spoken first piped up in response,
"You're talking about the Arno River."

Then the other said to him, "Why'd he hide
The name of the river, the way you sweep
Something ugly under the rug?"

The one questioned gave back, tit for tat,
"I don't know but the name of that valley
Oughta be wiped off the face of the earth;

It's so big and swollen when it begins in the Alps,
From which Pelorus once got lopped off—one
'Expects' something since few get past that stage.

But at the end it's only a seaside breeze and a beer
Produced from whatever the coastal sky has sopped
Up, and the river gets the pissant little left over;

And every Tom, Dick, Harry, Moll, Nell, and Sue
There runs from virtue as if it's a snake in the grass;
Either the place is doomed to misfortune or else

Bad habits poke around and find their peers there.
Their very nature's been so mutated they seem
To be munching carpet in Circe's pasture.

Among butt-ugly swine, better at foraging in woods
Than sitting down to a homemade meal, the river
Moves itself along like some dismal back alley.

Farther down, it encounters yappy little dogs
With barks bigger than their bites; seeing these,
It looks down its nose and turns on its heel.

As it goes on falling, the more it swells
The more that blinking, effing ditch discovers
The yappy dogs have become big bad wolves.

Farther downhill it drops through dark gorges,
After which it finds trickster foxes so cunning
They're fearless that any wit could crush them.

I'm not gonna hold my tongue just because others
Can hear, plus it's a word to the wise for this guy,
If later he can see I'm setting out a real prophecy.

I see your grandson becoming a hunter
Of the wolves along the banks of that puffed-up river;
He stuns them into submission,

Sells their living flesh, then hacks them to death
Like old nags sent to the glue factory;
Countless lose their lives, he loses his honor.

Bloodied, he exits the pathetic forest; leaving it
In a such a state not even a thousand years
Could take it back to the prime wood it was."

At the report of a devastation, the face
Of a listener looks troubled—no matter which
Side the news is sinking its teeth into—

So I saw the other soul, who was listening
With his head tilted, become upset—then sad,
Once he'd made sense of the words.

What the one said, how the other looked,
Made me want to know their names, so I added
"I beg of you" to "Could you tell me?"

The one who'd first spoken started up again,
"You would have me do for you
What you are unwilling to do for me?

Well, since God sheds so much of His grace
On thee, I won't be petty, but will graciously
Make you aware that I was Guido del Duca.

My blood was such a fire-and-forget missile of envy
If I caught sight of someone acting happy, I'd go
Ballistic and scatter a payload of spite. Of course,

Seed-wise, you get what you give; me, spent shells.
O humanity, why set your heart on what you know
So well you've been forbidden to partner with?

This here's Rinieri, the wealth and pride of the house
Of Calboli, where there's never been an heir
That met or exceeded his measure

It's not just his bloodline that's gone barren.
Between the Po and the mountains, the marina and
The Reno—in the search for truth and the 'golden

Peace of the shady lane'—within these boundaries,
The area's so overgrown with toxic underbrush,
Any effort to cultivate it would come too late.

Where are good Lizio and Arrigo Mainardi,
Pier Traversaro and Guido di Carpigna? Those
From Romagna all turned to scumbag bastards.

When will a Fabbro again take root in Bologna?
When in Faenza, a Bernardin di Fosco, the refined
Offshoot of a blade of common couch grass?

Don't be shocked, Tuscan, if I sob
As I call to mind, along with Guido da Prata,
Ugolin d'Azzo, who was living with us then;

Federigo Tignoso and his group,
The Traversari family; the Anastagis—
One enormous in-crowd, all gone to nothing.

Ladies and knights, their cares
And comforts encouraged love of the courtly kind
Where hearts have now become depraved.

O Bretinora, why is it you don't run away,
Given that your tribe and so many others
Have been sent off, never to return?

Bagnacaval's doing well at not doing it again,
And Castrocaro's doing it badly, and the Conios
Even worse, yet they do push out the odd count.

The Paganis will do well once the two-faced
Devil turns around and takes off, although
They won't go unsullied while I'm here to testify.

O Ugolin de Fantolini, your name is safe,
Since there's no longer anyone expected
To tarnish it with degeneracy.

Okay, Tuscan, it's time for you to get going,
Our little talk has sent me over the edge;
I'd much rather cry now than go on chatting."

We knew those souls paying dearly
Could hear us go; their silence
Made us trust we'd gone the right way.

Once we were moving along by ourselves,
We walked smack-dab into an oncoming voice
That split the air like lightning, saying,

"Anyone who finds out will kill me on sight";
It then rolled away the way thunder
Moves out when a cloud breaks up.

As soon as our ears stopped ringing, here it came,
Another thunderous ruckus that resembled
The bolt from the blue that soon followed:

"I am Aglauros who was turned to stone."
Instead of moving ahead, I took a step to the right
And pressed as close I could to the poet.

When the air on every side was still again,
He said, "Those are the difficult but necessary bits
Meant to make humans stay within limits.

Even so, each of you goes for the bait;
Using a lure line, the ancient adversary reels you in,
With little to no resistance, and no outcry.

The sky calls your name and whirls around you,
A daredevil airshow of timeless beauty, and yet,
Your eyes are fixed only on the ground—which

Is why the all-discerning one gobsmacks you."

1–3. *Who's running rings around our mountain . . . Batting his eyes at whatever he wants*: The speaker, as we'll discover in v. 81, is Guido del Duca.

4–6. *I don't know, but I know he's not alone . . . talk nice, so he'll answer*: This second speaker is Rinieri da Calboli. His caution to "talk nice" might be because he is used to del Duca's arrogant manner of speaking.

8–9. *they then / Fawningly looked up at me to speak*: Dante, here and elsewhere, shows he is an extremely keen observer of the ways in which people use their bodies to inspire pity. In *Purg.* XIII, 64–66, he notes that others lean in not to catch the sound of a mendicant's words but for the sight, "which is better at begging." The language here suggests that the two have shrewdly composed their faces to look deferential, which is clearly not their natural tendency. Because it's not how they would usually act, Dante makes the point that they are over-obvious about it.

14. *you're now the very button on Fortune's cap*: Shakespeare, *Hamlet* (II.ii.228–229): GUILDENSTERN. "Happy in that we are not over-happy. / On Fortune's cap we are not the very button."

15. *How much one wants what they've never been*: While they are paying down the sin of envy, they are still not without envy here on the second terrace.

16–18. *Cutting Tuscany in two . . . born in Mount Falterona and goes on / . . . well over a hundred miles*: Dante charts the Arno River, which is 150 miles long, from where it begins in the Apennine Mountains.

20–21. *To mention my name would be useless / Since it still wouldn't ring a bell*: Aware now of how the proud suffer in Purgatory, Dante is practicing modesty.

25–26. *Why'd he hide / The name of the river*: Guido del Duca is well aware of which river.

31–33. *so big and swollen when it begins in the Alps / . . . one / 'Expects' something*: This tirade about the people living along the Arno focuses throughout on their failure to produce viable offspring who can take the country forward. Using the word *pregno* (pregnant), del Duca, clearly speaking for Dante, begins by personifying the alpine mountain range as a pregnant abdomen that, as it goes forward, fails to deliver on its promise.

32. *Pelorus once got lopped off*: It is thought that Pelorus was at one time the tail of the chain of mountains that form the Apennine range but was cut off by the formation of the Strait of Messina, perhaps by the action of an earthquake. It is now Mount Pelorus on the Sicilian side of the strait. The language again suggests there was an interference with what the range might have produced.

34–36. *a seaside breeze and a beer . . . the river gets the pissant little left over*: A river's water cycle consists of the sun's heat and wind turning seawater to vapor via evaporation; the vapor rises and forms clouds, which move inland; when the water droplets become heavy enough, the water is returned to the river in the form of rain, which the river returns to the sea.

37. *Tom, Dick, Harry, Moll, Nell, and Sue*: "This expression is first recorded in an eighteenth-century song: 'Farewell, Tom, Dick, and Harry. Farewell, Moll, Nell, and Sue.' It is generally used in mildly derogatory contexts (he didn't want every Tom, Dick, and Harry knowing their business) to suggest a large number of ordinary or undistinguished people" (*Farlex Idioms and Slang Dictionary*, "Tom, Dick, and Harry").

38. *a snake in the grass*: The snake is a nod to the Garden of Eden, another doomed place.

41–42. *Their very nature's been so mutated they seem / To be munching carpet in Circe's pasture*: Daughter of Helios (the sun god) and Perse (an Oceanid nymph), Circe is variously depicted in Greek mythology as a goddess, magician, enchantress, or nymph. In Homer's *Odyssey* (10, 11), she uses drugs and spells to change Odysseus's drunken men into swine. After Odysseus convinces her to make them human again, they all live with her for a year on her island and she has two sons by Odysseus. She also appears in Virgil's *Aeneid* and Ovid's *Metamorphoses*.

43. *Among butt-ugly swine*: This is the Casentino Valley, where the Arno begins. Calling these people *porci* (literally, "swine" or "pigs"; figuratively, "degenerates," "lechers," "slimeballs," or "sleazebags") is a bit of wordplay that gestures to the Conti Guidi and his family branch, the lords of Porciano, a fortified town at the base of Mount Falterona alongside a stream that joins up with the Arno. The swine are foraging in the woods for acorns rather than sitting down to a home-cooked meal with a family.

46–48. *Farther down, it encounters yappy little dogs / . . . seeing these, / It . . . turns on its heel*: The Arno moves toward the city of Arezzo but a few miles before reaching it makes a sharp turn and heads northwest toward Florence. Singleton makes the point that Dante may be mocking the Aretines because they had adopted as their official motto "A cane non magno saepe tenetur Aper." (A dog that's not that large can often hold down a wild boar.)

51. *The yappy dogs have become big bad wolves*: The wolves represent Florence and especially the Florentine Guelphs. While wolves play an integral role in the history of early Italy—a she-wolf suckles Romulus and Remus, the legendary founders of Rome—in *Inf.* I, a she-wolf serves as the signifier of greed that only the messianic *veltro* (greyhound) will be able to slay.

52. *Farther downhill it drops through dark gorges*: Between the upper and lower valleys of the Arno, the river narrows as it passes through the gorge of La Golfolina; in that area, there are deep hollows.

53. *trickster foxes so cunning*: These foxes are the Pisan Ghibellines, who were said to make up in shrewdness what they lacked in military might.

57. *If later he can see I'm setting out a real prophecy*: The prophecy, which concerns a close relative of Rinieri da Calboli, also foretells Dante's future exile from Florence.

58–59. *I see your grandson becoming a hunter / Of the wolves*: The word *nipote* can mean "niece," "nephew," "grandson," or "granddaughter." Commentators lean toward grandson and one Fulcieri da Calboli. Vernon (1:493): "Messer Fulcieri da Calboli was then, we will suppose, grandson of Rinieri, and was called in as podestà of Florence in 1302. Being bribed by the *Neri* [Black Guelphs], he seized the persons of the chief *Bianchi*, and Ghibellines, and having put them to the torture, had them beheaded. On the *Bianchi* generally, he inflicted severe penalties; torture, death, confiscation of goods, or exile." Dante was a Bianchi (White Guelph).

65–66. *not even a thousand years / Would take it back to the prime wood it was*: Another lost paradise that looks back to Eden.

77–78. *You would have me do for you / What you are unwilling to do for me*: Dante had withheld his name when asked and said only where he was from.

79–80. *Since God sheds so much of His grace / On thee*: The lyrics of the song "America the Beautiful," with the verse, "America, America, God shed His Grace on thee," were originally written as a poem by Katherine Lee Bates (d. 1929), a YA novelist, poet, essayist, social activist, scholar, and professor of English literature at Wellesley College. The poem was first published in 1895 as "Pike's Peak" in the Independence Day issue of a church periodical, the *Congregationalist*; it was revised and reprinted in the *Boston Evening Transcript* in 1904, and collected in her volume, *America the Beautiful and Other Poems* (1912). In 1903, a publisher set the poem to music that had been previously composed for the hymn "O Mother Dear, Jerusalem," a poem first published in 1864 by William Cowper.

81. *I was Guido del Duca*: Commentators are uncertain of the identity of Guido del Duca. He is described as a judge to the podestà of Rimini in a document dated May 4, 1199. He was a follower of Pier Traversaro, who, with the help of Ghibellines, expelled the Guelphs of Ravenna and imposed himself as master there. The Guelphs retaliated by seizing Bertinoro and expelling any who were loyal to Pier Traversaro, including del Duca, who then moved with his family to Ravenna. His name appears as a witness on a land deed in Ravenna dated 1229. No further information is available.

82. *a fire-and-forget missile*: The coordinates of a fire-and-forget missile are generally set before firing.

83–84. *I'd go / Ballistic and scatter a payload of spite*: Go ballistic: "1775, 'pertaining to construction and use of thrown objects,' ultimately from Greek *ballein* 'to throw' . . . Of rockets or missiles (ones that are guided while under propulsion, but fall freely), from

1949. *Ballistic missile* first attested 1954; they attain extreme heights, hence figurative expression *go ballistic* (1981) 'become irrationally angry'" (*Online Etymology Dictionary*).

86–87. *Why set your heart on what you know / So well you've been forbidden to partner with.* Dante will ask another soul about the meaning of this statement in *Purg.* XV, 45.

88–89. *This here's Rinieri . . . the house / Of Calboli*: The soul's full name was Rinieri dei Paolucci da Calboli di Forli. He was a podestà of Faenza in 1247; of Parma in 1252; and of Ravenna in 1265, the year of Dante's birth. Vernon (1:498) quotes Tommaséo as saying that Rinieri was "of a noble Guelph family, a man of gentle and valiant manners, and a credit to his distinguished house, whose virtues were inherited by none of his descendants."

92–93. *Between the Po and the mountains, the marina and / The Reno*: Guido is referring to the territory of Romagna, which Hollander and Hollander (294) describe as "a large area on the right-hand side of Italy, separated from Tuscany (subject of the first half of the canto's exploration of sins along the Arno) by the Apennines, lying south and west of Romagna. The rough boundaries include the river Reno, just to the west of Bologna, the river Po, flowing into the Adriatic north of Ravenna, the Adriatic of the eastern limit, and the hills of Montefeltro at the southern edge."

93–94. *'golden // Peace of the shady lane'*: The phrase comes from a poem, "I due fanciulli" (The two children), by Giovanni Pascoli (d. 1912), an Italian poet and classics scholar also known for his Dante studies. He held an appointment as professor of Italian literature at the University of Bologna.

97. *good Lizio and Arrigo Mainardi*: Lizio da Valbona, a Ghibelline nobleman from Romagna, was a contemporary of Rinieri and, reportedly, an extravagant host; Arrigo Mainardi, from Bertinora, was similarly a Ghibelline nobleman given to social largess. Mainardi's son married da Valbona's daughter. The couple figures in an amusing story by Boccaccio.

98. *Pier Traversaro and Guido di Carpigna*: Pier Traversaro, of Ravenna, was an ally of Guido del Duca, a patron of poets and a strong supporter of the empire. His family had been involved in politics for generations but with his death, his son became a Guelph and the family lost influence. Guido di Carpigna, of Montefeltro, like the others mentioned here, was known for his political stature, lavish entertaining, and generosity.

100. *When will a Fabbro again take root in Bologna*: Fabbro de' Lambertazzi was another distinguished Ghibelline nobleman of Bologna. Upon his death, his sons became involved in a conflict with a rival faction, the Geremi. As a result, the Lambertazzi family and the Ghibelline party lost influence.

101–102. *in Faenza, a Bernardin di Fosco, the refined / Offshoot of a blade of common couch grass*: Bernardin di Fosco was a farmer's son who rose to become a podestà. He was appreciated for his humor and goodwill and treated as an equal by the noble families of Faenza.

104. *Guido da Prata*: Guido da Prata was a friend of Ugolin d'Azzo and a property owner of some importance in Ravenna.

105. *Ugolin d'Azzo*: Ugolin d'Azzo was another gentleman landowner; originally from Tuscany, he relocated to Faenza.

106. *Federigo Tignoso and his group*: Singleton (2:305) quotes Benvenuto: "[Federigo Tignoso] was a rich nobleman of Rimini whose house was a fountain-head of liberality, its door closed to no honest man. He enjoyed conversation with all worthy men and so Dante characterizes him from the company he kept, an altogether admirable group."

107. *The Traversari family; the Anastagis*: These two noble families exerted profound influence in the area until each experienced a reversal of fortune. See note to v. 98.

112. *O Bretinora, why is it you don't run away*: Bretinora was a small town in Romagna with a hilltop castle once occupied by the Malatestas, a family known for its hospitality. The family had departed by the time of the poem. Dante appears to be suggesting that the rest of the inhabitants may as well also leave, since none measure up to those who have left.

115. *Bagnacaval's doing well at not doing it again*: Bagnacaval was another castle town, this one ruled by the Malvicini family, who referred to themselves as the Counts of Bagnacaval. The male line had ended by 1300.

116–117. *Castrocaro's doing it badly, and the Conios / Even worse, yet they do push out the odd count*: The Ghibelline Castrocaro family had become extinct. The Guelph Conio family, where the men self-styled as counts, still existed but their fortunes had diminished.

118–119. *The Paganis will do well once the two-faced / Devil turns around and takes off*: The Paganis were a noble Ghibelline family of Romagna. The head of the family at the time of the poem, Maghinardo Pagano da Susinana, was a cunning statesman and military man nicknamed "the Devil." Dante faults him for his habit of changing sides. He was said to support the Florentine Guelphs when he fought on one side of the Apennines, and the Ghibellines when he fought on the other side.

121–123. *O Ugolin de Fantolini, your name is safe, / Since there's no longer anyone expected / To tarnish it with degeneracy*: The two sons of Ugolin de Fantolini had both died before 1300, so there was no one left to possibly damage the family's reputation.

133. *"Anyone who finds out will kill me on sight"*: This is the voice of Cain, after having killed his brother, Abel, out of envy. Genesis 4:13–14: "And Cain said unto the Lord, My punishment is greater than I can bear. Behold, thou hast driven me out this day from the face of the earth; and from thy face shall I be hid; and I shall be a fugitive

and a vagabond in the earth; and it shall come to pass, that every one that findeth me shall slay me."

139. *"I am Aglauros who was turned to stone"*. Ovid (*Metamorphoses* 2.708–832) tells the story of Aglauros, the daughter of King Cecrops of Athens, who became envious after Mercury became infatuated with her sister, Herse. Minerva, seeing Aglauros extract money from Mercury to allow him access to Herse, enlists Envy to poison Aglauros with its venom. When Aglauros stood outside her sister's bedroom door with the intent of turning Mercury away, she was turned into "a bloodless statue, not white stone but stained by envy."

CANTO XV

As much of that part of the sun that's always
Bouncing like a baby could be seen between
The end of the third hour and the start of day

As what would remain as the sun slid toward
Evening: it's ever the same: six o'clock vespers
There, the middle of the night down here.

We'd come so far around the mountain
We were now walking straight into the sun's rays,
Which were hitting me right between the eyes,

When a looming radiance came into sight—
Much brighter than what I'd been seeing.
I felt stunned, not knowing what it meant.

To dial down the blinding glare,
I made a sunshade by raising my hands
And tenting them over my eyebrows.

Just like a beam hitting water, or a mirror,
Ricochets opposite, then comes back down,
Bouncing over and over—each time departing

Equal distance from the stone bob
That dangles from the plumb line—as, in fact,
Has been shown by scientific experiment—

I felt like I was being pummeled by a sun-hatchet
Made of refracted light right in front of me;
I looked away as fast as I could.

"What's that, sir," I asked, "that I can't
Get it out of my face or shield my eyes—
And which seems to be coming straight at us?"

"It's no surprise," he said, "that you're still blinded
By the light of those from the company of Heaven;
It's the messenger that delivers the invite to go up.

Pretty soon, seeing these things won't be unbearable;
Instead, they'll give as much pleasure
As nature intends for you to feel."

Once we met up with the God-sent angel,
Which said, by way of a welcome, "Enter here,
This stairway isn't as steep as the others."

Setting out from there and climbing,
"Blessed are the Merciful" and "Rejoice
You are victorious" being chanted behind us,

As we went along, my teacher and I—alone
Together—I began to think I could benefit
From whatever he might have to say.

I posed a question to show I'd been paying
Attention, "What did that spirit from Romagna
Mean when he said 'forbidden' and 'partner with'?"

To that he said, "He knows the damage done
By his greatest flaw; it's no wonder
If he reproaches himself in order to suffer less.

When you invest all your desires
In a partnership, you lose something by sharing;
Jealousy acts like a bellows to your sighs,

But if a love of the highest order
Twists your desire and bends it upward,
There'd be no dread pounding in your chest.

Because the more who say 'ours,' each
Has more and all are better off and that cloister
Colonnade glows with more generous giving."

"I'm closer to fasting and further from being
Full," I said, "than if I'd kept quiet,
And now more doubts are gathering in my mind.

How is it that a good, distributed so that more
Will have it, will enrich those who have it
With more than if it is had by a few?"

"Because your mind is getting stuck on how
Things work on earth," he told me, "where light
Gets bent as it goes through dense matter.

That infinite and ineffable goodness
That's up there rushes toward love, just like light
Shoots through anything transparent.

It gives as much passion as it has,
So that however far love extends itself,
Eternal goodness increases to the same extent.

There are so many more 'beloveds' to love up there;
The more there are for you to love well, the more
To love you; it's like a mirror, each gives back another.

If my reasoning doesn't totally meet your needs,
You'll see Beatrice and she'll pull back the curtain
And fully satisfy this and every other constant craving.

For now, just work on finding a way to finish off,
Like the other two, the five remaining abrasions—
Whose edges can only meet through your agonizing."

I had intended to say, "You *are* satisfying me,"
But seeing we'd arrived at another level, I fell silent,
My eyes darting here and there, taking in the scene.

I felt immediately drawn into an ecstatic vision
Where there was a crowd
Of people in a temple up ahead,

And standing in the doorway, a woman
Who was acting like a caring mother,
"You're our son, why would you do that to us?

Your father and I were frantically searching
Everywhere for you."—And then, silence,
And whatever had seemed to be there, split off.

Then another woman appeared, tears distilled
From grief and nurtured by a great spite
Flowed down her cheeks like a steady stream of fire.

She was saying, "If you're the ruler of the city of Athens
Where the gods kept bickering over the name,
And from whose flame came all forms of knowledge,

Then avenge yourself, O Pisistratus, on the one
Who dared take our daughter in his arms."
The mister, who seemed kind and even-tempered,

Responded with a look marked by self-restraint,
"What should we do to the ones who hate us,
If we give a death sentence to those who love us."

I then saw a mob fired up in anger, stoning
A baby-faced man to death, shouting loudly
To no one but themselves, "Suffer! Suffer!"

I saw him bend over as death weighed on him,
Pressing him deeper into the dirt,
While his eyes stayed facing Heaven,

Begging the Lord above, in the heat of battle,
With that pleading look that unleashes pity,
To please forgive his persecutors.

Once my mind returned to the things that are
True beyond it, I realized
My not actually false, false impressions.

My guide, watching me act like Houdini
Escaping the straps of sleep, said, "What's up
With you, that you can't keep it together?

For more than a half mile, you've had your eyes
Half-closed, weaving like someone
Who's either half-drunk or half-asleep."

"My dear padre," I said, "if you'll listen,
I'll tell you what I thought I saw
When my legs were pulled out from under me."

"Countless canvas masks could be over your face,"
He said, "and I still wouldn't be locked out of
All that's going on under that thinking cap of yours.

You were shown all this because you're not excused
From opening your heart to the peace that spreads
In all directions, like water from an eternal spring.

You'll notice, I didn't ask you, 'What's up?'
Like someone who looks down but doesn't register
The obvious fact that the corpse at their feet is lifeless.

I was only asking as a way to nudge your feet;
You have to poke the lazybones
To use what's left of an evening once they get home."

We kept going through the hour of vespers,
Straining our eyes to see as far as we could
Through the blazing light of the dying day.

Suddenly, little by little, thick smoke,
Like nighttime darkness, began to move toward us.
There was no place to escape it.

That took away not only our sight but also our air.

1–3. *As much of that part of the sun that's always / Bouncing like a baby could be seen between / The end of the third hour and the start of day*: Unlike the moon, the sun is a constant sphere; it doesn't wax or wane, but only, like a perennial baby, bounces up and down. The simile invites us to see the sun as a round-faced—or from another angle, a round-bottomed—baby, being bounced, perhaps on someone's knee. The infant reference continues the theme of healthy offspring, and the lack of it, that dominated the preceding canto.

4–6. *As what would remain as the sun slid toward / Evening: it's ever the same . . . vespers / There, the middle of the night down here*: Where Dante and Virgil are, it is now 3:00 p.m. The end of the third hour is 9:00 a.m. The point of these comparisons between the time in Purgatory and on earth is to demonstrate that the sun remains a circle whatever time it is and in whatever place; it won't change, even as it slides toward midnight, when we no longer see it. The Catholic Church's Liturgy of the Hours consists of specific prayers that correspond to seven daylight hours and one nocturnal hour. At 6:00 p.m., the hour of vespers (evening prayers) on Mount Purgatory, it will be midnight in Purgatory. And yet, in both places, although the times vary, the sun will remain a circle. This constancy metaphor will come into play as devotedness later in the canto when Virgil explains how one avoids the pitfalls of earthly love, which waxes and wanes, by directing one's love toward Heaven.

18–21. *Bouncing over and over—each time departing // Equal distance from the stone bob . . . shown by scientific experiment*: The sun is constant both in its spherical nature and in the way its light acts; that constancy, Dante points out, can even be demonstrated scientifically.

38–39. *"Blessed are the Merciful" and "Rejoice / You are victorious" being chanted behind us*: According to the gospel, the fifth of the eight blessings Jesus delivered in his Sermon on the Mount is Matthew 5:7: "Blessed are the Merciful: for they shall obtain mercy." Matthew 5:12 instructs: "Rejoice, and be exceedingly glad: for great is your reward in heaven: for so persecuted they the prophets which were before you." The Rig Veda, a compilation of ancient Sanskrit hymns of the Brahmins, contains a similar injunction: "Let the gods rejoice in you as you are victorious." It is not clear who is chanting the *Beati misericordes*, the angel or the penitents, nor is it clear why the phrase that follows is in Italian, unless the angel is specifically addressing Dante, perhaps as a gesture of encouragement. Commentators point out that mercy, which shows compassion, is the opposite of envy, which delights in the misfortunes of others.

40–41. *alone / Together*: Dante and Virgil have left the angel behind and have yet to meet up with a new group of penitents. Samuel Beckett, *Ohio Impromptu*: "Could he not now turn back? Acknowledge his error and return to where they were once so long alone together. Alone together so much shared. No."

44. *that spirit from Romagna*: Dante is referring to Guido del Duca.

45. *when he said 'forbidden' and 'partner with'*: Dante is asking Virgil to explain what Guido del Duca meant when in *Purg.* XIV, 86–87, he posed the rhetorical question: "[W]hy set your heart on what you know / So well you've been forbidden to partner with?"

47–48. *his greatest flaw . . . he reproaches himself in order to suffer less*: Since envy is vanquished on this cornice, that sin must be del Duca's "greatest flaw." Self-awareness and self-reproach are part of penitence—until they occur, one is confined to one's current level.

49–50. *When you invest all your desires / In a partnership, you lose something by sharing*: Many commentators interpret this moment as a caution not to invest in "worldly goods," but there is nothing in the language that suggests materiality. Rather, it appears Dante is talking about relationships. The Italian word for envy (*invidia*) is a synonym for jealousy. Further evidence of this reading is that love is evoked in the next verse.

52–54. *But if a love of the highest order . . . bends it upward, / There'd be no dread*: One fears losing anything earthly, goods or people, but Heaven, like the sun's sphere, is invariable.

76–77. *If my reasoning doesn't totally meet your needs, / You'll see Beatrice*: Virgil again cautions Dante, as he did in *Purg.* VI, 43–48, that his knowledge is limited; for complete understanding of matters of faith, he must wait until he meets Beatrice at the top of the mountain.

79–80. *For now, just work on finding a way to finish off, / Like the other two, the five remaining abrasions*: We are meant to understand from this that the angel they encountered earlier erased one of the Ps on Dante's forehead.

88–92. *a woman / Who was acting like a caring mother . . . searching / Everywhere for you*: The Gospel according to Luke relates the story of how Mary and Joseph, after having traveled to Jerusalem for Passover, realized during their return trip that their son Jesus was not in the caravan. They returned to Jerusalem and, after frantically searching for three days, discovered him at the temple, listening to the rabbis and asking them questions. Luke 2:48–49: "And when they saw him, they were amazed: and his mother said unto him, Son, why hast thou thus dealt with us? behold, thy father and I have sought thee sorrowing. And he said unto them, How is it that ye sought me? wist ye not that I must be about my Father's business?"

94–95. *Then another woman appeared, tears distilled / From grief and nurtured by a great spite*: In contrast to the charitable, maternal Mary, driven only by concern for her son, the second woman's emotions are bound up with resentment.

97. *If you're the ruler of the city of Athens*: Pisistratus, the son of Hippocrates, overcame the democracy of Athens and ruled as a benevolent dictator between 561 and his death in 527 BCE. He is remembered for reducing income inequality and initiating the Panathenaic Games, which consisted of athletic, musical, and equestrian events. He is also said to have been responsible for compiling the loose collection of Homeric writings into the epic poems of the *Iliad* and the *Odyssey*. He was twice ousted and sent into exile. The importance of Athens declined after his death.

98–99. *Where the gods kept bickering over the name, / And from whose flame came all forms of knowledge*: During the reign of Cecrops, the city of Cecropia was renamed Athens, in honor of the goddess Athena. Ovid and several other writers tell the story of a contest between Poseidon and Athena to have the city named after them. Poseidon offered the gift of a spring, signifying naval power; Athena promised the olive tree, signifying peace and prosperity. Athens was the birthplace of Socrates and the location of Plato's Academy. Aristotle founded a lyceum there called the Peripatetic School. It continued to be a center of study during the Roman era.

100–101. *avenge yourself, O Pisistratus, on the one / Who dared take our daughter in his arms*: The Roman author Valerius Maximus, in *Facta et dicta memorabilis* (5, 1), tells the story of a young man who comes up to one of Pisistratus's daughters in public and kisses her. The wife's and husband's reported responses are just as Dante describes them.

102–103. *The mister, who seemed kind and even-tempered, // Responded with a look marked by self-restraint*: As Dante does so many times in *Purgatorio*, he draws from multiple sources to make the point that a phenomenon isn't limited to any single sex or social group or religion. Mary, the biblical mother, is here paired with Pisistratus, a male figure from history who behaves with a Mary-like restraint and generosity, in contrast to his wife, whose spitefulness prods her to overreact to what she perceives as a social slight.

106–114. *I then saw a mob fired up in anger, stoning / A baby-faced man . . . please forgive his persecutors*: This scene describes the stoning of Saint Stephen and illustrates the biblical mandate to "love one's enemies" regardless of their extreme cruelty.

116–117. *I realized / My not actually false, false impressions*: Dante's point is that these ecstatic visions, while having no material basis outside of the mind, are in fact real because the mind itself is real and capable of processing even a conjured reality.

118–119. *like Houdini / Escaping the straps of sleep*: Harry Houdini (d. 1926) was a pseudonym used by Erik Weisz, a Hungarian-born American illusionist/escape artist. Houdini would frequently perform a stunt in which he would escape the straps of a straitjacket while he hung from a crane.

127–128. *Countless canvas masks . . . and I still wouldn't be locked out*: Virgil reiterates the claim he made in *Inf.* XXIII, 25–27, which is that he has complete access to Dante's thoughts.

141. *Through the blazing light of the dying day*: The canto circles back to its beginning statement about the sun's constancy. Here, even as the day dies, the sun, like God, remains.

142–145. *Suddenly, little by little, thick smoke . . . not only our sight but also our air*: The smoke is the result of the fire of anger. It is so pervasive that it blocks out the constant sun, creating a state of complete darkness. It further robs the person of the very essence of life, literally, the ability to breathe; figuratively, the ability to be close to God.

Canto XVI

Gloom of Hell and night deprived
Of every star, the light-poor sky
Covered to the max with dark clouds

Never pressed a veil over my face
As thick as the one that smothered us there,
Nor has anything felt so like a hair shirt.

No open eye could endure it. My loyal escort,
Ever aware, moved his shoulder closer,
Offering me his upper arm.

The way a sightless person follows a guide,
So as not to get lost or crash into something
That may hurt, or even kill them—

So, I moved through the caustic grimy air,
Listening to my leader, who was making it clear,
"See that we don't get separated."

I heard voices; each appeared to beg the Lamb
Of God for tender mercies and the peace
That would take away their sins.

Their Agnus Dei kept beginning "Lamb
Of God," sung in unison and in one rhythmic
Mode making it seem they were all in accord.

I said, "Those are spirits I'm hearing, right, sir?"
And he to me, "So, you're learning what's real,
And also, that irascibility's a tough nut to crack."

"Well, now, who are you that you can crack
Our smoke and mirrors and speak as if
You're one of us, but still tell time by a calendar?"

Just like that, a single voice asserted itself,
After which my leader told me, "Answer it,
Then ask if this is the way to go up."

I said, "O being, revising yourself to be sent back
To your maker a corrected copy, if you get in line
Behind me, you'll be amazed at what you hear."

He said, "I'll come along with you as far as I can;
If the smoke doesn't let us see,
Hearing will still keep us coupled."

I said, "I'm making my way up
With those bands that death will dissolve;
I came here via the ghastly Hellish route

And if God in His grace has taken me in
By a method totally outside the modern way,
It's because He wants me to witness His court.

So, don't hide who you were before death; just tell me,
And also say whether I'm headed the right way;
Your words will act like an usher for us."

"I was a Lombard, called Marco; I was worldly-wise
And loved that spunkiness—which is why
Everyone's slack bow is now shooting blanks.

To go up, go directly ahead."
He paused, then added, "I beg of you,
That you'll pray for me when you get up there."

I told him, "I'm bound by faith to do whatever
You ask but I've been holding in a doubt
And I'm going to burst if I can't let it out.

First it didn't mean much, but now it's doubled
By your statement, which makes me sure that if
I heard it here *and* elsewhere, I have to connect the two.

As you told me, the way the world is now,
Everyone lacks any kind of character and is birthing
A litter of mischief behind every curtain,

But I'm asking you to tell me why, so I can watch
Out for it and point it out to others; one calls out
The cosmos, the other lays the blame below."

He sighed, which wrung a grief-stricken "Dear me!"
Out of him—then began, "Brother, the world
Is wearing a blindfold, and you clearly come from it.

You living ones connect the reason for everything
To the heavens, as if when they move,
Everything else has to move with them.

If that were the case, the idea of free will
Would be shredded and there'd be no equity
To good-equals-joy and bad-equals-grief.

It's true, the heavens start the ball rolling:
I'm not saying it does it all, just that it plays a role,
Light shines equally if you act well, or with malice,

Or with free will. Even if you fight to the point of fatigue
In your initial battles with a crushing cosmic fate,
Later, if well nurtured, you can overcome anything.

You're the free subject of a greater force,
And a better nature, which creates the mind inside you,
And the heavens don't act as a doctor to that.

But if the contemporary world deviates,
The cause is yourself; you have to question yourself,
And I'll be standing by like a truth-telling spy.

Formed by the hand of Him who looks upon it
Fondly even before it exists—a little girl doll,
Flip-flopping between laughing and crying,

A simplistic miniature soul that knows nothing
Except that, once set in motion by an auspicious maker,
It happily comes back to what it loves.

It has a first taste of the good that has charmed it;
Then beguiled, it keeps following it
Unless a hand or curb bends it away.

This is why laws were laid down and agreed upon,
Rules were stipulated, so one could discern,
At the bare minimum, the true city's watchtower.

The laws exist, but whose hand's behind it? No one's.
The shepherd may be capable of ruminating,
But it's not enough if the hoof isn't split in two.

Then people, seeing how their guide helps itself
To what looks good but does harm, get so greedy
They scarf it down, without even a 'Do I dare?'

So, you can clearly see that bad behavior
Is the reason the world is the guilty party,
And not that human nature is inherently corrupt.

Back when Rome was the model of an ideal world,
It had two suns, one made visible the worldly way,
And the other, the Godly way.

One has switched the other off, and the switchblade
Has been connected to the shepherd's crook, and
When joined that way, the twosome is a terrible idea,

Since, once coupled, the one no longer dreads
The other. If you don't believe me, keep in mind
An ear of corn: every blade of grass is known by its seed.

In the land scored by the Adige and the Po,
One used to find courage and kindness,
Before Frederick II got into trouble.

Now you're better off just passing through,
Embarrassed because you never know whether
Someone's good enough to approach or talk to.

There are actually three older men so convinced
That the ancient era rebukes the new, they think
God's late in taking them back to a better life.

Currado da Palazzo and the good Gherardo,
And Guido da Castel, who like me is called,
As the French quite simply say, the Lombard.

From today on, you can say the Church of Rome,
Having muddied the waters by merging two armies,
Has fallen into the mire—its ugly animal self *and*

What's on its back." "Well argued, like-minded Marco,"
I said, "and discerning enough that I now see why
The sons of Levi were spared from inheriting land.

But which Gherardo is it who serves
As a living example of the extinct group of people
Whose lives take our barbarous era to task?"

"You're either playing word games or teasing me,"
He said, "because the way you're talking, Tuscan,
Suggests you've never heard of good Gherardo.

I'm not aware of any nickname, except for the one
I might nick from his daughter, gay Gaia.
God be with you. This is as far as I can go with you.

The light rays are already whitening
Through the smoke; I need to leave
(The angel is there) before I'm seen."

He turned, like he didn't want to hear me anymore.

1–2. *night deprived / Of every star*: In the medieval era, planets were considered stars. Not only is the sun obscured but even those "stars" that might be seen at night, like Venus.

6. *Nor has anything felt so like a hair shirt*: A literal hair shirt is a garment made of haircloth worn next to the skin as penance; figuratively, it's any hidden affliction.

16–17. *I heard voices; each appeared to beg the Lamb / Of God*: These are the voices of the penitents chanting a prayer addressed to the "Lamb of God," a title for Jesus given in John 1:29: "The next day John seeth Jesus coming unto him, and saith, Behold the Lamb of God, which taketh away the sin of the world"; and in John 1:36: "And looking upon Jesus as he walked, he saith, Behold the Lamb of God!"

19–21. *Their Agnus Dei kept beginning "Lamb / Of God," sung in unison . . . making it seem they were all in accord*: The Agnus Dei, a three-line liturgical prayer said during the Catholic Mass, begins, "Lamb of God, who takest away the sins of the world, have mercy upon us," then repeats that line and ends with, "Lamb of God, who takest away the sins of the world, grant us peace." The idea that the penitents chant in unison in a single mode suggests they are practicing the sense of concord that their wrath prevented them from achieving on earth.

22–23. *I said, "Those are spirits I'm hearing, right, sir?" . . . you're learning what's real*: Dante is both asking for confirmation and demonstrating, for Virgil's approval, that he now knows the difference between reality and the imagination.

24. *irascibility's a tough nut to crack*: The original is "a knot that's tough to untangle"; both idioms speak equally to the difficulty of controlling the tendency to irascibility. Evidence of the difficulty is that it's impossible to see anything through the obscuring smoke.

25–27. *who are you that you can crack / Our smoke and mirrors and speak as if / You're one of us*: Dante uses *fendi*, "to split," "cleave," or "crack." The soul wants to know who Dante thinks he is that he can literally split the smoke—and so must still have a human body that measures earthly time—but also presumes that he can, without having gone through penance, fathom the smoke that represents the anger that consigned the souls to this level of Purgatory.

30. *Then ask if this is the way to go up*: Virgil continues to try to find the shortest way to the top. As he said in *Purg.* III, 77–78, "the more one knows, / The more one hates to waste time."

34. *I'll come along with you as far as I can*: The soul has to remain inside the cloud of smoke until he completes his penance.

38. *With those bands that death will dissolve*: Dante uses the word *fascia*, meaning "band," generally, but also "swaddling bands," narrow gowns or strips of cloth once used to restrain the limbs of infants. Luke 2:7 describes the infant Jesus as having been so wrapped: "And she brought forth her firstborn son, and wrapped him in swaddling clothes, and laid him in a manger; because there was no room for them in the inn." The bands "that death will dissolve" represent Dante's mortal body.

41. *a method totally outside the modern way*: Dante is possibly pointing out that trips to the afterworld were similarly taken by Aeneas and by Saint Paul but that those were in the distant past. Commentators note this is the first established usage in Italian of the word *moderno* (modern). Another possibility is that Dante is suggesting, self-referentially, that imagined journeys to the afterworld are no longer in literary fashion.

46. *I was a Lombard, called Marco*: Place was an important means of identification in Dante's era. There is ambiguity here: the soul may be named Marco Lombardo, or his name is Marco and he comes from lower Lombardy. Early commentators identify him as a Venetian gentleman, generous and well educated but with a propensity to anger.

46–48: *I was worldly-wise . . . Everyone's slack bow is now shooting blanks*: While Singleton (2:348) notes that the bow, a frequent metaphor in Dante, signals good intentions, the use of "worldly-wise" suggests Cupid—the arrows that leave his taut bow incite love.

53. *I've been holding in a doubt*: This is the doubt planted by Guido del Duca in *Purg.* XIV, 85–87, and about which Dante asked Virgil in *Purg.* XV, 44–45. Virgil's answer, however, left Dante feeling unsatisfied. Virgil had suggested Dante wait until Beatrice could explain but Dante can't hold in his uncertainty any longer.

55: *First it didn't mean much, but now it's doubled*: Dante says he had been able to exercise patience until Marco said essentially the same thing as del Duca, which is that what someone wants doesn't always get them what they are really looking for, which is love.

61–63. *I'm asking you to tell me why . . . one calls out / The cosmos, the other lays the blame below*: Dante says he wants to understand the root cause so he can guard against sinning and so he can save others through his writing. He asks, does the problem lie with fate (the cosmos) or with human frailty?

70–71. *If that were the case, the idea of free will / Would be shredded*: Marco says if the problem was simply cosmic fate, humans would have no agency.

83–84. *The cause is yourself . . . And I'll be standing by like a truth-telling spy*: Marco appears to be suggesting that he and his words will now serve as Dante's conscience, always reminding him that he has choices.

102. *without even a 'Do I dare?'*: T. S. Eliot, "The Love Song of J. Alfred Prufrock": "And indeed there will be time / To wonder, 'Do I dare?' and, 'Do I dare?'"

109–110. *the switchblade / Has been connected to the shepherd's crook*: There are no longer checks and balances since the Church has claimed absolute power and now also controls the military through the emperor.

114. *every blade of grass is known by its seed*: Luke 6:43–44: "For a good tree bringeth not forth corrupt fruit; neither doth a corrupt tree bring forth good fruit. For every tree is known by his own fruit."

115–116. *In the land scored by the Adige and the Po, / One used to find courage and kindness*: This is essentially the area from which Marco comes. Like Guido del Duca, he invokes the "good old days."

117. *Before Frederick II got into trouble*: As Holy Roman emperor (1220–1250), Frederick II resisted the power of the papacy and was twice excommunicated. Dante consigned Frederick II to Hell (*Inf.* 10, 119) as a heretic. In *De vulgari eloquentia* (On eloquence in the vernacular) 1.12.4, however, Dante praised his nobility and integrity, and that of his son, Manfred, and noted the importance of Frederick's support of Sicilian vernacular poetry, which would influence Dante's own poetic development.

121. *There are actually three older men*: These three Guelph noblemen are all from Lombardy in northern Italy: Currado da Palazzo, a Guelph from Brescia, who was active in the political life of Florence and Piacenza; the "good" Gherardo (da Cammino), who was from Padua and a captain-general of Treviso; and Guido da Castel, who was a vernacular poet from Reggio Emilia.

127–128. *the Church of Rome, / Having muddied the waters by merging two armies*: The Church's merger of the religious with the secular, by forcing the emperor to be subordinate to the pope, has led not only to its downfall but the downfall of the state that rests on the back of the Church.

131–132. *I now see why / The sons of Levi were spared from inheriting land*: Dante agrees with Marco that it was the failure to maintain the separation of Church and State that led to the ruin of the Catholic Church and of the State. He points out the wisdom of God's forbidding the Levites, who served in the temple, to inherit wealth insisting instead that they be supported solely by the tithes of the congregation. Only in this way, God said, would they remain free of corruption (Numbers 18:20–32).

133. *But which Gherardo*: Marco is so certain that Dante would know of Gherardo da Camino by reputation that he suspects Dante is putting him on. Marco, however, didn't give Gherardo's surname, only noting his "goodness."

140. *his daughter, gay Gaia*: The word *gaia*, also a girl's name, means gay. Commentators differ on the reputation of Gaia da Camino, the daughter of "good Gherardo" and his second wife. Some maintain she was a delightful young woman; Benvenuto, how-

ever, described her as a lascivious idler who offered to procure girls for her brother if he would in turn procure boys for her.

141–142. *This is as far as I can go with you. // The light rays are already whitening*: The soul is not allowed to exit the smoke and enter the light before he completes his penance.

144. *(The angel is there)*: God's angel represents God's light, as well the light of the setting sun that has begun to shine through the darkness.

Canto XVII

Bear in mind, Reader, if you ever find yourself
Caught by the fog in the Alps, and seeing
As I was, as if through moleskin,

The spherical disk of the sun
Dimly filtering in through the thick
And sticky-wet haze slowly beginning to lift,

Then you'll be able to quickly imagine
How the sun looked when I first saw it again,
Just at the point of setting.

Matching my pace to that of my confident guide,
I came out of that haze to find the sun's rays
Had already faded from the lower shore.

O imagination, that so carries us away
From what's outside, we're not even aware
When a thousand trumpets blare.

Who excites you, if sensuality's hand is empty?
You're moved by heavenly enlightenment, in and
Of itself, or the wish to be led by it here below.

An echo of the brutality of the one
That turned into the bird that so loves to sing
Appeared in my head like an earworm.

My one-track mind, locked inside itself,
Didn't fathom that what I was hearing
Wasn't coming from outside.

Then, a man on the gallows
Dropped into my lofty fantasy,
Looking fierce and spiteful, even in death.

Around him were the great Ahasuerus,
His wife Esther, and righteous Mordecai,
Who spoke and acted with utter integrity

As this mental image burst under its own
Weight, like a bubble bottoms out
When let down by the water that formed it,

A vision of a young woman rose up,
Sobbing uncontrollably and saying, "O Queen,
Why would fury make you want to be nothing?

You killed yourself so you wouldn't lose Lavinia.
But you have lost me! I'm the one, Mother,
Mourning your ruin before the other's."

When you're suddenly smacked in the face
By a light that wrecks your sleep,
You snap back—and it all collapses.

The second my eyes were struck by a light
Far brighter than anything we're used to,
Just like that, my fantasy fell apart.

As I spun around to see where I was,
A voice said, "Here's the way up,"
Which ended any other idea I may have had.

It made me so eager to see the speaker,
I knew the wish would persist
Until I could come face-to-face with it.

But like the sun, agonizing to look at,
Its shape obscured by its excess,
So here, the strength I needed was lacking.

"This is the divine spirit, without our even asking,
They're going to indicate the way to go up;
They hide inside their own light.

They're doing for us what anyone does.
If someone sees a need and waits to be asked,
You can bet they're cynically waiting to say no.

Let's take the offer and get on our way now
And finish going up before dark;
If we can't, we'll have to wait for day again."

After saying this, my leader and I turned
And headed toward the stairs.
As soon as I was on the first step,

I felt something like a wing near my face,
Brushing my forehead, and heard, "Blessed are
The peacemakers, for their anger isn't abusive."

The last rays of light, after which night
Was sure to follow, were already so high above us,
Everywhere we looked, there were stars.

"O stamina, why are you vanishing?"
I kept saying to myself,
Feeling like my legs were demanding a ceasefire.

We were finally where the stairway stops rising,
Anchored there like a ship
Stranded on the shore.

I waited awhile, to see whether I could hear
Anything coming from the new roundabout;
Then turned to my teacher and said,

"Tell me, dear father, which offense
Is cleared here on the round where we are?
The lessons can go on, even if our feet can't."

He said, "The love of good that clowns around
And doesn't do its work is revived right here.
Here, the slowpoke oar is made to answer.

But if you're open to learning even more,
Pay attention to what I'm saying
And you'll get something from our stay

No creator nor any creature," he began,
"Was ever without the desire for love, biological
Or intellectual; and you, my surrogate son, know this.

The natural can't ever be in error,
But with the other, you can choose badly,
Or have too much drive, or too little.

In the first place, as long as it's well directed
And secondly, if one is moderate,
It can't result in a pleasure that's wrong.

However, when it gets badly twisted,
Or there's too much or too little intensity,
That one works against their own best interests.

From this, you should be able to see how love
Sows the seed of all your virtues, *and* any schemes
For which you'll later have to pay the piper.

Since love can't bear to turn its face away
From the well-being of its object
the thing-in-itself is safe from self-hatred.

And because no self can manage to be divided
From itself and stand, it's a given that no human
Can opt for their one half to hate the other half.

If I'm doing the math right, I'd say what sickens
Love is the relationship to the other. This love
Arises in three ways in the clay you're made from:

There's the ego trip: diminishing the other
To build yourself up, and, for all that snarling,
You're the one that looks bad in the end.

Then, there're those with clout, favor, glory,
And fame, but fear losing it: if outdone, they wallow
In their grief and love it when the other loses.

Then, those outraged by perceived slights:
They get so greedy for the sweet taste of revenge,
They ingeniously fabricate errors in others.

Those below us cry tears over this tri-form
Love. Now, I'll teach you about another kind,
Well intended but not well regulated.

Each of us has a fuzzy notion of goodness,
Which calms the spirit, and one wants that,
And each of us struggles to achieve it.

But if some dimwitted love catches your eye
And you buy into it, once you've repented,
This cornice is where you'll suffer for it.

Another good that doesn't make a person
Happy—it's not happiness, not the essence
Of good, its edible fruit and root—

Love that gives too much of itself to that,
Is cried over in the three circles above us.
But about why it's considered tripartite,

I'll keep quiet, so you can figure it out."

2–3. *seeing / As I was, as if through moleskin*: During Dante's lifetime, Florence was a major center of the textile trade. The fabric known as moleskin is a tight-weave heavy cotton with a brushed surface that evokes the suede-like fur of the burrowing mammal of the Talpidae family. In the medieval era, because it was comfortable, warm, and wind resistant, the fabric was worn by farmers, hunters, and others who worked outdoors. This line is traditionally read by commentators as a refutation of the medieval belief that moles were sightless. Researchers have recently established that moles do have retinas and neural pathways to the brain so, although short-sighted, moles can see.

8–9. *the sun . . . Just at the point of setting*: It is early evening (around 6:30 p.m.) on Easter Monday.

19. *the brutality of the one*: See the note to *Purg.* IX, 14–15, for the story of Philomela's rape by her sister Procne's husband and Procne's subsequent revenge killing of her own son. It is her act of brutal cruelty that makes her an apt example of vengeful rage.

20. *the bird that so loves to sing*: Myths vary in terms of which sister Jupiter saved from death by turning her into a nightingale and which sister he saved by turning her into a swallow. Since it's the nightingale that has a particularly beautiful song, Dante clearly assumes that Procne became the nightingale. While the nightingale is named the "night songstress," only the males of the species sing.

25–27. *a man on the gallows . . . Looking fierce and spiteful, even in death*: The man is Haman, prime minister of the Persian King Ahasuerus (the Hebrew name of Xerxes, or Artaxerxes).

28–30. *Ahasuerus, / His wife Esther, and righteous Mordecai, / Who spoke and acted with utter integrity*: The story of Ahasuerus, Esther, and Esther's cousin (or uncle) Mordecai, is told in the book of Esther. The orphaned Esther, a ward of Mordecai, marries Ahasuerus without telling him she is Jewish. Mordecai exposes a plot to kill Ahasuerus, thereby earning his gratitude. The king's prime minister, Haman, insulted because Mordecai refused to bow to him, discovers the refusal is because Mordecai is Jewish. For the slight, Haman vows to kill not only Mordecai but all the Jews in the kingdom. Esther appeals to Ahasuerus, who rescinds the order and instead has Haman hung from the very gallows built to hang Mordecai. It is in the additions to the book of Esther, not in the Hebrew Bible (where the secular book of Esther doesn't mention God), that Esther and Mordecai are described as being pious.

34–36. *A vision of a young woman rose up, / Sobbing . . . "O Queen, / Why would fury make you want to be nothing*: In the *Aeneid* (12, 595–608), Virgil tells of the death by suicide of Amata, queen of Latinum. The speaker in this tercet is her daughter, Lavinia.

37–39. *You killed yourself . . . I'm the one, Mother, / Mourning your ruin before the other's*: Amata, favoring Turnus as a husband for her daughter, hides the daughter in the forest after Aeneas asks to marry her. She then instigates a war, hoping Aeneas will die in battle. When Aeneas prevails in the war, Amata mistakenly thinks Turnus has been killed. She then kills herself in fury. The "other" that Lavinia will have to mourn later is Turnus, since he is not dead yet, but will later be killed by Aeneas.

45. *Just like that, my fantasy fell apart*: As the sudden brightness of the sun through the shutters jolts sleepers from their dreams, the angel jolts Dante from his daydreaming.

49–51. *so eager to see the speaker, / I knew the wish would persist / Until I could come face-to-face with it*: Dante continues to be blinded by the celestial light since he has not yet completed his penitential journey. He also makes the point that a wish persists until one masters what it takes to realize it.

63. *we'll have to wait for day again*: As Sordello told them (*Purg.* VII, 44–60), one can't ascend the mountain in the dark but must wait for daylight.

66–68. *on the first step, // I felt something like a wing near my face, / Brushing my forehead*: The angel is erasing another P from Dante's forehead, signifying that he is now absolved of the sin of wrath.

68–69. *Blessed are / The peacemakers, for their anger isn't abusive*: Dante adds *mal* (evil, wicked, painful, damaging, pathological) before *ire* (anger). The suggestion here is that anger is a normal passion when it's not vindictive. Vengeful anger damages not only the sufferer but others as well, thus making it a sin.

73. *O stamina, why are you vanishing*: This continual "talking-to" that Dante has to give his legs is because darkness is coming and when it does, one can no longer climb. It also foreshadows the sin of sloth that is purged on the terrace toward which Dante and Virgil are moving.

75. *my legs were demanding a ceasefire*: Use of the word "ceasefire" illustrates the continual battle against laziness required to climb the mountain and reach celestial Heaven. One remembers Belacqua, procrastinating in the shade of a boulder in *Purg.* IV, 122–126.

79. *I waited awhile, to see whether I could hear*: Upon entering the previous two terraces, Dante heard voices, so he expects to hear them here as well.

82–83. *which offense / Is cleared here on the round where we are*: This cornice is devoted to the capital sin of *accidia* (sloth), which includes laziness, slowness, indolence, idleness, and lateness. In spiritual terms, it's a weariness that affects both the body and soul; the word, formed from the Greek, means "to not care"; sadness, boredom, and bitterness are all associated with it, as is negligence, sluggishness, and excuse making.

84. *The lessons can go on, even if our feet can't*: Dante is demonstrating that he has taken to heart Virgil's continual urging not to waste time.

85–87. *The love of good that clowns around . . . the slowpoke oar is made to answer*: The lack of attention to one's spiritual state is at the heart of the sin of sloth, which is defined by the Church as spiritual apathy, indifference, or negligence. The marine analogy circles back to the beginning of *Purgatorio*, where Dante, wanting to make good time, since he knows this is where things improve, lifts the sails of the boat of his intellect. In Virgil's metaphor, those rowers who dawdled, instead of using their oars to steadily propel the boat forward, are forced to face the consequences here; there is a sly implication that the oar might be used as a paddle for the tardy ones. The apt punishment on this circle is to continuously run the course without stopping.

91–93. *No creator nor any creature . . . Was ever without the desire for love, biological / Or intellectual*: Virgil starts his discourse on love and sin by advancing the idea that in every living thing, and in God (since God is love), there are two kinds of love, *naturale o d'animo*. The cognate *naturale* translates as "innate" or "biological." The word *animo* can mean "spiritual" or "mental"; either way, it is mediated by the mind and involves choice. Dante's ideas about love draw heavily on Thomas Aquinas's *Summa theologica* (ca. 1265–1274), which he is known to have read.

94–96. *The natural can't ever be in error, / But with the other, you can choose badly, / Or have too much drive, or too little*: Since natural love is instinctual, and thus God-given, it's impossible to develop a sinful attachment. With love that is self-directed, however, one can invest psychic energy in an unhealthy object (or activity, or idea), or one can over- or underinvest in a healthy object.

97–98. *as long as it's well directed / And . . . moderate*: As long as the attachment is to an appropriate object, and the charge of libidinal energy isn't extreme (too much or too little), the love won't lead to harm.

100–101. *when it gets badly twisted, / Or there's too much or too little intensity*: When the attachment to another isn't straightforward but twisted, presumably away from God, and it is either anemic or, conversely, neurotically obsessive, then the attachment doesn't bring about a sense of being closer to God and is thus harmful.

103–105. *love / Sows the seed of all your virtues,* and *any schemes / For which you'll later have to pay the piper*: Love, directed toward God, through the right choice of an object, and balanced in its emotional significance, leads to a life of virtue. The wrong choice, or a supercharged or flaccid attachment, leads to one of the seven deadly sins, for which one will have to pay in Purgatory. On the previous three cornices, Dante has seen what is required to purge the sins of pride, envy, and wrath, and now, on this, the fourth level, he is about to see the punishment for sloth. Above, he'll witness the payback for avarice (and its opposite, prodigality), gluttony, and lust. Virgil's point is that all these sins are a corruption of the attachment humans call love.

114. *the clay you're made from*: Psalm 40:2: "He brought me up also out of an horrible pit, out of the miry clay, and set my feet upon a rock, established my goings."

115–117. *the ego trip . . . To build yourself up, and, for all that snarling / You're the one that looks bad in the end*: This is the sin of pride, where one's self-worth depends on mocking and belittling others, especially those whose talents one secretly wishes one had.

118–120. *those with clout, favor, glory, / And fame, but fear losing it . . . and love it when the other loses*: This is the sin of envy, which causes the sufferer to delight in other people's losses. Since their own sense of self-worth is fragile, no matter how successful they are, they feel that another's gain diminishes their standing.

121–123. *those outraged by perceived slights . . . They ingeniously fabricate errors in others*: This is the sin of wrath, or vengeful anger. If the sufferer perceives any lack of respect, imagined or real, they seek revenge. Once they develop a sadistic sense of pleasure in punishing others, they manufacture situations so they can inflict that pain.

138. *But about why it's considered tripartite*: Virgil is referring to the fact that while the sins punished on the first three cornices (pride, envy, and wrath) make up one three-part corruption of love, the three remaining sins (avarice/prodigality, gluttony, and lust) punished on the next three cornices make up another tripartite misapplication of love.

canto XVIII

The esteemed doctor, having finished
His train of thought, studied my face
To see if I seemed satisfied,

While I, baited by a new thirst, kept quiet
While inwardly saying, "He might
Be getting tired of all these questions."

But true father that he was, aware of the wish
And of the silencing fear, had, by speaking,
Given me a model for daring to speak.

So, I said, "Teacher, I see a lot in the light
You've thrown; I get the logic
Behind what you've outlined, or described,

But please, dear kindly father, I want to know
What love is, I want you to show me how
It's the basis of any positive act, *and* its opposite."

"Prick up your ears," he said, "and look here
And the logical fallacy
Of a blind leader will be made crystal clear.

The mind was made for love at first sight
With whatever moving target delights it, and
As soon as pleasure shows up, it goes to town.

One's perception of the material-actual
Creates an image that gets mirrored
In one's consciousness, the mind gets drawn to it;

And when drawn, it reaches out to it. That
Reaching out, i.e., cathexis, is love. That's how
Nature binds you to a new object of desire.

Then, the same way fire moves upward
To reach what makes it last,
Since nature built that pattern into its matrix

The now-smitten mind opens the door
Of desire, a spectral exercise it never tires of
As long as the beloved still makes it jump for joy.

Now you can see how much truth is hidden
From those who actualize their love
Of any and every object they find appealing.

It might seem that the situation will always
Be ideal, but not every seal is a good one,
No matter how pliable the wax."

"I've been able to follow everything you've said,"
I told him, "and it has unmasked love for me,
But it's also planted more seeds of doubt.

If love arises outside of us, and the mind
Only has the feet it's been given, it can't take
Any credit for going the right or wrong way."

He told me, "Whatever's in the realm of reason,
I've laid out for you—anything past that,
Wait to get to Beatrice, she works with faith.

Each essence has its own substantial form,
Distinct from matter and one with it, and
Has within its makeup a specific quality,

Which isn't sensed unless it's acting, and which
Only reveals itself through its effect: the way
You know a plant's alive by its green leaves.

How our minds pick up on and interpret
The initial hints, no one knows, nor how we
First fathom our appetite for a kind of affection.

Those are in you, just like the bee is driven
To pollinate an apple blossom, a primal impulse
That merits no praise nor admits any fault.

Since this is true of all who harvest whatever,
Given that it's innate, virtue must caution you
When you're about to cross a threshold.

This is the principle of 'you get what you deserve,'
Depending on which good and guilty loves
You welcome and which you send packing.

The ones who reasoned their way
To the bottom of this saw that freedom is innate,
And passed on their moral code to the world.

So, let's suppose that whatever love
Turns you on is dictated by an urgent necessity,
Still, you are your own policeperson.

This noble virtue is what Beatrice means
By free will, so keep that in the forefront
Of your mind, if she talks to you about it."

The late-night moon, nearing midnight,
Glowed like a molten ladle, making it appear
That the sky had been shaved of its stars.

Its track against the sky followed the streets
The sun sets fire to when in Rome one sees
Darkness descend between Sardinia and Corsica.

That obliging shade, who'd made Pietola
More famous than any other Mantuan city,
Had managed the weight of my baggage,

So that I'd absorbed his clear and candid
Answers to my questions but now,
My drowsy mind kept wandering off.

This Land-of-Nod lapse was abruptly ended
By a group who, although they'd once been
In front of us, were now at our backs.

What the Ismenus and Asopus Rivers witnessed
On their banks at night, a rave of party monsters,
When the Thebans felt a need for Bacchus,

Ditto these from what I saw in the twilight,
Their scythe-like strides whipping that curve,
Driven by goodwill and the right kind of love.

Soon they were even with us, all running
Together as one turbulent moving mass,
Two at the front shouting, in tears:

"Mary ran fast to the mountain.
And Caesar, to tame Lérida,
Stabbed at Marseille, then raced off to Spain."

Nearby others cried, "Soon, we'll see you soon,
So no time is lost due to too little love
As we try to make grace green again."

"O people, who so earnestly aim to make up
For the previous negligent delays
Of your halfhearted attempts to do good,

This guy, who's alive, and I'm in no way lying,
Wants to go up, once the sun is shining—only
Please tell us, how close are we to the opening?"

Those are the words my leader used,
And in response, one of the spirits spoke up,
"Come behind us, and you'll find the hollow.

We're so brimming with the desire to move,
That we can't stay. Pardon us, please,
If by obeying the law we seem disrespectful.

I was abbot in San Zeno in Verona
Under the good Emperor Barbarossa,
A sore spot for those who think about Milan.

A guy with one foot already in the grave
Will soon boo-hoo over that monastery there
And regret ever having been in charge of it;

Because he installed his son—entire body
A mess, even worse mind, and baseborn—
In lieu of the place's true pastor."

I don't know if he said more or fell silent,
He was already that far ahead of us, but
I'd heard that much and happily held on to it.

The one always there when I needed help
Then said, "Turn around, look at these two
Taking a bite out of apathy's reality-sandwich."

The two latecomers were saying,
"The people the sea opened up for were dead
Before Jordan set eyes on those they had bred.

Those who couldn't endure till the end
Working alongside the son of Anchises
Accepted a life without glorious dividends."

Once those shades were so distant from us
It was no longer possible to see them, a new
Thought popped up, and that one gave birth

To more, each different, until delirious,
My eyes were clouded by a cuckoo-land mist
That transformed the insubstantial pageant

Into the stuff as dreams are made on.

13–15. *I want to know / What love is*: The song "I Want to Know What Love Is" was written by Mick Jones of the British-American rock band Foreigner for their 1984 album, *Agent Provocateur.*

16. *Prick up your ears*: *Prick Up Your Ears* was a 1984 film about the life and murder/suicide death of playwright Joe Orton and his partner Kenneth Halliwell, based on a biography of Orton by John Lahr that was inspired by Orton's diaries.

17–18. *the logical fallacy / Of a blind leader*: Matthew 15:14: "Let them alone: they be blind leaders of the blind. And if the blind lead the blind, both shall fall into the ditch."

19. *The mind was made for love at first sight*: The innateness of desire is necessary for the propagation of the species. This is a reiteration of the statement with which Virgil began his discourse on love in *Purg.* XVII, 91–93: "No creator nor any creature . . . Was ever without the desire for love, biological / Or intellectual."

21. *as soon as pleasure shows up, it goes to town*: Since the desire for pleasure is instinctive, the natural inclination, once an object has been identified as pleasurable, is to want immediate gratification.

22–24. *One's perception of the material-actual / Creates an image . . . mirrored / In one's consciousness*: This aligns with the Freudian notion of cathexis. The word in German (*Besetzung*) means "filling a vacancy" or "occupation," and is used by Freud to describe the libidinal energy invested in an object outside the self.

26–27. *Reaching out, i.e., cathexis, is love. That's how / Nature binds you to a new object of desire*: Later object-relation thinkers (post-Freud) differentiate between cathexis and love, identifying the initial libidinal attachment as cathexis and reserving the term "love" for a prolonged attachment.

28–30. *fire moves upward / To reach what makes it last, / Since nature built that pattern into its matrix*: Even nonsentient aspects of nature behave according to plan, each element according to the properties that further its existence. Thus, in this example, fire behaves the way God designed it to behave—flames rise in order to reach the oxygen that sustains it. Fire is one of the four essential elements (along with air, water, earth), so this example can stand for all of nature.

35–36. *those who actualize their love / Of any and every object they find appealing*: Not all objects are appropriate and some people, Virgil points out, cathect to any and all objects, to their eventual detriment—if not on earth, then later in Purgatory.

43–45. *If love arises outside of us, and the mind / Only has the feet it's been given, it can't take / Any credit for going the right or wrong way*: Dante's question is, if each spiritual intellect brings to the situation whatever it has been given by God, and desire gets triggered by what is outside of a person, then how can we be judged for what we cathect to?

46–48. *the realm of reason . . . anything past that, / Wait to get to Beatrice, she works with faith*: Virgil's point is that there are things beyond reason. These are in the realm of faith, Beatrice's domain. He has no access to that realm since he lived and died prior to Christ's death and resurrection.

49–54. *Each essence has its own substantial form . . . a specific quality, / Which . . . Only reveals itself through its effect: the way / You know a plant's alive by its green leaves*: *Forma substantialis*, a concept espoused by both Plato and Aristotle, argued that there were specific properties that were natural to all elements of nature—fire, insects, but also humans. In the medieval era, the concept became bound to Christian theology as an argument for the existence of the individual soul. The soul has been given properties by God and those properties form the character of the spiritual mind/soul, but they can only be demonstrated through action or behavior.

56–60. *no one knows . . . a primal impulse / That merits no praise nor admits any fault*: There is no way to understand what incites desire in any person, nor how a person recognizes the first stirrings of desire. Since desire is innate (God-given), no desire should be judged, nor praised, any more than a bee should be judged for doing what is natural for a bee to do (pollinate flowers).

62–63. *Given that it's innate, virtue must caution you / When you're about to cross a threshold*: This, Virgil cautions, is the reason one needs a moral code, to mediate instinct. As he will say in v. 72, "you are your own policeperson."

67–69. *The ones who reasoned . . . saw that freedom is innate, / And passed on their moral code to the world*: Dante is referring to Aristotle and Plato; the moral philosophy and ethics they passed on were highly principled and based on an understanding of free will. As Virgil tells Sordello in *Purg.* VII, 34–36, he and the other pre-Christians in Limbo "were never vested / With the three holy virtues; [but], of course, / Knew and flawlessly followed all the others."

73–74. *This noble virtue is what Beatrice means / By free will*: Beatrice will speak to Dante about free will but only after he has reached the Empyreal Heaven (*Paradise* V, 19–24).

80–81. *in Rome one sees / Darkness descend between Sardinia and Corsica*: The moon is following the path of the sun as it sets in the west. Neither the island of Sardinia nor the island of Corsica is visible from Rome; Dante seems to be using them simply as directional markers. The two islands were part of the Roman province of Sardinia and Corsica and often used as places of exile. It's possible that Dante is drawing on his time in Rome in 1301, after which he was forced into exile. During the thirteenth century, the Guelphs and Ghibellines sparred over control of Corsica and Sardinia. In 1297, Boniface VIII made James II of Aragon the nominal king of Corsica and Sardinia.

Only in 1323, after Dante's death, was James able to wrest control of Sardinia from the Pisans.

82–83. *Who'd made Pietola / More famous than any other Mantuan city*: Legend has it that Virgil was born in the Roman village of Andes, later known as Pietola, located two or three miles southeast of Mantua.

89–90. *they'd once been / In front of us, were now at our backs*: This is how quickly the group is running: they were just in front of Dante and Virgil, and now, having run the full circle, they are suddenly coming up behind them.

91–93. *the Ismenus and Asopus Rivers witnessed . . . a rave of party monsters, / When the Thebans felt a need for Bacchus*: The river Ismenus in Boeotia, named after a river god in Greek myth, was located near Thebes. The Asopus, a smaller Boeotian river, borders Thebes. The area was a center for Dionysian (Roman: Bacchus) cults. A "rave" is an all-night, often raucous, dance party. A "party monster," according to the *Oxford English Dictionary*, is "a person who parties frequently and without restraint, typically to excess."

100. *Mary ran fast to the mountain*: Luke 1:39: "And Mary arose in those days, and went into the hill country with haste, into a city of Juda." This event, called the Visitation, follows the Annunciation; Mary, pregnant with Jesus, runs to congratulate Elizabeth on her pregnancy (the future child will be John the Baptist). Mary serves here as an example of charitable promptness.

101–102. *And Caesar, to tame Lérida, / Stabbed at Marseille, then raced off to Spain*: In the civil war against Pompey the Great, Caesar, in 49 BCE—on his way to subdue Lérida (ancient Ilerda) in Spain—besieged the rebellious city of Marseille (ancient Massalia). He left troops there under Brutus and moved on.

107–108. *the previous negligent delays / Of your halfhearted attempts to do good*: The sloth that resulted in the penitents' failure to take advantage of opportunities to behave in ways that would result in goodness is now being atoned for by their continual action in the form of circling the fourth terrace at a fast clip and without stopping.

118. *abbot in San Zeno in Verona*: The San Zeno basilica was constructed between 967 and 1368. The monastery connected to it is said to have been built on the site where San Zeno, a Catholic martyr, was buried. The abbot may have been Gerardo II (d. 1187), who served during the reign of Frederick I.

119. *Under the good Emperor Barbarossa*: The red-bearded (*barbarossa*) Frederick I was crowned Holy Roman emperor in 1155. He was a charismatic figure who revived the Justinian Code of law, to which Dante refers in *Purg.* VI, 88–90.

120. *A sore spot for those who think about Milan*: In 1162, after having previously quashed several Milanese rebellions, Frederick I ordered the walls of the city of Milan to be

razed and the ground sown with salt. With the support of Pope Alexander III, the Lombard League began to rebuild Milan in 1167.

121–125. *A guy . . . Will soon boo-hoo over that monastery there / And regret ever having been in charge of it; // Because he installed his son . . . baseborn*: The current abbot, appointed in 1292 for a lifetime term, is Giuseppi (d. 1313), the "illegitimate" son of the lord of Verona, Alberto della Scala. The father is described as having "one foot in the grave" because Dante is aware that while della Scala is still alive in 1300, when the poem is set, he will die the following year. Cangrande, his youngest son, will host Dante in Verona during his exile and serve as his protector (1312–1318). Benvenuto describes Giuseppi as mean, violent, and given to marauding at night with armed companions and "filling the place with prostitutes."

126. *In lieu of the place's true pastor*: Dante gives no indication who the true pastor might have been, possibly one of della Scala's other three "legitimate" or "true" sons.

134–135. *The people the sea opened up for were dead / Before Jordan set eyes on those they had bred*: The penitents, as they run, are all citing examples of when sloth caused significant consequences. First mentioned are the Israelites who, after the Red Sea parted so they could escape the pursuing Egyptians, didn't directly cross the River Jordan to reach the Promised Land but instead remained in the wilderness and died there. Only Joshua and Caleb, who had urged the group to proceed to Canaan without delay, were allowed to survive and later cross over with the descendants of those who had perished.

136–138. *till the end / Working alongside the son of Anchises / Accepted a life without glorious dividends*: The Trojan companions of Aeneas, the son of Anchises, weary of travel, burned their ships on the banks of the Tiber rather than proceed to the founding of Latium, the city that would eventually become Rome and would thereby establish Aeneas's glory.

142. *To more, each different, until delirious*: Dante appears to be setting up the next canto, which will begin with fantasy encounters with two women, one pure and one "twisted."

143. *My eyes were clouded by a cuckoo-land mist*: Sylvia Plath, "The Ghost's Leavetaking": "To the cloud-cuckoo land of color wheels . . . O keeper / Of the profane grail, the dreaming skull."

144–145. *the insubstantial pageant / Into the stuff as dreams are made on*: Shakespeare, *The Tempest* (IV.i.155–157): PROSPERO. "And, like this insubstantial pageant faded, / Leave not a rack behind. We are such stuff / As dreams are made on."

CANTO XIX

At the hour when the day's heat, held captive
By the ground, and sometimes by Saturn,
Can't take the chill off the moon—

When seers see Fortuna Major in dots
And fears in a handful of dust, predawn
In the east, on a path that's not dark for long—

A woman came to me in a dream, talking
Doubletalk: the corner of her eye a twisted pin,
Bent-back hands, turned-in toes, dull skin.

I got her attention and—like the sun that's kind
To stiff limbs the cold night's been cruel to—
The look on my face made her decide

Which language she wanted to speak,
And that quickly straightened everything out
And painted her face whatever color love likes it to be.

Once she got her tongue untied,
She began to sing with such ease
I couldn't make myself look away.

"I am, I am," she sang, "a sweet-sweet-sweet-tea
Siren, I mislead sailors mid-sea;
They like it when I *do-re-mi*. Once I began,

O, O, Odysseus! He turned and gawked like a fan.
Those who come can hardly stand, much less leave.
I suit them like a sleeve, a skin we all fit in."

Before her mouth was even closed, a woman,
Ladylike, saintly even, quickly popped up
Beside me, to mess with the other one's head.

"O Virgil, Virgil, who *is* this?" she said,
Quite up in arms. He then came onstage,
Eyes entirely focused on the respectable one,

Grabbing the other, ripping her bodice, tearing
The fine linen and showing me her underbelly,
I woke to a stench that blew me away.

I blinked and the good teacher said,
"I called you at least three times. Get up,
Let's go find the opening where you go in."

I got up. All the rounds of the holy mountain
Were already filled with daylight;
We walked with the new sun low on our backs.

I followed him, head down, neck extended,
The way one with a lot on their mind
Enacts the first half of a bridge arch.

Then I heard, "Come, here's the crossing,"
In a soft voice infused with kindness
Not heard in these transient borderlands.

With swan-like, wide-open wings,
The one who'd spoken led us up
Between two side-by-side boulders,

Moving its feathers and gently fanning us,
Affirming that those "who mourn"
Will be blessed with an empress of consolation.

"What's with you, trying to outstare
The ground?" my guide began asking,
When we'd gotten a little above the angel.

"I'm hung up on that annoying dream
I just had. It's got me so bent out of shape
I can't stop thinking about it."

"You saw," he said, "that classic wicked witch
Who's causing all the crying above us,
You also saw how someone gets untangled.

But enough. You need to pound the pavement,
Your eyes focused on the lure the Eternal King
Spins with the great celestial wheel."

Like the falcon that first looks at its feet,
Then turns to the call, pulling at the tether
In its lust for the food that drew it there,

So I did, and kept doing as far as the split rock
Made way for someone to climb through it,
All the way up to where the circling begins again.

Arriving at the fifth round, I came out
Into an open area where I saw people
Lying facedown on the ground, sobbing.

"My soul lies down on the pavement,"
I heard them say, with such deep sighs
I could barely make out the words.

"O God's select few, whose suffering
Is lessened by hope and justice,
Point us to where the steps begin to rise."

"If you've arrived exempt from lying here
And want to find the quickest way,
Keep your right always on the outside."

So asked the poet and so came the answer
From a little ahead of us. I could tell
From his voice where he was tucked away.

I turned my eyes to the eyes of my escort
Whose satisfied nod said yes
To what my wishful look was asking.

Now free to do what I was thinking,
I went over to that poor creature
Whose words first made me notice him,

Saying, "Spirit, whose crying brings to maturity
What you can't go back to God without,
Pause your getting-better regimen for me,

Who were you and why're your backs
Turned up and do you want me to pray for you
When I'm moving around alive down there?"

He said to me, "You'll know why
Our backsides are aimed at Heaven, but first,
You should know I was an heir of Peter, a pope.

The Lavagna, a lovely river, comes to life
Between Sestri and Chiavari;
The top of my bloodline took its name as a title.

For a month plus, I felt how the great mantle
Weighs on any who'd protect it from the mire,
And how featherlight the other burdens feel.

My conversion, O me! was very late.
Only after having been made a Roman pope
Did I discover for myself what a liar life is.

I saw you couldn't quiet the heart down there,
And how you'd never rise above that life,
Which was what triggered my love of this.

Until that point, a miserable soul, cut off
From God, nothing but greed.
Now, as you can see, I'm punished for it here.

What greed does is made clear
Here in the overturned soul's detox;
The mountain has no pill more bitter than this.

Even as our eyes never looked up,
Fixed instead on earthly things,
So, justice here is an immersion in the earth.

Since greed blew away our love of anything
Good, we missed out on doing good works.
That's why justice holds us tight here,

Hands and feet captive for as long
As the fair-minded sovereign sees fit, that's
How long we'll lie facedown without moving."

I was on my knees and ready to speak,
But as I began, he became aware,
Just by listening, of my respectful attitude.

"What's wrong," he said, "that you're bent over?"
"Because the awe of your high office," I said,
"Gave me a guilty conscience when I was standing."

"Stand up, get up, brother!" he said,
"Don't get the wrong idea, I, with you and
With the others, uphold and espouse one power.

If you ever got the drift of that holy Gospel
Passage that says, 'Neither shall they marry,'
Then you know what I'm talking about.

Now go away. I don't want you to stay here
Any longer, you're interfering with my mourning,
That necessary 'maturing' you mentioned.

I have a niece back there, named Alagia,
Goodness personified, if our house
Hasn't ruined her by its bad example.

She's all that's left to me back there."

NOTES TO CANTO XIX

1–3. *At the hour when the day's heat . . . Can't take the chill off the moon*: Saturn was once thought to be the coldest planet (then called a star). Virgil, *Georgics* 1, 335–336: "This dread, notice the months and signs in the sky, Saturn's icy star retreats."

4–5. *When seers see Major Fortuna in dots / And fears in a handful of dust*: T. S. Eliot, *The Waste Land*: "I will show you fear in a handful of dust." Dante uses the term *geomanti*, practitioners of geomancy, "a method of divination which interprets markings on the ground or how handfuls of dirt land when tossed" (wiktionary.org/wiki/geomancy). Fortuna, the Roman goddess of luck, chance, fate, and fortune—often pictured with a wheel of fortune—was popular in the medieval era. According to Benvenuto, *Maggior Fortuna* (Major Fortuna) was an astrological configuration based on the appearance of stars seen in the east at the end of Aquarius and beginning of Pisces (Vernon 2:106).

7–8. *A woman came to me in a dream, talking / Doubletalk*: To describe the woman's speech, Dante uses *balba*, a capacious term that can describe stammering, stuttering, mumbling, gibberish, babbling, or baby talk. Doubletalk is likewise a form of non-sense speech. It's sometimes used by politicians to avoid speaking the truth.

8–9. *The corner of her eye a twisted pin, / Bent-back hands, turned-in toes, dull skin*: T. S. Eliot, "Rhapsody on a Windy Night": "Regard that woman . . . you see the corner of her eye / Twists like a crooked pin."

14–15. *that quickly straightened everything out / And painted her face whatever color love likes it*: The woman, her body initially bent in multiple ways and her speech twisted, is straightened out by Dante's look, at which point she begins to speak clearly and then to sing a song filled with sexual innuendo. It appears that it's only Dante's libidinal investment that makes her appear beautiful. Her face, which had been *scialba* (dull, colorless, pasty), now takes on whatever aspects the onlooker finds attractive, demonstrating that beauty is, indeed, in the eye of the enamored beholder.

17–18. *She began to sing with such ease / I couldn't make myself look away*: Like the sailors who were inextricably drawn to the Sirens of myth, Dante is finding it impossible to turn away.

19. *a sweet-sweet-sweet-tea*: Gertrude Stein, "Susie Asado": "Sweet sweet sweet sweet sweet tea. / Susie Asado."

20–21. *Siren, I mislead sailors mid-sea; / They like it when I* do-re-mi: Here, the songstress/witch not only admits to being a Siren but also brags about her ability to seduce sailors into following her voice and dying on the rocks.

22–24. O, O, Odysseus! *He turned and gawked like a fan. / Those who come can hardly stand, much less leave. / I suit them like a sleeve, a skin we all fit in*: Commentators suggest

Dante may not have read the *Odyssey* since he has the woman say that she "turned Ulysses from his wandering path" ("Io volsi Ulisse del suo cammin vago"). In the *Odyssey*, Odysseus, anticipating the Sirens, has his men tie him to the mast and then sends them belowdecks so no one will steer the boat toward the rocks on which the Sirens sit and sing. It's also possible that Dante does know the story and is simply describing Odysseus turning his head to listen as the boat goes by.

25–26. *Before her mouth was even closed, a woman, / Ladylike, saintly even*: Only in contrast to the saintly "lady" does the seductress now get revealed, a moment that echoes Virgil's lesson in *Purg.* XVIII, 34–36: "Now you can see how much truth is hidden / From those who actualize their love / Of any and every object they find appealing."

28–29. *Virgil, Virgil, who is this?" she said, / Quite up in arms*: This tone of indignation foreshadows the tone Beatrice will take with Dante in the opening of *Purg.* XXXI.

33. *I woke to a stench that blew me away*: Virgil, called onstage by the Beatrice figure, is required for Dante to come to his senses and see that the woman is not a worthy object of affection.

35. *I called you at least three times*: Matthew 26:34: "Jesus said unto him, That this night, before the cock crow, thou shalt deny me thrice."

37–38. *All the rounds . . . Were already filled with daylight*: Dante and Virgil are walking toward the west, so the just-risen sun is low and behind them.

43–45. *Come, here's the crossing, / In a soft voice infused with kindness / Not heard in these transient borderlands*: The angel ushers Dante and Virgil onto the crevice that leads to the next cornice. This angel's voice is infused with kindness, rare in Purgatory, and its tone matches the consolation to which the penitent can look forward once they complete their contrition.

50–51. *Affirming that those "who mourn" / Will be blessed with an empress of consolation*: Matthew 5:4: "Blessed are they that mourn: for they shall be comforted." Boethius, in his *Consolation of Philosophy*, which Dante is known to have read and admired, describes a Lady Philosophy (an allegorical figure Dante also uses in *Convivio*) that helps him process the psychic confusion he feels and who, through various questions, reflections, and proposed enigmas, helps him resolve his existential angst.

52–53. *What's with you, trying to outstare / the ground*: Shakespeare, *Antony and Cleopatra* (III.xiii.194–195): Enobarbus. "Now he'll outstare the lightning. To be furious / Is to be frighted out of fear."

58–59. *that classic wicked witch / Who's causing all the crying above us*: Dante uses *strega*, "witch," "hag," "harpy," "sorceress," from the Latin *strix*, "screech owl." The figure is meant to be seen as the timeless carping greed for what isn't good for one, which goes all the way back to Eden. The Wicked Witch of the West appears in L. Frank

Baum's *The Wonderful Wizard of Oz* (1900) and in the subsequent films (1910, 1914, 1939) based on the book. She pursues Dorothy in hopes of stealing the Silver Shoes (Ruby Slippers in the 1939 film, which starred Judy Garland as Dorothy), which had previously belonged to the Wicked Witch of the East, in order to increase her power.

60. *You also saw how someone gets untangled*: One appears to get untangled by looking at the rottenness hidden beneath the attractive surface. And, in Dante's case, by looking to Beatrice as a model for pure goodness and comparing any desired object with her.

62–63. *Eternal King / Spins with the great celestial wheel*: Muslim astronomers, beginning in the ninth century with al-Farghānī (whose name was given to the lunar crater Alfraganus), used Ptolemy's model of nesting spheres, with earth at the center, to determine the distance to other cosmic bodies. For the next several centuries, Muslim thinkers, and later European academics, continued to use the system of nesting spheres as a predictive map of the universe. In his *Opus majus*, Roger Bacon used it to consider the time it would theoretically take to walk to the moon. That work, written in medieval Latin, was requested by Pope Clement IV and sent to Rome in 1267, two years after Dante was born.

64. *Like the falcon that first looks at its feet*: The concentric circles of the cosmos are now compared to a falcon. When the falcon looks at its feet, it sees the straps, called jesses, that tether him to the falconer. When released by the falconer, the falcon circles until it strikes prey; it then returns to the falconer's arm, its perch. This image of the hawk is used multiple times in the *Commedia*.

69. *All the way up to where the circling begins again*: The circles of the Celestial Spheres echo the circular terraces of Purgatory, each connected by a vertically angled stone stairway.

70–72. *Arriving at the fifth round . . . people / Lying facedown on the ground, sobbing*: This is the cornice where the sin of avarice or greed (and its opposite, profligacy) is paid down. Since the penitents' eyes were focused only on earthly gains (or spending) when they were living, never looking up at God's Heaven, they now remain face-to-face with the earthly ground.

73. *My soul lies down on the pavement*: Dante uses the Vulgate Latin, "Adhaesit pavimento anima mea," from Psalm 119:25: "My soul cleaveth unto the dust: quicken thou me according to thy word." This psalm is included in the lessons and psalms said for the canonical hours found in the Roman Breviary, the first complete manuscript of which dates back to 1099.

81. *Keep your right always on the outside*: After exiting the stairway, the outside edge of each cornice will be on the right.

83–84. *I could tell / From his voice where he was tucked away*: Because the soul is lying facedown among rows of penitents in the same prone position, Dante would not have been able to see who had spoken but could only locate the voice based on hearing it.

94–95. *Who were you and why're your backs / Turned up*: The soul will wait until v. 115 to begin to answer the second part of the question, why their backs are turned up; he first addresses the issue of who he was.

99. *You should know I was an heir of Peter, a pope*: The original, "scias quod ego fui successor," is said in Latin, which would be fitting for a pope.

100–102. *The Lavagna . . . Between Sestri and Chiavari / The top of my bloodline took its name as a title*: The upper echelon of the Fieschi family used the name of the river to refer to themselves as Counts of Lavagna. Chiavari was a castle town near Genoa. Sestri, controlled by the Fieschi family, was located some thirty-five miles south of Genoa on a promontory on the Ligurian coast.

103. *For a month plus*: The election of Adrian V to pope, on the death of Pope Innocent V, took place on July 11, 1276. He died thirty-eight days later, on August 16, so was never crowned.

106. *My conversion, O me! was very late*: Lacking any historical evidence of a belated conversion, commentators speculate that Dante has attributed to Adrian V words that were supposed to have been said by Adrian IV. Petrarch similarly confused the two popes but later corrected the error.

115–126. *What greed does is made clear / Here in the overturned soul's detox . . . facedown without moving*: Since the souls were so addicted to earthly delights when alive that they turned their back on Heaven, refusing to face the place where true value resides, they must now go through withdrawal (detox) by remaining facedown, immersed in the earth so they will see it for what it really is, simply dirt.

134–135. *I, with you and / With the others, uphold and espouse one power*: Two biblical verses echo Pope Adrian's emphatic demand that Dante not bow down to him but treat him as an equal. Revelation 19:10; and Acts 10:25–26: "And as Peter was coming in, Cornelius met him, and fell down at his feet, and worshipped him. But Peter took him up, saying, Stand up; I myself also am a man."

136–137. *that holy Gospel / Passage that says, 'Neither shall they marry'*: Dante uses the Vulgate Latin, "Neque nubent" (they neither marry), from the Greek "to not be a bride." Jesus, when asked by the Sadducees, a Jewish sect that rejected the idea of the resurrection, to whom would a wife belong in Heaven if she sequentially marries seven brothers, responds (Matthew 22:30): "For in the resurrection they neither marry, nor are given in marriage, but are as the angels of God in heaven." Adrian appears to be using this quote to again emphasize that in Heaven one's only allegiance is to God.

142–144. *I have a niece back there, named Alagia . . . if our house / Hasn't ruined her by its bad example*: Alagia Fieschi, the niece of Pope Adrian V, was married to Moroello Malaspina, a Guelph military man and, notably, a friend of Dante's. The family extended hospitality to Dante in Lunigiana early in his exile. The two men both supported Henry VII's coronation as Holy Roman emperor in 1312. It is recorded that the women of the family were not held in high regard. Dante appears to want to make certain that Alagia, who was said to be a very devout woman, will not be included with the other women, whom Benvenuto refers to as "noble prostitutes."

145. *She's all that's left to me back there*: Only prayers said by his niece, since she alone is in a state of grace, might facilitate his journey up the mountain. An anonymous Florentine commentary on the *Commedia* (*Anonimo fiorentino*), written in the fourteenth or early fifteenth century, states that Alagia gave alms, offered up prayers, and had masses said for her uncle's salvation.

canto XX

The will fights badly against a better will;
Instead of pleasing myself, I pleased him,
And lifted the sponge before it was filled.

I started to move and my leader moved over
Siding into the space next to the rock face,
The way one stays close to a parapet edge.

This because the ones whose eyes, tear by tear,
Are dissolving the evil that eats up the world
Were there on the outer edge of the precipice.

Damn you, timeless she-wolf,
You need more victims than all the other beasts
To fill your bottomless pit.

O Heaven, in whose roundabouts
Some seem to think change takes place,
When will someone come and get her out of here?

We made our way with small deliberate steps,
All of my attention focused on the shades
Who were pitifully moaning and sobbing.

I happened to hear one ahead call out in tears,
"Sweet Mary," like when the mother
And child reunion is only a motion away,

Followed by, "How poor you were
Can be seen by the poorhouse-inn
Where you delivered your holy cargo."

Following that, this, "O good Fabricius,
You chose an order of virtuous poverty
Rather than a helping of wealth-*avec*-vice."

I so enjoyed the wordplay,
I pulled ahead in order to see for myself
From which soul it seemed to have come

He went on to talk about the largess of Nicholas
Who conducted three young things
Toward conduct better suited to young women.

I said, "O spirit who has a way with words,
Tell me who you were, and why only you
Look back again at these admirable acts.

Whatever you say won't go unthanked,
If I go back and finish that little putt-putt
Through that life that goes *pfft* at the end."

He said, "I'll tell you, not for any support
From back there, but because you haven't died
And yet such grace is shining in you.

I was the root of that invasive plant that blew
Through the entire Christian territory—
So that now, decent fruit rarely falls from the tree.

But if Douai, Lille, Ghent, and Bruges can keep
A can-do attitude, there'll soon be payback—
That's what I'm asking for from the all-judging one.

I was called Hugh Capet back there;
The Philips and Louies came from my line, at least
The most recent ones that propped up France.

I was the son of a Pan-loving Parisian meat-man.
When the ancient kings had all died out—
But for one, a monkish loafer who liked dirty linen—

I found I held the reins of the government
Tight in my hands. I had so much more
Buying power, and such a boatload of friends,

That I was able to offer up my son's head
For the widow's crown,
And from that, the sacred bones began.

Until the huge Provençal dowry wiped away
Any sense of shame, my bloodline wasn't worth
A lot but it also didn't do much damage.

It all began right there, using influence and lies
To rip everyone off, and then, as recompense,
Land grabbing Ponthieu, Normandy, and Gascony.

Then Charles came into Italy and, as recompense,
Made a martyr of Conradin; and then,
Sent Thomas off to Heaven, as recompense.

I see a time, not long from now,
That draws another Charles out of France,
So he and his line can become better known.

He comes out with only the jousting lance
Judas used, and with one thrust, the underbelly
Of Florence bursts like a dropped melon.

He won't gain ground, only sin and shame,
Which are much more profound,
Considering how little the real damage matters.

I see another Charles, having left his ship, dickering
Over the price as he pimps out his daughter,
The way pirates do with hostages.

O greed, what more can you do to us:
How is it my bloodline, so tied up with your DNA,
Doesn't care about its own flesh?

So that the past and future may not seem as bad,
I see the fleur-de-lis entering Alagna
And Christ, as his own vicar, taken captive.

I see him mocked again;
I see a rerun of the vinegar-and-gall scene,
And his getting killed between two living thieves.

I see a new Pilate so cruel that just this
Is not enough; with no authority,
He sails his greedy boat right into the Temple.

O my Lord, when will I be delighted
To see your revenge, which, still hidden,
Sweetens your wrath in its secrecy?

The way I spoke about that one Bride
Of the Holy Spirit, which then made you
Turn toward me for some gloss,

That's the proscribed form our prayers take
As long as it's day, but once night falls,
We play a different tune.

Then we replay the story of Pygmalion,
Traitor, thief, and parricide,
Who did it all out of a greed for gold;

And the misery of greedy Midas,
After his piggish wish for a golden touch,
We just have to laugh about that.

Each of us then remembers mad Achan,
How he stole the swag, so Joshua's anger
Still bites him in the I won't say but you-know-what.

Then we accuse Sapphira, with her husband;
We cheer the kicker that had Heliodorus;
And all around the mountain goes the infamous

Name of Polymestor, who killed Polydorus.
Lately we've been yelling, 'Crassus, do tell,
Since you know so well, what flavor is gold?'

Sometimes one speaks loud, another soft.
We go from major to minor, depending
On how attached we are to our anger.

But those daytime reflections on goodness,
It wasn't only me, it's just that none
Of those near me were raising their voices."

We'd already moved off from him,
And were trying to put the path behind us,
As much as possible, given the furrowed tract,

When, as if something were falling, I felt
The mountain trembling. A chill came over me—
Like someone arriving at death's door.

Delos Island surely couldn't have shaken more
Before Latona made a nest there to deliver
The two eyes of the sky, Diana and Apollo.

Then on all sides, such a hue and cry went up,
That my teacher came toward me, saying,
"Don't worry, while I'm here to guide you."

"Gloria in excelsis Deo," they were all shouting,
As far as I could make out from those nearby
Whose shouts I could actually decipher.

We stood motionless and in a state of suspense,
Like the shepherd who first heard that song,
Until the shaking stopped and it was over.

Then we started back on our hallowed path,
Eyeing the shades lying on the ground
Who'd resumed their usual crying.

Never has ignorance been so at war
With everything I wanted to know,
At least if my memory of it isn't mistaken.

I kept wondering what was possible right now;
I couldn't dare ask while we were rushing,
Neither could I, on my own, gain any insight:

So, I went on, timidly lost in thought.

10. *Damn you, timeless she wolf*: Dante meets a she-wolf in *Inf.* I, 49–54, shortly before he encounters Virgil; Virgil tells him that the wolf has ruined countless lives and her constant craving will be stopped only when the *veltro* (greyhound) arrives to drive her out of Italy, and that that moment will occur *tra feltro et feltro* (between felt and felt). Commentators have speculated for over seven hundred years about who or what the "greyhound" is meant to represent and what "between felt and felt" might mean. The wolf is *antica* (timeless or ancient) because she derives from Adam and Eve. Pluto, who stands guard over the fourth circle of Hell, where Greed is punished, is addressed by Virgil in *Inf.* VII, 8, as *maladetto lupo* (damned wolf) and told to be quiet when he begins to yell at Dante.

11–12. *You need more victims than all the other beasts / To fill your bottomless pit*: The one thing certain about the she-wolf is that she represents avarice. It also seems clear, from the references in *Inferno*, and what is said here, that Dante believed greed destroyed more people than any other sin—which follows New Testament teaching. 1 Timothy 6:10: "For the love of money is the root of all evil: which while some coveted after, they have erred from the faith, and pierced themselves through with many sorrows."

13–14. *O Heaven, in whose roundabouts / Some seem to think change takes place*: In *Purg.* XVI, Dante asks Marco, the Lombardi soul, which is responsible for earthly failure, Heaven or humans. Marco's answer (vv. 67–69) is that the heavens don't control the fates of humans, because "If that were the case, the idea of free will / Would be shredded and there'd be no equity / To good-equals-joy and bad-equals-grief."

15. *When will someone come and get her out of here*: This someone may be the greyhound noted above. Over time, possible identities for the greyhound have included Henry VII; Cangrande della Scala, a Ghibelline Lord of Verona (designated Imperial Vicar in 1312 by Henry VII) who was a known protector of Dante during the years Dante resided in Verona (from 1312 to 1318, after which, he left for Ravenna); a future monarch; a future pope; Christ; or Dante himself.

20–21. *like when the mother / And child reunion is only a motion away*: The song "Mother and Child Reunion," with the refrain, "Oh, the mother and child reunion / Is only a motion away," was the lead track on the 1972 album *Paul Simon*. The song, written by Simon, is said to have been at least partly inspired by a translation of a Japanese dish called *Oyakodon*, literally, "parent and child rice bowl"—so called because it contains both the chicken and the egg; on the American menu, the dish was translated "mother and child reunion." Other inspirations for the song include the death of Simon's pet dog; Simon's wife, Peggy Harper; Jimmy Cliff's backup musicians, with whom Simon recorded the song; and reggae dance music.

25–27. *Fabricius, / You chose an order of virtuous poverty / Rather than a helping of wealth-avec-vice*: The "one-eyed" Gaius Fabricius Luscinus, originally from a plebeian family from the town of Aletrium in the Lazio region, made his way to Rome and became a general, a consul, and a censor. When serving this last role, he tried to rein in Roman overindulgence. He was said to refuse bribes and political gifts. He was not only free of greed but practiced such austerity that he died in poverty and the government had to pay for his funeral. Both Virgil and Petrarch write about Fabricius. Dante mentions him not only in *Purgatorio* but also in *Convivio* (4, 5, 13) and in *De monarchia* (2, 5, 11).

31–33. *Nicholas / Who conducted three young things / Toward conduct better suited to young women*: Nicholas (d. 343) was an early Christian bishop, recognized as a saint by the early Roman Catholic Church and by the Russian and Greek Orthodox Churches, known for making secret gifts to those in need. He famously threw purses of gold through the window of a house where a gentleman who had fallen on hard times was considering prostituting his three daughters in order to support the family. The purses served as dowries so the daughters could instead marry. Saint Nicholas's gift giving, and the custom of giving children gifts on his name day (December 6), inspired the invention of the character known as Father Christmas, or Santa Claus.

43–45. *that invasive plant that blew / Through the entire Christian territory— / So that now, decent fruit rarely falls from the tree*: The invasive plant is the Capetian dynasty, also known as the House of France, which includes Hugh Capet (who will identify himself in v. 49), king from 987 to 996, and his thirteen male descendants, who sequentially ruled until the death of Charles IV in 1328. Matthew 7:18: "A good tree cannot bring forth evil fruit, neither can a corrupt tree bring forth good fruit."

46–47. *if Douai, Lille, Ghent, and Bruges can keep / A can-do attitude, there'll soon be payback*: These are the four principal cities of Flanders. In 1297, Guy of Dampierre, Count of Flanders, was imprisoned by Philip the Fair of France because of an alliance he'd made with Edward I of England. Philip forced Guy to renounce the alliance, which he did while captive, but then reneged as soon as he was released. Philip then sent his brother, Charles of Valois, to occupy Flanders. While the French were initially welcomed, the harsh conditions they imposed resulted in an uprising. On July 11, 1302, the French were defeated at the Battle of the Golden Spurs at Courtrai. Guy was briefly freed, then sent back to prison to die.

52–53. *the son of a Pan-loving Parisian meat-man. / When the ancient kings had all died out*: Legend had it that Hugh Capet's father, Hugh the Great, descended from a Parisian butcher. Commentators assume Dante is confused about which man had this humble background. Even so, some commentators suggest that the man wasn't a mere butcher but more likely a rich man who dealt in cattle.

54. *a monkish loafer who liked dirty linen*: There is no evidence that Charles of Lorraine, who would have been the only candidate for this figure since he was heir to the throne

before Hugh Capet, ever became a monk. Imprisoned in 991, he died the following year. Singleton (2:478) suggests Dante confused Charles of Lorraine with Childeric III, described by Villani (II.12) as "a no account man sent off to be monk."

58–60. *my son's head / For the widow's crown, / And from that, the sacred bones began*: Hugh Capet's son, Robert II, ruled France from 996 to 1031. After having been crowned king, Hugh Capet lobbied for his son to be declared his successor. When the son was sixteen, Hugh arranged for him to marry Rozala of Italy, daughter of the king of Italy and the widow of Arnulf II, Count of Flanders. Her exact age isn't known, but she would have been somewhere between the ages of twenty-eight and thirty-eight. The marriage was unhappy and produced no offspring. After the death of Hugh Capet, Robert II repudiated Rozala and married his second cousin, which resulted in his excommunication from the church until he arranged for that marriage to be annulled. In 1001, he married Constance of Arles and had seven children with her. He also fathered one child out of wedlock. The bones are sacred because they were consecrated by the archbishop of the cathedral of Reims, where French kings were crowned and entombed upon their deaths.

61–63. *Until the huge Provençal dowry . . . my bloodline wasn't worth / A lot but . . . didn't do much damage*: The territory of Provençe came under French control in 1245, when Charles of Anjou married Beatrice, the youngest daughter of the Count of Provençe, Ramon Berenguer IV. Charles was the son of Louis VIII and brother of Louis IX—who, in 1234, had married Ramon Berenguer IV's eldest daughter, Margaret.

66. *Land grabbing Ponthieu, Normandy, and Gascony*: During a period of French expansionism, these three regions, previously under the English Crown, were annexed by Philip of France and Charles Valois.

67–68. *Charles came into Italy and, as recompense, / Made a martyr of Conradin*: Conrad V of Germany became the heir to the throne of Naples and Sicily upon the death of his father, Emperor Conrad IV, in 1254. Since he was only three years old, his uncle, Manfred, whom we met in *Purg.* III, 104–116, reigned in his stead. Upon the death of Manfred in 1266, Charles I of Anjou was crowned King of Sicily. Conradin, age sixteen, was then persuaded to try to wrest his rightful crown from Charles but was defeated in 1268 and beheaded in Naples.

69. *Sent Thomas off to Heaven, as recompense*: Dante believed, as did Villani and others, that Charles of Anjou had arranged for Thomas Aquinas, philosopher, theologian, Dominican priest, Doctor of the Church, and author of the *Summa theologica*, to be poisoned on his way from Naples to attend the Second Council of Lyons—having been summoned there by Gregory X to present his work. Thomas fell and sustained a head injury on the way and died two months later on March 7, 1274, at the Cistercian Fossanova monastery near Terracina.

71–72. *another Charles out of France, / So he and his line can become better known*: This is Charles of Valois, who was engaged by Pope Boniface VIII to mediate between the Bianchi (White) and Neri (Black) factions of the Guelph party in Florence. In exchange, Boniface had agreed to support Charles's election as Holy Roman emperor. Following Charles's entrance into Florence on November 1, 1301, the pro-papacy Neri took control of the city, causing massive destruction and exiling a number of influential Bianchi, Dante among them. See the note to *Purg.* VI, 143–144.

73–75. *the jousting lance / Judas used, and with one thrust, the underbelly / Of Florence bursts like a dropped melon*: Dante conflates the lance used by the soldiers to pierce the side of Jesus and the betrayal by Judas that led to Jesus's crucifixion. Similarly, Charles for his own gain has put in motion events that rip Florence apart and cause the city to lose the very citizens that made the city work.

76–78. *He won't gain ground, only sin and shame, / . . . much more profound, / Considering how little the real damage matters*: The punishment Charles will endure in the afterlife is much greater than any military or political damage he may have effected. He won't gain any ground because he won't be made Holy Roman emperor. His derisive nickname after the Italian campaign was "Landless" (*Sans terre*), because he was never crowned king of any territory.

79–80. *another Charles, having left his ship, dickering / . . . as he pimps out his daughter*: This is Charles II, the son of Charles of Anjou and the king of Naples from 1285 to 1309. When his father went to raise troops to avenge the 1282 Sicilian Vespers (an anti-French rebellion on the island of Sicily), he allowed himself, against the express command of his father, to be drawn into a battle with a general of Pedro III, king of Aragon. He was defeated and held prisoner on his ship. In 1305, he agreed to the marriage of his youngest daughter, Beatrice, to the much older, and disreputable, Azzo VIII, Marquise of Este, for a large bride price (variously reported as 30,000, 51,000, or 100,000 florins).

85–86. *So that the past and future may not seem as bad, / I see the fleur-de-lis entering Alagna*: Anagni (then Alagna) was where Pope Boniface VIII's palace was located. The fleur-de-lis is the insignia of French royalty.

87. *And Christ, as his own vicar, taken captive*: Philip the Fair, after his excommunication by Pope Boniface VIII, "Christ in the form of a vicar," had Boniface arrested, roughed up, and detained in his own palace for three days, while soldiers ransacked it. After a popular uprising, the pope was released. He traveled to Rome, where he died a month later.

89. *I see a rerun of the vinegar-and-gall scene*: Matthew 17:34 says that the Roman soldiers offered Christ "vinegar to drink mingled with gall: and when he had tasted thereof, he would not drink." Vinegar was nonsweet wine; gall was either myrrh (Mark 15:23) or wormwood, which contains thujone, a stimulant that is mood elevating at low doses.

91–93. *a new Pilate so cruel . . . with no authority, / He sails his greedy boat right into the Temple*: The "new Pilate" is Philip IV, "the Fair" (*le Bel*), who delivered Boniface into the hands of his enemies the way Pontius Pilate, Roman governor of Judea and overseer of the trial of Jesus, delivered Christ into the hands of the Jews. The Knights Templar were a Catholic military order founded in 1119. By 1307, they had accrued tremendous wealth, especially by plundering the Holy Land during the Crusades. They also enjoyed tremendous power, since they were exempt from paying taxes and from following local laws. Their headquarters was called the Temple of Solomon. In 1307, Philip had huge numbers of the knights killed on false charges of heresy. In 1311, Philip pressured Pope Clement V to abolish the order.

103–105. *Pygmalion, / Traitor, thief, and parricide, / Who did it all out of a greed for gold*: In the *Aeneid* 1, 340–364, Virgil tells the story of Pygmalion, king of the Phoenician city of Tyre, who killed his wealthy uncle, Sichaeus (Sycharbas), who was also his sister Dido's husband, in an effort to gain the family wealth. Sichaeus appears to Dido in a dream and tells her to take the money and leave; she does. She eventually establishes the city of Carthage.

106–108. *Midas, / After his piggish wish for a golden touch, / We just have to laugh*: In *Metamorphoses* 11.100–193, Ovid tells the story of King Midas, who returned the satyr Silenus, who had wandered off after drinking, to Bacchus. Bacchus rewarded Midas by granting him the wish that everything he touched would turn to gold; unfortunately, "everything" included whatever he would eat or drink. When Midas asked to be relieved of the gift, he was told to bathe in the river Pactolus—when he did, the river sands turned to gold. In another story, Midas is given the ears of an ass by Apollo, as punishment for choosing Pan over him as the one who was best at the flute and lyre.

109–111. *mad Achan, / How he stole the swag, so Joshua's anger / Still bites him*: Joshua 7:1–26 tells the story of how Achan took some of the spoils of the battle of Jericho, after Joshua had explicitly said they were to be given to the temple. Although Achan eventually confessed and returned the treasure, Joshua had him stoned to death.

112. *Sapphira, with her husband*: Acts 5:1–10 tells the story of how Sapphira and her husband sold their possessions to support the apostles but held back part of the price for themselves. When each was separately confronted by Peter, they fell dead at his feet.

113. *We cheer the kicker that had Heliodorus*: 2 Maccabees 3:21–2:28 tells the story of how Heliodorus—when sent to Jerusalem by Seleucus IV Philopator (king of Syria) to claim treasure stored in the Temple so that Seleucus could pay taxes to the Romans—was repelled by three mystical beings on horseback who had assumed human forms. The horse ridden by the first man kicked him with its front hooves; the other two men then beat him until he had to be carried out on a stretcher.

115. *Name of Polymestor, who killed Polydorus*: Both Virgil and Ovid tell the story of how during the Trojan War, Polydorus, the son of King Priam, was sent for safekeeping,

along with a great deal of treasure, to Polymestor, the king of Arcadia who was married to Priam's eldest daughter. Polymestor killed the boy and threw his corpse into the ocean.

116–117. *Crassus, do tell . . . what flavor is gold*: The Roman consul and general Marcus Licinius Crassus was known for both his wealth and his greed. He, Caesar, and Pompey formed the political alliance known as the First Triumvirate. As commander of Syria, he tried to take over Parthia (ancient Iran) but was killed in 53 BCE. Legend had it that when Crassus died, the Parthians poured molten gold into his mouth to mock his love of money.

119. *from major to minor*: Cole Porter, "Ev'ry Time We Say Goodbye": "There's no love song finer but how strange / The change from major to minor / Every time we say goodbye."

130–132. *Delos Island surely couldn't have shaken more / Before Latona made a nest there to deliver / The two eyes of the sky, Diana and Apollo*: Apollo, the sun, and Diana, the moon, are the "two eyes of the sky." Leto (Roman: Latona), having been impregnated by Zeus, incurred the jealous wrath of Hera, who forbade any land to take in the pregnant woman. Leto discovered a floating island—Delos Island, a very real island in the South Aegean—where she could deliver her twin offspring. Later, Apollo is said to have fixed it in place. Because the island, battered by the wind and waves, moves, it is imagined as shaking like the vibration caused by the resounding cheers that go up the mountain to celebrate the admission of a penitent into Heaven.

136. *"Gloria in excelsis Deo," they were all shouting*: The Vulgate Latin phrase is said by the multitude of angels who appear with the Angel Gabriel to announce the forthcoming birth of Christ. Luke 2:13–14: "And suddenly there was with the angel a multitude of the heavenly host praising God, and saying, Glory to God in the highest, and on earth peace, good will toward men." Here in Purgatory, the phrase is shouted when a soul is purified and made Christlike, a form of rebirth.

140. *Like the shepherd who first heard that song*: Luke 2:8–10: "And there were in the same country shepherds abiding in the field, keeping watch over their flock by night. And, lo, the angel of the Lord came upon them, and the glory of the Lord shone round about them: and they were sore afraid. And the angel said unto them, Fear not: for, behold, I bring you good tidings of great joy, which shall be to all people."

150. *Neither could I, on my own, gain any insight*: Dante still must rely on Virgil to make sense of this new realm, even knowing by now that Virgil's comprehension is limited by his lack of faith and that some questions will have to wait until he is reunited with Beatrice in Heaven.

CANTO XXI

The natural thirst—that is never satisfied
With water but only with the grace
The Samaritan woman ended up asking for—

Tormented me and rushing on the obstructed
Path behind my leader was a pinprick,
Plus, I was sympathizing with those just deserts,

When whoa, just like Luke writes about Christ
Appearing to two on the road when
He was just-risen from the sepulchral cave,

A shade appeared, coming up behind us
As we kept our eye on the crowd at our feet.
We didn't see him until he spoke,

Saying, "May God give you peace, brothers."
We immediately turned our heads.
Virgil made a fitting gesture,

Then said, "May the one true court,
Which relegates me to eternal exile, accept you
Into the peace of the blessed assembly."

"What!" he said, as we kept hurrying.
"If you shades aren't worthy of God's attic,
Who brought you this far up the stairs?"

My doctor, "If you look at the marks
The angel incised on this one, you'll clearly see
It's been agreed he's to reign with the good.

But because the one spinning day and night
Hasn't yet measured the thread
That Clotho spools and files away for everyone,

His soul, which is your and my sister,
Couldn't manage the coming up alone,
Since his eyes can't see what our eyes can

I was fished out of Hell's commodious throat
To act as his docent and, by having him follow
Where my teaching leads, show him the beyond.

But tell me, if you know, why did the mountain
Shake just now and why did an all-for-one shout
Seem to go up and back down to its damp feet?"

His asking the question threaded the eye
Of my needlelike longing; and now the mere
Hope of knowing made my throat less of a desert.

The other one began, "The religious creed
Of the mountain allows nothing here
That's not preordained or that lies outside its rites.

Here, one's free from any modifications.
Heaven only gets what it grants itself,
And 'no other' means no other causality:

Ergo, no rain, no hail, no snow, no dew,
No ice-white frost over and above
What falls on those first three short steps.

No clouds, thick or thin, come out, no bolt
From the blue, no Thaumas and Electra's daughter,
Whose rainbow will often change neighborhoods.

Dry vapors don't rise any higher
Than the three steps I just mentioned, which is
Where Saint Peter's vicar plants his feet.

It may quake down below, a lot or a little,
But the wind that escapes the earth down there,
I have no idea how, has never stirred here.

There's trembling when a soul senses it's pure
And can go up, set off for the summit; the outcry
Seconds it, a way of saying, 'yes, you're next.'

Of its purity, the will alone is evidence;
Now free to change its level, the soul
Is pleasantly surprised: it's getting its wish!

From the beginning, it wants it but divine justice
Opposes the will, because it was in a state of sin,
And sets it to suffering instead.

I, having lain on this bed of thorns
For over five hundred years, only now,
Of my own free will, wanted that better threshold.

That's why you felt the tremor, and the pious
Spirits of the mountain paying tribute
To the man upstairs, that he'll soon invite them up."

So he said, and since one enjoys a drink
So much more if they're thirsty, it's beyond saying
How much good this one did me.

My wise leader said, "Now that I see the web
You're caught in, and how one escapes it, and
Why the shaking, and what's with the celebration,

I'd be interested now in knowing who are you,
And why you had to lie here for so many centuries?
In your own words works for me."

"In the era when good Emperor Titus, with
The highest sovereign's help, avenged the wounds
That shed the blood that Judas bartered,

I made a name for myself back there,
The longest lasting, most honored," said the spirit,
"A great deal of fame, but no faith yet.

My voice was so fresh and delicate that,
While from Toulouse, I was drawn to Rome,
Where I was honored with a laurel crown

Statius is what people down there still call me;
I sang of Thebes and then of the great Achilles,
Only I stumbled under the weight of that one.

The seeds of my passion, the sparks that warmed
Me, came from that same divine flame
Of which there are more than a thousand alumni.

I'm talking about the *Aeneid*, my poetic mama
And nanny, without which my work wouldn't
Weigh a dram, or equal even a closet drama.

To have lived back there, when and where
Virgil lived, I'd agree to extend
By one whole solar year my coming out of exile."

At this, Virgil turned to me with a face
That said, without saying, "Keep quiet!"
But, you can't always get the goodness you want—

Tears and smiles are tagalongs to the feelings
They go up on stage with; they're less likely
To hide the truth if the will is open and honest.

I must have given a split-second smile
Because the shade went silent and looked
Me in the eye, where sentiment can best be read,

And said, "So your hard work will come
To a good end, why did I just detect
The hint of a smile dart across your face?"

Now I'm stuck between a rock and a hard place:
One says shut up, the other begs me
To say something; so, I let out a sigh,

Which my teacher perfectly gets, and says,
"Don't worry, go ahead, address the issue
He's so preoccupied with."

So I go, "You may be wondering why,
Ghost of antiquity, I was smiling; but now
Get ready to be even more amazed.

This one, who my eyes look up to,
Is that same Virgil you used to closely pattern
Your songs of humans and gods;

If you suspect another reason for my smile,
Let it go, it's just not true. Trust me,
It's only what you just said about him."

He was already bending to touch the doctor's feet,
But he told him, "Brother, don't do that,
You're a shadow and a shadow is what you see."

Getting up, he said, "You can understand
The depth and breadth and height of the love
For you that burns in me when I delude myself as to

Our emptiness, treating shadows like solid things."

1. *The natural thirst—that is never satisfied*: This is the thirst for knowledge. In *Convivio* I, I, I, Dante writes: "Just as the Philosopher says at the beginning of *First Philosophy*, everyone naturally wants to know. The reason for this is that every single thing, driven by its primary providential nature, inclines toward its own perfection. Therefore, since learning is our soul's ultimate perfection, and that's our ultimate source of happiness, everyone naturally wants to experience it." The "Philosopher" is Aristotle; the "*First Philosophy*" is his *Metaphysics*.

2–3. *the grace / The Samaritan woman ended up asking for*: John 4:4–42 tells the story of how Jesus, having stopped at Jacob's well on his way to Galilee, asks for a drink of water from a lower-status woman from Samaria. She asks how it is that he, a Jew, asks her, a Samaritan, for water; he tells her that with water one just thirsts again but with salvation one is satisfied forever; he further says he is the Messiah come to bring salvation, at which point (15), "The woman saith unto him, Sir, give me this water, that I thirst not, neither come hither to draw."

4–5. *the obstructed / Path*: The path is obstructed because the penitents' bodies are all lying on it, facedown. Dante and Virgil, confined to the free area along the wall, have to be careful not to step on them.

7–9. *Luke writes about Christ / Appearing to two on the road when / He was just-risen from the sepulchral cave*: Luke 24:13–16: "And, behold, two of them went that same day to a village called Emmaus, which was from Jerusalem about threescore furlongs. And they talked together of all these things which had happened. And it came to pass, that, while they communed together and reasoned, Jesus himself drew near, and went with them. But their eyes were holden that they should not know him."

10. *A shade appeared*: The shade, the Roman poet Statius, won't be named until v. 91.

22–23. *If you look at the marks / The angel incised on this one*: The seven Ps the angel traced on Dante's forehead are now reduced to three. Virgil points these out as evidence that Dante has been granted permission to travel up the mountain, in spite of the fact that Virgil himself isn't worthy of Heaven.

25–27. *the one spinning . . . Hasn't yet measured the thread / That Clotho spools and files away for everyone*: In Greek myth, at the moment of birth, the Three Fates, daughters of Darkness and Night, determine how long one will live; Lachesis spins the thread, Atropos cuts it off, and Clotho wraps it around the distaff, makes a record of it, and puts it away for safekeeping.

28. *His soul, which is your and my sister*: In *Purg.* XVI, 85–86, the newborn soul is described as exiting, "Formed by the hand of Him who looks upon it / Fondly even before it exists—a little girl doll." This anticipates, by some six hundred years, Carl

Jung's notion of the anima, the female spirit within each human consciousness that exists alongside the animus, the male spirit.

30. *Since his eyes can't see what our eyes can*: Dante's vision is limited to what human eyes can see; the dead no longer have material bodies, so they sense through other means.

31. *Hell's commodious throat*: This, of course, is Limbo, which we know from *Inf.* IV. It is the widest circle of the funnel-shaped Hell and the "throat," because it leads to the lower levels. In Limbo, the inhabitants feel no pain but only sigh over the fact that, because they lived before the redemption of Christ, or died in infancy before being baptized, they will never be admitted to Heaven.

40–42. *The religious creed . . . allows nothing here / That's not preordained or that lies outside its rites*: Throughout Purgatory each penitent will have the same preordained experience; no favor will be shown to any, nor will there be unexpected events that might temporarily worsen or better conditions.

43–45. *free from any modifications. / Heaven only gets what it grants itself, / And 'no other' means no other causality*: The weather is used as an example of the unpredictability of earthly experience—the unexpected snowfall, the sudden electrical storm—versus Purgatory, where the design is unchanging and preset for uniform penitence and purification.

46–48. *Ergo, no rain . . . above / What falls on those first three short steps*: Variable weather elements do exist at the base of Mount Purgatory, which accounts for the dew Virgil used to wash the miasma from Dante's face, but they come to an abrupt halt after the three steps leading to the gate that is opened by the angel who serves as Saint Peter's stand-in.

50–51. *no Thaumas and Electra's daughter, / Whose rainbow will often change neighborhoods*: Isis, the winged daughter of Electra and Thaumas, sister to the Harpies, and goddess of rainbows, is a personified rainbow that serves as a messenger of the gods. The rainbow is seen as the connection between Heaven and earth, and it acts like a tracer for her flight between the two.

61. *Of its purity, the will alone is evidence*: There is no final exam or appearance before a tribunal that determines whether someone has achieved purification. The soul alone recognizes that it is now free of sin and fit to be welcomed into Heaven.

67–69. *I, having lain on this bed of thorns / For over five hundred years, only now . . . wanted that better threshold*: The still-unidentified soul offers himself as an example, saying his moment of recognition came only after five hundred years of suffering. Having died in 96 CE, he has been dead for some twelve hundred years—five hundred of them have been spent on this cornice; four hundred, we will learn in *Purg.* XXII, have been spent on the fourth cornice, and the rest were spent either on the three levels below that or waiting to be admitted through the gate. The awareness of wanting to cross a "better threshold" suggests the tradition of carrying a bride over the threshold, which existed in the medieval era. The penitent will now no longer be wedded to sin, or to penitential suffering, but to only God.

70. *That's why you felt the tremor*: It was this soul's success that inspired the celebratory shout that went up and down the mountain, and the shaking that was the result of the sonic vibrations.

81. *In your own words works for me*: The phrase "in your own words" has confused commentators: Does Virgil mean that if Statius speaks in Latin, Virgil, who is also Roman, will understand, or that Statius shouldn't recite theological chapter and verse, but should instead tell of his own experience? Or is this a veiled bard, suggesting Statius should use his own words instead of Virgil's?

82–84. *good Emperor Titus . . . avenged the wounds / That shed the blood that Judas bartered*: Titus, the son of Emperor Vespasian, was put charge of the "Jewish war" in 70 CE; after a siege of five months, he destroyed the Second Temple in Jerusalem. When Vespasian died in 79 CE, Titus became emperor. Suetonius, the Roman historian (*Lives of the Caesars*), referred to Titus, who was handsome, affable, and generous, as "amor et deliciae generis humani" (the darling and delight of the human race). During the eruption of Vesuvius, Titus initiated humanitarian measures. In 70, when Titus did his "avenging," Statius would have been approximately twenty-five years old.

85–86. *I made a name for myself back there, / The longest lasting, most honored*: The enduring name gestures to the fact that the speaker was a poet.

89–90. *While from Toulouse, I was drawn to Rome, / Where I was honored with a laurel crown*: Statius was not from Toulouse but from Naples. Commentators note that this was a common misconception; Boccaccio and Chaucer, who were both influenced by Statius, make the same claim. The confusion may have come from the fact that a famous rhetorician with the same last name, Lucius Statius, born ca. 58, came from Toulouse.

91–92. *Statius . . . I sang of Thebes*: Publius Papinius Statius (ca. 45–ca. 96) was the author of the *Thebaid*, a twelve-book Latin epic poem that focused on the story of the Seven against Thebes, the story of Oedipus and the struggle for power between his two sons that followed his death. The style shows the influence of Virgil. Only fragments of the original exist.

92–93. *and then of the great Achilles, / Only I stumbled under the weight of that one*: Statius's second epic, the *Achilleid*, about the Trojan War and early life of Achilles, remained unfinished at his death, with only the first and second books completed. He also published a collection of thirty-two verses called *Silvae*; the poems are divided into five books, each book introduced by a prose prologue. The fifth book may have been published posthumously. The lyrics have many Virgilian references, as well as obvious debts to Lucan, Horace, and Ovid, authors Dante admired and paid homage to in his *Commedia*.

97. *I'm talking about the* Aeneid: Virgil's poem, the *Aeneid*, a twelve-book Latin epic poem, was written between 29 and 19 BCE. Influenced by Homer's *Iliad*, it begins, "I sing of arms and the man," and covers the Trojan War and Aeneas's journey from Troy to Rome. It was unfinished at the time of Virgil's death. It remains, even today, a classic work of the Roman era.

98–99. *my work wouldn't / Weigh a dram, or equal even a closet drama*: There is punning here since *dramma*, in Italian, means a play or any other kind of drama, as well as the apothecary weight of a dram (1/16 of an ounce), a silver coin, and, figuratively, a tragedy or any dramatic situation. A closet drama is a play not meant to be performed but only read aloud by one or a few people.

130–132. *bending to touch the doctor's feet . . . Brother, don't do that, / You're a shadow and a shadow is what you see*: While Virgil and Sordello do, as fellow countrymen, cordially embrace in *Purg.* VII, 1–2, 15, that scene is not at all like this one. This scene is more like the one between Dante and Casella in *Purg.* II, 76–81, where Dante realizes that Casella's body is only an illusion. In the Dante/Casella scene, and in this scene, where Virgil stops Statius from trying to touch him, there is a declaration of the love felt on earth. When Dante asks Casella to stay and talk awhile (*Purg.* II, 88–89), Casella responds, "The way I loved you when I wore my mortal state, / . . . I love you the same released from it."

Statius declares his love for Virgil in vv. 133–136, and in *Purg.* XXII, 16–17, Virgil will reciprocate with, "no one / Has ever felt closer to someone they'd never met." In Purgatory, and in Heaven, the deep love felt by two people on earth is sublimated into a love of God; the body that was once desired is now only a shadow. There is something exquisitely painful in this scene; in pathos, it comes close to the scene in *Purg.* XXX, 49–50, when Dante looks around for Virgil and finds he has disappeared. In moments like these, we are meant to feel what it is to love and to take the measure of what it is to lose the physical aspects of the beloved.

134–135. *The depth and breadth and height of the love / For you that burns in me*: Elizabeth Barrett Browning, Sonnet 43, *Sonnets from the Portuguese*, dedicated to her husband, the poet Robert Browning: "How do I love thee? Let me count the ways / I love thee to the depth and breadth and height / My soul can reach."

135–136. *when I delude myself about // Our emptiness, treating shadows like solid things*: Vernon (2:211) points out that this is the only time Dante uses the word *dismentare*—which has its roots in the Latin verb *dementare*, "to go crazy" or "to be deluded"—for forgetting. Statius is saying, "I delude myself into thinking that a soul still has a body."

Canto XXII

We'd already left the angel behind, the angel
Who'd erased the mark on my forehead
And then led us to the steps to the sixth round.

It had quoted the beatitude about the ones
Who desire righteousness, ending its recitation
On the word "thirst," leaving us to fill in the rest.

I was lighter now than I'd been
At the other openings, no fatigue whatsoever
And easily able to keep up with the faster spirits,

When Virgil began, "Love, when turned on
By virtue, always turns on another,
Provided the flame is out in the open.

Ever since that time Juvenal
Came down to Hell and joined us in Limbo,
And made your affection for me clear,

My goodwill toward you is such that no one
Has ever felt closer to someone they'd never met,
So these stairs will seem all too brief.

But tell me—and as a friend forgive me
If overconfidence leads me to push the limits,
And just explain to me now as a friend—

How could you, filled with all the insight
You worked tirelessly to foster, find inside
Your deepest reaches a place to harbor avarice?"

At this, Statius first gave a half smile,
Then responded, "Anything you say
To me is a treasured amorous token.

In fact, an appearance will often
Create false suspicions about some matter,
While the real reason stays hidden.

I imagine your question comes because
You supposed I was greedy in my other life,
Perhaps because of the circle where I was.

You should know I wasn't greedy, instead,
I gave too much away and for that excess,
I've been punished for thousands of lunar cycles.

If I hadn't straightened myself out when I got
What *you* meant when you angrily addressed
What is essentially inherent in human nature:

'Why don't you mortals restrict
The heart's wicked hunger for gold,'
I'd still be riding Hell's grim merry-go-round.

I realized that spreading one's wings too wide
Could make the hands overspend;
I repented of that and of my other wrongs.

How many with tonsured hair will rise up,
Ignorant of the fact that with this sin 'I'm sorry'
Won't work, not in life nor at the extreme end.

And you should know that when any sin
Is essentially the opposite of another sin,
Both have their green zapped here.

In this way, I was one with those people
Lamenting greed while I was being punished
For its opposite, extravagance."

"Now when you sang about the brutal warfare
Behind Jocasta's double sorrow,"
Said the singer of the bucolic *Eclogues*,

"From what, with Clio's help, you dealt with,
I don't think you believed yet in that faith,
Without which good deeds aren't enough.

If so, what sun or handmade candles
So illuminated the darkness that afterward
You raised your sails to follow the fisherman?"

He told him, "You first sent me to Parnassus
To drink from the springs; you also first
Lit the way that brought me close to God.

You did it like a guide at night carries a light
Behind them—they don't benefit directly,
But make the ones who follow smarter—

When you said, 'The great cycle begins anew;
Justice returns, the Golden Age comes back,
A new lineage descends from Heaven.'

Through you I was a poet, through you,
A Christian; for you to better see
What I'm sketching, I'll fill in the colors.

The whole world was already far along
In terms of true believers, the seeds sown
By the messengers of the eternal kingdom

And those words of yours I just alluded to
Corresponded so closely to the view of the new
Preachers, I got in the habit of visiting them.

They came to seem so holy to me
That when Domitian began to persecute them,
Whenever they cried, my tears mixed with theirs.

For as long as I stayed in that world,
I supported them, and their upstanding ways
Made me disparage all the other sects.

Before I'd led the Greeks to the rivers of Thebes,
Poetically speaking, I got baptized,
But, out of fear, remained a hidden Christian,

Posing for a long time as a pagan; it's for this
Lack of enthusiasm that I had to loop around
The fourth circle for more than four centuries.

You then, who lifted the lid that hid from me
The good of which I've just spoken,
Since we have a lot of climbing left to do,

Tell me, if you know, where's Terence,
Cecilius, Plautus, and Varius, all from our era;
Are they damned, and if so, on which track?"

"They, plus Persius and I, and many others,"
Obliged my leader, "are with the Greek to whom
The Muses fed the most mother's milk.

On the first circle of the dead-end prison;
We often talk about Mount Parnassus, which still
Has the spring that served as our wet nurse.

Euripides is with us, and Antiphon, Simonides,
Agathon, and many other Greeks
Whose foreheads were once gem-set with laurels.

One sees some of your people there,
Antigone, Deipyle, Argia,
And Ismene, as sad as ever.

There, one sees Hypsipyle, who led some
To Langia; there, Historis, the daughter of Tiresias;
Also, Thetis, and Deidamia with her sisters."

Both poets now fell silent, closely scrutinizing
Their new surroundings, freed now
From the steep ascent and the walls.

The day's first four serving girls had been sent
Below and right now, the fifth was making
The blazing noon-hour pole ever more erect.

When from my leader, "I think it makes sense
For us to turn right at the outer edge,
Circling the mountain like we've been doing."

So, we let habit act like a green light—
And went on our way with less doubt,
Since that noble spirit had given the go-ahead.

They went in front and I, alone,
Behind them. Listening to their conversation
Gave me an idea for a poem.

The enlightening TED Talk soon broke off
When we came to a tree in the middle of the way,
With real fruit, which was sweet smelling.

Like a fir narrows as it goes up, from branch
To branch, this narrowed downward—
I imagined so no one would climb it.

From the sidewall that closed off our path,
A clear liquor fell down from the high rock
And spread over its leaves.

As the two poets approached the tree,
A voice from inside the foliage called out:
"This is the food you'll wish you had."

Then, "Mary was only about making the wedding
Feast honorable and complete, not
About her own mouth, which she now uses for you.

The ancient Romans were content
To drink water; and Daniel wanted nothing
To do with food and got smarter.

The first age was as lovely as gold:
Hungry, acorns tasted good;
Thirsty, each stream seemed like nectar

Wild honey and locusts were the edibles
That kept the Baptist fed in the desert,
For which he's glorious and every bit as great

As is clear to you who open up the Gospel."

3. *the steps to the sixth round*. Offstage, as it were, the fifth P on Dante's forehead has been erased by the angel and the group has been directed to the stairs up to the sixth round, the cornice devoted to the sin of gluttony.

4–6. *It had quoted the beatitude . . . ending . . . On the word "thirst," leaving us to fill in the rest*: The fourth beatitude is found in Matthew 5:6: "Blessed are they which do hunger and thirst after righteousness: for they shall be filled." Dante is possibly punning by saying they were left to complete or fill in (*fornire*) "for they shall be filled."

7. *I was lighter now than I'd been*: The sense of feeling lighter is consistent with Virgil's explanation in *Purg.* IV, 90, "The higher you get the less painful the effort." Having completed five of the seven cornices, Dante has been lightened considerably. Since the two spirits don't have human bodies, they are naturally faster; plus, Statius has completed his purgation and Virgil isn't weighed down by sins that must be expunged.

10–12. *When Virgil began, "Love, when turned on / By virtue, always turns on another, / Provided the flame is out in the open*: In his *Georgics* (3, 242), Virgil states, "Amor omnibvs idem." (Love is the same for all of them.)

13–15. *Juvenal / Came down to Hell and joined us in Limbo, / And made your affection for me clear*: Juvenal (Decimus Junius Juvenalis) was a Roman poet (d. ca. 140) whose collection of satirical poems, *Satires*, was composed of five books (sixteen poems in all). Statius would have been some ten to twenty years older than Juvenal; Juvenal satirically refers to Statius in his Book 3, Satire 7. It's impossible to know exactly why Dante chose Juvenal to act as the go-between who informs Virgil of Statius's affection, perhaps because of that mention.

23–24. *filled with all the insight / You worked tirelessly to foster*: All poets were assumed to be wise.

26–27. *Anything you say / To me is a treasured amorous token*: Shakespeare, *All's Well That Ends Well* (V.iii.68): King of France. "Send forth your amorous token for fair Maudlin."

34–35. *You should know I wasn't greedy . . . I gave too much away and for that excess*: In Hell and in Purgatory, avarice and prodigality are punished in the same circle; to hold too much back is viewed as sinful as giving too much away. The argument is for moderation in all things.

38–41. *when you angrily addressed / What is essentially inherent in human nature: // 'Why don't you mortals restrict / The heart's wicked hunger for gold'*: Dante uses Virgil's Latin from *Aeneid* 3, 56–57: "Quid non mortalia pectora cogis, auri sacra fames."

46–48. *How many with tonsured hair will rise up . . . at the extreme end*: Similarly, in *Inf.* VII, Virgil tells Dante that the avaricious and prodigal popes, cardinals, and others with tonsured hair, will continue to be punished for this type of sin until they rise from their graves on Judgment Day.

55–56. *the brutal warfare / Behind Jocasta's double sorrow*: In Greek myth, when King Laius of Thebes marries Jocasta, he's told that if he fathers a son, the son will kill him. In an act of uncontrolled passion, he fathers Oedipus; because of the prophecy, the child is left in a field to die of exposure. A shepherd from Corinth rescues him and raises him as his own child. As an adult, Oedipus, in a "road rage" altercation about right-of-way on a path, fulfills the prophecy by killing Laius. Without realizing that Jocasta is his mother, he marries her. The two have four children, two girls and two boys. After Oedipus's error is brought to light, he gouges out his own eyes, making literal his figurative blindness. He is subsequently exiled from the kingdom, leaving it to be ruled by his two sons, Eteocles and Polynices, with the stipulation that each is to rule in alternate years. Eteocles, however, refuses to relinquish the throne at the end of his reign and the two young men go to war, killing one another. This is Jocasta's double sorrow.

57. *the singer of the bucolic* Eclogues: The term "Eclogues" was not used by Virgil but only applied later. Virgil's collection of bucolics (ca. 43–36 BCE), pastoral poems, partly represent imitations of the *Idylls of Theocritus*, written by a Sicilian Greek poet whose work dates to around 280 BCE. Virgil weaves in elements of Roman politics.

58–59. *From what, with Clio's help, you dealt with, / I don't think you believed yet in that faith*: In *Thebaid* 1, 40, Statius invokes Clio, the Muse of history who celebrates greatness: "Which hero will you make introduce my theme, Clio?"

63. *You raised your sails to follow the fisherman*: Matthew, Mark, and Luke all tell the story of Jesus's encounter with the brothers Simon Peter and Andrew on the banks of the Galilee Sea. Jesus encouraged them to leave their nets, saying (Matthew 4:19): "Follow me, and I will make you fishers of men."

64–66. *You first sent me to Parnassus / To drink from the springs; you also first / Lit the way that brought me close to God*: The ancient Greeks considered Mount Parnassus, an actual twin-peak mountain in central Greece, with the Delphic oracle located at its base, to be the center of the world. In Greek mythology, the mountain was the home of Apollo and the Muses, and therefore associated with poetry. Statius is claiming that Virgil's writing first inspired him to become a poet and also inspired him to become a Christian.

70–73. *The great cycle begins anew; / Justice returns, the Golden Age comes back, / A new lineage descends from Heaven*: In *Eclogues* 4, 5–7, Virgil has the Cumaean Sibyl say: "Magnus ab integro saeclorum nascitur ordo. / Iam redit et Virgo, redeunt Saturnia regna; / Iam nova progenies coelo demittitur alto." Dante follows this closely but replaces Virgil's Latin *Virgo* (virgin, maiden), a reference to Astraea, the Greek goddess of justice, with *giustizia* (justice). He replaces *Saturnia regna* (the reign of Saturn) with *primo tempo umano* (the first age of man). In Roman mythology, the reign of Saturn, the "first or Golden Age" of man, is the time of plenty and of germination. Dante keeps Virgil's word *progenies* (*progenie*)—"lineage," "offspring," "descendants"—that descends from on high. To Dante, and to others before and after him, this single Virgilian mention of a future progeny from on high is read as prophesying the birth of Christ.

73–74. *Through you I was a poet, through you, / A Christian*: There is no evidence that Statius was a Christian. Commentators believe Dante is using a moment in a Statius text that echoes that moment in the *Eclogues* 4, 5–7, noted above to construct that reading.

78. *messengers of the eternal kingdom*: These messengers would have been the Apostles.

83. *when Domitian began to persecute them*: Statius dedicated the *Thebaid* to Domitian, the autocratic Roman emperor who reigned from 81 to 96 CE, when he was assassinated by Senate members whom he had marginalized. The accepted belief during Dante's time was that Domitian had persecuted Christians; that belief has been called into question since.

97–99. *where's Terence, / Cecilius, Plautus, and Varius . . . Are they damned, and if so, on which track*: Terence, a comic playwright, was born in Carthage, sold as a slave to a Roman senator who educated him, and then freed by him. Cecilius Statius, a comic playwright, poet, and translator, was also a freed slave. Plautus was a comic playwright. Varius, a comic poet and a friend of Virgil and of Horace, edited a volume of the *Aeneid* after Virgil's death.

100–102. *They, plus Persius and I, and . . . the Greek to whom / The Muses fed the most mother's milk*: Persius was a follower of Stoicism and a poet and satirist. The one the Muses favored is Homer, the ancient Greek presumed to be the author of the *Iliad* and the *Odyssey*; Dante describes him in *Inf.* IV, 88, as the *poeta sovrano* (the reigning poet).

103. *On the first circle of the dead-end prison*: This first circle is Limbo.

104–105. *Mount Parnassus, which still / Has the spring that served as our wet nurse*: The spring may be the Castilian spring on the southern slope above Delphi, whose waters Roman poets associated with poetic inspiration. It could also be the springs at Corycian Cave, which were considered sacred and associated with Pan and the Muses.

106. *Euripides . . . Antiphon, Simonides, / Agathon, and many other Greeks / Whose foreheads were once gem-set with laurels*: Euripides was a well-known and prolific Greek tragedian. Antiphon, ancient Greek poet and tragedian, was mentioned by Aristotle and praised by Plutarch; only fragments of his work survive. Simonides was a lyric poet and the inventor of the "memory palace" system of mnemonics: imagined objects linked to specific words are placed in imagined rooms; walking through the rooms and allowing the objects to cue the words associated with them is a way to enhance recall. Agathon was another Greek tragedian whose work survives only in fragments.

109–110. *One sees some of your people there, / Antigone, Deipyle, Argia*: "Your people" are characters in Statius's poems. Antigone is one of the two daughters of Oedipus and Jocasta; Deipyle and Argia are daughters of King Adrastus of Argos. These three, and the next three, appear in the *Thebaid*.

111. *Ismene, as sad as ever*: Ismene, the second daughter of Oedipus and Jocasta, would have been mourning many events: the self-blinding and exile of her father; the suicide of her mother; the murder of her two brothers, Eteocles and Polynices; the loss of the kingdom; and her sister Antigone's suicide by hanging (rather than succumbing to being buried alive by Creon).

112. *Hypsipyle who led some / To Langia*: In Book 5 of the *Thebaid*, Statius tells how Hypsipyle, when she was serving as nursemaid to the infant son of Lycurgus, king of Nemea, laid the child down in order to lead the seven Argive generals marching toward Thebes to the spring called Langia. In her absence, the child was killed by a snake.

113. *Historis, the daughter of Tiresias*: Pausanius, in his *Description of Greece* IX.11.3, gives Tiresias a second daughter, in addition to Manto, whom Dante placed with the soothsayers in Hell. When Alcmena was delivering Heracles, having been impregnated by Zeus, Hera jealously sent witches to interfere with the birth. Historis feigned the birth moment by giving a cry of joy, causing the witches to give up and leave. The delivery then proceeded. There is, however, no actual evidence that Dante ever read Pausanius, leading some commentators to believe that he either forgot that he put Manto in Hell, or that he means the named ones are below, but not necessarily in Limbo.

114. *Thetis, and Deidamia with her sisters*: See the note to *Purg.* IX, 34–38, for the story of how, during the Trojan War, Thetis dressed her son Achilles as a girl and secreted him in the court of King Lycomedes of Skyros and how, when the boy was fifteen, he fell in love with Deidamia, one of the king's seven daughters, and fathered a child with her.

118–120. *The day's first four serving girls had been sent / Below . . . the fifth was making / The blazing noon-hour pole ever more erect*: The morning hours are personified as servants to the day; the fifth-hour serving girl would have been from 10 to 11. The *temo* (pole) is the tongue of a wagon or chariot, in this case, the chariot of Helios, the sun god.

126. *that noble spirit had given the go-ahead*: Dante assumes Statius's silence means he agrees with Virgil that they should turn right. In *Inferno*, the travelers always turned left; in Purgatory, the "right way" is always to the right.

130. *enlightening TED Talk*: From the TED homepage: "TED is a nonpartisan nonprofit devoted to spreading ideas, usually in the form of short, powerful talks. TED began in 1984 as a conference where Technology, Entertainment and Design converged, and today covers almost all topics—from science to business to global issues—in more than 110 languages."

131–134. *a tree in the middle of the way, / With real fruit, which was sweet smelling . . . this narrowed downward*: Dante may have modeled the tree on the *Malus florentina* (Florentine crabapple), native to Italy. The wild tree, which can grow to be twenty six feet high, is said to be upright-spreading with a wide canopy and branches that angle upward, making the tree look like an upside-down triangle. The fruit are called pomes, which is what Dante calls the fruit of this tree.

141. *This is the food you'll wish you had*: The fruit of this tree, like that of the Tree of Knowledge in the Garden of Eden, must not be eaten. The penance for overindulging one's earthly appetites is to be tormented by the wish to consume the fruit of the tree, while having to resist doing so.

142–144. *Mary was only about making the wedding . . . not / About her own mouth, which she now uses for you*: This mention of Mary's magnanimous behavior at the marriage feast at Cana, where she thinks only of the wishes of the guests, links to the disembodied voice in *Purg.* XIII, 29, that says, "They have no wine."

145–146. *the ancient Romans were content / To drink water*: Dante's *le Romane antiche* (the ancient Romans) is universally translated as "ancient Roman women." The word "women," however, is not present in the text. The argument offered in commentaries for adding "women" is that several sources, including Thomas Aquinas (*Summa theologica*), claimed that Roman women "used not to drink wine, lest they might be led into any breach of good manners." Since there is no other evidence in this verse, or in the surrounding ones, I prefer to believe that all the ancient Romans, as Boethius wrote, and which Dante himself will imply in v. 150, when thirsty, "potum quoque lubricus amnis" (drank from a stream as it flowed by).

146–147. *Daniel wanted nothing / To do with food and got smarter*: Daniel 1:8 tells how Daniel refused to eat the king's meat or drink his wine in order not to defile himself. After ten days, Daniel (and the other three children he enlists in the refusal) are tested by the king (1:20): "And in all matters of wisdom and understanding, that the king enquired of them, he found them ten times better than all the magicians and astrologers that were in all his realm."

151–152. *Wild honey and locusts . . . kept the Baptist fed in the desert*: Matthew 3:4: "And the same John had his raiment of camel's hair, and a leathern girdle about his loins; and his meat was locusts and wild honey."

153–154. *he's glorious and every bit as great // As is clear to you who open up the Gospel*: Both Matthew (11:11) and Luke (7:28) praise John the Baptist.

CANTO XXIII

While my eyes were glued to the green foliage,
Like one who wastes a lifetime
Of shoe leather chasing little birdies,

The one who was more than a father to me said,
"Okay kiddo, come on, we have to be savvy
Now about how to divvy up the allotted time."

I turned my head, and quickened my steps
Behind the wise ones, who spoke so well
I felt I lost nothing by going along with them.

And then, Hello! we heard chanting
Infused with tears . . . "Lord, open thou my" . . .
The effect was equal parts pleasure and grief.

I'd begun, "O dear father, what I'm hearing is—"
When he broke in with, "Possibly souls
Working to undo the knots in the ties that bind."

Just then, the way pilgrims deep in thought
Turn without stopping to sneak a peek
At those on the path they don't know—

From behind and moving more quickly,
The crowd of pious troubled spirits paying dearly
Came even, then passed, looking amazed.

Each had eyes like bottomless pits.
Their faces were ashen and so gaunt
The bones told on what the skin was up to.

I doubt that Erysichthon, whittled down
To nothing but skin and fearing the worst,
Was more dried out from starving.

I said to myself, yes, just like the people
Who lost Jerusalem
When Maria took a bite out of her baby boy

Their eye sockets were like rings, the precious
Stones now lost; those who saw HUMAN
On their faces would have easily made out the M.

Who would have thought that the fragrance
Of little pomes mixed with a water
Would produce, who knows how, such cravings?

I was wondering if they were starving or whether
There was another cause that I wasn't yet
Aware of for their emaciation and sad scaling skin

When a shade turned and looked directly
At me with his hollowed eyes, then shouted
Loudly, "What'd I do to be granted *this*?"

I would never have recognized his features;
It was the voice that brought home
How badly his looks had been ravaged.

That spark revived my sense of what lay behind
That changed appearance and, just like that,
I recognized the face of Forese.

"Oh, don't be put off by the scabs
Making my skin look all blotchy," he begged,
"Or that I have next to no meat on my bones,

Just tell me your news; tell me,
Who are those two souls acting as escorts?
Don't just stand there and not tell me *everything*."

"Your body, which I cried over when you died,"
I said, "is causing me no less pain now;
I want to cry again seeing you so bent out of shape.

For God's sake, tell me how you became
A flaky pastry. I'm too shocked to speak, plus
Someone with a craving may say the wrong thing."

He told me, "Virtue falls from the Eternal Council
Into the water, then onto the tree behind us,
And that makes me keep getting slimmer.

All these crying people are singing
As a way to sanctify their hunger and thirst,
After their previous unrestrained gorging.

The pomes' fragrance is added to the sprinkler
Spritzing the greenery. That acts like an aperitif,
Switching on our wish to eat and drink.

The sprinkler doesn't make just one turn,
It keeps sweeping so each time we pass, it refreshes
Our pain—did I say pain, I meant solace.

The same will that keeps leading us by the trees
Led no less than Christ to gladly say, 'My God,'
When he freed us with his blood."

I said to him, "Forese, it's been less than
Five years since that day
You traded in the world for a better life.

If your willingness to go on sinning only ended
Just before the hour of the blessed sorrow
That reweds us to God,

How can it be that you're already here?
I would have expected to find you down below,
Where taking time is repaid by doing time."

He said, "Yes, what led me to so quickly drink
The sweet absinthe of the martyrdom
Is my Nella, with her deluge of bitter tears.

With her pious prayers and sighs, she negotiated
How long I had on the slope where one waits,
And freed me completely of the other rounds.

She is one of God's dearest and most delightful,
That little widow of mine, whom I loved so much;
She's doing such good work, and all by herself!

Because even the females in the Barbagia
Of Sardinia have more discretion
Than those in the Barbagia where I left her.

O sweet brother of mine, what can I say?
Time-future is already visible in front of me,
When this hour won't be all that ancient,

Then there will be sanctions from the pulpit
For saucy Florentine women who go around
Showing their breasts as if they were briskets.

Which barbarians, which Saracens,
Ever needed spiritual, or some other discipline,
To be made to cover themselves up.

But if the shameless hussies knew the scheme
Being readied in that lightning-like heaven,
They'd have their mouths open, ready to scream,

Because, if the foresight here doesn't deceive,
They'll be sorry before there's a hint of hair
On the cheeks of those being sung lullabies.

Okay, brother, stop hiding things from me!
You can see it's not only me, but all these people
Who're staring at where you're hiding the sun."

I said to him, "If you recall what you were
With me, and what I was with you,
That memory will still be troublesome.

The one up ahead, he turned me from that life
Some days ago, when the sister of that," I pointed
To the still visible sun, "was completely round.

He's led me through the darkest night,
Through the land of the truly dead;
I followed him, dressed in my real flesh,

I've reached this level with his support,
Climbing and circling the mountain
That straightens what the world made crooked.

He promised we'd remain partners
Until I get to where Beatrice is;
I'll have to stay there without him.

Virgil's the one who says this," I pointed
To him. "The other's the shade for whom,
Just now, on every slope the kingdom shook

As if it were sending him off all by itself."

NOTES TO CANTO XXIII

2–3. *one who wastes a lifetime . . . chasing little birdies*: Commentators point out that bird hunting was an aristocratic pastime during the Middle Ages. Additionally, since 1200, birds and especially young birds were also used to refer to girls, women of noble birth, ladies, and even to the Virgin Mary. This appears to be a moment of sly humor.

6. *about how to divvy up the allotted time*: Just as Virgil and Dante had limited time in Hell, so here, the two have to complete the journey in a predetermined amount of time.

11. *Lord, open thou my*: Psalm 51:15: "O Lord, open thou my lips; and my mouth shall shew forth thy praise." Dante assumes his readers will recognize the beginning of the psalm and fill in the rest on their own. This verse is a continuation of the "Miserere" sung by the penitents in Ante-Purgatory in *Purg.* V, 24.

13–15. *dear father, what I'm hearing is . . . Possibly souls / Working to undo the knots in the ties that bind*: These knots are the penitents' attachments to earth and to the sinful desires that resulted in their current situation, where they have to pay down the accumulated debt of their overindulging.

21. *Came even, then passed, looking amazed*: As in the other circles, the penitents are amazed because they can see that Dante's living body is blocking the sun.

25–27. *I doubt that Erysichthon, whittled down . . . Was more dried out from starving*: Ovid (*Metamorphoses* 8.740–880) tells the story of how Erysichthon, son of the king of Thessaly, chopped down a giant oak tree that embodied a nymph in Cerces's sacred grove; as punishment Cerces called on Famine to infuse him with unappeasable hunger. He sold his shape-shifting daughter Mestra several times but still could not get enough food. Finally, he began to eat his own flesh and died.

28–30. *like the people / Who lost Jerusalem / When Maria took a bite out of her baby boy*: This secondhand story, included in Flavius Josephus's *De bello judaico* (*The Jewish War*) (6, 201–213), maintains that during Titus's siege of Jerusalem a noblewoman named Maria, mad with hunger, despair, and anger, rather than leave her infant son to be killed by the Roman occupiers, strangled him, took a bite out of him, and then offered his body to the horrified soldiers who'd come looking for food. For "bite," Dante uses a word that also means a bird's beak, continuing the extended bird metaphor set up in the first tercet.

31–32. *Their eye sockets were like rings, the precious / Stones now lost*: Shakespeare, *King Lear* (V.iii.187–189): EDGAR. "Met I my father with his bleeding rings, / Their precious stones new lost; became his guide, / Led him, begged for him, saved him from despair."

32–33. *those who saw HUMAN . . . would have easily made out the M*: Dante uses the Latin *OMO* (meaning man, human, or mankind). The M would be easily recognizable because with the rest of the face sunken, the beak-like nose would be prominently centered between the cheeks in a manner that would suggest the letter M, especially as that letter was handwritten with curved sides during the medieval era: **m**. The arches at the top of the rounded emme suggest the arched eyebrows; the Os on either side of the M in OMO can be seen as ears, or they can be imagined as the eyes removed from their emptied sockets.

35. *little pomes mixed with a water*: Job 14:9: "Yet through the scent of water it will bud, and bring forth boughs like a plant."

48. *I recognized the face of Forese*: Forese Donati, nicknamed Bicci Novello by his intimates, was a Florentine nobleman and poet friend of Dante's. The two lived together for a while and, between ca. 1293 and 1296, they exchanged at least six sonnets (three apiece) seeped in teasing sarcasm. One of Dante's sonnets was about Forese's wife and the coldness she experiences—she's even frozen in mid-August—which can't be addressed by simply pulling up the covers because they're too "short"; the problem, the poet says, clearly comes "per difetto che ella feels al nido" (from the shortcomings she's felt in the nest)—another bird reference. Forese's brother, Corso Donati, was the leader of the Florentine Black Guelphs and one of those responsible for Dante's banishment. Dante places a sister, Piccarda, in *Paradiso* III. Dante's wife, Gemma Donati—who is never mentioned in the *Commedia*, unless she is the missing *gemme* (gemstones) in vv. 31–32—was related to this family.

61–63. *Virtue falls from the Eternal Council . . . then onto the tree . . . And that makes me keep getting slimmer*: The *etterno consiglio* (eternal council) is God plus his intimate circle in Heaven.

73–75. *The same will that . . . Led no less than Christ to gladly say, 'My God' . . . with his blood*: Matthew 27:46: "And about the ninth hour Jesus cried with a loud voice, saying, Eli, Eli, lama sabachthani? that is to say, My God, my God, why hast thou forsaken me?" In the Vulgate Bible, the "Eli, Eli, lamma sabachthani," the last words of Christ on the cross, are in the original Aramaic.

76–82. *less than / Five years since that day . . . How can it be that you're already here*: Forese Donati died on July 28, 1296; since the poem is set in 1300, it has actually been less than four years since he died.

87–90. *my Nella, with her deluge of bitter tears . . . freed me completely of the other rounds*: There is no archival record of Forese's wife. Nella is possibly a familiar form of Giovanella. Forese refers to her as "La Nella"; Vernon (2:276) points out that attaching the definite article "La" to a woman's name was a Florentine custom, especially among the lower classes. The fact is, however, that Forese's family was upper class.

92–93. *That little widow of mine, whom I loved so much . . . and all by herself*: Commentators treat Forese's comments about his wife as dead earnest; however, if one keeps in mind the insult humor at the heart of the sonnets the two poets exchanged when Forese was alive, it's possible to view this exchange as a humorous homage to his friend. Asking Forese (vv. 58–60) how he became a puff pastry (*sfoglia*), followed by "someone with a craving may say the wrong thing," invites us to read that moment and those that follow, including Forese's tirade about the Florentine women who go around with their breasts out like briskets, as the type of mannered humor that underlies camp!

94–96. *the females in the Barbagia / Of Sardinia have more discretion / Than those in the Barbagia where I left her*: The mountainous Barbagia district of Sardinia, an island in the Mediterranean off the coast of central Italy, was occupied by "unbelievers" (Vandals and Byzantines). The women there were said to wear dresses with plunging necklines in the summer due to the extreme heat. Forese is saying that Florence is a type of Barbagia, where all the women, except for his beloved Nella, lack discretion in their dress.

100–102. *Then there will be sanctions from the pulpit / For saucy Florentine women who go around / Showing their breasts as if they were briskets*: The comic wordplay of saucy/brazen women who advertise their (edible) breasts is embedded in the alliterative phrase *le poppe il petto*. Both words can mean "breasts," but there is a strong echo in *petto* of *punta di petto*, literally "breast meat" or beef brisket. *Pappa di ciccia* is an idiom (roughly, food and fat) for chumminess, or those who are as thick as thieves. *Pappa* (mush, porridge, baby food) additionally means pimp. It's clear that Dante is having fun by slyly putting words in the mouth of Forese, words that possibly suggest what the gluttonous Forese may have liked to put in his mouth when he was alive, especially since, like Queen Gertrude in Shakespeare's *Hamlet*, Forese "doth protest too much" about these women with lax morals. All of this must be read against Dante's poem (see note to v. 48) about Forese's pious wife freezing from a "lack" in bed.

103. *Which barbarians, which Saracens, / Ever needed spiritual, or some other discipline, / To be made to cover themselves up*: In the early medieval era, Saracens referred to Arab Muslims. In time, it came to mean any nonbaptized person, excluding those who were Jewish. Singleton (2:555) quotes Villani (9, 245) as saying that in Florence, arbitrators were established in April 1234 to issue directives on the excessive trimmings on women's clothes and that in 1300 (10, 150), women "could not wear a coronet or a garland of gold, silver, pearls, jewels, or silk, nor anything even resembling a coronet or garland, even of colored paper; nor could they wear nets or braids of any sort, unless they were very simple . . . nor could they wear more than two rings on their fingers, or any kind of belt or girdle that had more than twelve silver links."

108. *They'd have their mouths open, ready to scream*: The extended metaphor of the open mouth/hungry bird continues. Here the open mouth of gluttony is turned on its head,

so to speak, by having it screaming, like the greedy, childish penitents around the tree, begging for fruit that isn't theirs to have.

109–111. *if the foresight here doesn't deceive . . . sorry before there's a hint of hair / On the cheeks of those being sung lullabies*: The mouth here is singing the infant to sleep. Those dulcet sounds, Forese says, will later become screams. All of these comments are bound up in Forese's prophecy ("if the foresight here doesn't deceive"), which may concern the destruction of Florence. That will occur in November 1301, when Charles of Valois, supported by Boniface VIII, enters the city and installs the Black Guelphs as overseers (the prelude to Dante's exile in 1302). There is no indication, however, about how this political prophecy relates to the indecency of the women of Florence—unless he is crudely suggesting that what the women are wearing will lead to their being sexually assaulted, a sexist fallacy that still exists in the contemporary era.

115–117. *I said to him, "If you recall what you were / With me, and what I was with you, / That memory will still be troublesome*: The inherent suggestion is that the relationship was more than merely a friendship; it may have been a homosexual relationship—which fits with Dante's agitated state at the beginning of *Inferno*, when he comes to in a dark forest and finds the "right path" has been lost. Most commentators read the tercet that way. A series of sonnets called the *Tenzone*, believed to have been exchanged between Dante and Forese, explicitly allude to homosexual sex.

119–120. *when the sister of that," I pointed / To the still-visible sun, "was completely round*: In Greek myth, Selene, the goddess of the moon, is the sister of Helios, the god of the sun. They each have a chariot they drive across the sky.

132–133. *Just now, on every slope the kingdom shook // As if it were sending him off all by itself*: The wordplay here rests on agency—Dante says it is as if the mountain, by vibrating, shook Statius free of itself, as opposed to Statius freeing himself of the mountain through the exculpatory work he did there.

CANTO XXIV

Talking didn't set our pace, nor did our pace
Slow that down, we just chatted as we went
At a clip, like a ship driven by a strong wind.

The shades, looking like death warmed over,
Aware I was alive, were drawn to me, staring
In wonder through the hollows of their eyes.

And I, continuing where I'd left off, said,
"He might be going up later than he would have,
For the sake of the other one.

But can you tell me where Piccarda is, if you know;
And same, whether I'm seeing anyone notable
In this group that's so interested in me?"

"My sister, who between beauty and goodness,
I don't know which she had more of, triumphs
Up on Olympus, delighted to have her reward."

He first said that, then, "There's no ban here
On going by our given names, since our looks
Have been sucked dry by the abstinence diet.

This," he pointed with his finger, "is Bonagiunta,
Bonagiunta from Lucca; and that one,
Whose face is more lined than a wrinkled quilt,

From Tours, he held the Holy Church in his arms;
He wastes away refusing the Lake Bolsena eels
And the white wine he once washed them down with."

He named many others for me, one by one,
And they all seemed fine with the naming,
Not one gave us a look like "bugger off."

I saw Ubaldino dalla Pila, and Archbishop Boniface,
Who'd shepherded so many with his rooky crook,
Both grinding a pasture of air between their teeth.

I saw Lord Marchese, who had plenty of leisure time
For a cocktail at Forlì, even when his throat
Wasn't that dry, and yet oddly never felt satisfied.

Even so, the way you look around and prize one
More than others, for me, it was one from Lucca,
Who acted like he might know me.

He was mumbling, and I could only make out
"Riffraff-scum" coming from over there, where
He was feeling raw from justice nibbling at him.

"Soul," I said, "you seem to want to talk to me
But you're rambling. If you could stay on topic,
You and I might both get your drift."

"There's a woman from there," he said, "not yet
Wearing a veil who'll make you adore my city,
However much others love to dis it.

You'll leave here with this prediction:
If you misconstrue my mutterings,
Actual events will make things clear.

But tell me, do I see before me the one
Who brought out the new verse that begins,
'You women who have the intellect of love'?"

I answered him, "I am that one for whom,
Notably, when love inspires me,
I go deep inside and make meaning signify."

"O brother, I can now see," he said, "the knot
That held Notaro, Guittone, and me back
From what I can hear in the sweet new style.

I also see very well how your pen strokes
Track more closely the inner dictator,
Which certainly didn't happen with ours,

Beyond putting in more of whatever you like,
One style looks much like the other."
Then, as if satisfied with that, he fell silent.

Like migrant birds wintering along the Nile
Will sometimes mass in the air,
Then, in a sudden rush, settle into a single line,

So the people there, light as birds
In their leanness and longing, were turning
Their faces, then quickening their pace,

While Forese—like a man exhausted by his run
Who then lets the group go on ahead
And walks until his chest stops heaving—

Had let that holy flock pass
And, coming along with me behind them,
Said, "When will I see you again?"

"I don't know," I said, "how long I'll live,
But my return won't be so soon
That I won't already wish I were at the shore.

The place where I was set to live
Is day by day being picked clean of its worth;
Sadly, the site seems to be tipping toward ruin."

"So it goes," he said. "I see the one most at fault
Being dragged by the tail of a beast
Toward the Valley of No Absolution.

With each step the beast speeds up, more
And more; it keeps thrashing him about until
Finally his flesh is hideously stripped off.

It doesn't take much to turn those screws—"
He looked to the heavens, "Something I can't say
More about will become crystal clear.

You stay where you are; time's so precious
In this realm that I'm losing too much
By going with you side by side like this."

Sometimes a knight on the tournament team
Comes galloping out, and straightaway
Achieves honors at the first encounter.

Likewise, he hotfooted it off to overcome obstacles
While I stayed on the path with those two
Who were such worldly grand marshals.

And when he'd moved so far ahead
That my eyes had to strain to make him out,
The way my mind was doing with his words,

Rounding the bend, I found in front of me,
And not that far off, what looked like another
Living tree, the boughs heavy with pomes.

Under it, I saw people shouting, I couldn't
Make out what, and raising their hands toward
The leaves, like greedy, grabby little kids

Begging in vain, their prayers unanswered.
To make their desire clear, they hold nothing back
But keep screaming for what they want.

Then they left, as if they'd changed their minds,
And we now stepped up to the huge tree
That refuses to address all that tearful pleading.

"No closer, keep moving: there's a tree higher up
From which Eve pinched a piece of fruit;
This plant was raised from that seed."

So said an unrecognizable voice from the branches,
Which caused me, Virgil, and Statius
To shrink over to the side where the cliff rises.

"Remember," it said, "the damned, cloud-born
Centaurs Theseus tussled with when
Their binary chests were puffed up with wine.

And the Hebrews who got soaked guzzling water
So Gideon didn't want them as comrades
When he went down the hill to Midian."

So, we passed by, hugging the inside track
Between the two edges, listening to how the guilt
Of gluttony was now paying its dismal dividends.

Then we spread out across the open road,
Some thousand steps on, each a step forward,
Each of us silent, deep in our thoughts,

"What are you thinking, you three all alone?"
A sudden voice startled me.
Like a frightened, downcast Eeyore,

My head snapped back to see who it was;
Never before, not even in a forge, has anyone
Seen red glass or brass as bright

As the one I saw, which then said, "If you wish
To go up, you need to make the turn here—
Whoever seeks peace goes this way."

Since its appearance had left me totally blinded,
I moved over behind my caretakers and went on
Like someone led only by what they can hear.

The way the May breeze, the deejay of dawn,
Moves its milky fragrance,
Gravid with grass and flowers, through the air,

Like that, I felt a current of air on only half
Of my forehead; sensing the drift
Of downy feathers, I inhaled a hint of ambrosia

I heard, "Blessed are they so lit by Grace
That their love of taste doesn't light their hearts
On fire but makes them, like Goldilocks,

Forever hungry for whatever is just right."

8–9. *He might be going up later than he would have, / For the sake of the other one*: Statius might be slowing his going up in order to walk alongside Virgil, just like Forese is slowing his penitential circling to walk at Dante's side.

10. *can you tell me where Piccarda is, if you know*: Piccarda, Forese's sister, as we'll learn in vv. 13–15, is in Heaven, the Christian equivalent of Mount Olympus of Greek myth. Dante will encounter her in *Paradiso* (III.34–123), where she will explain that she's on the lowest level, reserved for those who broke their religious vows.

13–15. *My sister . . . triumphs / Up on Olympus, delighted to have her reward*: After having entered a convent, Piccarda was forced by her brother Corso Donati to leave in order to marry an influential Florentine. She died shortly after the marriage. Heaven, Forese is saying, is her just reward for the piousness she wanted to devote her life to.

16–18. *There's no ban here / On going by our given names, since our looks / Have been sucked dry*: Since these penitents are so emaciated and desiccated, there would be no way to recognize them except by their earthly names.

20. *Bonagiunta from Lucca*: Bonagiunta was a Tuscan poet and an acquaintance of Dante's. In his essay *De vulgari eloquentia* (On eloquence in the vernacular), Dante criticized his poems as being overly indebted to his local dialect instead of using the more widely shared vernacular. Benvenuto writes about him, "He was the greatest master of gluttony . . . a splendid orator in his mother tongue, with much facility in the matter of rhymes, but of greater facility in that of wines." Benvenuto quoted in Vernon (2:293).

22–24. *From Tours, he held the Holy Church in his arms; / He wastes away refusing the Lake Bolsena eels / And the white wine*: Jacopo della Lana, an early Dante commentator, wrote in 1324 about this gourmet pope, Martin IV: "He was most depraved by gluttony and other food-inspired greed, to the point that he had eels brought from Lake Bolsena which he put to drown in Vernaccia wine, then had then roasted and ate. So fond was he of this morsel that he kept wanting them brought up to drown in his room." Pope Martin was said to have died of indigestion in Perugia on March 28, 1285.

28–29. *I saw Ubaldino dalla Pila and Archbishop Boniface, / Who'd shepherded so many with his rooky crook*: Ubaldino of La Pila, a castle located in the alpine region north of Florence, was a member of a powerful aristocratic Ghibelline family, two members of which Dante placed in Hell—his brother, Cardinal Ottaviano degli Ubaldini (*Inf.* X), and his father, Archbishop Ruggieri degli Ubaldini of Pisa (*Inf.* XXXIII). Ugolin d'Azzo (*Purg.* XIV, 105) was his nephew. Boniface, of the Fieschi family of Genoa, was the archbishop of Ravenna from 1274 to 1294, during which time he accrued tremendous wealth that he used to reward his relatives and friends and amass decorative collections (plate and embroidery). His staff was topped with a chess rook.

30. *Both grinding a pasture of air between their teeth*: Singleton (2:565) notes the double meaning of pasture in this verse; one, as the place where the archbishop should have been spiritually feeding his Christian flock; and two, the flock of courtiers in his inner circle with which he shared elaborate meals. Dante may have been inspired by Ovid's description of Erysichthon's hunger in *Metamorphoses* (8.824–857):

The jawed mouth moving, going through the motions,
Wearily grinding tooth against tooth,
Exercising the throat through deluded swallowing
A banquet of empty air

31–33. *I saw Lord Marchese, who had plenty of leisure time / For a cocktail at Forlì . . . and yet oddly never felt satisfied*: Marchese, of the Argogliosi family of Forlì, was a podestà. Sources claim that when he questioned a servant about what the people said about him, the servant answered that they said he did nothing but drink; to which he responded, why don't they simply say I'm always thirsty?

37–38. *I could only make out / "Riffraff-scum"*: Dante uses the word *gentucca*, similar to *gentuccia*, common people or lowlifes. Early commentators read it that way; later commentators, however, read this as a proper name, possibly the name of the young woman from Lucca mentioned in vv. 43–45. There is historical evidence of two women living in Lucca around the time that Dante might have lived there in exile (1308), both married, so any relationship would have been platonic. In 1300, when the poem is set, one or both of the women may have been unmarried, and thus not yet wearing a veil. I've chosen to translate it as the early commentators.

43–45. *a woman . . . not yet / Wearing a veil who'll make you adore my city / However much others love to dis it*: The *benda* (veil) was a headdress worn by married aristocratic women. It only later came to be the word used for a nun's wimple.

46–48. *this prediction . . . Actual events will make things clear*: The actual matters that will in time make things clear are the events leading up to and including Dante's exile from Florence. His exile is why he goes to Lucca and accepts the hospitality of those who live there.

50–51. *verse that begins, / 'You women who have the intellect of love'*: *Vita nuova*, XIX, begins with an apostrophe to "Donne che avete intelletto d'amore" (You women who have the intellect of love) and continues "i' vo' con voi de la mia donna dire." (I would speak with you of my woman.)

54. *I go deep inside and make meaning signify*: In *Vita nuova*, the above canzone follows a prose section in which Dante talks about looking for a new style that would allow him to speak about his feelings; he says he decided to use the second-person pronoun "you" as a way to establish more intimacy than possible when writing in the third person.

55–56. *the knot / That held Notaro, Guittone, and me back*: Jacopo (or Giacomo) da Lentino (*il Notaro*), a poet of the Sicilian school and a notary at the court of the Holy Roman Emperor Frederick II, is credited with inventing the fourteen-line sonnet. Dante praises one of his poems (without attribution) for its elegance in *De vulgari eloquentia* 1.12.8. Fra Guittone d'Arezzo (d. 1294) was a Tuscan poet who is said to have rediscovered the sonnet and adapted it to the Tuscan language; in the late 1260s, although married with children, he entered the Order of the Frati Gaudenti. Dante will mention him again in *Purg.* XXVI, 124–126, saying that he was unquestionably admired past the time he should have been.

57–60. *the sweet new style . . . your pen strokes / Track more closely the inner dictator, / Which certainly didn't happen with ours*: In time, the style in which Dante and his Tuscan contemporaries composed verse was referred to as the *Dolci stil novo* (Sweet new style). This mention is the first known use of the phrase. Poems written in the new style are more introspective, and, like those of the troubadour poets, they use the trope of the courtly woman as both inspiration and signifier. Since many of the women at the center of the poems are married, or, as in the case of Dante's Beatrice, deceased, they emphasize love as selflessness. Like the troubadours, these poets often exploit the ambiguity of language to talk sotto voce about things that might be hidden, in the realms of love and politics.

61–63. *putting in more of whatever you like, / One style looks much like the other," / . . . satisfied with that*: Bonagiunta's defensive position is to say that the so-called new isn't all that new; the poet is just more indulgent in terms of what he or she includes compared to poets who adhere more closely to received conventions.

79–81. *where I was set to live . . . seems to be tipping toward ruin*: Dante had, of course, been set to live in Florence for his entire lifetime. After the Guelph victory over the Ghibellines at the Battle of Campaldino in 1289, the Guelph party began to fracture into the Bianchi (Whites), who opposed Pope Boniface VIII, and the pro-papacy Neri (Blacks).

82–84. *the one most at fault / Being dragged by the tail of a beast / Toward the Valley of No Absolution*: The one Forese considers most to blame is his brother Corso Donati, the head of the Black Guelph party. The story of Corso's death differs among sources. In 1301, the White party, including Dante, in order to quell the internecine fighting, banished the leadership of both parties. Corso went to Rome and appealed to Boniface VIII to send Charles of Valois to Florence. Charles entered the city on November 1, 1301, and Corso and the Neri followed soon afterward. For five days and nights, they attacked the homes of the Bianchi. Charles withdrew, leaving the Neri in charge. Corso's arrogance, however, caused him to be eventually called before the courts and condemned to death. In 1308, he was placed under house arrest, escaped, captured, and died while being brought back to Florence. He either intentionally threw himself from his horse and was stabbed by one of those entrusted with returning him, or slipped from the horse with one foot caught in a stirrup and was dragged.

88–89. *It doesn't take much to turn those screws—" / He looked to the heavens*: The word Dante uses (*ruote*) means wheels, which gestures to the rotation of the celestial spheres, but the word can also imply the medieval torture device called the rack: wheels, at either end of a frame on which a victim was tied down, were turned to stretch the victim to the point of dislocating their joints. In this moment, Forese is suggesting the divine retribution in store for his brother Corso, but also the torture he'll suffer in Hell.

104–105. *what looked like another / Living tree, the boughs heavy with pomes*: This tree, as with the previous one, is living and producing fruit. Not since Ante-Purgatory has there been anything living. We can presume this tree is likewise watered by liquid coming from the cliff face.

106–109. *people shouting . . . and raising their hands toward / The leaves, like greedy, grabby little kids // Begging in vain, their prayers unanswered*: The gluttonous are like children who have not yet learned to control their desires. Singleton (2:582) quotes Seneca's similar description of the punishment of Tantalus (*Thyestes*, vv. 162–168): "But then the whole grove lets its riches down nearer still, and the mellow fruits above his head mock him with drooping boughs and whet again the hunger, which bids him ply his hands in vain. When he has stretched these forth and gladly has been baffled, the whole ripe harvest of the bending woods is snatched far out of reach."

115–117. *a tree higher up / From which Eve pinched a piece of fruit; / This plant was raised from that seed*: The original tree, from which Eve stole the metaphoric apple, is in Heaven. This purgatorial tree, and presumably the tree encountered earlier, is an offshoot, identical in that its highly desirable fruit is forbidden.

121–123. *the damned, cloud-born / Centaurs Theseus tussled with when / Their binary chests were puffed up with wine*: In Greek myth, half-man, half-horse centaurs (thus having binary chests), were the offspring of the Ixion king of the Lapiths in Thessaly and a Hera-shaped cloud, which Zeus substituted for his consort. Ovid (*Metamorphoses* 12.210–212, 215–225) tells the story of the centaur Eurytus, drunk on wine, leading the centaurs to abduct the bride and her bridesmaids at the wedding of Pirithous and Hippodamia. Theseus and other Lapiths overcame the centaurs and saved the women.

124–126. *the Hebrews who got soaked guzzling water / So Gideon didn't want them as comrades . . . down the hill to Midian*: Judges 7:2–8 relates how the Lord instructed Gideon to cull the troops he would take with him to fight the Midianites by observing who cupped their hands to drink water from the river and who greedily got down on their knees and lapped water directly from the river.

133. *What are you thinking, you three all alone*: The speaker appears to notice the group of three because they are not part of a larger group of penitents.

135. *a frightened, downcast Eeyore*: Eeyore, an "old grey donkey," is a stuffed-animal character in the two *Winnie-the-Pooh* books written by A. A. Milne (1926, 1928). In the books, he lives in a part of the Hundred Acre Wood that is marked on the map as "Eeyore's Gloomy Place: Rather Boggy and Sad."

138–141. *red glass or brass as bright // As the one I saw . . . "If you wish / To go up, you need to make the turn here— / Whoever seeks peace goes this way*: As with the other angels, the radiance of this one is too much for Dante's human eyes. The way of peace, toward which Dante must turn if he wishes to continue to gain Heaven, is the path of moderation. The immoderate can never be at peace but will always be troubled by unsatisfied desire.

148–150. *I felt a current of air . . . I inhaled a hint of ambrosia*: The angel is erasing another P from Dante's forehead. In Homer's *Odyssey*, ambrosia is something eaten by the gods and goddesses; in Virgil, it appears to be a perfumed balm used to anoint the body.

151–153. *Blessed are they so lit by Grace / That their love of taste doesn't light their hearts / On fire*: Matthew 5:6: "Blessed are they which do hunger and thirst after righteousness: for they shall be filled." In the beatitude that introduces *Purg.* XXII, we were told the listeners were left to fill in what followed the word "thirst"; here, hunger is made explicit in v. 154.

153–154. *like Goldilocks, // Forever hungry for what is just right*: "The Story of the Three Bears," written by Robert Southey (poet laureate of England 1813–1843), is known today as "Goldilocks and the Three Bears." The story originally featured an old woman who visits the home of three bachelor bears, one large, one medium, and one small; she tries out the beds, chairs, and bowls of porridge. In every case, the smaller bear's objects are the ones that feel "just right." In 1849, with Southey's permission, Joseph Cundall changed the old woman to a young girl when he included the story in his *Treasury of Pleasure Books for Young Children*. Over successive publications by other writers, the girl's hair changed from silver to gold, and the bears became a family consisting of Papa Bear, Mama Bear, and Baby Bear. Throughout, the protagonist prefers those things belonging to the smallest bear. The idea of finding a best solution through trial and error is now referred to as the "Goldilocks principle."

Canto XXV

At this hour, the going up didn't want any
Slowing down: the sun had given the meridian
To Taurus, and night had left it to Scorpio,

Which is why—like someone who doesn't
Get stuck where they are but goes on their way,
No matter what, whenever need acts as a catalyst—

We entered a fissure in the rock face,
One in front of the other, taking a staircase
So tight it uncouples the climbers.

Like the little storklet that wants to fly,
So raises its wing, then gives up
Trying to leave the nest and lets it drop,

My need to ask was similarly an on-again
Off-again effort, my mouth going so far
As to form an O, as if it were about to speak.

We were going rather fast, but even so, my kind
Father figure said, "You've drawn the arrow
Back to the breastplate, go ahead, shoot."

Then, of course, I did open my mouth
And began, "How can this be, getting skinny
In a place where you never feel the need to eat?"

"If you remember how Meleager fizzled out
In the burning up of the sizzling ember," he said,
"It may not seem such a bitter pill to swallow.

And if you consider how when you rush by,
Your image in a mirror also rushes by,
What now seems hard would be a piece of cake.

But, so that you can put to rest what's
Eating at you, here's Statius. I'm asking him nicely
To apply his expert balm to your sore spot."

"If I build the case of the eternal viewpoint,"
Statius said to him, "while you're right here,
Let it be because I can't say no to you."

He began, "If you can get your head around this,
Son, and closely examine the words I use,
That will answer your, 'How can this be?'

Perfect blood, which the greedy veins
Can't get directly, keeps its potential, a bit like
Food brought to the table that goes uneaten;

An instructive power acquired in the heart
Is taken through the veins to all the human limbs
And that's what directs the limbs to be themselves.

More dissolved, it descends to a place,
Better left unmentioned, where it covers
The blood of another in nature's ready vessel.

That's where the one and the other get together,
The one willing to suffer, the other to serve,
Given the perfect place in which they were made.

The two joined together now begin to work,
First through thickening, then by quickening
The substrate the matter is made to consist of.

The active virtue, having been made a soul—
Like a plant but different in that this one is still
Making its way, the other has already landed—

Is in a position to work; it already moves
And feels, much like a sea sponge, but then
It must learn to organize the intel that's in the seed.

Now that, son, explains how virtue extends
Directly from the heart of the generator
To all the members, exactly as nature intended.

But how the animal becomes the immortal
Diamond Jack or Jill, you don't see that yet; this
Is where someone wiser than you once got lost

By theorizing that, since there was no single
Organ recruited for its use, the intellect
Had to be disjoined from the idea of the soul.

Be open to the truth inside your heart:
As soon as the unborn can articulate
What's in its brain, it's been perfected;

The Prime Mover turns to it, delighted
That there is so much artistry in nature, and
Breathes into it a new spirit, replete with power,

Which, activated, draws on what nourishes
And sustains it—and that makes the soul a self,
A living feeling self that can examine itself.

If you're not awed yet by what I'm saying,
Look at the way the sun's heat causes a wine
To manifest the particular essence of a vine.

When Lachesis runs out of thread, the flesh
Is dissolved of itself; the essence that's left
Carries with it both the human and the divine.

The other faculties all go silent—memory,
Intelligence, and the will, remain in place,
Becoming more acute than they were before.

The soul doesn't stay, but falls, miraculously
By itself, to the bank of one of the rivers; where
It first learns which path it will be made to take.

As soon as the location is set, an intrinsic
Force radiates around it and creates a shape,
As it does in the limbs of the living.

Like when the moist air is supersaturated
It reflects the rays of the sun and becomes
A decorative entity of iridescent colors,

So too, here, the surrounding air
Adopts a form that is inimitably that one's,
Virtually sealing in the soul adhered to it.

And like the flame that follows a fire
That continuously changes direction, so too
Its new form seamlessly tracks the soul.

In this way, it has a semblance, which is
Referred to as a shade; and with that,
Organs for every sense—even up to sight.

So we talk, and then we laugh;
We cry, then make sighs of the sort
You undoubtedly heard on the mountain.

The shade takes shape according to its wants
Or what afflicts it; anything that affects it
Creates the effect you pointed out."

Now we had come to the last twist of the knife;
Turning to the right, we were quickly aware
We had something else to worry about.

Flames shoot out here from the cliff face,
While along the cornice, a blast of fresh air
Deflects them and reclaims the path.

Because of that, we had to go single file
Along the open side; I was afraid of the fire
Over there, and over here, of falling off.

My leader said, "Along here, keep your eyes
On the road and your foot on the brake,
Even a near miss can be a mistake."

When I heard "Father of Highest Mercies"
Coming from within the blazing fire,
I felt myself wanting, no less, to stop and stare.

I saw spirits going through the flames. Using
A split-screen approach, moment to moment,
I looked up at them, then down at my feet.

As soon as they came to the end of the hymn,
They shouted loudly, "I've known no man,"
Then quietly began to sing the hymn again.

Finishing, they again shouted, "In the woods,
Diana got to stay; Callisto, who'd had a venom-
Shot of Venus's intoxicant, was sent away."

They again returned to singing; then the women
Called out and were married to the chaste,
As virtue and marriage dictate.

I think this is the way it works the entire time
They're held in the arms of the fire:
It's with that cure, with that regimen,

That the last gaping wound is finally closed.

1–3. *At this hour, the going up didn't want any / Slowing down [illegible] meridian / To Taurus and night had left it to Scorpio*: Since the sun crosses the meridian at approximately noon, depending on where on earth one is, and Taurus and Scorpio are opposite one another on the Zodiac circle, it is now approximately 2 p.m. in Purgatory, and 2 a.m. back in Italy.

10. *Like the little storklet*: The migratory stork, a herald of springtime and of birth, is associated with the Annunciation and with Christ. Baby female storks are called storklets; males are called storklings.

20–21. *How can this be, getting skinny / In a place where you never feel the need to eat*: Since the shades no longer have material bodies, Dante wants to know how they can experience the emaciation that comes with unsatisfied hunger.

22–23. *how Meleager fizzled out / In the burning up of the sizzling ember*: Ovid (*Metamorphoses* 8.445–532) relates the story of how, upon the birth of Meleager, son of the king of Calydon, the Fates decreed that he would be brave and strong but live only as long as the log burning on the hearth remained unconsumed. His mother, to protect him, removed the log and hid it in a chest. She threw it back on the fire years later after he killed his two maternal uncles when they objected to his having given the skin of the Calydonian Boar to a woman named Atalanta—who'd been the first on the hunt to wound it with an arrow before Meleager killed it. As the log burned, Meleager, who was elsewhere, wasted away; once the log was nothing more than ashes over dying embers, he died. Virgil is asking Dante to understand that outside forces—in the parallel case of the penitents, God—can effect changes, even from afar, that satisfy divine retribution.

25–26. *when you rush by, / Your image in a mirror also rushes by*: Virgil offers a second example of how the mirrored reflection, which is an exact replica of the human, can exist independent of the material body and can track it exactly. As with Meleager, and with the mirror image, what represents you *is* you.

29. *here's Statius. I'm asking him*: Virgil's deference to Statius on the "eternal viewpoint" is presumably because Statius is a Christian and has, additionally, completed his purgation.

37–51. *Perfect blood . . . The two joined together now begin to work, / First through thickening, then by quickening the substrate the matter is made to consist of*: What Statius presents as an abbreviated and highly lyricized version of "the birds and the bees" will later in the canto be inflected by writings on the nature of the soul by Aristotle, Thomas Aquinas, Saint Augustine, Albertus Magnus, Christian doctrine, and the Old Testament. Charles Singleton's *Commentary* (2:594–619) gives detailed notes and attributions. Statius begins by describing how perfect blood is distributed by the arteries; it can't be gotten by the veins, whose sole job it is to return the exhausted (oxygen-poor) blood to the heart to be reinfused. The priceless information inherent in the arterial blood is distributed to the limbs and to the testicles (the "place better left unmentioned") and to nature's "ready vessel," the womb, where the job of creating a human being is begun in the meeting of the two, the man with his sperm, and the woman who is willing to (passively) suffer the pangs of labor. The seed deposited there is the beginning of the process by which flesh becomes the matter that forms a human being.

53. *Like a plant but different*: In the plant, the genetic material is in the seed, but everything is settled ("landed") while the human cell still has to develop, in utero, a soul.

58–62. *how virtue extends / Directly from the heart of the generator / To all the members . . . But how the animal becomes the immortal / Diamond*: The generator is the Heavenly Father, who implants the soul in the developing infant the same way the father implants his seed in the perfect place. That, however, is a mere beginning. More is necessary for the soul to be fully realized.

61–62. *the immortal / Diamond Jack or Jill*: Gerard Manley Hopkins, "That Nature Is a Heraclitean Fire and of the Comfort of the Resurrection":

In a flash, at a trumpet crash,
I am all at once what Christ is, | since he was what I am, and
This Jack, joke, poor potsherd, | patch, matchwood, immortal diamond,
Is immortal diamond.

63–66. *someone wiser than you once got lost . . . the idea of the soul*: This wiser person is Averroës (Ibn Rushd), a Muslim philosopher, physician, and jurist, from Córdoba, Spain, who was famous for his commentaries on Aristotle. He proposed a "unity of the intellect" theory that claimed the intellect is how the brain understands, based solely on an individual's unique experiences, and is not otherwise tied to the soul or to the material body—since there is no single organ dedicated to it, like the ear is for sound.

70–75. *The Prime Mover turns to it . . . Breathes into it a new spirit, replete with power, // Which, activated, draws on what nourishes / And sustains it . . . A living feeling self that can examine itself*: "Prime Mover" is Aristotle's term. This self-awareness, the conscious mind, in Freudian terms, is thought to distinguish humans from other animals or plants. In *Convivio* (4, 2, 18), Dante writes, "Because philosophy, which is . . . the loving practice of wisdom, is concerned with itself, when it catches sight of its own beautiful eyes; what else is there to say, except that the philosophizing soul not only contemplates its reality, but even contemplates its contemplating self and its beauty, interrogating itself and falling in love with itself through the beauty of its first look."

79. *When Lachesis runs out of thread*: See the note for *Purg.* XXI, 25–26, for Lachesis's role in determining the length of one's life.

91–96. *moist air is supersaturated . . . a decorative entity of iridescent colors . . . sealing in the soul adhered to it*: Like the rainbow that appears when the sun's rays are dispersed in water droplets, the soul's form after death is ephemeral, mediated by its environment, and impossible to separate from the space it occupies.

109. *the last twist of the knife*: T. S. Eliot, "Rhapsody on a Windy Night": "The bed is open; the tooth-brush hangs on the wall, / Put your shoes at the door, sleep, prepare for life. // The last twist of the knife."

118–120. *keep your eyes on the road . . . can be a mistake*: The danger of lust is that if one lets down one's guard, one can metaphorically get burnt by the passion that comes out of nowhere and is only deflected by the breath of fresh air that chastity represents.

121. *When I heard "Father of Highest Mercies"*: The Latin used by Dante is *Summae Deus clementiae*, the name of a seventh-century liturgical hymn ascribed to Saint Ambrose. The wording of the first verse, revised by Pope Urban VIII, was changed to *Summae Parens clementiae* in the 1632 Roman Breviary. The third stanza of the hymn, sung at Saturday matins, asks God to rid us of the worst of our twisted passions.

125. *Using / A split-screen approach*: The first known use of split-screen/parallel action in films is thought to be a British 1898 short film (1 minute, 16 seconds) titled *Santa Claus*, by George Albert Smith, who was, by all accounts, the first filmmaker to also use the close-up, double exposures, and soft-focus (for transitioning from dream scene to "reality"). According to his biography on IMDb, in 1906, he patented Kinemacolor, "the world's first commercial cinema color system."

128. *They shouted up loudly, "I've known no man"*: Dante uses the Latin, *Virum non cognosco*. These are the words spoken by Mary after being visited by the Angel Gabriel and told she would deliver a son (Luke 1:31–34): "And, behold, thou shalt conceive in thy womb, and bring forth a son, and shalt call his name Jesus . . . Then said Mary unto the angel, How shall this be, seeing I know not a man?"

130–132. *In the woods, / Diana got to stay; Callisto, who'd had a venom- / Shot of Venus's intoxicant, was sent away*: Ovid (*Metamorphoses* 2.453–465) tells the story of how one of the nymphs who'd sworn loyalty to Diana (Greek: Artemis) was seduced by Zeus, who had disguised himself as Diana, and subsequently became pregnant with a son (Arcas). When Diana discovered the pregnancy, she banished her from her circle. Juno, out of jealousy, transformed Callisto into a bear. Years later, Arcas encounters the bear in the forest and is about to kill it when Zeus intervenes and places both mother and son in the sky as the constellations Ursa Major and Ursa Minor. Since Venus is the goddess of love and lust, it's her "venom" that is responsible. Snake wine, used in traditional Chinese medicine since ca. 700 BCE, is made by steeping a venomous snake in rice wine, or grain alcohol mixed with herbs, for months, or by adding the blood or organs of the snake directly to the alcohol and consumed as a shot.

133. *the women / Called out and were married to the chaste / As virtue and marriage dictate*: Only women are mentioned, but, since the women have already said they had been with no men, the men are now assumed to be the chaste ones whom the women "marry" inside the fire. It appears that Dante, unlike the Catholic Church, which limits sex to a means of procreation, places no such restrictions on sex but sees monogamy as the appropriate vehicle for sexual passion.

136–139. *I think this is the way it works . . . That the last gaping wound is finally closed*: The metaphorical wound of sin, echoed in the Ps cut into Dante's forehead, has finally been healed by the rituals of contrition on this seventh cornice, which is devoted to the sin of lust.

Canto XXVI

The whole time on the edge, walking one
In front of the other, my teacher kept saying,
"Pay attention. Use what I've taught you."

The sun was striking my right upper arm,
Already scattering light over the Western sky,
Changing its original air-blue dress to white.

I, with my shadow, made the flames redder;
Such a small clue, but I could see quite a few,
Who were turning it over in their minds.

That's what got them started talking about me;
It began by someone saying, "That doesn't
Seem like a phantom body to me."

Then several came toward me, as much
As they could, taking care not to exit so far
They wouldn't continue being burned.

One said, "You, behind the others, I assume
From respect, not laziness, could you tell me,
Over here dying of thirst in this oven—

And it's not only me who needs the answer,
All of us here thirst for it more than those
In India or Ethiopia for ice water—

Tell us how it is you can turn yourself
Into a piece of sheetrock to block the sun,
As if you hadn't yet been caught in death's net."

I would have straightaway said who I was
Except that at that moment, an amazing
New development caught my attention.

Inside the blazing track, a crowd of people
Came from the opposite direction to meet
This group. Suspense held me in place

As I watched each quickly greet one another,
All kissing, not lingering, seemingly
Quite happy with a brief bit of partygoing.

The same as in a dark mass of ants,
One meets the mouth of another, perhaps
To find out about a food trail or treasure trove.

As soon as the friendly hello is finished,
Before the first step away from them is taken,
Each one tries to outshout the other.

The new group, "Sodom and Gomorrah";
The others, "Pasiphaë trussed herself up
In a cow, so the bullock could come to her lust."

Then, like cranes—the sun-shy ones
Winging their way to the mountains, the ones
Who dislike ice, running off to the Riviera—

The one group goes, the other keeps coming,
They all return, crying, to their first chant,
Ending with whatever shout suits them best.

The ones from before, who'd asked me
About myself, came over again. I could see
By their faces they were eager to listen.

Having twice now seen how keen they were,
I said, "O souls, certain to achieve,
Whenever that might be, a state of peace,

My limbs weren't left behind, not as a green
Infant, nor as ripe oblivion, but they're here
With me, their blood and their joints.

I'm going up so I'll no longer lack insight;
A woman above has gained permission for me,
A mortal, to go through your world.

But, so your greatest wish might soon
Be satisfied and you'll be housed in that Heaven
Filled with love and wider than the sky,

Tell me, so I can make a record of it,
Who are you, and who's in that crowd
Going back the other way behind your backs."

No different from any stick-in-the-mud,
Or rough-and-ready sore-headed bear,
Dumbstruck when visiting the big city,

That was the look on the faces of this group;
But once freed from their wonder, which
Is soon mitigated in everybody who has a heart—

"Lucky you," said the first who'd addressed me,
"You're blessed to have a better death,
Absorbing the experience of our orbits.

The ones who didn't come with us offended
The same way Caesar did, when a bystander
On parade day called out 'Hey, Queen.'

So, they go off scolding themselves, shouting
'Sodom,' as you heard; their self-shaming
Helps with the burning thirst.

Our sin was hermaphrodite; since
We didn't adhere to the one-way human law,
But followed our appetites like animals,

In our shame, when we go off we shout out
The name of the woman on all fours
On the splintery floor of a beast-shaped crate.

Now you know our acts and why we're guilty;
If you might want to know our names,
There's no time to say, and I wouldn't know.

In terms of me, I'll happily satisfy your wish:
I'm Guido Guinizzelli, I'd already begun
My cleansing by repenting well before the end."

The way Lycurgus's madman grief made the two
Sons behave when they saw their mother again,
I wanted that, if there'd been less to overcome,

The second I heard him give his name as the father:
Mine, and all the best among the rest of us—
Never have love poems been so freshly elegant—

I stopped listening, and went on, thinking
But not speaking, staring in amazement,
Not able to get closer because of the fire.

When my eyes had feasted long enough,
I said I was totally ready to be of service,
Swearing it in the most convincing way.

He said, "You make such an impression;
From what I hear, it's quite clear Lethe
Can't take it away from me or make it fade.

But if the vow you've sworn is true, tell me
Why you're making such a show—saying
And staring—of how much I've meant to you."

I said, "Your much-admired verses will,
As long as the poetic vernacular lasts,
Make even the ink they're written in precious."

"O brother," he said, "the one I'm pointing out
To you," he gestured to one up ahead,
"Was the best locksmith of the mother tongue.

His love poems and epic romances exceeded
Everyone else's; ignore the fools that claim
The one from Limoges was his better.

They turn toward hearsay rather than truth,
Then form their opinions before listening
To art or to reasoned arguments.

That was the case long ago for many with
Guittone, shout-out after shout-out added chits
To his value, until most people saw the light.

Now, if you have such exclusive license
That you're permitted to enter the cloister
Where Christ is Provost of the College,

Do something for me, say an Our Father;
That's the 'daily bread' we need in this world,
Since it's no longer possible to trespass."

Then, perhaps to give his place to the one
Close to him, he dove back into the fire,
Like a fish in a hurry to get to the bottom.

I moved up a little toward the one
I'd been shown; what I wanted, I said,
Was to prepare a special place for his name.

He began to speak with some frankness,
"I'm so pleased by your courteous request,
I could not nor would I go undercover;

I'm Arnaut, and I go, crying and chanting,
Sadly I see my past madness; I look forward
To that longed for day when I'll walk on air.

I pray you now, whatever the power
That guides you to the top of the stairs,
Recall my pain when you come to that hour!"

He then hid himself in the fire that refines them.

4–6. *The sun was . . . Changing its original air-blue dress to white*: In the absence of clouds, the sky is bluest in the early morning and near sunset; as the angle of the sun drops, after reaching its height at noon, it lightens so that by late afternoon it may even appear to be white. Thomas Hardy, "The Voice":

> Can it be you that I hear? Let me view you, then,
> Standing as when I drew near to the town
> Where you would wait for me: yes, as I knew you then,
> Even to the original air-blue gown!

7. *I, with my shadow, made the flames redder*: Because Dante's body is blocking the sun, the fire next to him isn't washed out by the bright sunlight; it thus appears a darker red.

21. *India or Ethiopia*: These two countries represent warm climates. Commentators note that Dante pairs these two countries in all three of the canticles of the *Commedia*, possibly following Aristotle in *On Sophistical Refutations*, a work Dante cites in *Monarchia* 3, 1, 4.

33. *a brief bit of party going*: *Party Going* (1939) is the title of the second novel by the British author Henry Green. The satirical plot revolves around a group of rich friends traveling by train to a house party who encounter fog and are forced to stay in a hotel.

34–36. *The same as in a dark mass of ants . . . the mouth of another, perhaps / To find out about a food trail or treasure trove*: Ants have interaction networks with advanced methods of communication. These include sounds, multiple forms of touch, and pheromone trails unique to a colony that enable others in the colony to return to a food source. If an ant has food to spare, two ants will meet and join mouths to exchange food by a liquid-regurgitation process called trophallaxis. Similar to the situation of the penitents, the ants can't spare too much time interacting or the colony would be put at risk.

38. *the first step away from them*: Frank O'Hara, "A Step Away from Them."

40. *"Sodom and Gomorrah"*: Sodom and Gomorrah are mentioned as "wicked" cities in Genesis 13:13. Genesis 19:24–25 tells the story of the destruction of the cities following a visit by two angels to Lot, during which the men of the neighborhood demanded Lot make the angels available for sex. Lot offered instead his two virgin daughters, but the men refused. The angels then told Lot to take his family and escape. When Lot's wife looked back, she was turned into a pillar of salt.

41–42. *Pasiphaë trussed herself up / In a cow, so the bullock could come to her lust*: King Minos prayed to Poseidon (represented by a bull) to send him a white bull, promising to sacrifice it to him. In the event, the king found it too beautiful and sacrificed a different bull. Angered, Poseidon punished Minos by having Pasiphaë, his queen (and daughter of Helios), fall in love with the bull and lust after it. To satisfy her lust, she had the craftsman Daedalus construct a wooden cow, covered in cowhide, into which Pasiphaë climbed and, according to Ovid's *Ars amatoria*, "Pasiphaë was overjoyed to become the bull's adulteress" ("Pasiphaë fieri gaudebat adultera tauri"). The offspring of that coupling is the half-man, half-bull Minotaur who had to be kept in a labyrinth and periodically fed seven youths and seven maidens—which is why Dante uses Pasiphaë to signify the monstrous outcome of an act of lustful indulgence. Pasiphaë is also mentioned in Virgil's *Eclogues* 6, 45–60.

43. *like cranes—the sun-shy ones*: The first known use of the word "sun-shy" is in *The Silmarillion*, by J. R. R. Tolkien (d. 1973), a posthumously published origin-myth fantasy (primarily 1914–1926): "Then Curufin said to Eol: 'What errand have you, Dark Elf, in my lands? An urgent matter, perhaps, that keeps one so sun-shy abroad by day.'"

45. *Who dislike ice, running off to the Riviera*: The Camargue, seventeen minutes by car from Arles, France (Mapquest), is a wetlands area on the migration route between Italy and Spain, where thousands of birds, including large numbers of cranes, begin their warm winter residency.

59–60. *A woman above has gained permission for me, / A mortal, to go through your world*: The woman is Beatrice.

63. *Filled with love and wider than the sky*: Emily Dickinson (632):

> The Brain – is wider than the Sky –
> For – put them side by side –
> The one the other will include
> With ease – and you – beside –

68. *rough-and-ready sore-headed bear*: To be "like a bear with a sore head" is a primarily British idiom meaning to be grumpy, irritable, or bad-tempered.

72. *soon mitigated in everybody who has a heart*: Lucie Brock-Broido, "Everybody Has a Heart, Except Some People." The title of Brock-Broido's poem is a quote from the 1950 film *All about Eve*, written and directed by Joseph L. Mankiewicz, based on a story, "The Wisdom of Eve," by Mary Orr; in both, an ingenue befriends an older established actress, Margo Channing, played by Bette Davis, in order to further her career. It's Davis who utters the statement.

77–78. *The same way Caesar did, when a bystander / On parade day called out 'Hey, Queen'*: There are multiple collaborating stories, including one by Uguccione of Pisa, which Dante is known to have read, of how Caesar, when he was twenty and serving as ambassador to Bithynia, was rumored to be having a sexual relationship with King Nicomedes VI. Upon his return to Rome, during a triumph parade, someone called out, "Hail King and Queen."

82–84. *Our sin was hermaphrodite . . . the one-way human law, / But followed our appetites like animals*: The term "hermaphrodite" derives from Ovid's story (*Metamorphoses* 4.285–388) of Hermaphroditus, the mythical son of Hermes and Aphrodite. The wood nymph Salmacis, infatuated with the beautiful young boy but rebuffed by him, wrapped herself around him and prayed to the gods to be united with him forever. The result was a winged figure with female breasts and male genitals. No one can know what Dante meant by this term, although countless have argued for various readings. One possibility is that the term relates to a person born with unassignable sexual characteristics, today referred to as intersex, who, once they chose to follow one gender, switched to another. Albert the Great included intersex "hermaphrodites" in his *De animalibus* (Treatise on animals), arguing that while the cause was "excess matter," "the prevailing sex should definitely be the one governed by the complexion of the heart" (Rubin, 102). Another possibility is that the term includes any sexual desire that is aberrant in its manifestation, including heterosexual positions. Since "Sodom" is what is shouted by those in the group presumed to be homosexual, commentators argue that this, the "Gomorrah" category, must be heterosexual. Ovid's tale, however, emphasizes the effeminacy of Hermaphroditus after his transformation and, moreover, states that anyone who subsequently bathed in the pool where the union occurred would "go soft." Thus, the second group could include both heterosexuals and homosexuals, all practicing various types of nonprocreative sexual behavior.

While we can't know what Dante had in mind, what is unarguable is that he does not consign homosexuals, nor heterosexuals with non-Church-sanctioned sexual predilections, to Hell but instead has them make amends on the highest level of Purgatory, right next to the Terrestrial Paradise. This is radically progressive for its time. An excellent comprehensive discussion of the historical context of the questions raised by Dante's use of the term *ermafrodito* can be found in Leon Jacobowitz Efron's "Hermaphrodite Trouble: Gender, Sex and Sexuality in Fourteenth-Century Italian Commentaries to the *Divine Comedy*."

92–93. *Guido Guinizzelli, I'd already begun . . . by repenting well before the end*: Guinizzelli was a Bolognese poet and a Ghibelline podestà. He was exiled when the Ghibelline party was expelled from Bologna and died ca. 1276 in Verona. Guinizzelli explains the fact that he has progressed from Ante-Purgatory through the first six lower cornices in less than twenty-five years by saying that he repented before his death; this presumably earned him credit toward his redemption. Although his lyrics were infused with Platonic ideals, he was known mostly as a love poet, which may be why Dante places him in the cornice devoted to the sin of lust.

94–96. *Lycurgus's madman grief made the two / Sons behave . . . I wanted that, if there'd been less to overcome*: Statius, in Book 5 of the *Thebaid*, tells the story of the death of Lycurgus's infant son due to the neglect of the nursemaid Hypsipyle (see the note to *Purg.* XXII, 112). When Lycurgus learns of his son's death, he orders Hypsipyle's execution. Before the act can be carried out, her twin sons, Thoas and Euneus, arrive and beg Lycurgus to spare her. When he does, her sons "rushed to greedily embrace her and crying pressed her to their chests." Dante, likewise, would embrace Guinizzelli with this same degree of ardor, but for the fire. This moment echoes that of *Inf.* XVI, 46–51, where Dante states that it's only the fire that keeps him from joining the group of runners who pay for the sin of offending God in the seventh circle of Hell.

97–99. *the father: / Mine, and all the best among the rest of us . . . so freshly elegant*: Dante credits Guinizelli's poems with being the inspiration for the *Dolce stil novo* (Sweet new style). The opening verses of Dante's famous sonnet "Amore e 'l cor gentil sono una cosa / si come il saggio in suo dittare pone" (Love and the noble heart are the same / as the wise one said in his poem) adapt the first verse of Guinizelli's "Al cor gentil ripara sempre amore" (Love always nests in the noble heart). What the new style derives from Guinizelli is the celebration of love as a type of salvation. His ideas supported Dante's belief that it was righteousness, not high birth, that was the essence of nobility and that a "lady" would play the role of a guide to self-realization, as Beatrice does in *Purg.* XXXIII.

107–108. *Lethe / Can't take it away from me or make it fade*: Virgil, Lucan, Statius, and Ovid all mention Lethe, the mythic river of oblivion that erases all earthly memory so the dead soul can begin its new life with a clean slate and not pine for what it left behind. In *Purg.* XXXIII, Dante will be immersed in Lethe; in Dante's version, however, Lethe erases only sinful memories, not all memories. Guinizzelli is saying that the memory of Dante's words won't be erased or lessened by his immersion in the river, when that time arrives, because the sentiment behind them is pure.

115. *the one I'm pointing out*: The poet, who will name himself in v. 142, is Arnaut Daniel, a troubadour poet from what is now the Dordogne region of France who wrote in Occitan between 1180 and ca. 1210. Inventor of the sestina form, he practiced a hermetic style of troubadour poetry called *trobar clus* (closed form): rhymed metrical poems that exploited multiple types of ambiguity and were thus only accessible to insiders who understood the principles guiding their composition. The poems, rife with sexual innuendo, celebrated a particular kind of love, called *fin'amour*, where *fin* can mean any number of things, including "shrewdness." The purpose of the coding may have been to slyly embed in the poems social criticism of the upper classes, upon whom the poets were dependent for support, or to conceal the identity of objects of their desire.

117. *the best locksmith of the mother tongue*: T. S. Eliot published his 1922 lyric sequence, *The Waste Land*, with a dedication: "For Ezra Pound / *il miglior fabbro*." Pound had radically edited Eliot's manuscript *He Do the Police in Different Voices* into a much shorter and far more cohesive poem and suggested the new title. The Italian word *fabbro* can mean "craftsperson," as it is usually translated in the Eliot dedication, but more accurately refers to a locksmith, blacksmith, or forger. Pound also used "Il Miglior Fabbro"

as a chapter title in his 1910 book of literary criticism, *The Spirit of Romance*. *Miglior* can mean "better" or "best." The mother tongue would have been any Latinate vernacular.

120. *The one from Limoges was his better*: This Provençal poet is Giraut de Borneil (d. ca. 1220). Dante mentions him three times in *De vulgari eloquentia* (On eloquence in the vernacular), identifying him as the poet of righteousness, and once in *Convivio* (*The Banquet*).

125–126. *Guittone . . . until most people saw the light*: Guittone (also mentioned in *Purg.* XXIV, 55–57) is credited with being the first poet to create a significant body of Italian lyric poetry. Highly celebrated in his own time, he wrote love poems until he entered a monastery, at which point he rejected carnal love. He was born in Arezzo but moved to Florence at some point and died there in 1294; Dante may have known him.

147–148. *Recall my pain when you come to that hour! // He then hid himself in the fire that refines them*: Dante uses the Provençal language for the eight verses Arnaut Daniel speaks. T. S. Eliot uses the canto's last verse, in Italian—"Poi s'ascose nel foco che gli affina"—as v. 427 of *The Waste Land*, one of the "fragments . . . shored against my ruins."

Canto XXVII

It's just like when its first rays vibrate the air
Where its Creator shed His blood, Spain settles down
Beneath Libra's scales hung to the height,

And noon scalds the Ganges's waves,
That's the sun's way; meaning, day was leaving
When happily the angel of God appeared.

Standing on the edge outside the flames,
It chanted, "Blessed are the pure of heart!"
In a much more uplifting voice than ours.

"No one goes farther, holy souls, without first
Feeling the sting of the fire. Enter it
And don't block out the distant singing."

It added that last bit when we were next to it,
Making me feel, once I got what it meant,
Like someone about to be buried alive.

I reached out my hands as if for protection,
Watching the fire and vividly picturing
The burnt bodies of people I'd seen.

My knowing escorts turned toward me;
It was Virgil who spoke, "True, son,
It might be an agony but it won't kill you.

Remember, remember! If I,
From high atop Geryon, guided you to safety,
What will I do now, even closer to God?

Rest assured, believe me, you could stay
A thousand years in the belly of this flame,
And your head wouldn't lose a single hair.

And if you suspect I'm putting you on,
Move closer, convince yourself
By holding the hem of your coat to it.

Starting now, let go, let go of every fear,
Turn and come here, enter with confidence."
I stood fixed, dead set against my conscience.

When he saw I was fixed and unbending,
He said, slightly annoyed, "What you're seeing,
Son, is the wall between you and Beatrice."

The same as at the name of Thisbe, dying
Pyramus opened his eyes and saw her,
Magically turning the mulberries vermilion,

So my inflexibility gave way, hearing
The name that always springs to my mind,
I turned to my sensible leader, at which,

His raised eyebrows dropped, "So! You still
Want us to stay here?" smiling now, the way
One does at a kid won over by fruit chew.

He then entered the fire before me,
Calling to Statius, who'd been between us
For quite a while, asking him to come last.

Once in, I would have gladly been recast
As molten glass in order to cool off,
That's how immeasurably hot the fire was.

My kind father, to soothe me, kept talking
Throughout about Beatrice, saying,
"I might just be able to make out her eyes."

From the other side, a chanting voice
Led us and, homing in on it,
We came out where one begins the climb.

The sound of "Come ye, blessed of my Father"
Came from within a light so intense
And overwhelming, I couldn't look into it.

"The sun's going down, evening's coming."
The angel went on, "Don't stop,
Just push on ahead, before the west goes dark."

The way went straight up through the rock;
In front on me, the sunlight
Being blocked by my body was already fading.

We'd only gone a few steps more before I
And my wise men sensed, since my shadow had
Gone out, that the sun was in bed behind us.

And before all the boundless parts became one
Continuous horizon, and the whole of night
Handed out in fair shares,

Each of us chose a level and made a bed.
Since the nature of the mountain took away
The strength to climb, as well as the wish to.

Like goats who'd been all bouncy
And head-butting on the peaks before
They'd eaten their fill, now meekly ruminating

Quiet in the shade, the sun in full swing,
Watched by a shepherd leaning on a crook,
Letting them take their rest.

Or like a cattle driver sleeping rough
All night long next to his silent livestock,
One eye open so no slasher animal scatters them.

So too with the three of us—I was the goat,
They were the shepherds—bounded
On all sides by high rock walls.

I could see little through the opening,
But in that little, I saw the stars,
Larger and brighter than usual.

Thinking and having my sights set on those,
I was taken by sleep, sleep that often knows
The news before the facts have happened.

I think it must have been near the time when
The rays of Venus, where the love-light
Is always burning, first touched the mountain,

That I saw in a dream what seemed
To be a beautiful girl walking on a heath,
Picking flowers and singing this song:

"If someone wants to know my name,
Say Leah, and say my good hands stay
Busy making daisy chains. I wear one:

See the pretty girl in the mirror there?
My sister Rachel, never caring
To leave her glass, is there all day, staring.

She's as eager to see her lovely eyes as I
To refine myself with my hands; for her,
It's seeing; for me, it's work that satisfies."

Now, with the predawn splendor—that rising
That makes a returning traveler more grateful
They're waking closer to home—

On all sides, darkness was scurrying off
And taking my sleep with it; I got myself up,
Seeing the grand masters were moving about.

"All that sweet fruit on so many branches
That mortals forever try so hard to reach,
Today you'll have your fill of it."

These were the words Virgil used,
And there's never been a graduation gift
That brought as much happiness as this one.

Wish upon wish to be up there kept coming
And with each step I grew lighter
Than a thing with feathers: I felt I could fly.

When the entire staircase, now beneath us,
Had been run up, and we were at the topmost
Level, Virgil fixed his eyes on me,

"You've seen the fire of Purgatory and that
Of Hell, son, and now we've come to a place
Beyond which I, on my own, have no insight.

I brought you this far with intellect and skill;
Now you can let your own pleasure lead you.
The steep path is over, the narrow is history.

Look at the sun shining on your face,
Look at the grass, the flowers, the shrubs,
Which the soil here produces all on its own.

Until the happy arrival of those lovely eyes,
The tears of which brought me to you,
You can sit here, or walk around among these.

Don't wait for a word or a sign from me.
Your will is free, upstanding, and healthy; and
It's wrong not to follow its judgment. And so,

I crown and miter you, emperor of yourself."

NOTES TO CANTO XXVII

1–5. *its first rays vibrate the air / Where its Creator shed His blood, Spain settles down / Beneath Libra's scales . . . And noon scalds the Ganges's waves . . . meaning, day was leaving*: Dante tracks the sun's position relative to where the group of three is standing, about to leave the seventh cornice: the sun is just rising in Jerusalem, the center of the Western world for Dante; it's midnight in the Strait of Gibraltar (marked by the river Ebro in Spain), above which one would see the constellation Libra; and it is high noon in India—all of which means it's 6 p.m. on Mount Purgatory. Vernon (2:403) notes that the phrase "from the Ebro to the Ganges" was, in Dante's era, the equivalent of saying "from one end to the other of the inhabited world."

3. *hung to the height*: Gerard Manley Hopkins, "Spelt from Sibyl's Leaves": "her wild hollow hoarlight hung to the height / Waste; her earliest stars, earl-stars, | stárs principal, overbend us."

6–8. *the angel of God appeared . . . "Blessed are the pure of heart!"*: This is the beginning of the final beatitude. Matthew 5:8: "Blessed are the pure in heart: for they shall see God."

10–12. *No one goes farther, holy souls, without first / Feeling the sting of the fire*: This final step in the purification process echoes the medieval "trial by ordeal," where guilt or innocence is determined by whether an accused survives an extreme situation such as burning or drowning. Trial by fire usually involved walking over red-hot ploughshares for a set distance or holding one for a set amount of time. Of course, in the eternal fire, there is no bodily harm, but Dante will have to be convinced of that by Virgil before he is willing to enter it.

12. *And don't block out the distant singing*: There are two angels, one on either side of the fire; by following the chanting of the second, those inside the fire will find their way across not by sight but by sound.

15. *Like someone about to be buried alive*: Commentators point to the form of medieval execution called *propagginazione*, suffocation by having one's head buried in a hole. Dante also refers to the practice in *Inf.* XIX, 49–51.

17–18. *vividly picturing / The burnt bodies of people I'd seen*: Burning at the stake was another form of medieval punishment. This was Dante's own sentence, levied by the tribunal in Florence, should he ever return to that city.

22–23. *If I, / From high atop Geryon, guided you to safety*: In *Inf.* XVII, 85–136, Virgil and Dante travel from the seventh circle down to the eighth on the back of Geryon, a monster from Greek myth, described by Virgil (*Aeneid* 6, 289) as "a three-bodied shade." Dante uses the monster as a symbol of fraud: honest face, reptilian body, dragon wings, lion paws, and a stinging scorpion tail.

26–27. *A thousand years in the belly of this flame, / And your head wouldn't lose a single hair*: Jesus reassures his disciples that while they will be hated, ostracized, and possibly even put to death, they will live on in the afterlife. Luke 21.18. "But there shall not an hair of your head perish."

30. *holding the hem of your coat to it*: Virgil suggests that if Dante can't trust in his word, he should use the scientific method of direct observation. Commentators point out that Dante's *fatti far credenza* (make a proof) was used to describe the practice of tasting a noble's food to make certain it hadn't been poisoned.

37–39. *Thisbe, dying / Pyramus opened his eyes . . . Magically turning the mulberries vermilion*: Ovid tells the story (*Metamorphoses* 4.55–166) of Thisbe and Pyramus, two Babylonian young people whose love was forbidden by their parents but who spoke through a hole in the shared wall of their adjacent homes. They arranged to meet one night, but Thisbe, who arrived first, interrupted a lion attacking an ox and ran away. In her haste, she dropped her cloak, which the lioness then soiled with blood. When Pyramus arrived, he mistakenly thought the lion had eaten Thisbe; griefstricken, he fell on his sword under a mulberry bush—splashing blood on the white mulberries and turning them red. Thisbe returned and begged Pyramus to show a sign of life; he opened his eyes, saw her, and breathed his last. She then used his sword to end her life. The myth inspired Shakespeare's *Romeo and Juliet*.

58. *The sound of "Come ye, blessed of my Father"*: Vernon (2:655) points out that the angel on the Purgatory side functions as Saint Peter at the gate and the angel on the Terrestrial Paradise side acts as Christ, since the words he chants are those Christ is supposed to speak on the Day of Judgment. Matthew 25:34: "Then the King will say to those on His right hand, 'Come, ye blessed of My Father, inherit the kingdom prepared for you from the foundation of the world." As with other Bible verses, Dante could expect his readers to know the rest of the Latin verse. Commentators beginning with Wilkins (1927) note that there is a mosaic in the Florentine Baptistery dating back to Dante's time that shows one angel at the gate to Paradise and a second angel leading a group of souls toward it, carrying a banner that reads: "Venite beneditti Patris mei possidete preparatum." (Come, ye blessed of the Father, inherit what has been prepared.)

70–72. *And before all the boundless parts became one / Continuous horizon, and the whole of night / Handed out in fair shares*: We are now at the end of the third day, Tuesday, April 12, and have left Purgatory and entered the Terrestrial Paradise.

80–86 *Watched by a shepherd . . . I was the goat, / They were the shepherds*: Since Dante is the only human among the three, only he requires sleep. The other two can serve as shepherds who watch over their flocks and keep them safe.

92–93. *sleep that often knows / the news before the facts have happened*: In *Inf.* XXVI, 7–8, Dante alludes to the common medieval belief that dreams experienced just before dawn are often prophetic. It would follow that since sleep brings dreams, sleep knows the news in advance.

95–98. *Venus, where the love-light / is always burning*: For Venus, Dante uses Citerea, the Aegean island of Cythera that is her birthplace (from sea foam). Venus is sometimes a morning star and other times an evening star. Due to an error in the *Almanac of Profacius*, widely believed to have been used by Dante, Venus was mistakenly said to be a morning star in 1300, the year in which the poem is set (Toynbee, 545).

101–102. *Say Leah, and say my good hands stay / Busy making daisy chains*: Leah, the first wife of Jacob and older sister of Rachel, is indirectly referred to in *Inf.* IV, 58–60, when Dante includes Jacob among those who were lifted out of Hell during the Harrowing; there he mentions that Jacob had to serve for a long time before marrying Rachel. In the Old Testament, Laban, the father of Leah and Rachel, forced Jacob to work for sixteen years, and to first marry Leah, before allowing him to marry Rachel. Leah is a signifier of the active life, one's whose hands stay busy.

103. *See the pretty girl in the mirror there*: "See the pretty girl in that mirror there: Who can that attractive girl be?" is from the song "I Feel Pretty," from the 1957 Broadway musical *West Side Story*, conceived, directed, and choreographed by Jerome Robbins, music by Leonard Bernstein, lyrics by Stephen Sondheim, book by Arthur Laurents, based on Shakespeare's *Romeo and Juliet*.

104–108. *My sister Rachel . . . is there all day, staring . . . for her, / It's seeing; for me, it's work that satisfies*: Rachel is the signifier of the contemplative life. The mirror into which she looks, commentators note, is not meant to suggest vanity but to suggest the satisfactions of contemplation. When Leah sees herself in a mirror, she sees what her hands have created; Rachel sees her own eyes, the vehicle of knowing.

109–111. *the predawn splendor . . . makes a returning traveler more grateful . . . closer to home*: The home that awaits Dante and Statius is the Terrestrial Paradise. For Dante, there is the added anticipation of being reunited with Beatrice.

115–117. *All that sweet fruit . . . mortals forever try so hard to reach, / Today you'll have your fill*: After completing their penance, each soul will have its fill of the Edenic fruit forbidden outside of Heaven.

122–123. *And with each step I grew lighter / Than a thing with feathers: I felt I could fly*: Dante's lightness is the result of the last P having been erased by the welcoming angel. Emily Dickinson (314):

> "Hope" is the thing with feathers –
> That perches in the soul –
> And sings the tune without the words –
> And never stops – at all –

127–129. *the fire of Purgatory and that / Of Hell . . . Beyond which I, on my own, have no insight*: Virgil uses the terms "temporal fire" and "eternal fire" to distinguish between the time-limited punishments (figurative fires) Dante witnessed in Purgatory and the everlasting punishments he witnessed in Hell. Commentators quote Thomas Aquinas as a likely source: "The punishment of the damned is eternal, according to Matth. XXV. 46, *These shall go into everlasting punishment* [Vulg.,—*fire*.] But the fire of Purgatory is temporary." Quoted in Singleton, *Purgatorio* (2:663).

130–132. *I brought you this far with intellect and skill; / Now you can let your own pleasure lead you. / The steep path is over, the narrow is history*: Virgil has used the intelligence nature granted him (intellect), plus the education he acquired (skill), to navigate the challenges of guiding Dante through the two realms. Virgil says Dante can now follow his own wishes because he can trust them to be pure.

135. *the soil here produces all on its own*: Adam's curse was having to work; in the Terrestrial Paradise, the vegetation is self-replicating and requires no effort on anyone's part. It's the gift God intended when he created Eden.

136–137. *Until the happy arrival of those lovely eyes, / The tears of which brought me to you*: This, of course, is Beatrice.

139–141. *Don't wait for a word or a sign from me. / Your will is free, upstanding, and healthy; and / It's wrong not to follow its judgment*: Dante uses the word *sano* (sound) to describe the healthy will, just as we use "of sound mind" as the essential measure of cognition required for legal competence in wills and testaments. In *Convivio* 4, 15, 11, Dante writes: "Onde è da sapere che lo nostro intelletto si può dir sano e infermo: e dico intelletto per la nobile parte de l'anima nostra, che con uno vocabulo 'mente' si può chiamare. Sano dire si può, quando per malizia d'animo o di corpo impedito non è ne la sua operazione." (There's a sense in which our intellect can be called healthy or sick: and by intellect I mean the noble part of our soul that can be described by the word "mind." We can say it's healthy when it's not impeded in its transactions by some malignancy of either body or soul.)

142. *I crown and miter you, emperor of yourself*: Vernon (2:428) quotes Giovanni Andrea Scartazzini (d. 1901), an Italian-Swiss literary critic and Dante commentator and translator (into German): "Scartazzini explains this: 'I place on thy head the mitred crown of the Emperors.' In early times it was usual to place on the head of the Emperor, first the mitre, and upon the mitre the Imperial crown. The ecclesiastical mitre is quite out of the question here, for two reasons. In the first place Virgil would have no power to confer it; and secondly, Dante was not to become from this moment bishop and pastor to himself, but was to be under the direction of his spiritual guide, Beatrice. Scartazzini sums up Virgil's last words thus: 'I pronounce thee to be Emperor of thyself, that is, director of thine own reason in the practice of moral and intellectual virtues: thou needest no longer a rider to bestride thee to direct thy will, to hold thee in check with bit and bridle, and to turn thy steps into the direct road.'"

CANTO XXVIII

I was eager by now to thoroughly explore
In and around the divine forest, its thick green
Softening the morning light in my eyes.

Without waiting any longer, I left the bank
And took the field, slowly, slowly, over
The rich floodplain, fragrant with alluvium.

The steady current of fresh air that struck
My face with an impact no greater
Than a gentle breeze

Caused the tree leaves to flutter and to tilt
As one toward the area where the holy
Mountain casts its first morning shadow.

They weren't bowed down so far
From the upright that the little treetop birdies
Stopped producing their popular operas,

But kept singing joyfully in the early hours,
The rustling leaves accompanying
Their rhymes with a harmonic drone effect,

Like the one that travels branch-to-branch,
Rallying in the pines along the Adriatic
Shore when Aeolus lets Sirocco loose.

In spite of my slow pace, I'd already
Been carried so far into the ancient forest
I could no longer see where I'd entered,

When hello! a stream stopped me in my tracks;
The rippling current made the grass
At its edge bend toward the left.

All the most crystalline waters on earth
Seem muddy compared to this,
Which hides nothing

Although the dark gets even darker as it flows
In the eternal shade, where no ray of sun
Or moonbeam is ever let in.

I'd stopped walking and stood there looking
Along the length of the stream at the vast
Variety of the freshest-ever blossoms,

When there appeared, the way something
Marvelous can pop up so suddenly
It pushes out any other thought,

A woman, totally alone, just singing
And picking this flower, that flower,
From those painted all along her way.

"Oh, Bella Donna, you seem to radiate
Love-light. In my experience, when one
Looks like you, the heart is usually involved.

Would you be willing to come closer,"
I asked, "toward this side of the stream,
So I can hear what you're singing?

You're making me recall where
Persephone was and what happened when
Her mother lost her, and she lost her spring."

Like when a woman turns to dance,
Her feet close to the ground and together,
Barely moving one foot in front of the other,

From the upturned red and upturned yellow
Blossoms she turned toward me—
Lowering her honest eyes like an innocent.

To make me happy, she did what I'd asked,
Coming near enough that I could understand
What was being sung so softly.

As soon as she was there, where the waves
Of the gentle stream just dampen the grass,
She gave me the gift of lifting her eyes.

I doubt the light under Venus's lashes
Was more glorious when she was aimlessly hit
By her son's archery, so unlike his usual mode.

She smiled shyly from the right bank—
In her hands, the many-colored flowers taken
From that lofty soil that doesn't need any seed.

The river was some three steps across,
But the Hellespont—where Xerxes bridged it,
Still inhibiting all the hotshot humans—

Didn't create more hatred in Leander
For the sea swell between Sestos and Abydos
Than I had because these waters wouldn't part.

"You're new here," she said, "and just maybe
Because I'm smiling in this place
That was chosen as a nest for human nature,

You're wondering and have suspicions,
But the light shed by Psalm 92, 'You have
Delighted me,' should demystify your mind.

Now you, in front of me, who asked me here,
Say if you want to know more; I've come ready
To field every question until you're satisfied."

"The water," I said, "and the treetop sounds
Contradict a recent belief I had about this place
Based on something I'd been told."

"I'll explain the cause and effect
Of what you're wondering about," she said,
"And get rid of that fog that's confusing you.

The Supreme Good, solely out of self-interest,
Made humans good, to do good, and created
This place as a down payment on eternal peace.

Due to their failings, they lived here briefly;
Due to their failings, they traded straight-up smiles
And Candy-Land games for tears and grief.

So that the atmospheric disturbances below,
Via moisture rising from bodies of water and soil
(As much as can be trapped in warm air)

Wouldn't bombard humans, the mountain rose
This far toward the heavens, so as to be free
Of the greenhouse effect above the gate.

Now, because all the air that began moving
In the first go-around continues to circulate,
Like a song sung in rounds that never gets broken,

At this height, the air, free of all impurities,
Moves at such a brisk pace, it makes a sound
As it passes through the forest, since it's so leafy.

The repeatedly struck tree is so potent
The air gets infused with its pollen,
Which the circulating wind then scatters

The same way seeds in the other world
Produce, subject to suitable climate and soil,
Diverse plants with diverse qualities.

Given this, it shouldn't seem so wondrous
When some plant below puts down roots
Without an obvious source for the seed.

Keep in mind, the holy field, where you are,
Is full of every kind of seed and has fruit in it
That doesn't fall from any tree down there.

The water you see doesn't spring from a vein
That's restored by vapor condensed by cold,
Like a river that gains and loses its velocity,

But comes from a constant reliable source,
And, through the will of God, it regains whatever
It loses as it divides into two running streams.

The virtue that flows from the one side
Wipes away all memory of sin; while what flows
From the other restores all the good done.

So, here, Lethe; while the other side is called
Eunoe; it won't work if you don't first drink
From this side before tasting that:

That flavor is better than any other.
Although your thirst might be satisfied already,
Even without my revealing more to you,

I'm going to give you an add-on bonus, gratis,
Which I don't think you'll value less, even if
What I say exceeds what we agreed upon.

For those in ancient times who poeticized
The Golden Age and its happiness, this place
May have been the Parnassian dream.

Here the human was rooted innocence;
Here, everlasting spring and every kind of fruit;
This is the nectar they all talk about."

I turned to my poets, who were standing
Behind me, and saw they were smiling
At having heard that last conjecture.

I then turned my eyes back to the Bella Donna.

2. *the divine forest*: The contrast between this forest, filled with the light of a literal and figurative *novo giorno* (new day), and the dark forest in which Dante found himself at the beginning of *Inferno*, dark "because the straightway was lost" ("ché la diritta via era smarrita"), says everything about the rewards of penance: this forest is the one he worked to achieve; the other forest was one he ended up in.

4. *Without waiting any longer, I left the bank*: Dante acts on his own for the first time since becoming totally reliant on Virgil, which is precisely what Virgil told him to do at the end of *Purg.* XXVII.

5. *slowly, slowly*: There is no longer any need to hurry, having finally arrived in this place that Dante will soon learn is the biblical Eden. It is also the morning of the seventh and last day of Dante's journey, the day of rest.

17–18. *The rustling leaves accompanying / Their rhymes with a harmonic drone effect*: The *burdone* (burden) is an unvarying drone pitch that underlies a melody, often compared to bagpipes. The forest air through the narrow openings between the moving leaves acts like air forced through a reed instrument, making this sound, which accompanies the melodic birdsong.

19–20. *Like the one that travels branch-to-branch / Rallying in the pines along the Adriatic*: Dante uses the place name *Chiassi* (today Classe) to refer to the famous pinewood forest that extends from that city all along the coast of the Adriatic Sea to south of Ravenna, the site of an Augustinian-era Roman naval base. The pine trees are primarily Italian stone pines, also called umbrella or parasol pines, for their huge broad canopies; like the pome trees on the sixth cornice, the top widens as it goes higher. They can grow to be eighty-two feet high. Dante knew them well from his stay in Ravenna during his exile.

21. *when Aeolus lets Sirocco loose*: In Greek myth, Aeolus was the god (or king) of the winds. He was said to keep the winds locked away in skin bags behind a bronze wall on his floating eponymous island, Aeolia. The Sirocco is a fierce wind that begins in the Sahara Desert, travels to the coast of northern Africa, crosses the Mediterranean Sea—where it picks up moisture—and sweeps across southern Europe.

23. *the ancient forest*: Commentators quote Virgil (*Aeneid* 6, 179) as a possible source: "Itur in antiquam silvam, stabula alta ferarum." (They pass into the ancient forest, the deep lairs.) This is the forest primeval, i.e., Eden.

25–26. *a stream stopped me in my tracks; / The rippling current made the grass / At its edge*: This stream is Lethe, as Dante will learn later in the canto. In Greek myth, Lethe, Greek for "forgetfulness" or "oblivion," is one of the five rivers in Hades. Drinking from it destroys all memory of life, so the dead won't pine for the world above. Virgil,

Georgics 4, 18–19: "At liquidi fontes et stagna virentia musco / Adsint, et tenuis fugiens per gramina, rivus." (But let there be clear springs and moss-green pools / And a narrow stream cutting through the grass.)

28–29. *All the most crystalline waters on earth / Seem muddy compared to this*: Shakespeare, *A Midsummer Night's Dream* (III.ii.138–139): DEMETRIUS. "To what, my love, shall I compare thine eyes? / Crystal is muddy!"

30. *Which hides nothing*: Nothing can be hidden in Eden, which is why the first couple's transgression was readily apparent.

40–41. *A woman, totally alone, just singing / And picking this flower, that flower*: The young shepherdess, alone in a bucolic landscape, is a traditional trope of the troubadour *pastorella* genre.

43–45. *Oh, Bella Donna, you seem to radiate / Love-light. In my experience, when one looks / Like you, the heart is usually involved*: Dante, mistakenly, he will soon learn, is making assumptions about this young woman's possible interest in him and using what's clearly a pickup line.

48. *So I can hear what you're singing*: Oddly, we are never told what the woman is singing, making Dante's request seem even more of a transparent ploy.

49–51. *You're making me recall where / Persephone was and what happened when / Her mother lost her, and she lost her spring*: In Greek myth, as told by Ovid (*Metamorphoses* 5.385–408), Persephone was similarly gathering flowers when Pluto carried her off to be queen of Hades. Her mother, Demeter, went to bring her home, but Persephone erred in eating a few forbidden seeds, which resulted in her having to forever spend spring in Hades and winter on earth. She lost her spring because she was taken during that season, and she can no longer come to earth during that season; but she also lost the spring of her life, her innocent girlhood, because she was raped by Pluto. This moment feels oddly self-indicting on Dante's part, especially given that he has just ended his tenure on the seventh cornice, which is devoted to lust. The woman will not be named until *Purg.* XXXIII, 119, when Beatrice deflects Dante's question about the stream called Eunoe by saying, "Ask Matelda."

52–54. *Like when a woman turns to dance, / Her feet close to the ground and together, / Barely moving one foot in front of the other*: Singleton (2:672), somewhat dryly, writes: "Apparently this for Dante represents a most beautiful manner of dancing, modest and becoming to a maiden. The feet are barely lifted from the ground and are kept close together." In the stately court dance called *basse danse* (low dance), dancers don't raise their feet far from the floor but instead walk slowly or glide. The first mention of the *basse danse* is found in a poem, "Quar mot orne fan vers," by Raimon de Cornet (fl. 1324–1340), a priest and troubadour poet. The form is considered to be precursor of the Renaissance *pavane*.

55–57. *From the upturned red and upturned yellow / Blossoms she turned toward me—Lowering her honest eyes like an innocent*: The blossoms are adamantly faceup, in contrast to the down-turned eyes of the modest girl.

63. *She gave me the gift of lifting her eyes*: There is a certain boldness in this "gift" of looking directly at Dante, which forecasts the way Matelda will soon take control of the situation and make clear to Dante that he has erred in reading her downcast eyes as evidence of submissiveness.

64–66. *the light under Venus's lashes . . . when she was aimlessly hit / By her son's archery, so unlike his usual mode*: Ovid (*Metamorphoses* 10.525–532) tells how, when she was accidently wounded by her son Cupid's arrow as he leaned in to kiss her, Venus fell in love with the mortal Adonis. This is unlike the intentional way Cupid usually works. Dante appears to misread the brightness in Matelda's eyes for availability; in the *pastorella* form, the shepherdess is not only available for lovemaking, but in the Cavalcanti poem, she initiates it. A verse from the Cavalcanti poem will begin the next canto. Dante appears to be acting in this scene according to that often-quoted verse in Virgil's *Eclogues* (10, 69): "Amor vincit omnia; et noa cedamus amori." (Love conquers all; so let's give in to love.) Shakespeare, *A Midsummer Night's Dream* (III.ii.103–107):

> OBERON.
> Hit with Cupid's archery,
> Sink in apple of his eye
> . . . .
> Let her shine as gloriously
> As the Venus of the sky.

71–74. *Hellespont—where Xerxes bridged it . . . Didn't create more hatred in Leander / For the sea swell between Sestos and Abydos*: In his attempt to conquer Greece, the Persian king Xerxes I built a bridge across the Hellespont, a strait known today as the Dardanelles that divides Europe from Asia Minor. When a storm destroyed the bridge, he was forced to retreat in a small boat. In *De monarchia*, Dante writes that Xerxes had military might and ambition, but even so, the bridge "got the upper hand." In Greek myth, Leander used to swim from Abydos across the Hellespont to Sestos to visit his beloved Hero, a priestess of Aphrodite. When the wind blew out the lamp she set in her tower window to guide him, he lost his way and was drowned by the waves. When she discovered his body, she threw herself from the tower in grief.

76–78. *You're new here and . . . I'm smiling in this place / That was chosen as a nest for human nature*: Matelda gently explains to Dante the possible reasons he may be misreading the situation: one, he's thinks her smile is a coy romantic overture; two, he's new to Eden so may not understand that coyness doesn't exist here, everything is forthright; and three, because they are in the place where mating began the entire human race, he wrongly has mating on his mind.

79–81. *You're wondering and have suspicions . . . the light shed by Psalm 92 . . . should demystify your mind*: From the medieval liturgical psalter: "Quia delectasti me Domine in factura tua et in operibus manuum tuarum exultabo." (For thou hast given me, O Lord, a delight in thy doings: and in the works of thy hands I shall rejoice.) Matelda uses the psalm to suggest that the pleasures in this place are not carnal but a delight in what God has created. This, and not an interest in Dante as a love partner, is the radiant warmth he recognized when he first saw her standing in the flowers.

82–83. *you, in front of me, who asked me here, / Say if you want to know more; I've come ready*: Matelda becomes a bit more confrontational: Dante indicated he wanted her to come over, well, here she is, and this is what she has to offer—knowledge, yes, although of a different sort than what he might have had in mind.

85–87. *The water . . . and the treetop sounds / Contradict a recent belief . . . Based on something I'd been told*: Dante is referring to having been told by Statius (*Purg.* XXI, 44–72) that there were no weather elements above the three steps leading up to the gate to Purgatory.

91–93. *The Supreme Good, solely out of self-interest . . . created / This place as a down payment on eternal peace*: The Terrestrial Paradise was created for humans—who were created to act in accord with God's wishes—as an earnest, a temporary paradise before the guaranteed-permanent Paradise.

94–96. *Due to their failings, they lived here briefly . . . they traded straight-up smiles / And Candy-Land games for tears and grief*: The Bible does not say how long the first family lived in Eden, but it appears they were banished before the birth of their first child. Having compromised their ideal existence, they inherited the myriad worries with which humans must contend. Candy Land, a simple board game in which gingerbread icons race one another to a Candy Castle, requires no reading and only simple math skills; it was designed in 1948 by Eleanor Abbot, who tested it on the children on the hospital ward where she was recovering from polio. It was sold to Milton Bradley and first produced in 1949.

100–102. *the mountain rose / This far toward the heavens, so as to be free / Of the greenhouse effect above the gate*: Matelda confirms what Statius said insofar as there is a complete absence of earthly weather events above the level of the gate.

121–126. *The water you see doesn't spring from a vein . . . And, through the will of God, it regains whatever / It loses as it divides into two running streams*: Matelda ends her explanation of how the mechanism of action for everything in the Terrestrial Paradise is God's will, as opposed to the earthly laws of nature.

127–132. *The virtue that flows from the one side . . . here, Lethe; while the other side is called / Eunoe; it won't work if you don't first drink / From this side before tasting that*: Dante alters the Greek idea of Lethe, a river that erases all memory, to having only the memories of sin erased. He invents the river Eunoe, which restores the memory of good acts. Lethe must be crossed first, and in both cases, the water must be actually swallowed.

133. *That flavor is better than any other*: To have all the good of a lifetime restored to memory, after having the sum of one's errors erased, is a taste beyond any others. In *Purg.* XXXIII, 137–138, Dante will say that the water is "the sweet drink / That never would've satisfied me."

139–144. *those in ancient times who poeticized / The Golden Age . . . This is the nectar they all talk about*: Matelda is suggesting that the Terrestrial Paradise embodies all the elements the Greek and Roman poets wrote about under the guise of a first Golden Age: the everlasting spring; the Parnassian streams; and the nectar, especially as described by Ovid (*Metamorphoses* 1.89–112): "flowers sprang up unplanted. Untilled earth produced silos filled with grain, and the fields, although unplowed, grew pale with thick bearded wheat. Streams of milk and streams of sweet nectar flowed, and golden honey was claimed from the green oak."

145–147. *I turned to my poets . . . Behind me, and saw they were smiling / At having heard that last conjecture*: Dante is obviously charmed by the possibility that these poets were prophetic, and clearly trusts that Statius and Virgil will be as well. And they are. That they have all found their way to this place of perfection, only imagined in the past, gives them all great pleasure. The fact that Dante instinctively turns to Virgil to share this moment reminds the reader of the bond between them.

Canto XXIX

Singing like a woman in love, she went on
At the end of her speech,
"Blessed are those whose sins are covered!"

And like the nymphs that used to go alone
Through shady sylvan glades, now
Wanting to see the sun, now escaping it,

She moved that way against the current.
Walking on the bank, I kept even with her,
Matching my steps to her smaller steps.

Together we hadn't gone more than
A hundred steps when the two banks both
Turned in a way that left me facing east;

We hadn't gone far along the next stretch
Before she turned to face me, saying,
"My monkish brother, look and listen."

Then hello! out of the blue a flash of light
Flooded every part of that enormous forest,
Making me think it must be lightning.

But because lightning's like there, then gone,
And this kept on, getting more and more bright,
I had to ask myself, "What *is* this?"

A lilting melody ran through
The luminous air; at which, a righteous
Zeal made me recall Eve's daring:

There, where all of Heaven and earth obeyed,
One woman, just formed, couldn't bear
To remain in a cloud of unknowing.

If she'd remained devout in it,
I would have felt these ineffable delights
From the outset and for a longer time.

As I went on among so many firstfruits
Of eternal pleasures, all deferred,
And wishing for still more happiness,

The air before us under the green boughs
Began to glow like a lit fire and the soft sound
Could now be made out as chanting.

O inviolable Virgins, if for your sake
I was ever hungry, cold, or awake all night,
I call on you now to show me mercy.

Let Helicon flow for me, let Urania
Send me a boatload of vocalists, so that
These mind-blowing ideas can be versified.

A little farther on, seven golden trees—
A false impression created by
The great distance between them and us—

When I was near enough, the distance
No longer messing with the senses, the common
Object no longer scrubbed of its purpose,

The faculty that readies thought to meet matter
Got that they were candelabras,
And that the voices were chanting "Hosanna."

The top of that lovely device
Blazed far brighter than a full moon
In the midst of a cloudless midnight.

I turned around, filled with awe,
To clever Virgil and he responded with a look
No less charged with amazement.

I turned back to wait for those tall objects;
They were taking so long to get to us,
Brides in lace would have outpaced them.

The woman scolded, "You're so turned on
By these bright lights, you don't even notice
What's coming up after them?"

I then saw people, coming behind
As if being led, dressed in white of such
Incandescence as has never been seen here below.

The water to my left picked up my image
And reflected back my left side
As if I were looking into a mirror.

When I was at a point on the shore
Where only the stream was between us,
I stopped to get a better look

And saw the flames go by, leaving the air
Behind them painted with a semblance
Of undulating brushstrokes;

Hovering above, seven distinct ribbons
In all the colors from which the sun makes
A rainbow and Diana her headband.

These banners stretched back farther
Than I could see; my best estimate said
Between the outer edges was maybe ten steps.

Below this beautiful sky, I separated out
Twenty-four elders, coming two by two,
Crowned with fleurs-de-lis.

They were all chanting: "Blessed art thou
Among the daughters of Adam,
And blessed be thine everlasting beauty."

After the flowers and lush greenery
On the bank opposite me
Were completely clear of that elite group,

Like in the sky, the way one light quickly follows
Another, a group of four animals came next,
Each with a crown of green leaves.

Each was feathered with six wings, feathers
Filled with eyes. Argus's one hundred eyes,
If alive, would look like these.

I can't spare any more rhymes to describe
Their forms, Reader—my other expenses
Are too pressing, I don't dare lavish more on these.

But read Ezekiel, who depicts them
As he saw them, coming from the cold side
With a whirlwind and fire in a cloud.

You can find that in his writings,
The same as here, except for the wings,
Where John is with me, and differs from him.

The interior space defined by the four
Contained a two-wheeled triumphal chariot,
That came drawn by the neck of a griffin:

It lifted both wings, isolating the center
Band from the three and three on either side,
Damaging nothing in the cutting through,

Raising them so high they were lost to sight.
Whatever was bird, those parts were gold;
The rest was white, mixed with red.

Rome never cheered Africanus or the great
Caesar Augustus with a chariot this stunning;
The sun's car couldn't even hold a candle to it:

The sun's which, sidetracked, was burned up
When pious Earth cried out and Jove
Mysteriously did what was right.

Next, came three women circle dancing
At the right wheel; one was so red,
She'd barely be noticed in a fire,

The other seemed as if she'd been made,
Flesh and blood, out of emerald,
The third looked like snow in motion.

Now the white one leads, now the red
And from what the red one sings, the others
Take their cues to go, and fast or slow.

On the left, four dressed in purple were
Court dancing, following the rhythm
Set by the one with three eyes in her head.

After the troupe I just described, I saw
Two elders, dissimilar in dress but similar
In bearing, upstanding and no-nonsense.

One revealed himself to be a follower
Of the great Hippocrates, whom Nature
Made for the creatures she holds most dear.

Another revealed the opposite tendency,
With a highly polished sword so sharp
Even on this side of the stream, I felt uneasy.

Then I saw four with an air of humility;
Bringing up the rear, an old man, alone,
Sleepwalking, but with a wide-awake face.

These seven were dressed just like those
In the first division, but they didn't have
Fleur-de-lis garlands on their heads,

Instead roses and other red flowers.
From not that far away, you'd have sworn,
From the eyebrows up, they were all on fire.

And when the chariot was in front of me,
A thunderclap was heard; it seemed
That august crowd, forbidden to go on,

Was stopping right there with the initial regalia.

1. *Singing like a woman in love*: This first line echoes a poem by Dante's friend, and the dedicatee of *Vita nuova*, the poet Guido Cavalcanti. Cavalcanti is describing a shepherdess he discovers in a grove: "Cantava come fosse 'namorata / Era adornata di tutto piacere." (She sang as if she were in love, / She was dressed in pure pleasure.) That poem contains a soft echo of Dante's poem "You women who have the intellect of love."

3. *Blessed are those whose sins are covered!*: The Penitential Psalm 21, one of the psalms for matins in the Roman Breviary, begins, "Beati quorum remissae sunt iniquitates, et quorum tecta sun peccata." (Blessed are they whose transgressions are forgiven, whose sin is covered.) The Latin *tecta* means "covered," as in to have a roof over, to be sheltered. The end of *Purg.* XXVIII and this new beginning are tied together by the dreamed-of "nectar" of the ancients. Lethe is the nectar and in this canto, Dante and Statius will have their memories wiped of sin by drinking of it; this is how their sins, atoned for on the seven levels of Purgatory, will be "covered."

4–6. *And like the nymphs that used to go alone / Through shady sylvan glades, now / Wanting to see the sun, now escaping it*: Dante invokes the ancient forest of Virgil's bands (*Georgics* 4, 382–383) of mythic "sister-nymphs who guard / the hundred forests and the hundred streams" to describe how Matelda, at the edge of the forest, is sometimes in sun, sometimes in shade. Like the nymphs, she goes alone and with great purpose.

12. *Turned in a way that left me facing east*: Dante is facing east, toward Jerusalem, and it is from that direction, appropriately, that the holy procession will come.

15. *"My monkish brother, look and listen"*: Matelda addresses him now as *Frate mio*, "my brother," not in the sense of a blood relative, but as the title used by a monk or friar. This both honors him, by including him in the brotherhood/sisterhood of those who belong in this place, and, equally, reinforces the platonic nature of their connection.

16–18. *a flash of light . . . Making me think it must be lightning*: Dante appears to have forgotten Matelda's explanation that the elements in this place are not earthly phenomena.

22–24. *A lilting melody . . . a righteous / Zeal made me recall Eve's daring*: We aren't told the nature of the melody, but its effect is to produce a sense of indignation. Dante uses the term *buono zelo*, a principle of the Benedictine brotherhood. Saint Benedict described good zeal as an expansive spiritual ardor, as opposed to evil zeal, a withholding bitterness.

26–27. *One woman, just formed, couldn't bear / To remain in a cloud of unknowing*: Dante describes Eve as unwilling to remain under any *velo*; *velo* in Italian means "veil," "cover," or anything that obscures; the verb *velare* can figuratively mean "to cloud." *The Cloude of Unknowyng* is a Middle English work of Christian mysticism of unknown authorship, thought to be written in the latter half of the fourteenth century: the premise is that only by remaining in the cloud of unknowing can one paradoxically know God.

28–30. *If she'd remained devout . . . I would have felt these ineffable delights / From the outset and for a longer time*: Had Eve not disobeyed, and in doing so consigned future generations to share in the guilt of original sin, Dante would have been born into a state of grace and enjoyed all the fruits of Eden throughout his life. Instead, he has led a sinful life and only now, with divine intervention on the part of Beatrice, and after achieving forgiveness by passing through Hell and climbing Mount Purgatory, has he been allowed into the Terrestrial Paradise.

32–33. *Of eternal pleasures, all deferred, / And wishing for still more happiness*: While there are many pleasures here, the eternal pleasures are deferred until he crosses both Lethe and Eunoe. The additional happiness he desires is the long-awaited reunion with Beatrice.

35–36. *the soft sound / Could now be made out as chanting*: The increasingly clear sound is being used to suggest that Dante is moving toward something slightly mysterious. He will soon realize that the mysterious something is also moving toward him.

37–39. *O inviolable Virgins, if for your sake / I was ever hungry, cold, or awake all night, / I call on you now to show me mercy*: As at the beginning of the poem, Dante invokes the Muses for help to translate his complicated thoughts into lyric utterance. In *Purg.* I, 9, he beseeched Calliope; here he asks first for help from the Mountain of Helicon, down which flowed two streams sacred to the Muses. He follows Virgil in that invocation: *Aeneid* 7, 641, and again in *Aeneid* 10, 163: "Pandite nunc Helicona, deae, cantusque movete." (Now, Helicon, place your goddesses at my disposal and inspire those songs.) He then appeals to Urania (Greek for "heavenly"), one of the nine Muses: the Muse of astronomy and goddess of music, song, and dance. Bacchylides, fragment 16: "Since fine-throned Urania has sent me from Pieria a golden cargo-boat laden with glorious songs."

43–45. *seven golden trees / A false impression created by / The great distance*: These illusionary trees, we will soon learn, are candelabras.

50. *they were candelabras*: The seven candalabras were presumably atop stands with shafts made of spindles and knobs on a clawed tripod base. There still exist parts of a twelfth-century seven-candle Milanese candelabra known as "the Virgin's tree" that is over eighteen feet high. How these are being moved is not clear. The seven-branch candlestick is rooted in biblical tradition (Exodus, Leviticus, Numbers).

51. *the voices were chanting "Hosanna"*: In both Matthew (21:9) and Mark (11:9–10), "Hosanna," a cry of praise or adoration, was said to have been shouted by the crowd when Jesus entered Jerusalem. In *Vita nuova* XXIII, Dante writes that upon hearing of

Beatrice's death, he imagined her rising to Heaven as a cloud, attended by a chorus of angels singing, "Hosanna in the highest."

55–57. *I turned around, filled with awe, / To clever Virgil and he responded with a look / No less charged with amazement*: Virgil, the pagan Roman poet, is being given a glimpse of the Christian Heaven, and is as impressed as Dante. The moment is yet another reminder of their enduring bond.

61–63. *The woman scolded, "You're so turned on / By these bright lights, you don't even notice / What's coming after them*: Dante, much to Matelda's annoyance, is still smitten by the first thing he sees and remains focused on that instead of taking in the bigger picture.

64–66. *people, coming behind / As if being led, dressed in white of such / Incandescence*: The seven candelabras, representing the sevenfold Spirit of God, appear to be leading people dressed in immaculate white. Christ's garments, after his transfiguration, were described in Mark 9:3 as being "exceeding white as snow; so as no fuller on earth can white them." From the appearance of the lamps onward, Dante draws heavily on Revelation (also called the Apocalypse), the final prophetic book of the New Testament. Revelation 4:5: "And out of the throne proceeded lightnings and thunderings and voices: and there were seven lamps of fire burning before the throne, which are the seven Spirits of God."

67–68. *The water to my left picked my image / And reflected back my left side / As if I were looking into a mirror*: Lethe is mirroring Dante's left side, as if to show him that sinful side of himself that will be erased by the water, once he swallows it.

73–75. *leaving the air / Behind them painted with a semblance / Of undulating brushstrokes*: These undulating bands of variously colored refracted light become airy banners that hang like a canopy over the entire procession.

76–78. *seven distinct ribbons . . . the colors from which the sun makes / A rainbow and Diana her headband*: Rainbows, created when water droplets create a prism of the sun's light, contain the entire spectrum of colors. Diana, the huntress (referred to by Dante as *Delia*, for her birthplace, the island of Delos), is goddess of the moon. Moonbows are rare. Aristotle mentions them in *Meteorologia* III.ii: "if there is to be one it must be at full moon, and then as the moon is either rising or setting. So, we have only met with two instances of a moon rainbow in more than fifty years." Revelation 4:3: "and there was a rainbow round about the throne, in sight like unto an emerald."

83–84. *Twenty-four elders, coming two by two, / Crowned with fleurs-de-lis*: Most commentators interpret the twenty-four elders as representing the twenty-four Old Testament books as well as the twenty-four elders described in Revelation 4:4: "And round about the throne were four and twenty seats: and upon the seats I saw four and twenty elders sitting, clothed in white raiment; and they had on their heads crowns of gold." The white fleur-de-lis flower crowns represent faith. The stylized fleur-de-lis emblem is used by French royalty, the Catholic Church, and the city of Florence. Dante associates the fleur-de-lis with French power in *Purg.* XX, 86.

85–87. *Blessed art thou / Among the daughters of Adam, / And blessed be thine everlasting beauty*: Dante has replaced the "blessed art thou among women" in Luke 1:28—where the angel appears to Mary to announce she's been chosen to produce a son—to "blessed art thou among the daughters of Adam," a gesture to the Edenic beginning.

92–93. *a group of four animals came next, / Each with a crown of green leaves*: Commentators agree these four animals are meant to represent the Evangelists, the authors of the four canonical New Testament gospels: Matthew, Mark, Luke, John, and their corresponding symbol animals; winged man, winged lion, winged ox, and eagle. Each animal is the "king" of its species: the lion, king of wild animals; the ox, king of domesticated ones. Green is the color of hope. The green leaves can also be imagined as laurel wreaths.

94–96. *six wings, feathers / Filled with eyes. Argus's one hundred eyes, / If alive, would look like these*: Dante draws on both Ezekiel and Revelation for the wings and eyes.

97–98. *I can't spare any more rhymes . . . Reader*: This is the fifth time Dante uses the literary device of direct address to the reader. These metapoetical moments create a sense of intimacy between the speaker and reader and heighten the illusion of authenticity.

100–102. *Ezekiel, who depicts them . . . coming from the cold side / With a whirlwind and fire inside a cloud*: Ezekiel 4:4: "And I looked, and, behold, a whirlwind came out of the north, a great cloud, and a fire infolding itself, and a brightness was about it, and out of the midst thereof as the colour of amber, out of the midst of the fire."

103–105. *in his writings . . . except for the wings, / Where John is with me, and differs from him*: In Ezekiel 10:21, the living creatures are described as having four wings: "Every one had four faces apiece, and every one four wings; and the likeness of the hands of a man was under their wings." The author of Revelation, thought to be John of Patmos, gives them six wings, as in the note to vv. 94–96.

107–108. *two-wheeled triumphal chariot*: Commentators throughout time have interpreted the chariot as the symbol of the Church Triumphant, the beatific vision of Heaven, based on the idea (from Plutarch's *The Life of Camillus*, 7.1) that the Romans considered the triumphal chariot to be sacred and reserved for the king and father of the gods. The Byzantine emperor John I Tzimiskes was said to have refused the two-wheeled triumphal chariot offered him at Constantinople after his victory over the Bulgarians and instead placed a captured icon of the Virgin in the carriage.

108. *That came drawn by the neck of a griffin*: The Greeks associated the griffin, a four-legged beast with the head and wings of an eagle and body of a lion, said to have enormous strength and very sharp claws, with Apollo, god of the sun and poetry; its role was to guard Apollo's treasures and to carry off anything that interfered with

the god's inspiration. Commentators have long assumed the griffin in *Purgatorio* was meant to represent Christ, since its biform nature is consistent with Christ's duality as man and god. Hollander and Hollander (614) note there have been recent opposing viewpoints.

In medieval heraldry, the griffin connects back to Imperial Rome; Peter Armour argues in the *Dante Encyclopedia* (455) that the figure represents "the union of the divine and human, the imperial and the popular powers in Dante's conception of ideal Rome, its empire and its Christlike prince, the agent of redemption at Christ's birth and death, and the guide to temporal happiness in the Earthly Paradise." Armour further develops this idea in his book *Dante's Griffin and the History of the World*.

109–110. *It lifted both wings, isolating the center / Band from the three and three on either side, / Damaging nothing*: The enormous wings of the griffin cut through the three streams of colored light on either side as they come up to frame the center band. Dante makes the point that the banners aren't disturbed by this, implying that if the phenomenon were not supernatural, they would have been. The three on either side are interpreted by some as the Trinity; others see the combined seven bands as the Seven Gifts of the Holy Spirit (or as some argue, a sevenfold gift): piety, fear of God, knowledge, fortitude, counsel, intellect, and wisdom (*Convivio*, 4, 21, 12); these gifts are meant to oppose, in the same order, envy, pride, anger, sloth, avarice, sensuality, and gluttony.

113–114. *Whatever was bird, those parts were gold; / The rest was white, mixed with red*: The fact that the creature is bicolored emphasizes its dichotomy; the gold bird elements are usually read as embodying Christ's divinity, while the white (sinew) and red (blood) lion elements emphasize his incarnate aspect.

115–116. *Rome never cheered Africanus or the great / Caesar Augustus with a chariot this stunning*: Scipio Africanus the Younger destroyed Carthage at the end of the Third Punic War and was rewarded in Rome with a triumphal procession. Augustus, the first Roman emperor, received three different triumphs after three victorious battles.

117–120. *The sun's car couldn't even hold a candle to it: // The sun's which, sidetracked, was burned up / When pious Earth cried out and Jove / Mysteriously did what was right*: The sun's chariot, driven across the sky in Greek myth by Helios, the sun god, was "sidetracked" when his son Phaeton insisted on driving it one morning. Phaeton lost control and when the fiery chariot got too near the plains of Africa, Earth prayed to Jupiter; he answered her prayer by killing Phaeton with a thunderbolt. The event was referred to in *Inf.* XVII, 106–108, and previously in *Purg.* IV, 71–72.

121–126. *three women circle dancing . . . one was so red . . . The other seemed . . . out of emerald, / The third looked like snow in motion*: The colors are believed to represent the three theological virtues: charity is red, because of its burning ardor; hope is green; and faith is pure white. When Dante finally encounters Beatrice in the next canto, she will be wearing a white veil, a red dress, and a green cloak.

127–129. *the white one leads, now the red . . . what the red one sings, the others / Take their cues*: Faith and charity take turns leading the dance but since charity is at the top of the hierarchy, her song sets the tempo and tells the group when to stop and start.

130–132. *the left, four dressed in purple . . . following the rhythm / Set by the one with three eyes in her head*: This second group, lesser since it's on the left, is said to be "making festival," which we can presume is also dancing, perhaps a form of chain dance or *ridda*, since the other was specifically a ring dance. This group is seen as representing the four cardinal virtues: justice, prudence, temperance, and fortitude. These were established by the Greek philosophers (Plato and Aristotle) and adopted by the early church. Prudence is at the top of this hierarchy, so she establishes the rhythm. Her three eyes represent her ability to see past, present, and future.

Dante may also have had in mind Brunetto Latini's poem *Il tesoretto* (*The Little Treasure*) (vv. 175–179), which features four women who represent social values: Cortesia, Larghezza, Leanza, and Prodezza (courtesy, generosity, loyalty, and prowess); the poem instructs: "But all in common [*per comune*] / Should pull together on a rope / Of peace and of welfare, / Because a land torn apart / Cannot survive." Dante places Latini in the seventh circle of Hell, for those who were violent against God (*Inf.* XV, 82–87), although he softens the judgment by saying that he too would join the group if it weren't for the fear of the fire that punishes them.

134–135. *Two elders, dissimilar in attire but similar / In bearing, upstanding and no-nonsense*: While the men's demeanors are similarly grave, their garments indicate their different occupations.

136–138. *a follower / Of the great Hippocrates, whom Nature / Made for the creatures she holds most dear*: This is clearly Saint Luke, the gospel author, physician, and author of the Acts of the Apostles; he appears twice in the procession because Dante wishes to present the entire sequence of the New Testament books. He would have practiced according to the Hippocratic oath, a set of principles outlined by Hippocrates, the "father of medicine." The oath, which today has been reduced to the catchphrase "First, do no harm," is actually a series of oaths sworn to the god Apollo and other gods and goddesses: to act ethically, to keep patient confidentiality, and to practice within the law. The creatures that nature holds most dear are, according to Aristotle and Dante, humans.

139–140. *Another revealed the opposite tendency, / With a highly polished sword so sharp*: This is thought to be the Apostle Paul. His sword represents his martyrdom, as well as the word of God.

142. *Then I saw four with an air of humility*: These are the authors of what some call the minor or "lesser" epistles: James, Peter, John, and Jude.

143–144. *an old man, alone, / Sleepwalking, but with a wide-awake face*: This final man, old and entranced, but with an animated face, is thought to be the mystic John of Patmos, author of Revelation; see note to vv. 103–105.

145–148. *These seven were dressed just like those / In the first division, but they didn't have / Fleur-de-lis garlands . . . Instead roses and other red flowers*: The red flowers have been variously interpreted by commentators, but all agree that the primary symbolic meaning is charity. The three crowns—the green (hope), the white (faith), and the red (charity or love)—echo the colors of the three theological virtues. Red also gestures to the passion of Christ, his arrest, trial, crucifixion, and death, and to the "blood of the new covenant" promised by Christ to his disciples at the Last Supper, and to the red wine of the Eucharist.

151. *And when the chariot was in front of me*: The entire pageant has now been seen, those elements that have passed by Dante and those still to come. Vernon (2:484) quotes Frederick Ozanam, author of a *Purgatorio* translation and commentary (into French, 1862), on how Dante's conception of the pageant is indebted not only to the Bible but also to the tropes of Christian art, especially the mosaics in the ninth-century Basilica of Saint Praxedes (called Santa Prassede) in Rome: "Dante doesn't work at random. He reproduces Ezekiel, the Apocalypse and the entire tradition of Christian art. In Rome, in the mosaics of the Basilica of Saint Praxedes, we see the lamb on the altar, the seven candelabras, the four animals, the twenty-four old men; at the Moissac portal, the facing griffins, Christ, the four animals, the old men."

152–154. *A thunderclap was heard; it seemed / That august crowd, forbidden to go on, / Was stopping right there with the initial regalia*: The thunderclap, like the bolt Jupiter threw when pious Earth called out for help, and like the biblical thunder in Revelation 6:1, 10:3, comes from above. It is a signal that brings the procession to a complete halt. The reader is reminded of the seven lamps at the front of the procession; when they stop, everything that follows them must also stop.

Canto XXX

At that moment, the highest Heaven's
Seven stars—which can't rise and can't set
And can't be veiled except by a film of guilt—

Were making everyone there hyperaware
(Like the lesser stars tell one to turn the rudder
Toward the port) of what they must do:

Stop and stand still. That truthful group
That had come before the griffin now turned
To the chariot, as if to its peace.

Then one, like a Heaven-sent messenger,
Singsong shouted three times, "Come, my bride,
From Lebanon," then all the others echoed him.

The way, at the trumpet's last blast,
Each blessed will step from its cave,
Singing Hallelujah with a regained voice,

So here, over the divine car there rose up,
At the voice of so great an elder, a hundred
Ministers and messengers of eternal life.

All of them saying, "Thou art blessed,"
While throwing flowers all over and around it,
"Oh, offer lilies, your hands filled with them."

I've seen how daybreak can begin
With a totally rosy eastern sector,
The rest of the sky stunningly clear,

While the shaded face of the rising sun,
Softened by mist, allows the eye to look at it
For a few breath-held seconds—

The same here, inside a cloud of flowers
Being tossed up by angelic hands, then
Tumbling down again, turning inside out,

I made out a woman: the top, a white veil
With a wreath of olive leaves; the bottom,
A naked-flame red dress under a green coat;

And my mind, even after it had been
Such a long time since I'd been stunned,
Trembling, and overwhelmed in her presence,

Even before my eyes recognized her
(The virtue she emanated hidden in the occult)
My mind felt the power of that ancient love.

As soon as I was struck by the sight
Of that sublime virtue that had transfixed me
Before I'd outgrown childhood,

I turned to my left, with the same expectation
With which a kiddo runs to its mother
When afraid or upset,

To say to Virgil, "There's not a cell
In my body that isn't shaking. I'm starting
To recognize the traces of my ancient flame."

But Virgil had slipped away, having left us
Dumbfounded after him. Virgil, dearest father,
Virgil, to whom I gave myself for my safekeeping.

However much our first mother'd lost, it wasn't
Enough to keep the cheeks the dew had washed
From being muddied again with tears.

"Dante, just because Virgil's run off,
Don't cry yet, save your crying;
There's another sword coming to make you cry."

A bit like an admiral who walks from stern
To prow, overseeing the crew managing
The other boats, urging: do the right thing,

From the left side of the chariot,
When I turned at the sound of my name—
Recorded here out of utter necessity—

I saw the woman who'd first appeared to me
Behind the curtain of that angelic free-for-all
Looking straight at me from across the stream.

Still, the veil that fell from her head,
Capped with a chaplet of Minerva's leaves,
Kept her appearance from being registered.

Regally, with a haughty attitude, she continued
Talking like someone who's holding back
The most searing critique for later.

"Look really well! I'm really Beatrice, I really am.
How were you able to access the mountain?
You know, don't you, everyone here is happy?"

I lowered my eyes to the clear stream; seeing
Myself in it, faced with the weight of such shame,
I looked awkwardly away at the grass.

It can seem to a child that the mother
Is on her high horse; that's how she seemed to me.
Such is the bitter taste of harsh pity.

She stayed quiet and the angels suddenly sang,
"In thee, O Lord, I put my trust,"
But they went no further than "my feet."

Like the snow between the living rafters
On the dorsal ridge of Italy, which freezes
Once it's blown and packed down by trapped winds,

Then liquefies, leaking and feeding off itself,
Just like the breath of a land with no shadows
Can act like a flame that makes a candle melt

Like that, I was without sighs or tears
Before the singing of those who are forever
In tune with the eternal spheres,

But when I sensed that their soft melodies
Were actually meant to show sympathy for me,
As in: "Lady, must you crush him?"

The ice around my strangled heart cracked,
And breath and water left my anguished chest,
Exiting through my mouth and eyes.

She, still standing firm on the same side
Of the stopped chariot, turned and addressed
The charitable angels with this:

"You are everlastingly vigilant all day,
You don't waste your time with night or sleep,
While the century ticks away.

I'm far more concerned that the sniveling one
Over there get the drift of what I'm saying,
Since his suffering still needs to equal his guilt.

Not only through the work of the great wheel
That breeds each seed for a unique end,
According to its own fixed stars,

But also through the largesse of divine grace—
Which makes rain clouds so high,
Try as we might, we can't ever see them—

This one here, potentially, still in his new life,
Having all of that quick-witted aptitude
Would've made an amazing demonstration.

If a bad seed can grow in wasteland soil,
The outcome in a landscape with assets
Is all the more malignant and thorny.

For a while, I had my character hold him up,
Let him see youth through my eyes,
Dragging him with me in the right direction.

As soon as I arrived at the doorway
Of my second phase and let go of life,
Bingo, he ran off and took up with others.

When I was moved up from flesh to spirit,
And had all-grown-up beauty and virtue,
I was less dear to him, less appreciated.

He changed direction and took a bad path,
Chasing false images of good, no promise
Ever met: a bolt of nothing, shot at nothing.

Nor was it worth my begging for and being given
Divine inspiration for him; I used it
To try to reach him in a dream: he didn't care!

He was so low, and all the earlier efforts
Toward his well-being had fallen so short,
Nothing was left but to show him the lost ones.

That's why I went down there to the door
Of the dead and, crying, directed my prayers
To the one who led him here;

God's supreme decree would be shredded to bits
If Lethe were crossed and a meal like that
Got eaten without the piper being paid

In scalding hot tears of remorse."

1–3. *At that moment, the highest Heaven's / Seven stars—which can't rise and can't set / And can't be veiled except by a film of guilt*: Dante uses *settentrïon*, the North, from the Latin *septentrio*, literally "seven plow oxen"—a term used to refer to Ursa Major, the great bear constellation. The smaller Ursa Minor constellation is the lesser bear. Unlike those stars, which rise and set, the Sevenfold Spirit of God, Heaven's seven stars signified by the seven candelabras, is steadfast. Those divine lights aren't obscured by earthly clouds, the way stars are, but only by the sinful nature of humans, which keeps them from knowing God. The negating *nè*, repeated three times, is the first of many emphatic triads in this canto.

5–6. *Like the lesser stars tell one to turn the rudder / Toward the port*: The brightest star in the Ursa Minor constellation is Polaris, also called the North Star or polestar. Throughout time, it's been used by sailors for nighttime navigation. Just as Polaris tells sailors at what point to turn the rudder toward the boat's port (left) side, so too the procession takes its cues from the seven candelabras.

7–8. *that truthful group / That had come before the griffin now turned*: By stopping, the seven candelabras have directed the twenty-four elders representing the books of the Old Testament to stop and turn toward the chariot. Dante refers to the group as truthful based on the belief that their Old Testament messianic prophecies were fulfilled in Jesus.

9. *To the chariot, as if to its peace*: Christ is the peace promised in the New Testament.

11–12. *Come, my bride, / From Lebanon, then all the others echoed him*: The triple invocation, first by a single elder, then repeated by the others, echoes King Solomon's appeal in the Song of Solomon 4:8: "Come with me from Lebanon, my spouse, [come] with me from Lebanon: [come] look from the top of Amana, from the top of Shenir and Hermon, from the lions' dens, from the mountains of the leopards." That book, called *Liber sapientiae* (book of wisdom) in the Vulgate Bible, is an allegorical poem in which the spouse means many things, one of which is a personification of the divine wisdom (the wisdom of Solomon) given to the righteous through the word of God. Beatrice, when she exits the car, becomes that personified wisdom. In *Convivio*, Dante similarly personified philosophy (knowledge) as a woman.

13–15. *at the trumpet's last blast, / Each blessed will step from its cave, / Singing Hallelujah with a regained voice*: The book of Revelation describes seven trumpet blasts by seven angels; the first six blasts prophesy plagues and call for repentance. The seventh announces the Second Coming of Christ. At this, the Last Judgment, the dead will be reunited with their bodies and regain their human voices; the faithful will then welcome this new state by praising God. "Hallelujah" is from the Hebrew *hal'luyáh*, meaning "Praise Yah[weh]."

16. *divine car*: Dante uses the Latin word *basterna* for the car, an enclosed bench with a privacy drape used by Roman noblewomen. King Solomon similarly built a chariot for his bride. Song of Solomon 3:9–10: "King Solomon made himself a chariot of the wood of Lebanon. He made the pillars thereof of silver, the bottom thereof of gold, the covering of it of purple, the midst thereof being paved with love, for the daughters of Jerusalem."

16–18. *there rose up, / At the voice of so great an elder, a hundred / Ministers and messengers of eternal life*: Singleton (2:732) interprets the use of *cento* (one hundred) as an indefinite "many," which is how the word is used elsewhere in the *Commedia*; Hollander and Hollander (663) take the number literally and add it to the forty-three members of the pageant, plus Beatrice, to arrive at the number 144, "the mystical number (144,000) of the Church Triumphant," which is said in Revelation to be imprinted upon the foreheads of the redeemed (Rev. 7:4, 14:1, 14:3). The "ministers and messengers of eternal life" are angels. In *Vita nuova*, Dante pictures Beatrice ascending to Heaven with angels; here she is surrounded by them (see note to *Purg.* XXIX, 51).

17. *At the voice of so great an elder*: Dante uses the Latin *ad vocem tanti senis* for this phrase. Some commentators argue that he wishes to rhyme *senis* with the Latin *venis* (v. 19) and *plenis* (v. 21). Vernon (2:504) rejects that claim and suggests that Dante is quoting an author now unknown to us. Hollander and Hollander (629) suggest that Dante is creating a trio of Latin writers, Virgil, biblical Mark, and himself. The hubris of that notion might be a sufficient argument against it.

19. *All of them saying, Thou art blessed*: Dante uses the Latin *Benedictus qui venis*. Commentators note that the masculine adjectival ending (*-dictus* instead of the feminine *-dicta*, which one would expect for Beatrice) matches the Vulgate *Benedictus qui venit* found in the description of Jesus entering Jerusalem in Mark 11:9. This is one of several moments when Beatrice is conflated with Christ.

20. *While throwing flowers on and around it*: On the occasion of the entry of Jesus, palm fronds were strewn along the way; here the carriage is strewn with flowers.

21. *Oh, offer lilies, your hands filled with them*: Dante also keeps the Latin for "*Manibus*, oh, *date lilïa plenis!*"—a verse appropriated from Virgil's *Aeneid* 6, 883—but Dante adds the Italian interjection "oh." In the *Aeneid*, the verse is spoken by Anchises, the father of Aeneas, when Aeneas encounters him in the underworld. Anchises is lamenting the premature death of Marcellus, the nephew and son-in-law of Augustus, who was the prospective heir to the Augustan throne. The funereal role of the lilies, to be scattered on the grave of the much-beloved Marcellus, foreshadows the Roman poet's own departure in v. 49 of this canto.

31–33. *a white veil / With a wreath of olive leaves . . . A naked-flame red dress under a green coat*: In ancient Greece, the winner of the Olympic games was crowned with a wreath of olive leaves from a sacred tree near the temple of Zeus. In the Roman era, the olive wreath, because of its association with Minerva, goddess of war and wisdom, was a triumphal crown conferred on military victors. The colors Beatrice is wearing are those worn by the three dancers that represent the three theological virtues, white (faith), green (hope), and red (charity or love), at the right wheel of the chariot in *Purg.* XXIX, 121–126. In *Vita nuova*, Dante says that Beatrice is dressed in red the first time he meets her (see note to vv. 39–42).

37–38. *before my eyes recognized her / (The virtue she emanated hidden in the occult)*: While Dante doesn't yet recognize the woman as Beatrice, since she is hidden by the veil and by the supernatural quality she radiates, he senses a presence that is as electrifying as Beatrice's once was.

39–42. *the power of that ancient love . . . that had transfixed me / Before I'd outgrown childhood*: In *Vita nuova*, Dante writes of the first time he saw Beatrice: "She was about to be nine, while for me, nine was almost over. She was wearing an extremely dignified little dress: demure, blood-red, belted and modestly trimmed in a manner that was perfect for a girl her age. I can honestly say that at that moment, the animating spark of life that lives in the deepest recess of the metaphoric heart exploded with such force that I felt it in every fiber of my being."

43–48. *I turned to my left . . . a kiddo runs to its mother . . . To say to Virgil . . . I'm starting / To recognize the traces of my ancient flame*: Dante now incorporates a second line from Virgil's *Aeneid* (4, 23), "Adgnosco veteris vestigia flammae." In this case, he translates Virgil's Latin into his own Italian: "conosco i segni dell'antica fiamma." (I recognize the traces of the ancient flame.) The verse in the *Aeneid* is spoken by Dido, the queen of Carthage, to her sister Anna about how her love of Aeneas caused her to break the vow of chastity she'd made to her late husband, Sychaeus, who had been slain by her brother, Pygmalion. Upon encountering Virgil and Dante on the sixth cornice (*Purg.* XXI, 97–98), and before realizing to whom he's speaking, Statius says that Virgil was both mother and wet nurse to his poetry. Here, Dante envisions Virgil as both the mother to whom a child would turn in distress and as the father who has kept him safe. The triple invocation of Virgil's name is echoed in yet another Virgilian verse; in *Georgics* 4, 525–527, Orpheus similarly calls out three times to his dead Eurydice.

52–54. *However much our first mother'd lost, it wasn't / Enough to keep the cheeks . . . From being muddied again with tears*: Dante appears to be arguing that however much the loss of Eden, through Eve's failure to forego knowledge, has caused countless tears, his loss of Virgil is worthy of adding a few more to the cheeks Virgil had washed with dew at the end of Canto I (vv. 125–127).

55–57. *just because Virgil's run off, / Don't cry yet, save your crying; / There's another sword coming to make you cry*: This detached response by the veiled woman argues that no,

Virgil's departure is not as worthy of tears as the loss of Eden and, moreover, the pain Dante is experiencing is nothing compared to what is coming.

58–60. *an admiral . . . overseeing the crew managing / The other boats, urging: do the right thing*: Dante appears to appreciate how the stern speaker might be holding him to a high standard, similar to an overseeing officer who is in charge of others, each with a responsibility.

61–63. *From the left side of the chariot . . . my name— / Recorded here out of utter necessity*: Exiting from the left side, she is now facing Dante. He records his name as an act of accountability. In *Convivio* 1, 2, Dante writes: "Experts in rhetoric say no one is allowed to talk about oneself without a compelling reason." In *Inferno*, he claimed to have rescued someone who'd fallen into a baptismal well but didn't explicitly give his name. In that case, it was to defend himself against an accusation; here, it is to serve as an example.

68. *a chaplet of Minerva's leaves*: Her imperious bearing, already compared to that of an admiral, echoes the combative aspect of Minerva, the goddess of war. Minerva, however, is also the goddess of wisdom and the speaker has already begun, in her caution to Dante to save his tears, to demonstrate that attribute as well.

73. *Look really well! I'm really Beatrice, I really am*: The mysterious woman, still veiled, now names herself, as she first named Virgil, and then Dante. The insistent, emphatic *ben* (really) is another trinity, like the negation in vv. 2–3; the crying in vv. 56–57; and the "Come, my bride, from Lebanon" called out three times by the elder in vv. 11–12.

74–75. *How were you able to access the mountain? / You know, don't you, everyone here is happy*: The first question is a cutting reminder that Dante was able to ascend the mountain only through her intervention. The second question, equally sarcastic, is to remind him that she was forced to intervene because his bad behavior had led to his great unhappiness.

76–78. *I lowered my eyes to the clear stream . . . faced with the weight of such shame, / I looked awkwardly away*: The mirrorlike aspect of the stream, which Dante delighted in, in *Purg.* XXIX, 64–66, now reveals to him how far he still has to go to achieve forgiveness.

81. *the bitter taste of harsh pity*: Throughout *Inferno* and *Purgatorio*, Dante has been motivated to overcome the many obstacles in order to be reunited with the mythologized Beatrice. This, however, is clearly not the reunion he has longed for and long imagined. Instead, he feels like a naughty child in front of a mother in a bad mood.

82–84. *the angels suddenly sang, / "In thee, O Lord, I put my trust," / But they went no further than "my feet"*: The hundred angels sing the Latin Vulgate beginning of Psalm 31, a prayer of praise mixed with a petition for deliverance; they sing the first seven verses through but stop at "*pedes mios*" (my feet) near the end of the eighth verse ("And hast not shut me up into the hand of the enemy: thou hast set my feet in a large room").

85–90. *Like the snow between the living rafters / On the dorsal ridge of Italy . . . liquefies . . . like the breath of a land with no shadows / Can act like a flame*: The long simile describes the thawing of Dante's well-defended heart by comparing it to the way snow packed between the still-living trees that will later become rafters at the top of the Apennine ridge, the backbone of Italy, seeps through the earth's crust if hot winds from Africa act like a fire that melts the snow as if it were candle wax.

92–93. *those who are forever / In tune with the eternal spheres*: The intuitive angels don't follow prearranged notes, as an earthly choir would, but instead sense what the universe requires and match their singing to that knowledge.

95–97: *meant to show sympathy for me, / As in: "Lady, must you crush him?" // The ice around my strangled heart cracked*: His defenses—she's a power-hungry military type; she's up "on her high horse"; she doesn't understand what a good parent Virgil's been—are suddenly overcome by the idea that the angels also may feel she has been too strict.

100. *standing firm on the same side*: Beatrice is standing above the linchpin of the left wheel. Such a device, a metal or wooden shank inserted through the axletree to keep the wheel attached, holds things together, just as she is holding to the divine principles that require that Dante understand the nature of his guilt and complete his penance.

101–102. *addressed / The charitable angels with this*: Beatrice wants to make certain the charitable angels don't rob Dante of the opportunity to achieve the necessary contrition. As she says in v. 108, his suffering has to equal his guilt.

105. *While the century ticks away*: The ticking occurs on earth; in Heaven, there is only the eternal present.

115–117. *still in his new life, / Having all of that quick-witted aptitude / Would've made an amazing demonstration*: Since *Vita nuova* is Dante's only previous complete text at this time, it's impossible not to read *sua vita nova* (his new life) as self-referentially referring back to that work, particularly since vv. 121–123 below appear to summarize it.

118–120. *If a bad seed can grow in wasteland soil, / The outcome in a landscape with assets / Is all the more malignant and thorny*: Seedling vigor is the ability of a seed to grow even in suboptimal conditions. Beatrice is making the point that if a *mal seme* (bad seed) can minimally grow in bad conditions, if grown under good conditions, the plant will have even more of its negative attributes. The corollary is that with Dante's good "soil," the devotion to Beatrice evidenced in *Vita nuova*, his wildness became all the more degenerate.

121–123. *For a while, I had my character hold him up, / Let him see youth through my eyes, / Dragging him with me in the right direction*: Commentators point out how these three verses present a concise nutshell summary of the narrative arc of *Vita nuova*.

124–126. *the doorway / Of my second phase and let go of life, / Bingo, he ran off and took up with others*: A noblewoman named Beatrice ("Bici") di Folco Portinari, one of five daughters of Folco Partinari, a wealthy Florentine banker, is believed by many scholars to be the historical figure that inspired both Dante's *Vita nuova* and his *Commedia*. She married Simone dei Bardi (ca. 1287), a banker, and died in 1290 at the age of twenty-four. In *Vita nuova*, Dante says that they saw one another only twice: once when he was nine and taken by his father to a May Day party at her parents' house and a second time when she greeted him on the street nine years later, specifically at the ninth hour. Boccaccio was the first person to insist upon an autobiographical reading of Beatrice, and for *Vita nuova* in general. Benvenuto, writing fifty years after Dante's death, argued that while there was a real Beatrice, one whom the nine-year-old boy and young adult man idealized, she was also a ready emblem when he needed a sacred object. In the event, Dante allegorizes Beatrice.

In *Convivio* (4, 24), Dante divides a life span into quarters; the first quarter, he says, lasts up until the twenty-fifth year. Since Beatrice dies in her twenty-fourth year, she was about to enter her second phase. The *altrui* (others) to whom Dante then devotes himself are left unnamed. He admits in *Vita nuova* that he was drawn to a young and very beautiful woman after Beatrice died. This, however, could have been the personified Lady Philosophy that forms the subject of the unfinished *Convivio*.

127–128. *When I was moved up from flesh to spirit, / And had all-grown-up beauty and virtue, / I was less dear to him, less appreciated*: The movement from flesh to spirit is her death. At that point, her beauty is that of a fully grown woman and her virtue is fully developed.

132. *a bolt of nothing, shot at nothing*: Shakespeare, *Cymbeline* (IV.ii.300–302): IMOGEN. "'Twas but a bolt of nothing, shot at nothing, / Which the brain makes of fumes. Our very eyes / Are sometimes like our judgements, blind."

138. *Nothing was left but to show him the lost ones*: This is exactly what Virgil says to Cato in *Purg.* I, 62–63, when he explains how and why it is that he and Dante are arriving on foot at the shore of Purgatory instead of by the boat piloted by an angel.

139–141. *I went down there to the door / Of the dead and, crying, directed my prayers / To the one who led him here*: This is the visit to Limbo in *Inf.* II, 116, when Beatrice tearfully appealed to Virgil to rescue Dante. She reduces Virgil here to his role in the story, the one who led Dante here.

142–145. *God's supreme decree would be shredded to bits / If Lethe were crossed . . . without the piper being paid // In scalding hot tears of remorse*: Dante uses *fato di Dio* (God's fate) for the Christian idea of God's decree. The pre-Christian idea of fate pervades the *Aeneid*; that poem begins with the proclamation that the poet will tell the story of one who was forced by fate to leave Troy and come to Italy, a fate that is tied to the anger of a goddess (Juno), who is herself trying to influence the fate of her favorite city, Carthage. Christian theology revamps the idea of fate into the natural order of the divine mind, while leaving room for the exercise of free will and for the consequences of the misuses of free will. The idiom "to pay the piper" means to suffer the consequences. Dante uses the word *scotto*, meaning to pay up or settle an account.

Canto XXXI

"O you, on the other side of the holy stream,"
Getting right to the point, as if the edge
Of what she'd already said wasn't sharp enough.

She went on, without missing a beat, "Speak up,
Say if you plead guilty—the accusation
And confession have to be linked."

My faculties were so disorganized,
I'd go to speak but when the organ stops opened,
Nothing would come out.

She tolerated this for a bit, then said, "Answer me.
What are you thinking? The water hasn't yet
Damaged your regrettable memories."

At that, confusion and fear joined forces
And pushed out a "yes"—but to decipher it,
You had to be a lip-reader.

Like a crossbow under too much tension,
The string frays, the bow breaks, and now
With too little force, the shaft can't meet its mark.

Similarly, I burst beneath that heavy burden;
Tears gushed out and my sobbing voice
Worked its way through the weakened gap;

At which, she to me: "As per my earlier wishes,
Which were leading you to love goodness,
Beyond which there's nothing left to hope for,

What holes did you have to dig yourself out of,
Or what chains did you wind up in, that in order
To keep going, you had to strip away all hope?

What well-oiled silver spoons or hustler bonuses
Were advertised on the face of the others
That you felt obliged to hang out with them?"

After letting out a bitter sigh, I barely
Had a voice left with which to answer;
My quivering lips struggled to shape a reply.

Crying, I said, "These things,
With their bogus pleasures, led me astray
As soon as your face was hidden."

"If you'd kept quiet or denied
What you're confessing, your guilt would be
No less evident. This judge knows things!

In our court, when an accusation of guilt
Spills out onto the sinner's cheek, he can address
The rostrum and deflect the cutting edge.

All the same, so you'll now be ashamed
Of your errors, and be stronger
The next time you hear the Sirens,

Sow the seeds of your sorrow and listen:
You're going to hear how my buried carnal body
Should have moved you in the opposite direction.

Neither nature nor art ever offered you anything
As delightful as the beautiful flesh I was held in,
And which is now buried in the ground.

And if this supreme delight fell through
With my death, what drew you
Into a love match with a mothlike living thing?

At the first misleading pinprick,
You should have gotten up and come looking
For me, who was no longer one of those.

While waiting for more slings and arrows,
You shouldn't have let your wings be pinned down
By some young thing or fly by night novelty.

A fledgling might wait around a few times,
But a full-grown feathered friend isn't taken in
By a spread net and flees at the sight of an arrow."

Like children stand listening, shamefaced,
Speechless, eyes glued to the ground, owning up
To what they've done, overcome by remorse,

I stood there. She said, "Since mere listening
Has made you sad, lift up your beard,
And have a good look at some serious labor pains."

A sturdy oak is uprooted with less resistance
By one of our northern winds,
Or by one from the land of Iarbas,

Than my reluctant chin rose at her command;
By her saying "beard" and meaning "face,"
I felt all the venom behind the pretext.

Having lifted my head and composed myself,
I looked squarely at those highest beings
Who had stopped sprinkling their flowers around.

By my lights, which were still a bit shaky,
I saw Beatrice turn toward the beast
That is one person with a twofold nature.

Although under her veil, and across the stream,
She seemed to outdo even her former self, even more
Than she'd surpassed all others when she was here.

I was so pricked by the stinging nettle of regret,
The more something other had bent my love to it,
The more it became my nemesis.

So much self-recognition gnawed at my heart
That, overwhelmed, I fell. What caused it
Is only known by her who had a hand in it.

Once my beating heart brought me back
To myself, the woman I'd found earlier by herself
Was over me, saying, "Hold on to me, hold on."

Eventually she got me into the river
And I was up to my neck in it; she was pulling me
Behind her lightly over the water, like a shuttle.

When I was near the sacred edge, I might
Have heard "Cleanse me" being sung, but faintly;
I barely remember, not well enough to record it.

The Bella Donna opened her arms, embraced
My head, and plunged me under, which,
As it was meant to, made me swallow the water.

She helped me out and took me, sopping wet,
Over and presented me at the center of the four
Beautiful dancers. Each elevated an arm over me.

"Here we are nymphs, in the sky we are stars;
Before Beatrice descended to the world,
We were ordained her handmaiden darlings.

We'll lead you to her eyes, but once inside
That smiling light, those three over there,
Who aim farther, will sharpen your sight."

They began with that chant, then brought me
With them over to the front of the griffin
Where Beatrice was standing facing us.

"Don't be sparing," they said, "take in the view;
We've placed you in front of those emeralds
From which Cupid once shot his arrows at you."

A thousand desires hotter than fire
Kept my eyes locked onto those bright shining eyes
That remained fixed on the griffin.

Like the sun in a mirror, the two-natured beast
Was reflected in them: now showing
One mode, now showing another.

Think, Reader, how I must have marveled
As I watched this thing-in-itself stay as it was,
While its image kept morphing back and forth.

Meanwhile, my soul, full of amazement
And delight, tasted of that food which,
As it's satisfying, the thirst for it grows.

Demonstrating they were of a higher order,
The other three moved forward,
Dancing one of those angelic circle dances.

"Turn Beatrice, turn your holy eyes,"
Was their song, "to the one who is true
And who went through so much to see you.

As an act of merciful grace, for our sake,
Unveil your mouth for him—so he can see
The second beauty you keep behind a key."

O splendor of everlasting living light, who
Among those who grew pale beneath the shadows
Of Parnassus, or drank from its fountains

Wouldn't have been driven to distraction
Trying to convey what you appeared to be,
Matching the heaven casting a shadow over you,

When there in the open air you showed yourself.

1. *O you, on the other side of the sacred stream*: While Beatrice was clearly talking both about Dante and implicitly to him, when she was addressing her handmaidens at the end of *Purg.* XXX, she now addresses him directly. She gets straight to the point, confronting him about his wayward behavior.

11–12. *The water hasn't yet / Damaged your regrettable memories*: Since Dante hasn't drunk from the river Lethe yet, she's suggesting that he is still aware of his sins and should still be suffering remorse.

40–42. *In our court . . . he can address / The rostrum and deflect the cutting edge*: The highest ecclesiastical tribunal, the Sacra Romana Rota, was the papal court from the twelfth to the sixteenth century. While the ultimate authority was the pope, bishops and cardinals could serve as auditors and make recommendations. The court is named Rota (the wheel) because it was originally held in a round room. Punishment in the twelfth century often took the form of cutting, especially that part of the body associated with the offense: the hand of a thief might be cut off; someone found guilty of slander might have their tongue cut off; a rapist's eyes might be cut out.

44–45. *and be stronger / the next time you hear the Sirens*: In Greek myth, the Sirens were mermaids whose songs lured sailors onto the rocks. In the *Odyssey*, Odysseus has his men go belowdecks after tying him to the mast to prevent his being lured into steering the ship toward them.

60. *By some young thing or fly-by-night novelty*: *Pargoletta* is a female child. Some commentators suggest this might be the same woman celebrated in one of Dante's four *Rime petrose* (Stone Rhymes, ca. 1296). *Petrose* means both "hard" and also "cold," "rocky," and "stormy." There may have been an actual woman or she could simply have been a conceit in the tradition of the troubadour poets, whose poems were addressed to an unavailable woman. Another possibility is that this is meant to be the "young and very beautiful" woman Dante admits in *Vita nuova* to having been attracted to after Beatrice's death.

70–72. *A sturdy oak is uprooted with less resistance / By . . . winds . . . from the land of Iarbas*: The land of Iarbas is North Africa. Iarbas, a king in Roman mythology who appears in both Virgil's *Aeneid* and Ovid's *Metamorphoses*, tried to persuade Dido, queen of Carthage, to marry him; she, however, preferred Aeneas. When she entreated Aeneas to stay with her, he resisted, "like a deep-rooted tree that withstands strong northern winds." Dante reuses the simile but reverses the effect: he succumbs to the wind because his "Dido," Beatrice, deserves his devotion.

74–75. *by her saying "beard" and meaning "face," / I felt all the venom behind the pretext*: Dante gets the full sarcasm behind Beatrice's telling him to lift his "beard," instead of just telling him to raise his face and look at her; she is suggesting that he should act like an adult and not a prepubescent child.

77–78. *I looked squarely at those highest beings / Who had stopped sprinkling their flowers around*: These are the one hundred (or many) angels who had been hovering above the chariot and showering it with flowers. They are the highest beings because they were created before humans and because they reside with God in the highest realm.

80–81. *I saw Beatrice turn toward the beast / That is one person with a twofold nature*: The beast is the dual-natured griffin—part eagle and part lion—who represents the duality of Christ, part human and part divine.

88–90. *So much self-recognition gnawed at my heart / That, overwhelmed, I fell. What caused it / Is only known by her who had a hand in it*: Dante faints twice in *Inferno*: in *Inf.* III, when he witnesses an earthquake, fire, and lightning while sitting on the boat rowed by Charon to Hell proper; and in *Inf.* V, after having spoken to Francesca and Paolo in the second circle, where lust is punished, and being moved by their story. Beatrice's harsh interrogation has made Dante feel the full weight of his remorse. It may be that only she knows the cause of his collapse because only she knows the nature of his sins. It's also possible that only she understands the mysterious workings of the Terrestrial Paradise and that the collapse might be a part of the final stage of penance.

91–92. *Once my beating heart brought me back / To myself*: The beating heart reminds us that Dante is still alive, unlike those who usually reach this stage. It also suggests the importance of love. 1 Corinthians 13:13: "And now abide faith, hope, love, these three; but the greatest of these is love."

92–93. *the woman I'd found earlier by herself / Was over me, saying, "Hold on to me, hold on"*: Once Dante recovers, he finds he's in the arms of the woman from the riverbank. This is the opposite of the beginning of *Inferno*; when he comes to there, he's alone in a lightless forest and the path is lost.

95–96. *she was pulling me / Behind her lightly over the water, like a shuttle*: The specificity of Dante's description, "like a shuttle," makes it clear that he's not been completely submerged and has, therefore, not yet swallowed the cleansing water of Lethe.

97–99. *near the sacred edge, I might / Have heard "Cleanse me" being sung but . . . not well enough to record it*: "Asperges me" is a thirteenth-century liturgical plainchant refrain derived from Psalm 51: "Purge me with hyssop, and I shall be clean: wash me, and I shall be whiter than snow." While it is being chanted, the congregation is sprinkled with holy water by the celebrant of the mass.

100–102. *The Bella Donna opened her arms, embraced / My head, and plunged me under, which, / As it was meant to, made me swallow the water*: Finally, having drunk from the river Lethe, Dante will have the memory of his sins erased.

103–105. *took me, sopping wet, / Over and presented me at the center of the four / Beautiful dancers. Each elevated an arm over me*: These are the cardinal virtues, prudence, temperance, fortitude, and justice. The four raise their arms and form the promised "cover" over the now-purified Dante.

106–108. *Here we are nymphs, in the sky we are stars; / Before Beatrice descended to the world, / We were ordained her handmaiden darlings*: As he so often does, Dante draws here on multiple references. These four may be the four stars Dante saw in *Purg.* I, 23–24, which he says had not been seen by anyone since the first human beings. They are also mythological Virgilian nymphs, young women associated with nature, especially woodlands, rivers, and streams, who served as attendants to the gods and goddesses. They say they were assigned to serve as Beatrice's handmaidens even before they came down to earth, which suggests that Beatrice, like Christ, was born sanctified. As Hollander and Hollander point out (654), only the lyric allows for what would otherwise be theological heresy.

109–111. *We'll lead you to her eyes, but once inside / That smiling light, those three over there . . . will sharpen your sight*: While the cardinal virtues can lead Dante over to stand before Beatrice, it will require the three theological virtues, faith, hope, and charity (or love), the bedrock of moral rectitude, to sharpen his sight so he can see into the depths of her purity.

116–117. *those emeralds / From which Cupid once shot his arrows at you*: The emeralds are Beatrice's green eyes. Cupid, the Roman god of love (Greek: Eros), was the son of Venus (the goddess of love) and Mars (the god of war). His golden arrows incite desire; his lead arrows cause a sense of revulsion.

121–123. *the two-natured beast / Was reflected in them: now showing / One mode, now showing another*: There are actually two dual natures, and they flash back and forth: lion and eagle on the one hand, human and divine on the other.

124–126. *Think, Reader, how I must have marveled / As I watched this thing-in-itself stay as it was, / While its image kept morphing back and forth*: Once again, the metapoetical address to the reader. By inviting the reader to suspend disbelief and accept a fantastical reality, Dante is asking the reader to engage in an act of faith, which demonstrates how faith works.

127–129. *my soul, full of amazement / And delight, tasted of that food which, / As it's satisfying, the thirst for it grows*: This, the poet is saying, is the reward of faith—absolute confidence in the knowledge one has gained, a confidence that feeds upon itself. In Ecclesiasticus 24:21, Wisdom speaks, saying: "They that eat me shall be hungry, and they that drink me shall yet be thirsty."

130–132. *Demonstrating they were of a higher order, / The other three moved forward, / Dancing one of those angelic circle dances*: The higher-order theological virtues now come forward. Commentators have been puzzled by the word (*caribo*) used for the dance since there is no such word. Most interpret the dance as a roundelay, a medieval circle dance, based on the *carole* or *carola*, a dance accompanied by music popular in the twelfth and thirteenth centuries in Western Europe. Boccaccio describes a *carola* danced in Florence in the *Decameron* (ca. 1350–1353).

133–138. *Turn Beatrice, turn your holy eyes . . . As an act of merciful grace, for our sake, / Unveil your mouth for him—so he can see / The second beauty you keep behind a key*: The virtues, like the angels, argue for leniency for Dante. In *Convivio,* speaking of Lady Philosophy, Dante says wisdom can only be read in her eyes and her smiles. The "second beauty" of Beatrice is her smile.

139–143. *O splendor of everlasting living light . . . those who grew pale beneath the shadows / Of Parnassus . . . Trying to convey what you appeared to be*: Even the great Latin poets, who exhausted themselves to the point of pallor on the Parnassian mountain and drank from the fountains of the Muses, even they couldn't have adequately described the splendor that Dante is witnessing.

144–145. *Matching the heaven casting a shadow over you, // When there in the open air you showed yourself*: The reader is reminded, by the mention of the shadow cast over her, of the rainbowlike ribbons that rise from the seven candelabras and overlie the entire procession. She matches the beauty of those as well as the radiance of Heaven. Beatrice's loveliness, as she unveils herself, is equal to all of that.

Canto XXXII

As the ancient net drew my eyes
To that saintly smile, my eyes were so fixed
And focused on satisfying the ten-year thirst

That all my other senses were switched off
And held on either side
Behind a wall of indifference.

Only because I heard those goddesses say,
"*Way* too fixated!" did I feel the need
To turn my face and look to my left.

That tendency of the eyes to be blinded
When struck by the sun,
That's what had happened to me.

But then, as the eyes adjust a little
(And I say a little out of respect for the greater
Radiance I was forced to look away from),

I saw that that glorious troupe, the seven flames
At its head, had swung around to the right
And was now headed back toward the sun.

The same way, to save themselves, troops turn tail
Behind their shields, yet wait for the standard
Bearer to pivot before they change position,

So the militia of the celestial kingdom
Advanced, all of them passing by
Before the cart's wooden pole swung around.

Then the women went back to their wheels,
And the griffin moved its blessed cargo
Without so much as a ruffled feather.

The Bella Donna who had pulled me across,
And Statius and I, followed the inside wheel,
Which made its orbit with a smaller arc.

Walking through the empty vaulted forest,
Which was *her* fault for believing the snake,
Our measured pace set by an angelic note,

We were maybe three times the distance
Of a let-loose arrow from where we'd begun
When Beatrice stepped down.

I heard everyone murmuring "Adam,"
Then they circled a barren tree, every branch
Stripped of its leaves, even the unopened buds.

The canopy of it, which expands more
The higher it rises, would go through the roof
Of the tallest trees in the admirable forests of India.

"Bless you, griffin, that you don't tear into it
With your beak and eat the tasty softwood,
Which then makes the belly cramp so badly,"

The others around the robust trunk called out.
And then from the binatured animal, "Yes!
The seed of all righteousness must be preserved."

To that end, he dragged the wooden pole
That he'd pulled over to the foot of the widowed tree
And left it tied to the branch it had come from.

The same as our plants—when the strong light
That falls on them gets mixed with
The shining light next in line after Pisces,

They begin to swell, and, even before the sun
Has time to race its steeds over to other stars,
Each rediscovers its own color.

This plant, unfurling its colors, less like roses
And more like violets, was similarly restored,
The bare branches now as they'd been before.

I didn't know what it meant, nor is the hymn
The group then sang anything we sing here,
Nor could I get through the whole thing.

If I were able to sketch how the relentless-eyed
Argus dozed off while hearing about Syrinx,
Eyes which if alert could cost someone dearly,

Like a painter who paints from life,
I'd make a self-portrait: Me, falling asleep—
But who wants a picture of pretend sleep?

I'll just skip ahead to when I woke up and say
That a dazzling light pierced the veil of my sleep,
And a call: "Get up, what are you doing?"

When taken to see the apple blossoms—the pomes
Of which the angels crave, and from which
Heavenly wedding wine is eternally made—

Peter, John, and James were overwhelmed
And then brought back by the word
That has shattered even deeper sleeps;

They then saw their group had been reduced
By Moses, and likewise by Elias, and that
The Master's garments had been changed.

I came back like that and saw,
Standing over me, the devoted one
Who'd earlier been my guide along the stream.

Completely at sea, I asked, "Where's Beatrice?"
And she: "Look over there under the new leaves,
See her sitting on the roots?

See how her handmaidens are circling her?
The others followed the griffin up,
Singing more softly, but with deeper feeling."

If she went on making more small talk,
I wouldn't know; I only had eyes for the one
Who held all my attention.

Sitting by herself on the bare ground,
As if she'd been left to guard the chariot
I'd seen the binatured animal attach there,

In a circle, the seven nymphs formed a cloister
For her, the candles in their hands safe
From any winds, Aquilo or Auster.

"Here, in a little while, you'll be sylvan,
And you'll be, until the end, a citizen with me
Of that Rome, where Christ is Roman.

This is why, although evil lives in the world,
You need to keep your eye on the chariot, and,
Once back there, make yourself write what you see."

That was Beatrice, and I, like all those at her feet
Devoted to her commands, dedicated
My mind and sight to whatever she wanted.

A blaze never zigzagged down so fast
From a thick cloud of rain at the border
Of the highest sphere of fire

As the bird of Jove that I saw crash down
Through the tree, tearing off not only the bark
But the flowers and new leaves as well.

It struck the chariot full force, tipping it
Like a ship in a tempest pummeled by waves,
Now starboard right, now larboard left.

Then I saw a fox pounce on the cradle
Of the triumphal two-wheeler; it looked like
It had fasted through every decent meal.

My lady, lighting into the filthy sinner,
Put it to flight, at least as far as possible
For bones missing their meat.

Then, from where it had come to rest before,
The eagle plunged into the ark of the chariot
And left the better part of its feathers there.

At which, sounding like a heart filled with regret,
A voice came out of Heaven and said,
"O my little boat, what a heavy burden."

Then it seemed to me the earth opened up
Between both wheels, and I saw a dragon emerge
And stick its tail end up through the chariot.

And like a wasp retracts its stinger, it drew back
Its vicious tail, taking with it part of the bottom,
Then wandered around it, just wandering.

What was left were a few feathers,
Offered perhaps with benign good intentions.
Like crabgrass in fertile soil,

These quickly spread over it: one wheel,
Then the other, then the pole, in less time
Than a sigh holds a mouth open.

Transformed like that, the holy edifice
Grew a head for each of its parts,
Three over the pole and one on each side.

The three had oxen-like horns; however,
The four had only one horn on their foreheads:
No monster like this has been seen before.

Certain, almost like an alpine fortress,
A free-and-easy whore was perched on it,
Batting her lashes and looking around.

As to how and why she hadn't been run off,
I now saw, standing next to her, a giant;
From time to time, they cozied up and kissed.

But because her amorous wandering eye
Had been pointed at me, her barbaric lover boy
Read her the riot act, top-down and bottom-up.

Then, filled with suspicion and coarse rage,
He untied the monster and dragged it so deep
Into the woods that only that fact shielded me

From the whore and the strange new beast.

NOTES TO CANTO XXXII

1–3. *As the ancient net drew my eyes / To that saintly smile . . . satisfying the ten-year thirst*: Dante's long-standing attachment to the flesh-and-blood Beatrice, the Freudian object of libidinal cathexis, pulls him in. Since the poem is set in 1300, it has been ten years since the death of Beatrice in 1290.

7–9. *Only because I heard those goddesses say, / "*Way *too fixated!" did I . . . turn my face and look to my left*: The three theological virtues, still standing with Dante in front of the griffin, understand that the attachment Dante is demonstrating is regressive. In addition, he is not seeing what else is going on around him (the same complaint Matelda made in *Purg.* XXIX, 61–63). The Three Graces of Greek myth were minor deities representing beauty, charm, and grace, collectively known as the Charities and often depicted as handmaidens to Aphrodite, the goddess of love. By calling the virtues "goddesses," Dante appears to be conflating, as he so often does in the *Commedia*, pre-Christian and Christian symbols.

16–18. *that glorious troupe, the seven flames / At its head . . . was now headed back toward the sun*: The procession is turning to face east, to return to Paradise from which it came; in this case, the sun is God.

19–24. *The same way . . . troops turn tail . . . the militia of the celestial kingdom / Advanced . . . Before the cart's wooden pole swung around*: The military simile gestures toward what is called the Church Militant, the struggle of the earthly Church against evil and misuses of power. The history of the Church Militant will be symbolically enacted later in this canto.

25–27. *Then the women went back to their wheels, / And the griffin moved its blessed cargo / Without so much as a ruffled feather*: Until now, all seven virtues have been standing with Dante, Matelda, and Statius at the front of the chariot. The fact that the griffin moves the chariot, without so much as disturbing a feather, suggests that when Christ was in charge of the Church, all was well. After the griffin returns to Paradise, we'll see the chariot/Church transform into a monster.

28–30. *The Bella Donna . . . And Statius and I, followed the inside wheel . . . with a smaller arc*: The procession has turned to the right and now Dante, Matelda, and Statius join the theological virtues at the right wheel, which makes a smaller arc because it's turning right. Statius being named reminds us that he is still there.

31–33. *Walking through the empty vaulted forest, / Which was* her *fault for believing the snake, / Our measured pace set by an angelic note*: The loss of Eden, which left the forest empty of inhabitants, was the fault of Eve for having been convinced by the serpent to disobey the limitations placed on the couple.

34–36. *We were maybe three times the distance / Of a let-loose arrow . . . when Beatrice stepped down*: A medieval arrow would have traveled one hundred yards; three times that distance would equal three American football fields. In *Thebaid* 6, 354, Statius measures a distance as being equal "four times a javelin throw, three times an arrow's flight."

37–38. *everyone murmuring "Adam," / Then they circled a barren tree*: While Dante has just indicted Eve, it's Adam that the group associates with the denuded tree.

40–42. *The canopy of it, which expands more / The higher it rises . . . the tallest trees in the admirable forests of India*: Like the two trees on the cornice of gluttony (*Purg.* XXII, 131, and XXIV, 105), this tall, wide-canopied tree may be a crabapple, which can reach forty feet. In *Georgics* 4, 122–124, Virgil describes trees in India as being so tall that even an arrow shot full force can't reach the top.

47–48. *then from the binatured animal, "Yes! / The seed of all righteousness must be preserved."*: The griffin answers in words attributed to Jesus in Matthew 3:15: "for thus it becometh us to fulfil all righteousness."

49–51. *he dragged the wood pole . . . over to the foot of the widowed tree . . . the branch it had come from*: The pole is usually interpreted as the cross on which Christ died, the wood of which is linked to the Tree of Knowledge via legend (*The Legend of the Cross*).

54–57. *The shining light next in line after Pisces . . . Each rediscovers its own color*: Aries, March 21 to April 20, follows Pisces; because it's spring, the sunlight in Aries is stronger and warmer, which causes the trees to bud and plants to turn green.

58–59. *less like roses / And more like violets*: Many crabapple cultivars, including the *Malus florentina*, have dark purple-red foliage in the fall. The Latin noun *malus* means "evil," while *mālus* is "an apple tree"; the slippage between the two words may be how the biblical Tree of Knowledge became thought of as an apple tree. Deep red and purple in the medieval era were often thought of as the same color. Purple is what the cardinal virtues wear and is the color associated with the blood of Christ and with communion wine.

64–66. *the relentless-eyed / Argus . . . Syrinx, / Eyes which if alert could cost someone dearly*: Ovid (*Metamorphoses* 1.568–747) tells the story of Argus, the "all-seeing" hundred-eyed giant enlisted by Juno to keep Io—whom Jupiter had turned into a calf in an attempt to deceive Juno—tied up and away from Jupiter. Mercury, engaged by Jupiter to kill Argus, puts Argus to sleep by telling him the story of Pan's pursuit of the nymph Syrinx; once Argus is asleep, Mercury beheads him.

71–72. *That a dazzling light pierced the veil of my sleep, / And a call: "Get up, what are you doing?"*: Dante compares his falling asleep to Argus's being lulled into ignoring his responsibility; the sudden light that wakes Dante is possibly his own enlightenment.

73–75. *When taken to see the apple blossoms—the pomes . . . the angels crave, and . . . Heavenly wedding wine is eternally made*: The pomes, which delight the angels and are made into wedding wine for the never-ending marriage of Christ and his Church, represent Christ's ascent to Heaven. The pomes of a crabapple tree can be eaten raw or cooked; wine or strong cider can be made from them, as was mentioned as far back as Pliny.

76–78. *Peter, John, and James were overwhelmed / And then brought back by the word . . . even deeper sleeps*: Dante now compares his awaking to that of Peter, James, and John in Matthew 17:1–8, when they were taken to the mountain by Jesus to witness his transfiguration. They witness a light shining on him and his garments turning white and see him talking to Moses and Elias. Peter proposes setting up a test to make sure Moses and Elias are who they say they are. At that point, a dark cloud overshadows them and God speaks, saying to trust Jesus, his son. The disciples then fall on their faces in fear.

79–81. *saw their group had been reduced / By Moses, and likewise by Elias . . . The Master's garments had been changed*: Jesus comes over and reassures them, after which the three look up and discover Moses and Elias are gone.

82–84. *I came back like that and saw / Standing over me, the devoted one . . . my guide along the stream*: Matelda, who has so far played the role of a devoted helper—getting the just-revived Dante into the river Lethe, making certain he swallows the water, getting him out and presenting him to the theological virtues—wakes him, as Jesus similarly brought his disciples around.

85. *Where's Beatrice*: Dante's first thought is for the one he will now rely on to find his way, as he once relied on Virgil.

87–88. *See her sitting on the roots? // See how her handmaidens are circling her*: Beatrice is pictured as sitting on the roots of the Tree of Knowledge, a position of guardianship and of humility, especially as compared to the rapaciousness of the Catholic Church. The seven virtues form a protective circle around her.

89. *The others followed the griffin up*: The griffin, Christ, has led the rest of the procession back to Heaven.

97–99. *the seven nymphs formed a cloister . . . the candles in their hands safe / From any winds, Aquilo or Auster*: The lights held by the virtues aren't affected by earthly phenomena like wind; similarly the candles of the true Chuch can't be put out. Aquilo is the Greek name for the north wind; Auster, for the south. In *Georgics*, Virgil talks about cold Aquilo and dark Auster "which makes the sky sad."

100–102. *Here, in a little while, you'll be sylvan, / And you'll be, until the end, a citizen with me / Of that Rome, where Christ is Roman*: By "here," Beatrice means that when Dante returns to the Terrestrial Paradise after his death, he will truly belong in that Edenic place, as a sylvan or woodland creature naturally belongs in a forest. Dante will then join Beatrice in Paradise, where Christ, the head of the Roman Church, lives for time everlasting. The word "sylvan" comes from Silvanus, a Roman deity who oversaw the boundaries of fields and protected woodlands.

105. *Once back there, make yourself write what you see*: Revelation 1:11: "What thou seest, write in a book."

109–114. *A blaze never zigzagged down so fast . . . at the border / Of the highest sphere of fire*: In medieval cosmology, it was believed that there were four "spheres" (earth, water, air, and fire), which, at the point of the moon, met a system of nine spheres that contained the rest of the solar system. Dante and Beatrice will travel through those nine spheres in *Paradiso*. This extra-fiery lightning came from the border between the outermost terrestrial sphere of fire and the second set of spheres.

115–117. *As the bird of Jove that I saw crash down . . . tearing off not only the bark . . . new leaves as well*: The bird of Jove is the eagle, the symbol of Imperial Rome and also of the later Holy Roman Empire. This destruction of the tree by the eagle is thought to represent the persecution of the early Christians by the Roman emperors, especially Nero and Domitian.

118–122. *I saw a fox pounce on the cradle / Of the triumphal two-wheeler . . . It had fasted through every decent meal // My lady . . . Put it to flight*: The fox is interpreted by commentators as being those who created divisive schisms in the early Church and who were thus seen by the Church as heretics. The fox has no meat on its bones because whatever heretical belief it represents, it is unsustainable. Beatrice, in her rôle as the guardian of the Church, disposes of it quickly.

124–126. *from where it had come to rest before, / The eagle plunged into the ark of the chariot / And left the better part of its feathers there*: The Imperial eagle's "donation" of some of its feathers inside the chariot may refer to the Donation of Constantine, a document of questionable authenticity that granted land, wealth, and political power to the papacy. The word *arca* (ark) suggests the Ark of the Covenant, the legendary gold-covered casket that was said to have held the Ten Commandments.

128–129. *A voice came out of Heaven and said, / "O my little boat, what a heavy burden"*: There was a legend that when the Donation of Constantine was made, a voice from Heaven called out, "Today poison is poured into the Church of God." ("Hodie diffusium est venenum in Ecclesia Dei.")

130–132. *the earth opened up . . . I saw a dragon emerge / And stick its tail end up through the chariot*: The dragon is usually thought of as representing Satan in his serpentine form; the word *drago* derives from the Latin *draco*, which, to the Romans, was a dragon or a particularly large and exotic snake. Revelation 12:3–4 describes a dragon with seven heads and ten horns and seven crowns on its heads. "And his tail drew the third part of the stars of heaven, and did cast them to the earth." In its action on the chariot, the dragon gestures to the corruption inside the Church.

133–135. *it drew back / Its vicious tail, taking with it part of the bottom, / Then wandered around it, just wandering*: The calamity appears to enact some type of phallic penetration and withdrawal. Self-indulgent clergy now symbolically sow seeds of destruction from within, raping the Church, corrupting those around them, and then wandering about looking for more victims.

136–140. *a few feathers . . . benign good intentions . . . quickly spread over it: one wheel, / Then the other, then the pole*: This weed-like, rapid spreading of the leftover feathers gestures to the further corruption, possibly that caused by well-intentioned kings; commentators mention the French king Pepin, who made the eighth-century land grants that established the Papal States (Donation of Pepin, 756), and Charlemagne, who protected Pope Leo III when he was accused of misconduct and tyranny, in exchange for Leo's crowning him emperor on December 25, 800.

142–147. *the holy edifice / Grew a head for each of its parts, / Three over the pole and one on each side . . . three had two oxen-like horns . . . four had only one horn . . . No monster like this has been seen before*: See note to vv. 130–132 for the apocryphal imagery from which Dante drew for the heads and horns. There is no way to know what the specifics meant to Dante; some commentators suggest the seven deadly sins, but others refute that idea. All, however, agree that these aberrations represent a further defilement of the chariot/Church.

148–150. *almost like an alpine fortress, / A free-and-easy whore . . . Batting her lashes and looking around*: Beatrice as guardian of the Catholic Church has now been replaced by a *puttana sciolta* (a loose woman/whore). In the year in which the poem is set, the Church is ruled by Boniface VIII, whom Dante blamed for the continued political tumult in Italy and for his own exile. The whore also prefigures the transfer of the Church from Rome to France. The quasi-fortress description may gesture to the grand and austere Palais de Papes (Palace of the Popes) in Avignon, which sits on a rocky prominence overlooking the Rhône River.

152. *standing next to her, a giant*: The giant is thought to represent earthly kings, especially the French kings with whom the prostituted Church, now monstrously corrupt, has allied itself. Of special note is Philip IV ("the Fair"), who supported the move of the papacy from Rome to Avignon and who suppressed the Knights Templar, a powerful monastic military power within the Catholic Church. Dante refers to Philip in a letter (*Epistola* VII) as "Goliath."

154–155. *But because her amorous wandering eye / Had been pointed at me*: It is not clear what role in Church history Dante sees himself playing. It's possible he felt "flirted with" when called to Rome by Boniface VIII in 1301 to discuss resolving the political situation in Florence. He was then held there while the pope sent Charles of Valois to make peace with the Black Guelphs, who ransacked the city and exiled Dante.

158–159. *He untied the monster and dragged it so deep / Into the woods that only that fact shielded me*: Boniface died in 1303. Pope Benedict XI had a brief eight-month tenure and then, in 1305, Clement V of France was elected pope and moved the papacy to Avignon. The move was referred to as the Babylonian Captivity, which makes the whore inhabiting the chariot the biblical Whore of Babylon (Rev. 17:2), "with whom the kings of the earth have committed fornication."

160. *From the whore and the strange new beast*: Had the papal court remained in Italy, Dante might have kept an eye on the intrigues and conspiracies; now, since they take place in distant France, they are out of his sight.

Canto XXXIII

The handmaidens began, sweetly singing
The psalm, "God, the nations came," alternating,
Now three, now four—eyes welling up.

And Beatrice, plaintive and pious,
Listening so attentively—Mary at the cross
Looked only slightly more altered.

But when the maidens made room for her
To speak, she rose, blushing fire-red,
To her feet and responded,

"In a little while, you will no longer see me,
And in another little while,
My beloved sisters, you will see me again."

She positioned all seven in front—then
With a gesture, moved me, the Bella Donna,
And the wise one who'd stayed, behind her.

So off she went. I don't think
She'd put her foot down more than ten times
When her eyes locked onto mine.

Looking cool, calm, and collected, she said,
"Walk faster, at least enough so that if I speak
To you, you'll be able to hear me."

When I was where I *should* have been, with her,
She said, "Now, Brother, since you're with me,
Why aren't you trying to ask me questions?"

The way those faced with talking to a better,
When they're way too much in awe,
Can't drag a living voice past their teeth,

That's what happened to me. I began, hemming
And hawing, "My mistress, it's you . . .
Who know what I need and what's good for it."

And she, "I want you to let go
Of this fear-shame routine, and stop talking
Like a man in the middle of a dream.

Face the facts: the vessel the dragon fractured
Was and is no more, but for those at fault,
Believe me, God's vengeance won't be bought off.

The eagle that left its feathers in the chariot,
Turning it into a monster, then a victim,
Won't be forever without an heir.

I'm clear-sighted, so I'm telling the story:
Stars already close at hand, and safe
From any delay or obstacle, will bring a time

When a five hundred ten and five,
Sent by God, will kill that hell-on-wheels
And that complicit giant soliciting with her.

Perhaps my 'midnight dreary' story is even less
Convincing than Themis or the Sphinx
Since like those, the mind has to find the key.

But soon, actual events will become an Oedipus
That unravels this tight-lipped enigma
Without damaging any flocks or fields.

Mark my words, and just like I'm doing,
Chalk-talk them for those who are living the life
That's a race toward death.

And keep in mind when you write them,
Not to hide what you saw happen back there
At the tree, which has now been robbed twice.

Whatever steals from it, or slams into it
Swearing like a trooper, actually shocks God,
Because He made it sacred solely for His use.

For taking a bite out of that, the first soul
Suffered more than five thousand years, in pain,
And longing for the one who redeemed that bite.

You're asleep at the wheel if you don't see that
That is the curious reason the tree towers like it does
With the top so wide it overwhelms the rest.

And if your idle thoughts didn't keep churning
Like the waters of Elsa, getting fixed on whatever
They meet, like Pyramus's blood on the mulberry,

You would have morally recognized,
At least in the distinctive features of the tree,
The Divine Justice behind the ban.

But since I see your mind is made of stone,
So indoctrinated and ingrained
That the light of what I'm saying is dazzling you,

I also want it, if not written, at least outlined.
And carry that with you, like the staff wrapped
In a palm leaf a pilgrim brings back."

"Yes," I said. "Like with sealing wax,
Where the stamped image doesn't change,
My brain is now marked by you.

But why are your instructions, which I need,
Going so over my head that I can't grasp them?
It's all try again, fail again."

"So that you'll become aware," she said,
"Of that school you've been going to—and see
How much of its doctrine follows my teachings,

And you'll see that between your way
And the divine equals the difference between
Earth and the highest, fastest-whirling heaven."

To which I responded, "I don't recall
Ever being estranged from you,
Nor is my conscience pricking me."

"If you can't remember that,"
She said, smiling, "Let me remind you
That just today you drank from Lethe.

And if that 'where there's smoke, there's fire'
Claim is true, your forgetting cinches it,
Your faulty will was focused elsewhere.

Actually, from now on my words will be
As bare naked as needed, so you can
Make them out with your crude eyesight."

Now with more glittering and slower steps,
The sun paced the noonday circle, which is
Here or there, depending on one's perspective.

The way an escort at the front of a company
Stops short if it catches sight
Of a news flash, or even hints of one,

The seven handmaids halted under green leaves
And wet, black boughs at the edge of ashy shade,
Like that which mountains cast over cold streams.

In front of them, what seemed to be the Tigris
And Euphrates flowed from a single spring
And, almost like friends, idly wandered off.

"O light, O glory of human inheritance,
What's this water unfolding here from one source,
Then self from self at a distance?"

To this earnest inquiry, I was told,
"Ask Matelda to tell you." And here, piping up
Like a guilty party trying to shift the blame,

The Bella Donna, "This and other things
Were told to him by me, and I'm sure
The Lethe River water hid none of it from him."

And Beatrice, "Perhaps some major preoccupation,
The kind that can rob us of our memory,
Has pulled a shade over the eyes of his mind.

But look over there where Eunoe springs up—
Lead him to it and, however you see fit,
Revive his out-for-the-count consciousness."

Like an obliging soul that makes no excuses
But takes another's desire as their own
As soon as the slightest hint of it's revealed,

I was led over, and then the Bella Donna,
Like a mistress to the manner born,
Said to Statius, "Come along with him."

If I had, Reader, a longer time to write, I would
As far as possible sing of the sweet drink
That never would've satisfied me,

But because all the cards
Of the second canticle have been laid out,
The limits of art won't let me go further.

I came back from those most holy waters
Remade, no longer past repair,
A new plant, renewed with new leaves—

Pure and ready to climb the stairway to the stars.

2. *The psalm, "God, the nations came"*: The first verse of Psalm 79 is "O God, the nations have come into your inheritance; your holy temple they have defiled; they have laid Jerusalem in ruins." For Dante, in the time in which the poem is set, Italy is in a state of similar defilement. It is particularly so in the actual time that he is writing the second canticle, which is thought to have been finished somewhere between 1313 and 1314; the papacy has been moved to Avignon and Clement V is consistently cooperating with Philip the Fair.

4. *plaintive and pious*: Beatrice is initially presented as a sorrowful Mary figure, but lest the reader underestimate her, in v. 9, the indignation that prompts her to get to her feet, literally to take a stand, will turn her face fire-red with ardor and fury.

10–12. *In a little while, you will no longer see me . . . you will see me again*: John 16:16: "A little while, and ye shall not see me: and again, a little while, and ye shall see me, because I go to the Father." In this echo of Christ's words, we again see Beatrice as the guardian of the Church.

15. *the wise one who'd stayed*: The wise one is Statius. The statement that he had stayed behind is a reminder that Virgil is no longer present.

23. *Now, Brother*: Beatrice uses *Frate*, the term for a religious brother or friar.

34–36. *the vessel the dragon fractured / Was and is no more, but for those at fault . . . God's vengeance won't be bought off*: The vessel is the chariot, which, now that it's been violated, signifies the corrupted Church. The *serpente* is the dragon of *Purg.* XXXII, 131, figuratively Pope Clement V and Philip the Fair.

43–45. *When a five hundred ten and five, / Sent by God, will kill that hell-on-wheels / And that complicit giant soliciting with her*: The prophecy is in a code that one assumes would have been clear to at least some of Dante's readers. Chronograms were very popular in the Middle Ages. Beatrice says, as with any oracular pronouncement, "the mind has to find the key." Frequent suggestions by commentators as to how to read the "five hundred ten and five" have included a strong secular leader, especially Henry VII (who would have failed to fulfill the prophecy, since he died in 1313); the Second Coming of Christ; a pope; or Dante himself. Some have suggested that the numbers gesture to a year: 515 added to the year 800, when Charlemagne was crowned Emperor of the Romans, would be 1315. What was meant to happen in 1315, however, is not clear. It's possible that since Pope Clement V died in April 1314, Dante thought the papacy would be returned to Rome by then; in a letter sent to the cardinals (in May or June of 1314), he implored them to do just that (*Epistola* VIII).

46. *my 'midnight dreary' story*: Edgar Allan Poe, "The Raven": "Once upon a midnight dreary, while I pondered, weak and weary, / Over many a quaint and curious volume of forgotten lore."

47–48. *Themis or the Sphinx / Since like those, the mind has to find the key*: The goddess Themis, the daughter of Uranus (heaven) and Gaia (earth), was one of the Oracles of Delphi. The Sphinx—a hybrid creature with a woman's head and breasts, lion's body, and eagle's wings—ruled the countryside around Thebes, devouring any who couldn't solve the riddle of "what creature walks with four legs in the morning, two legs at noon, and three legs at night." Oedipus solves the riddle by answering "humans"; the Sphinx, in her fury, throws herself off a cliff and the townspeople rejoice. Oedipus then unknowingly marries his mother, the queen, after having killed the king, before knowing it was his father—all of which fulfills a prophecy made at his birth.

49–50. *actual events will become an Oedipus / That unravels this*: Due to a textual error in the transmission of Ovid in Dante's lifetime, the word "Naïades," mythological wood nymphs, was substituted for "Laïades," which signifies "Oedipus, the son of Laius." Because of that mistake, Dante errs in writing that the Naïades do the "unraveling," when he actually means Oedipus.

51. *Without damaging any flocks or fields*: Most commentators explain the damage to flocks and fields (literally, "the sheep and corn") as having been caused when Themis, furious that Oedipus solved the riddle of the Sphinx, sends a monster to destroy the flocks and fields around Thebes. It's possible, however, that the notion of the destruction comes from Hesiod's *Works and Days* (2, 163), where one finds the phrase "fighting for the sheep of Oedipus" in a description of the struggle between Polynices and Eteocles, the two sons of Oedipus, for control of the kingdom after Oedipus is self-blinded and self-exiled.

53. *Chalk-talk them*: A chalk-talk is a lecture illustrated in real time in order to make the points more memorable.

56–57. *what you saw happen back there / At the tree, which has now been robbed twice*: The two occasions when the tree was robbed were when Eve took a bite of its fruit and when the chariot was removed from the tree; this second instance is possibly meant to signify the papacy being moved from Rome to France.

61–62. *For taking a bite out of that, the first soul / Suffered more than five thousand years, in pain*: The first soul, Adam, had to wait for Christ to redeem his sin. How long he had to wait is based on the notion that he lived for 930 years (Genesis 5:5) and then spent 4,302 years in Limbo before being released during the Harrowing of Hell—Christ's descent into Hell to free the early patriarchs.

68–69. *Like the waters of Elsa, getting fixed on whatever / They meet, like Pyramus's blood on the mulberry*: The Elsa River, fed by mineral springs, flows into the Arno. The carbonic acid in the water precipitates and forms limestone deposits. Beatrice is saying that Dante's thoughts are without direction and simply light on whatever's nearest, and then get fixed there. See the note to *Purg.* XXVII, 37–39, for how Pyramus's blood turned the mulberries red. After Pyramus's death, the gods honored Thisbe's mourning by making the color change permanent.

70–72. *You would have morally recognized, / At least in the distinctive features of the tree, / The Divine Justice behind the ban*: Dante should have recognized that the tree's enormous height, spreading canopy, and the fact that the branches point up were signifiers of Divine Justice. And that in the divine plan, the prohibition against eating of the Tree of Knowledge is just one part of the required obedience to an entire code of ethics and morality.

77–78. *the staff wrapped / In a palm leaf a pilgrim brings back*: The palm frond is evidence of the pilgrim having visited the Holy Land. The walker's staff, since it functions as a third leg, represents the Trinity. It was also useful to the pilgrim for keeping away dogs and other animals—in that way, it represents the Christian victory over death.

84. *It's all try again, fail again*: Samuel Beckett, "Worstward Ho": "Ever tried. Ever failed. No matter. Try again. Fail again. Fail better."

86–87. *that school you've been going to—and see / How much of its doctrine follows my teachings*: This is the school of pure, pre-Christian philosophy, which Dante explored in *Convivio*. The teachings of Beatrice are instead theological.

104–105. *The sun paced the noonday circle, which is / Here or there, depending on one's perspective*: As throughout *Purgatorio*, the spherical sun is unchanging: it is a complete circle regardless of where one stands or where one travels. That said, Dante appears to believe it moves more slowly when overhead than when it's lower in the sky. It is now noon on April 13, 1300, the first Wednesday after Easter Sunday.

110. *wet, black boughs at the edge*: Ezra Pound, "In a Station of the Metro": "The apparition of these faces in a crowd: / Petals on a wet, black bough."

112–113. *the Tigris / And Euphrates flowed from a single spring*: In Genesis 2:14, the Euphrates and the Tigris (ancient name Hiddekel) are two of the four rivers said to go out of Eden. Both the Tigris and Euphrates begin in Turkey; the Tigris joins the Euphrates in southern Iraq and the conjoined rivers then empty as one into the Persian Gulf. Dante takes the idea of these two rivers coming from one source from *The Consolation of Philosophy*, a treatise by the Roman statesman and philosopher Boethius written while he was awaiting execution by Theodoric the Great. The work is an apostrophe to Lady Philosophy. Dante uses this same conceit in his *Convivio*, as well as the formal device of having a poem follow each of the prose sections. Dante appropriates two verses

(5, 1, 3–4) from Boethius's poem "Chance": "Tigris et Euphrates uno se fonte resolvunt, / Et mox abjunctis dissociantur aquis." (From one spring the Tigris and Euphrates both are freed / But soon the waters get detached and go off separately.) Boethius took the two verses from a preserved fragment by Seneca; Lucan also uses it in *Pharsalia* 3, 258.

114. *like friends, idly wandered off*: Dante adds *quasi amici* (like friends) to the Boethius, creating an image of two who wander for a while, reluctant to part.

119–120. *Ask Matelda to tell you. . . / Like a guilty party trying to shift the blame*: This is the first time Dante has named Matelda. Previously, she's only been referred to as the "Bella Donna," the beautiful lady, a trope in troubadour poetry and a virtual catchphrase in Italian (pretty woman). Commentators have searched for a possible historical figure who may have inspired the character. One possibility is Matilda of Tuscany, crowned imperial vicar and vice-queen of Italy by Henry V, the Holy Roman emperor, in 1111. A second is Mechthild (Matilda) of Magdeburg, a Beguine Christian mystic (died ca. 1282–ca. 1290s) who wrote a seven-part book titled *Das fließende Licht der Gottheit* (*The Flowing Light of the Godhead*) in a German dialect. Around 1290, the work was translated into Latin by Dominican monks. A third is Saint Mechthilde (Matilda) of Hackeborn (d. 1298), a Benedictine nun also from Saxony. She approved and corrected a book of her visions recorded by her confidantes that was published as *Liber specialis gratiae* (*The Book of Special Grace*). That book has a conceit of a seven-terrace mountain, each level devoted to the purgation of one of the seven deadly sins with a seventh stairway ending in a blissful pre-Paradise similar to Dante's Terrestrial Paradise. According to Boccaccio, the book was popular in Florence as *La laude di donna Matelda* around the time Dante was finishing *Purgatorio*. Regardless, in *Purgatorio*, she is only an allegorical figure.

122–123. *I'm sure / The Lethe River water hid none of it from him*: The fact that Dante can't recall his estrangement from Beatrice, she says, proves that that period was, in fact, sinful. Matelda refuses to take responsibility for Dante's failure to understand that Lethe would erase not only the sins of which he was aware but also those of which he was unaware.

127–129. *But look over there where Eunoe springs up— / Lead him to it and, however you see fit, / Revive his out-for-the-count consciousness*: Dante's purely invented river, *Eunoè* (Eunoe), combines the ancient Greek *eu* (well or good) and *nous* (mind or memory). The combination literally means "well minded" (or "good memories"); figuratively, it translates as peace of mind, nirvana, or bliss.

135. *Said to Statius, "Come along with him"*: This moment establishes that Matelda is not only Dante's attendant but she also facilitates the journey across the two rivers for each purified soul. Whatever Dante experiences, we are to presume Statius will also.

141. *The limits of art won't let me go further*: The limits, in this case, are thirty-three cantos. The cantos range in length from 115 to 160 lines, which means Dante could go on

for a few more lines. He appears to be saying, however, that it would take not just a few more lines but at least another whole canto to adequately describe the experience of Eunoe and the sense of tranquility that follows.

142–144. *I came back from those most holy waters . . . no longer past repair, / A new plant, renewed with new leaves*: The sense of renewal comes from both the absolution of past sins and a preparedness to be in the world in a new form. Mark Strand, "The Other Rose": "'Oh no,' they said. / 'We are what we are—nothing else.' // How perfect. How ancient. How past repair."

145. *Pure and ready to climb the stairway to the stars*: Like *Inferno*, *Purgatorio* ends on the word *stelle* (stars). *Paradiso* will likewise.

BIBLIOGRAPHY

ENGLISH TRANSLATIONS OF DANTE'S *PURGATORIO*

Cary, Henry Francis. *Purgatorio*. London: Printed for James Carpenter, 1814.

Cayley, C. B. *Dante's Divine Comedy*. 4 vols. London: Longman, Brown, Green and Longmans, 1851–1855.

Ciardi, John. *The Purgatorio: A Verse Translation for the Modern Reader*. New York: New American Library, 1961. First published 1954 by Mentor.

Durling, Robert M., and Ronald L. Martinez. *Purgatorio*. Oxford: Oxford University Press, 2003.

Hollander, Robert, and Jean Hollander. *Purgatorio*. New York: Doubleday, 2003.

Kirkpatrick, Robin. *Purgatorio*. Vol. 2 of *The Divine Comedy*. London: Penguin, 2007.

Longfellow, Henry Wadsworth. *Purgatorio*. Edited by Matthew Pearl. New York: Modern Library, 2003. First published 1867.

Mandelbaum, Allen. *The Divine Comedy: Purgatorio: A Verse Translation*. Drawings by Barry Moser, notes by Allen Mandelbaum and Gabriel Marruzzo, with Laury Magnus. New York: Bantam, 2004.

Merwin, W. S. *Purgatorio: A New Verse Translation*. New York: Alfred A. Knopf, 2001.

Musa, Mark. *Purgatory*. Vol. 2 of *Dante Alighieri's Divine Comedy*. London: Penguin, 1985.

Norton, Charles Eliot. *Purgatory*. Vol. 2 of *The Divine Comedy of Dante Alighieri*. Champaign, IL: Project Gutenberg, 1999. First published 1891.

Okey, Thomas. *Purgatorio. The Divine Comedy of Dante Alighieri*. The Carlyle Okey Wicksteed Translation, with an introduction by C. H. Grandgent. New York: Illustrated Modern Library, 1944. First published 1901.

Sinclair, John D. *Purgatorio* 2. of *The Divine Comedy*. 3 vols. New York: Oxford University Press, 1961. Originally published as *The Divine Comedy of Dante Alighieri*, London: John Lane, 1939.

Singleton, Charles S. *Purgatorio*. Vol. 2 of *The Divine Comedy of Dante Alighieri: Translation, and Commentary*. 2 vols. Princeton, NJ: Princeton University Press, 1973.

Thomas, John Wesley. *Purgatorio: or, The Vision of Purgatory*. London: Bohn, 1862.

Vernon, William Warren. *Readings on the Purgatorio of Dante: Chiefly Based on the Commentary of Benvenuto da Imola*. 2 vols. London: Methuen, 1907. First published 1889.

SOURCES CITED IN THE NOTES

All quotations from the Bible are from the King James Version, with a few exceptions mentioned in the notes. All translations within the notes are by the translator, unless otherwise credited.

Abbot, Eleanor, designer. *Candy Land*. Milton Bradley Company, 1949.

Alighieri, Dante. *Convivio*. Digital Dante website. https://digitaldante.columbia.edu/text/library/convivio-italian.

———. *De monarchia*. The Latin Library website. www.thelatinlibrary.com/dante.html.

———. *De vulgari eloquentia*. The Latin Library website. www.thelatinlibrary.com/dante.html.

———. *Epistolae: The Letters of Dante*. Translated and edited by Paget Toynbee. Oxford: Clarendon Press, 1920.

———. *Vita nuova*. The Latin Library website. www.thelatinlibrary.com/dante.html.

American Heritage Dictionary of the English Language. 5th ed. Boston: Houghton Mifflin Harcourt, 2016.

Andersen, Hans Christian. "The Princess and the Pea." *Tales, Told for Children*. Copenhagen: C. A. Reitzel, 1835.

Anonymous. *The Cloude of Unknowyng*. Late 14th century. Cambridge University Library Kk.vi.26.

Armour, Peter. *Dante's Griffin and the History of the World; A Study of the Earthly Paradise*. Oxford, UK: Clarendon Press, 1989.

Ashbery, John. "Soonest Mended." *Paris Review*, no. 47 (Summer 1969).

Assefi, Seema L., and Marryanne Garry. "Absolut® Memory Distortions: Alcohol Placebos Influence the Misinformation Wffect." *Psychological Science* 14, no. 1 (January 2003): 77–80.

Aubrey, Elizabeth. "References to Music in Old Occitan Literature." *Acta Musicologica* 61, no. 2 (May–August 1989): 110–49.

Bacchylides. *The Poems and Fragments*. Edited by Richard Claverhouse Jebb. Cambridge, UK: Cambridge University Press, 1905.

Barney, Natalie Clifford. "A Parisian Roof Garden in 1918." *Poems & Poèmes: Autres Alliances*. Paris: Émile-Paul Frères, 1920.

Barthes, Roland. *Camera Lucida: Reflections on Photography*. Translated by Richard Howard. New York: Hill & Wang, 1981.

Baseball Almanac website. "Guinness Book of Baseball World Records." www.baseball-almanac.com/recbooks/rb_guin.shtml.

Bates, Katherine Lee. "America the Beautiful." *America the Beautiful and Other Poems*. New York: Crowell, 1912.

Baum, L. Frank. *The Wonderful Wizard of Oz*. Chicago: George M. Hill, 1900.

Beckett, Samuel. "Echo's Bones." New York: Grove Press, 2014.

———. *Collected Shorter Plays*. New York: Grove Press, 1984.

———. *How It Is*. New York: Grove Press, 1964. First published as *Comment c'est*. Paris: Éditions de Minuit, 1961.

———. *Malone Dies*. New York: Grove Press, 1956. First published as *Malone meurt*. Paris: Éditions de Minuit, 1951.

———. *Molloy*. New York: Grove Press, 1955. First published Paris: Éditions de Minuit, 1951.

———. *Ohio Impromptu*. First performed May 9, 1981, at the Stadium II Theater in Columbus, Ohio.

———. *The Unnamable*. New York: Grove Press, 1958. First published as *L'innommable*. Paris: Éditions de Minuit, 1953.

———. "Worstward Ho." *Nohow On*. New York: Grove Press, 1995.

Bergvall, Caroline. "Via: 48 Dante Variations." From *Fig*. Cambridge, UK: Salt, 2005.

Berryman, John. "Dream Song 20: The Secret of the Wisdom." *77 Dream Songs*. New York: Farrar, Straus and Giroux, 1964.

Boccaccio, Giovanni. *Decamerone* (*The Decameron*). Florence: Filippo and Bernardo Giunti, 1353.

Boethius, Anicius Manlius Severinus. "Chance." *The Consolation of Philosophy*. Book IV, song I. https://faculty.georgetown.edu/jod/boethius/jkok/4m1_t.htm.

Bolaño, Roberto. *By Night in Chile*. Translated by Chris Andrews. New York: New Directions, 2003.

Brock-Broido, Lucie. "Everybody Has a Heart, Except Some People." *AGNI* 39 (January 2018).

Brooker, Gary, Keith Reid, and Matthew Fisher. Lyrics and music. "A Whiter Shade of Pale." From *Procol Harum*. Performed by Procol Harum. Olympic Studios, 1967.

Browning, Elizabeth Barrett. "Sonnet 43." *Sonnets from the Portuguese and Other Love Poems*. Originally published 1850. New York: Doubleday, 1990.

Browning, Robert. *Sordello*. London: Edward Moxon, 1840.

Bruegel, Pieter the Elder. *Census at Bethlehem*. C. 1566. Oil painting, 115.5 cm × 164.5 cm. Royal Museums of Fine Arts of Belgium, Brussels.

Byrne, David, Chris Frantz, Jerry Harrison, and Tina Weymouth. Lyrics and music. "Burning Down the House." From *Speaking in Tongues*. Performed by Talking Heads. Sire Records, 1983.

Byron, Lord. "Don Juan." *The Poetical Works of Byron*. Boston: Houghton Mifflin Harcourt, 1975.

———. *Manfred*. London: John Murray, 1817.

———. "The Prisoner of Chillon." *The Prisoner of Chillon and Other Poems*. London: John Murray, 1816.

———. *The Prophecy of Dante*. Philadelphia: M. Carey and Sons, 1821.

Camus, Albert. *The Plague*. Translated by Stuart Gilbert. New York: Vintage Books, 1991.

Carroll, Lewis. *Through the Looking Glass and What Alice Found There*. Philadelphia: Henry Altemus, 1895.

Cavalcanti, Guido. *The Complete Poems*. Edited and translated by Marc Cirigliano. New York: Italica Press, 1992.

Cervantes, Miguel de. *The Ingenious Gentleman Don Quixote of La Mancha* (*El ingenioso hidalgo Don Quixote de la Mancha*). Francisco de Robles, 1605–15.

Chaytor, Henry John. *The Troubadours and England*. Cambridge: Cambridge University Press, 1923.

Chutes and Ladders. Milton Bradley Company, 1943.

Ciabattoni, Francesco. *Dante's Journey to Polyphony*. Toronto: University of Toronto Press, 2014.

Coltrane, John. Liner notes. *A Love Supreme*. Performed by the John Coltrane Quartet: John Coltrane, McCoy Tyner, Jimmy Garrison, and Elvin Jones. Impulse! Records, 1965.

Confucius. *The Analects*. Translated by D. C. Lau. New York: Penguin, 1998.

Conington, John. *The Works of Virgil: With a Commentary*. London: Whittaker, 1876.

Cowper, William. "O Mother Dear, Jerusalem." New York: Anson D. F. Randolph, 1864.

Cundall, Joseph. *Treasury of Pleasure Books for Young Children*. First published 1850. Morrisville, NC: Lulu Press, 2010.

David, Hal, and John Barry. Lyrics and music. "We Have All the Time in the World." From *On Her Majesty's Secret Service* (soundtrack). Performed by Louis Armstrong. EMI, 1969.

di Bondone, Giotto. *Paradiso*. C. 1335. Fresco. Chapel of the Palazzo del Podestà, Bargello Museum, Florence, Italy.

Dickinson, Emily. *The Complete Poems of Emily Dickinson*. Boston: Little, Brown, 1960.

Dietz, Howard, designer. "Leo the Lion." Metro-Goldwyn-Mayer, 1916.

Dodge, Mary Mapes, ed. "The Little Red Hen." First collected in *St. Nicholas Magazine*, New York, 1874.

Doolittle, Hilda (H.D.). *Collected Poems 1912–1944*. New York: New Directions, 1986.

Dunbar-Nelson, Alice. "The Idler." *Violets and Other Tales*. Boston: Monthly Review, 1895.

Dylan, Bob. Lyrics and music. "Sad-Eyed Lady of the Lowlands." From *Blonde on Blonde*. Performed by Bob Dylan. Colombia Records, 1966.

Efron, Leon Jacobowitz. "Hermaphrodite Trouble: Gender, Sex and Sexuality in Fourteenth-Century Italian Commentaries to the Divine Comedy." *Gender & History* 25, no.1 (April 2013): 65–85.

Eliot, T. S. *Collected Poems, 1909–1962*. New York: Harcourt Brace, 1963.

———. *Selected Prose of T. S. Eliot*. Edited by Frank Kermode. New York: Harcourt Brace Jovanovich, 1975.

Ellison, Ralph. *Invisible Man*. New York: Random House, 1952.

Eyes on the Prize. Directed by Orlando Bagwell, Sheila Curran Bernard, Callie Crossley, James A. DeVinney, Madison D. Lacy, Louis Massiah, Thomas Ott, Samuel D. Pollard, Terry Kay Rockefeller, Jacqueline Shearer, Paul Stekler, and Judith Vecchione.

Narrated by Julian Bond. Fourteen episodes airing January 21, 1987, to March 5, 1990. PBS series, 1990.

Farlex Idioms and Slang Dictionary. Dublin. Farlex International, 2017.

Figueroa, Dante. "The Rehabilitation of Dante Alighieri, Seven Centuries Later." *In Custodia Legis* (blog). Law Librarians of Congress, April 13, 2016. https://blogs.loc.gov/law/2016/04/the-rehabilitation-of-dante-alighieri-seven-centuries-later.

Flanner, Janet. *Darlinghissima: Letters to a Friend*. Edited by Natalia Danesi Murray. New York: Random House, 1985.

Fudgé, Thomas A. *Medieval Religion and its Anxieties: History and Mystery in the Other Middle Ages*. New York: Palgrave Macmillan, 2016.

Gaye, Marvin. *Here, My Dear*. Tamla Records, 1978.

Gilmore, David, and Polly Samson. Lyrics and music. "Lost for Words." From *The Division Bell*. Performed by Pink Floyd. EMI Records, 1994.

Ginsberg, Allen. "Part III." *Howl and Other Poems*. San Francisco: City Lights, 1956.

Green, Henry. *Party Going*. London: Hogarth Press, 1939.

Hardy, Thomas. "The Voice." *Collected Poems of Thomas Hardy*. Ware, UK: Wordsworth Editions: 1998. First published in *Satires of Circumstance*, 1914.

Heinlein, Robert A. *Stranger in a Strange Land*. New York: G. P. Putnam's Sons, 1961.

Hesiod. *Work and Days*. Translated by H. G. Evelyn-White. https://en.wikisource.org/wiki/Hesiod,_the_Homeric_Hymns_and_Homerica/Works_and_Days.

Herodotus. *The Histories*. Translated by George Rawlinson. New York: Alfred A. Knopf, 1997.

Hollander, Robert, and Jean Hollander, trans. *Purgatorio*. New York: Doubleday, 2003.

Hopkins, Gerard Manley. *The Poems of Gerard Manley Hopkins*. Edited by W. H. Gardner and N. H. MacKenzie. Oxford: Oxford University Press, 1976.

The Humpty Dumpty Circus. Directed by J. Stuart Blackton and Albert E. Smith. 1897. Distributed by Kalem Company, 1908.

Huxley, Aldous. *Brave New World*. London: Chatto & Windus, 1932.

IMDb. "George Albert Smith." www.imdb.com/name/nm0808310.

James, William. *Principles of Psychology*. New York: Henry Holt, 1890.

Jansen, Leo, Hans Luijten, and Nienke Bakker, eds. *Vincent van Gogh: The Letters*. Amsterdam & The Hague: Van Gogh Museum & Huygens, 2009.

John, Elton, and Bernie Taupin. Lyrics and music. "Candle in the Wind." From *Goodbye Yellow Brick Road*. Performed by Elton John. MCA, 1993.

———. Lyrics and music. "Candle in the Wind 1997." Performed by Elton John. Rocket Record Company, 1997.

Jones, Mick. Lyrics and music. "I Want to Know What Love Is." From *Agent Provocateur*. Performed by Foreigner. The Hit Factory, 1984.

Josephus, Flavius. *The Great Roman-Jewish War (De bello judaico)*. New York: Dover, 2012.

Juvenal. *The Satires of Juvenal*. Introduction and notes by A. F. Cole. London: J. M. Dent, 1906.

Keats, John. "Ode on a Grecian Urn," "Ode to Psyche," "On First Looking into Chapman's Homer." In *The Norton Anthology of Poetry*. Edited by Margaret Ferguson, Mary Jo Salter, and Jon Stallworthy. 5th ed. New York: Norton, 2004.

Klein, Francesca, ed. *Book of Chiodo in the Florence State Archive* (*Il Libro del Chiodo, Archivio di Stato di Firenze*). Italy: Edizioni Polistampa, 2004.

Lahr, John. *Prick Up Your Ears: The Biography of Joe Orton*. New York: Alfred A. Knopf, 1978.

Lansing, Richard H., and Teodolinda Barolini. *The Dante Encyclopedia*. New York: Garland, 2000.

Lear, Edward. "The Owl and the Pussycat." From *Nonsense Songs, Stories, Botany, and Alphabets*. London: Robert John Bush, 1872.

Lennon, John, and Paul McCartney. Lyrics and music. "Getting Better." From *Sgt. Pepper's Lonely Hearts Club Band*. Performed by the Beatles. Parlophone, 1967.

Living in Oblivion. Written and directed by Tom DiCillo. With Steve Buscemi and Catherine Keener. Sony Pictures Classics, 1995.

Lucan. *Pharsalia*. Translated by Jane Wilson Joyce. Ithaca, NY: Cornell University Press, 1993.

Lynch, Patricia Ann, and Jeremy Roberts. *Native American Mythology A to Z*. Philadelphia: Chelsea House, 2010.

MapQuest. "The Camargue to Arles, France." https://www.mapquest.com/directions.

"Mary Jo Bang Discusses Purgatorio." Interview with Kevin Young, December 23, 2019. Poetry Podcast. Produced by Michele Moses. The *New Yorker*. www.newyorker.com/podcast/poetry/mary-jo-bang-discusses-purgatorio.

Maximus, Valerius. *Memorable Deeds and Sayings* (*Facta et dicta memorabilis*). Translated by Henry John Walker. Indianapolis: Hackett, 2004.

Mayakovsky, V. V. "A Cloud in Trousers." *Russian Poetry: The Modern Period*. Edited by J. Glad and D. Weissbort. Translated by P. Lemke. Iowa City: University of Iowa Press, 1978.

McCartney, Paul, and Linda. Lyrics and music. "Band on the Run." From *Band on the Run*. Performed by Paul McCarney and Wings. Apple Records, 1973.

Mechthild of Hackeborn. *The Book of Special Grace* (*Liber specialis gratiae*). Translated by Barbara Newman. Mahwah, NJ: Paulist Press, 2017.

Merrick, Jerry. Lyrics. "Follow." From *Mixed Bag*. Performed by Richard P. "Richie" Havens. Verve Records, 1966.

Milne, A. A. *The House at Pooh Corner*. London: Methuen, 1928.

———. *Winnie-the-Pooh*. London: Methuen, 1926.

Milton, John. *Paradise Lost*. London: Samuel Simmons, 1667.

O'Hara, Frank. "A Step Away from Them." *Lunch Poems*. San Francisco: City Lights, 1964.

Online Etymology Dictionary website. www.etymonline.com.

Ovid. *The Metamorphoses*. Translated by Allen Mandelbaum. New York: Harcourt Brace, 1993.

Page, Jimmy, and Robert Plant. "Stairway to Heaven." From *Led Zeppelin IV.* Performed by Led Zeppelin. Atlantic Records, 1971.

Pascoli, Giovanni. "The Two Children (I Due Fanciulli)." *Il fanciullino.* First published 1897. Wikisource website. https://it.wikisource.org/wiki/Pagina:Primi_poemetti.djvu/161.

Pausanius. *Description of Greece.* Translated by W. H. S. Jones. London: William Heinemann, 1918.

Plath, Sylvia. *The Bell Jar.* London: Heinemann, 1963.

———. "Elm" and "The Ghost's Leaving." *Collected Poems.* Edited by Ted Hughes. London: Faber and Faber, 1981.

Plato. *Republic.* Translated by Christopher Rowe. New York: Penguin, 2012.

Plutarch. *Lives of the Noble Grecians and Romans.* New York: Dell Laurel, 1959.

Poe, Edgar Allan. "The Raven." First published in *Evening Mirror,* January 29, 1845. *The Raven and Other Poems,* New York: Wiley and Putnam, 1845.

Porter, Cole. Lyrics and music. "Ev'ry Time We Say Goodbye." London: Chappell & Company, 1944.

Pound, Ezra. "In a Station of the Metro." *Poetry,* April 1913.

———. *The Spirit of Romance.* Letchworth, UK: J. M. Dent & Sons, 1910.

———. "Three Cantos" and "Canto LXXXI." *Cantos of Ezra Pound.* New York: New Directions, 1993.

Prick Up Your Ears. Directed by Steven Frears. Written by John Lahr and Alan Bennett. With Gary Oldman and Vanessa Redgrave. Zenith Productions, 1987.

Quartieri, Franco. "Previous 'colleagues.'" *Benvenuto da Imola.* Ravenna, Italy: Angelo Longo Editore, 2001.

Riley, Henry T. *The Pharsalia of Lucan, Literally Translated into English Prose with Copious Notes.* India: Alpha Editions, 2019.

Rinaldi, Mariangela, and Mariangela Vicini. *Buonapetito, Your Holiness: The Secrets of the Papal Table.* New York: Arcade, 2012.

Rubin, Miri. "The Person in the Form: Medieval Challenges to Bodily Order." *Framing Medieval Bodies.* Edited by Sarah Kay and Miri Rubin. Manchester: Manchester University Press, 1994.

Said, Edward. *Orientalism.* New York: Pantheon Books, 1978.

Santa Claus. Directed by George Albert Smith. UK: 1898.

Santagata, Marco. *Dante: The Story of His Life.* Translated by Richard Dixson. Cambridge, MA: Harvard University Press, 2016.

Schildgen, Brenda Deen. *Dante and the Orient.* Champaign: University of Illinois Press, 2002.

Seneca, Lucius Annaeus. *Moral Letters to Lucillius (Ad lucilium epistulae morales).* Edited by Christopher Abrantes and Michael Abrantes. Translated by Richard Mott Gummere and J. C. Rolfe. Complete Classics: 2016.

———. *Select Letters of Seneca.* Edited by Walter C. Summers. London: Macmillan, 1910.

———. "Thyestes." *The Ten Tragedies of Seneca*. Translated by William Bradshaw. London: Swan Sonnenschein, 1902.

Simon, Paul. Lyrics and music. "Mother and Child Reunion." From *Paul Simon*. Washington, DC: Columbia Records, 1972.

Simpson, John, and Edmund Weiner, eds. *Oxford English Dictionary*. 2nd ed. Oxford, UK: Oxford University Press, 1989.

Sinclair, May. "The Novels of Dorothy Richardson." *Egoist* 5, no. 4 (April 1918).

Singleton, Charles S., trans. *The Divine Comedy II: Purgatorio*. 2 vols. Princeton: Princeton University Press, 1973.

Singleton, Charles S. "Stars over Eden." *Annual Report of the Dante Society, with Accompanying Papers* 75 (1957): 1–18.

Sondheim, Stephen, and Leonard Bernstein. Lyrics and music. "I Feel Pretty." From *West Side Story* (soundtrack). Performed by Marni Nixon, Yvonne Othon, and Suzie Kaye. Columbia Masterworks, 1961.

Southey, Robert. "The Story of the Three Bears." *The Doctor*. Harlow, UK: Longman, Rees, 1837.

Statius, Publius Papinius. *Silvae*. Internet Archive website. https://archive.org/stream/statiusstato1statuoft/statiusstato1statuoft_djvu.txt.

Stein, Gertrude. "Susie Asado." *Selected Writings of Gertrude Stein*. New York: Peter Smith, 1992.

Steinberg, Billy, and Tom Kelly. Lyrics and music. "True Colors." From *True Colors*. Performed by Cyndi Lauper. Portrait, 1986.

Strand, Mark. "The Other Rose." *New Yorker*, May 28, 2001.

Styron, William. *Lie Down in Darkness*. First published as *An Inheritance of Night*. Indianapolis: Bobbs-Merrill, 1951.

Tawney, C. H., trans. *The Kathá sarit ságara; or, Ocean of the Streams of Story*. 2 vols. First published in Calcutta: Baptist Mission Press, 1880. Project Gutenberg, 2012.

TED. "About: Our Organization." www.ted.com/about/our-organization.

Theocritus. *Idylls of Theocritus*. Translated by Robert Wells. London: Penguin Classics: 1988.

Thompson, Augustine. *Cities of God: The Religion of the Italian Communes, 1125–1325*. University Park, PA: Pennsylvania State University Press, 2005.

Tolkien, J. R. R. *The Silmarillion*. Australia: George Allen & Unwin, 1977.

Toynbee, Paget Jackson. *Concise Dictionary of Proper Names and Notable Matters in the Works of Dante*. Oxford: Clarendon, 1914.

Treccani, Giovanni, developer. *Italian Encyclopedia of Science, Letters, and Arts*. First published serially. Italy: Treccani, 1929–36.

Trench, Richard C. "On the Study of Words: Lectures Addressed (Originally) to the Pupils at the Diocesan Training School, Winchester." Newark, UK: J. W. Parker and Sons, 1852.

Van Gogh, Vincent. *The Letters*. Edited by Leo Jansen, Hans Luijten, and Nienke Bakker. www.vangoghletters.org.

Vernon, William Warren, trans. *Readings on the Purgatorio of Dante: Chiefly Based on the Commentary of Benvenuto Da Imola*. 2 vols. 3rd ed. London: Methuen, 1907.

Virgil. *Aeneid*. The Latin Library website. www.thelatinlibrary.com/verg.html.

———. *Aeneid*. Project Gutenberg. www.gutenberg.org/files/227/227-h/227-h.htm.

———. *The Aeneid of Virgil: A New Verse Translation*. Translated by C. Day Lewis. Oxford: Oxford University Press, 1953.

———. *The Aeneid of Virgil*. Edited by Thomas Chase. Philadelphia: Eldredge & Brother, 1870.

———. *Eclogues*. The Latin Library website. www.thelatinlibrary.com/verg.html.

———. *Georgics*. The Latin Library website. www.thelatinlibrary.com/verg.html.

Whitman, Walt. "The Song of Myself." *Leaves of Grass*. Brooklyn: Self-published, 1855.

Wikipedia. *"Agnus Dei."* https://en.wikipedia.org/wiki/Agnus_Dei.

———. "Hell in the arts and popular culture." https://en.wikipedia.org/wiki/Hell_in_the_arts_and_popular_culture.

———. "Te lucis ante terminum." Translated by J. M. Neale. https://en.wikipedia.org/wiki/Te_lucis_ante_terminum.

Wilde, Oscar. "Amor Intellectualis." *Poems*. Boston: Robert Brothers, 1881.

———. *The Works of Oscar Wilde*. New York: Lamb, 1909.

Williams, Maurice. Lyrics and music. "Stay (Just a Little Bit Longer)." Performed by the Zodiacs. Herald Records, 1960.

Wine, Alice. Lyrics. "Keep Your Eyes on the Prize."

Winehouse, Amy. Lyrics and music. "Tears Dry on Their Own." From *Back to Black*. Performed by Amy Winehouse. Island Records, 2006.

The Wizard of Oz. Directed by Victor Fleming. Screenplay by Noel Langley, Florence Ryerson, and Edgar Allan Woolf. Lyrics by E. Y. Harburg. Music by Harold Arlen. With Judy Garland, Frank Morgan, Ray Bolger, et al. Metro-Goldwyn-Mayer, 1939.

DANTE ALIGHIERI (1265–1321) is an Italian Florentine poet best known for his *Divine Comedy* (*La divina commedia*). The poem, written between 1308 and 1321 and composed using an interlocking rhyme scheme called terza rima, consists of three separate books that trace the poet's allegorical journey through Hell (*Inferno*), Purgatory (*Purgatorio*), and Paradise (*Paradiso*).

MARY JO BANG is the author of eight poetry collections, including *A Doll for Throwing* and *Elegy*, winner of the National Book Critics Circle Award and a *New York Times* Notable Book. She has also published an acclaimed translation of Dante's *Inferno*. Bang has received a fellowship from the Guggenheim Foundation, a Hodder Fellowship from Princeton University, and a Berlin Prize Fellowship from the American Academy in Berlin. She is a professor of English and teaches in the creative writing program at Washington University in Saint Louis.

The text of *Purgatorio* is set in Dante—a font designed by Italian printer, book designer, and typeface artist Giovanni Mardersteig. The fonts were first used in 1955 to publish Boccaccio's *Trattatello in laude di Dante*—hence the typeface's name. Hand lettering by Henrik Drescher. Composition by Bookmobile Design & Publisher Services, Minneapolis, Minnesota. Manufactured by McNaughton & Gunn on acid-free 100 percent postconsumer wastepaper.